A TWENTY-FIRST CENTURY US WATER POLICY

A Twenty-First Century US Water Policy

Juliet Christian-Smith and Peter H. Gleick
With Heather Cooley, Lucy Allen, Amy Vanderwarker,
and Kate A. Berry

OXFORD
UNIVERSITY PRESS

Oxford University Press, Inc., publishes works that further
Oxford University's objective of excellence
in research, scholarship, and education.

Oxford   New York
Auckland   Cape Town   Dar es Salaam   Hong Kong   Karachi
Kuala Lumpur   Madrid   Melbourne   Mexico City   Nairobi
New Delhi   Shanghai   Taipei   Toronto

With offices in
Argentina   Austria   Brazil   Chile   Czech Republic   France   Greece
Guatemala   Hungary   Italy   Japan   Poland   Portugal   Singapore
South Korea   Switzerland   Thailand   Turkey   Ukraine   Vietnam

Published by Oxford University Press, Inc.
198 Madison Avenue, New York, New York 10016

www.oup.com

Oxford is a registered trademark of Oxford University Press

Library of Congress Cataloging-in-Publication Data
Gleick, Peter H.
A twenty-first century US water policy / Juliet Christian-Smith and Peter H. Gleick ; with Heather Cooley . . . [et al.].
    p.   cm.
Includes bibliographical references and index.
ISBN 978-0-19-985944-3 (hardcover : alk. paper) 1. Water-supply—Government policy—United States.
2. Water-supply—United States—Management. I. Christian-Smith, Juliet. II. Cooley, Heather. III. Title.
IV. Title: 21st century U.S. water policy.
 ∟ TD223.C47   2012
   333.9100973—dc23   2011041073

9 8 7 6 5 4 3 2 1

Printed in the United States of America
on acid-free paper

Contents

Foreword

EXCEPTIONAL DROUGHT IN Texas. Massive flooding in the Northern Plains. Crumbling infrastructure across the country. Pharmaceutical residues in drinking water. Depletion of the agriculturally critical Ogallala Aquifer. Invasive species in the Great Lakes. Intersex fish turning up in the Corn Belt. Coastal erosion and sea level rise along the Gulf Coast, not to mention in Norfolk, Virginia. What in the world is going on? And what are we going to do about it?

Welcome to the real world of water in the 21st century. Among the natural resource challenges facing the country, perhaps none is more important than ensuring adequate supplies of clean water for all the many needs and purposes people have. Clean water is not just a requisite for health, as important as that is, but essential for a prosperous economy, for growing food, for recreation, and for maintaining productive, functioning ecosystems—the forests, lakes and rivers, wildlife, and other resources on which all human activity depends.

Water has long been a special interest of mine throughout a career in environmental affairs. While serving as administrator of the Environmental Protection Agency in the administration of President George H. W. Bush, I put a priority on expanding programs to restore important bodies of water. I had seen firsthand how people across the country would mobilize to protect special places in their own communities, the lands and waters they had come to treasure. After my work with the EPA, convinced that water would be a flashpoint in many places around the globe, I started a private equity investment fund dedicated to improving the way water and sanitation are provided in the developing world. In many developing countries, the consequences of the lack of these most basic services takes a steep toll on health and economic opportunity, limits the ability of girls to stay in school, and directly causes as many as 2 million deaths each year, mostly children under five years old. The sad commentary here is that many of these problems are preventable and advocates know what needs to be done, but domestic political will and often local technical expertise and financing are lacking.

Here at home, the United States today faces our own variety of persistent and emerging water troubles. Many key water laws are not well, or even adequately, enforced. Chesapeake Bay, the Great Lakes, Puget Sound, the Gulf of Mexico, the San Francisco Bay Delta, and any number of other important aquatic resources are struggling to avoid collapse notwithstanding significant federal and state investments. The Gulf and Chesapeake Bay are witnessing ever larger dead zones in recent years. Although the United States has made great strides in using water efficiently—total water use in the year 2005 was actually lower than in 1975 and per capita use is lower than it has been since 1955 despite a growing economy and population—many cities, businesses, and farms are not yet availing themselves of cost-effective technologies and practices that conserve water. Much of the nation's infrastructure is outdated. Treatment plants and underground pipes need repair and upgrading. The cost of reducing water pollution from stormwater runoff in major cities is staggering. Energy production requires large amounts of water, and demand is growing for water to produce biofuels such as ethanol and to expand natural gas production. What is more, climate change even now is altering the timing and magnitude of precipitation, putting new strains on current sources of water supply.

It is often emphasized that water problems are local and must be resolved at the local and state level. Much of the country's water law is state-based and that has been a jealously guarded prerogative. And yet, there is an essential role for the federal government to play in developing and implementing water policies. A score of diverse federal agencies are responsible for different aspects of water management and regulation, and typically they have not collaborated to any significant degree to craft a smart, coherent approach. Part of the problem is confusion over authority. Part of the problem is insufficient funds to protect and manage water resources, a situation that is, frankly, only likely to worsen as Congress tackles budget deficits and the national debt. Part of the problem is that the basic legislative authorities governing water have not been updated to account for today's water realities and for recent advances in scientific and technical understanding of both water problems and solutions. The Clean Water Act, to name one important law, was last updated in 1987 and the prospects for informed debate about reform options seem limited at best. Part of the problem certainly is that consumers do not pay anywhere near the full cost for the delivery of clean water and the collection and treatment of wastewater. Water is often underpriced and that has serious consequences for the ability of water utilities to meet a growing set of demands.

No one should doubt that current laws and regulations and the public agencies and private firms implementing them have had a beneficial effect. Many of the nation's waters are cleaner, safer, and more productive than they would have been without the past few decades' efforts. The rub today is that these many efforts are no longer sufficient to meet the needs for managing water resources in the United States in the 21st century.

Few people are more qualified in my view to spark a robust and thoughtful conversation about reforming water policy than Peter Gleick and the Pacific Institute. A leading independent nonprofit organization, the institute undertakes research and analysis on the related and pressing issues of environmental degradation, poverty, and political conflict. In 2012, the Pacific Institute celebrates 25 years of groundbreaking work, a generation spent addressing local, national, and international problems in the fields of freshwater resources, climate change, environmental justice, and globalization. The institute aims to fill an important role by integrating science, policy, and equity issues, an interdisciplinary approach critical to forging sustainable solutions. The quality and relevance of its work in the water sector has earned the Pacific Institute well-deserved recognition, including the 2011 US Water Prize.

For this book, the Pacific Institute worked with more than a dozen organizations across the country to examine, in a series of case studies, the human and environmental impacts of the nation's often out-dated and underenforced water laws. The book looks to the future as well, offering solutions and recommendations that can lead to more comprehensive and effective water policy. The agenda here could not be more timely: Better coordination among fragmented federal programs. Better scientific and base-level information on water supply, demand, and flows. Greater monitoring and stronger enforcement. More widespread use of innovative economic tools. Updating key statutes. Incorporating the risk of climate change into planning, design, and operations of water services. And more.

None of this will come readily at a time when the country is preoccupied with the economy, with overseas conflicts, with the role of the federal government and how the country pays for the services our fellow citizens want and demand. Fragmented congressional oversight, tensions between and among federal regulators and state programs, uncertainty about the impacts of a warming world—these and other pressures will make the challenge all the more arduous.

But what choice do we have really? Water is life. We ignore that simple truth at our peril. It may well take more widespread droughts, more massive spring floods, more shocking news of water contamination or other dramatic findings to galvanize action. The game now is to be armed with analyses and ideas so when the political moment is ripe, the country's political leaders know what they can and what they should do. Herein, *A Twenty-First Century US Water Policy*—a blueprint for reform. Those who care about the country's water resource policy in all its manifestations would do well to take the themes to heart and spread the word widely.

William K. Reilly
Chairman, Global Water Challenge
Administrator, US Environmental Protection Agency 1989–1993

Acknowledgments

WE WOULD LIKE to thank the following individuals for their contributions to this book; we are incredibly grateful for their guidance and suggestions: Michael Ambrose, Dianne Bady, Carolina Balazs, Drew Beckwith, Dvija Michael Bertish, Roseann Bongiovanni, Lynn Broaddus, Edmund J. Cain, Michael Cohen, Jeff Conant, Debbie Davis, Martha Davis, Susana De Anda, Mary Ann Dickinson, Holly Doremus, Mark Franco, Andrew Fahlund, Rick Frank, Gary Grant, Martha Guzman, Steven M. Hilton, Dailan Jake, Rose Johnson, Julie Kiang, Aggie Lane, John Leshy, Myra Lewis, Kit Luce, Kathryn Mann, Jeff Opperman, Juan Parras, Nia Robinson, Doria Robinson, Michael Sarmiento, Ann Tartre, Mari Rose Taruc, Bradley Udall, Janice Varela, Doug Wallace, Michael Webber, and Henry Vaux.

We especially want to acknowledge the generous financial support of the following organizations: the Henry Luce Foundation, Conrad N. Hilton Foundation, Horace W. Goldsmith Foundation, William and Flora Hewlett Foundation, and the Flora Family Foundation.

List of Abbreviations

THE FOLLOWING ARE commonly used throughout this book.

AF	= acre-foot
BLM	= Bureau of Land Management
CSO	= combined sewage overflow
CWA	= Clean Water Act
EPA	= Environmental Protection Agency
ESA	= Endangered Species Act
FY	= Fiscal Year
GAO	= Government Accountability Office
GPCD	= gallons per capita per day
MCC	= Millennium Challenge Corporation
MHI	= median household income
NEJAC	= National Environmental Justice Advisory Council
NOAA	= National Oceanic and Atmospheric Administration
OCR	= Office of Civil Rights
SDWA	= Safe Drinking Water Act
SRF	= state revolving fund
TAS	= treated as states
TMDL	= total maximum daily load
USACE	= US Army Corps of Engineers
USAID	= US Agency for International Development
USDA	= US Department of Agriculture
USGS	= US Geological Survey

Introduction: The Soft Path for Water

AS WE MOVE through the second decade of the 21st century, the United States faces a complex and evolving set of freshwater challenges. Despite the fact that the nation is, on average, a comparatively water-rich country, we are approaching "peak water" limits in many places, for many water systems. We are reaching absolute limits on our ability to take more water from many renewable water systems like the Colorado, Sacramento-San Joaquin, and Klamath River Systems. We are overpumping non-renewable groundwater aquifers in the Great Plains and California's Central Valley. Water quality threats are poorly understood, monitored, or addressed throughout the country. Important federal water laws are out-of-date or are not effectively or equitably enforced. Aquatic ecosystems, fisheries, and wetlands are threatened with destruction. Much of our urban water infrastructure has not been adequately maintained, and confidence in our tap water system is falling. Rising energy demands and shifts toward domestic fuels are adding new demands for water, in competition with the production of food and fiber. Climate changes are already altering water availability and the risk of extreme events. And the institutions put in place in the 20th century to manage our water needs are often inadequate, inefficient, and uncoordinated.

The public cares deeply about water—it consistently polls as the most important environmental issue in people's minds, yet it remains largely neglected in the halls of Congress, the White House, and in our federal agencies. Most water management happens at the local or regional level through complex mixes of public and private actors and activities. But there are clear roles for the federal government: setting consistent national standards and regulations for water quality and environmental protection, deploying advanced monitoring systems that collect global and national data vital for disaster planning and response, providing funding for basic research on issues of national interest, intervening in legal disputes among the states, participating in international water policy and diplomacy, managing water on federal lands, and helping to ensure that states and municipalities are able to meet future water challenges. These objectives are not being adequately addressed by the federal agencies responsible for them. In some cases, agencies have overlapping and conflicting authorities. In other instances, the executive branch has failed to request sufficient funds to protect and manage our water resources, or the legislative branch has failed to appropriate and allocate those funds. And water policies have not been updated to account for advances in our scientific and technical understanding of both water problems and solutions.

It is time for a new 21st century United States water policy.

The need for national water policies and reappraisal of current strategies and approaches to water management is not new. Over 60 years ago, President Truman signed Executive Order 10095 to establish The President's Water Commission with the following charge:

> The President's Water Resources Policy Commission shall study, and make recommendations to the President with respect to, Federal responsibility for and participation in the development, utilization, and conservation of water resources, including related land uses and other public purposes to the extent that they are directly concerned with water resources. The Commission shall give consideration in particular to (a) the extent and character of Federal Government participation in major water-resources programs, (b) an appraisal of the priority of water-resources programs from the standpoint of economic and social need, (c) criteria and standards for evaluating the feasibility of water-resources projects, and (d) desirable legislation or changes in existing legislation relating to the development, utilization, and conservation of water resources.

That Executive Order led to "A Water Policy for the American People," published in 1950.

Over four decades ago, Congress acknowledged the need for a more rational, comprehensive approach to water resource planning and management, passing the National Water Commission Act (P. L. 90-515) on September 26, 1968. The act called for the creation of a National Water Commission to:

> review present and anticipated national water resource problems, making such projections of water requirements as may be necessary and identifying alternative ways of meeting these requirements—giving consideration, among other things, to conservation and more efficient use of existing supplies, increased usability by reduction of pollution, innovations to encourage the highest economic use of water, inter-basin transfers, and technological advances . . .

The commission's work culminated in a nearly 600-page report to Congress in 1973, concluding, among other things, that the federal government should improve collaboration among different agencies, collect and distribute more comprehensive water data, and replace the financial model of taxpayer-funded water projects with the principle that project beneficiaries should pay for those benefits (NWC 1973).

Things have changed again since the mid-1970s. We have seen important strides in water management, including significant improvements in wastewater treatment and reductions in point source pollution. There have been some remarkable reductions in per capita water use associated with increased water conservation and efficiency and changes in the structure of our economy. New technologies have been developed to measure, monitor, and evaluate water quality and use. Public appreciation of environmental values has grown along with efforts to slow the rate of ecosystem destruction. New collaborations between public and private entities have been developed. Some of the recommendations in those early national assessments were adopted, while others are outdated, based on assumptions about economic, social, and environmental values and priorities that are no longer true or valid. Some of the recommendations are as relevant today as they were decades ago, but they've never been successfully implemented. And new challenges not faced by earlier generations are emerging and are unaddressed and unresolved, including new contaminants in public drinking water supplies, increased competition among water users, continued population growth, infrastructure decay, and climate change.

These water challenges are not unique to the United States. Water problems are being felt worldwide and have prompted many governments to reassess their approach to water management (Christian-Smith et al., 2011). South Africa's water reform efforts in the mid-1990s included constitutional efforts to guarantee basic water requirements for all humans and the environment; Russia and the European Union have moved toward water laws that provide a common commitment to more holistic water management; Australia implemented widespread reforms to water rights policies, pricing structures, ecosystem protections, and conservation in the face of a decade-long severe drought. Chile, the Netherlands, the Philippines, and Great Britain have tested combinations of public and private management systems. There are many new experiments underway to move to more sustainable, equitable, and efficient water systems. It is time for the US to move in this direction as well—toward a soft path for water that satisfies both human and environmental needs within the constraints of a scarce and precious resource.

The Soft Path for Water

While diverse national initiatives have differing cultural dimensions and political imperatives, they share a commitment to many "soft path" water solutions. The "soft path for water" defines a new approach to managing water resources. The soft path begins with the recognition that with few exceptions people do not want to "use" water—they want complex combinations of goods and services. People want to drink and bathe, grow food, produce and consume goods and services, and otherwise satisfy human needs and desires. While many of these things require water, achieving these ends can be done in different ways, often with radically different implications for water. The soft path recognizes that there are two primary ways of meeting water-related needs, or, more poetically, two paths. The "hard" path relies almost exclusively on centralized infrastructure and decision making using technology and institutions developed in the 19th and 20th centuries: large dams and reservoirs, pipelines and treatment plants, public water departments and agencies, and private companies. The objective of the hard path is to deliver water, mostly of potable quality, and sometimes to remove wastewater.

The "soft path" has a different, broader set of goals—the delivery of water-related services matched to users' needs and resource availability. The soft path also uses centralized infrastructure, but as just one in an integrated series of tools. It also seeks to take advantage of the potential for decentralized facilities, efficient technologies, flexible public and private institutions, innovative economics, and human capital. It strives to improve the overall productivity of water use rather than seek endless sources of new supply. It works with water users at local and community scales and seeks to protect the critical ecological services such as nutrient cycling, flood protection, aquatic habitat, and waste dilution and removal that water also provides (Gleick 2002, Wolff and Gleick 2002).

Conventional management approaches in the US are based on the hard path and include a range of obstacles to the implementation of soft-path approaches, including ignorance of the links between human systems and ecological systems, the reliance on ineffective water-pricing structures and markets, and the segregation of agencies and policies into "silos" (Brooks et al. 2009). Many of the recommendations that we provide in the individual chapters of this book are part of a soft-path approach: they encourage better integration across sectors and scales, equitable access to water for both humans and ecosystems, proper application and use of technology and economics, incentives for efficient use, social objectives for water quality and delivery reliability, and public participation in decision making.

The soft path can also be defined in terms of its differences from the hard path (Wolff and Gleick 2002).

1. The soft path redirects government agencies, private companies, and individuals to work to meet the water-related needs of people and businesses, rather than merely to supply water. For example, people want to produce or consume goods and services, and increasingly to do so in cost-effective, environmentally sound, and socially acceptable ways. They do not fundamentally care how much water is used, and may not care whether water is used at all. If water utilities work to satisfy customers' demands for water-based services, rather than simply "sell" water, then new options open up for improving efficiency and implementing decentralized and more sustainable technologies. This book explores in great detail the differences between simply supplying water and the more complex objectives of satisfying the need for goods and services in a water-efficient manner. Among our conclusions are calls to expand efforts to

improve the efficiency and productivity of water use in agricultural and urban settings.

2. The soft path recognizes that different water qualities can satisfy different kinds of water demands and strives to reserve higher quality water for those uses that require it. Conversely, storm runoff, graywater, and reclaimed wastewater are explicitly recognized as water supplies suited for landscape irrigation and other nonpotable uses. The soft path recognizes that single-pipe distribution networks and once-through consumptive-use appliances are no longer the only cost-effective and practical technologies. This is almost never the case in traditional water planning: all future water demand in urban areas is implicitly assumed to require potable water. This practice exaggerates the amount of water needed and inflates the overall cost of providing it. We describe water quality challenges and solutions in chapter 5 and recommend new efforts to match water quality availability and needs – a key soft-path approach.

3. The soft path recognizes that investments in decentralized solutions can be just as cost-effective as investments in large, centralized options. For example, there is nothing inherently more reliable or cost-effective about providing irrigation water from centralized rather than decentralized rainwater capture and storage facilities. Decentralized investments are highly reliable when they include adequate investment in human capital, that is, in the people who use the facilities. And they can be cost-effective when the easiest opportunities for centralized rainwater capture and storage have been exhausted. Many of the recommendations here recognize the need for new forms of investment and financing, exploration of flexible pricing and markets, and more efficient use of limited federal funds for programs of truly national or international interest.

4. The soft path requires water agencies or company personnel to fully interact with water users and to effectively engage community groups in water management. Past water management was considered the purview of engineers and water professionals accustomed to meeting generic needs. But experience has shown that communities and water users can play vital roles in long-term planning and management of water. Users need help determining how much water of various qualities they need, and neighbors may need to work together to capture low-cost opportunities. By engaging in more effective and transparent communication, many of the objectives of the soft path will be easier to achieve, and many of the environmental justice and equity problems of the past, described in chapters 3 and 4, can be reduced.

5. The soft path recognizes that ecological health and the activities that depend on it (such as fishing, recreation, and natural water purification systems) are valuable services. Water that is not abstracted, treated, and distributed may still be "productive." The hard path, by ignoring or discounting these natural values leads to their destruction. A key conclusion of this book is that the trend toward

better integration of environmental values in federal water policies should continue. This includes continuing to improve methods for protecting and valuing ecosystem services, incorporating them into federal decision making and water management, and improving management of water on federally protected lands.

6. The soft path recognizes the complexity of water economics and management, including the power of economies of scope, by integrating across competing interests. The hard path looks only at projects, revenues, and economies of scale, and works with limited institutions. An economy of scope exists when a combined decision-making process allows specific services or benefits to be delivered at a lower cost than would result from separate decision-making processes. For example, water agencies, flood-control districts, and land use managers can often reduce the total cost of services (such as flood protection) to their customers by understanding and integrating factors that none of them can account for alone. This book recommends thinking about water in an integrated, not isolated, way, streamlining the complex and sometimes overlapping federal agencies with water-related responsibilities, and taking a broader view of the scope of water decisions.

Conclusions

In summary, the 21st century brings with it both persistent and new water challenges, including growing human populations and demands for water, unacceptable water quality in many areas, weak or inadequate water data collection and regulation, outdated laws and regulations, and growing threats to the timing and reliability of water supply from climate change. We have reached a fork in the road and we must now make a choice about how to address our water problems. Several countries have begun to reform their water policies to better address these challenges—it is time the US did as well. While the political and cultural contexts of these reforms have varied, international water reforms reflect a greater focus on "soft path" water solutions including new concepts of water supply, expanded efforts at improving water conservation and efficiency, smarter water pricing and economic strategies, and more participatory water management. The United States has not followed suit and continues to rely on a fragmented and outdated approach to water policy based on a patchwork of old laws, competing institutions, and aging infrastructure.

We know where the traditional, hard path leads us: to an impoverished environment, undemocratic decision making, and growing social, political, and economic costs. The soft path offers an alternative: a way to satisfy human and ecological needs, reduce pressure on limited resources, promote transparent and democratic decision making, and more efficient and rational economic choices. New and effective solutions are available and are being explored at local, state, regional, and national levels. That experience should be tapped in efforts to develop new integrated federal water policies. In this book, we have laid out a path towards such policies. Progress will be slow as we learn how best to identify and overcome barriers, but effective and sustainable water management is a necessity. It is urgent that the United States accelerate efforts to develop a new 21st century water policy.

References

Brooks, D. B., O. M. Brandes, and S. Gurman. 2009. *Making the Most of the Water We Have: The Soft Path Approach to Water Management*. London: Earthscan.

Christian-Smith, J., H. Cooley, and P. H. Gleick. 2011. "U.S. Water Policy." In *The World's Water*, Volume 7 (P. H. Gleick, ed.). Covelo, CA: Island Press.

Gleick, P. H. 2002. "Soft Water Paths." *Nature*, 418: 373.

———. 2009. "On 21st Century Water Planning: The Need for Integrated National Water Actions." Testimony to the House Committee on Science and Technology. US Congress. Washington, DC, March 4, 2009. http://www.pacinst.org/publications/testimony/gleick_testimony_hr1145.pdf.

National Water Commission (NWC). 1973. *Water Policies for the Future. Final Report to the President and to the Congress of the United States*. Washington, DC: US Government Printing Office.

Water Resources Policy Commission (WRPC). 1950. *A Water Policy for the American People: Volume 1: General Report.*" The Report of the President's Water Resources Policy Commission. Washington, DC: US Government Printing Office.

Wolff, G. and P. H. Gleick. 2002. "The Soft Path for Water." In *The World's Water 2002–2003* (Volume 3). Edited by P. H. Gleick, 1–32. Washington, DC: Island Press.

A TWENTY-FIRST CENTURY US WATER POLICY

THE WATER OF THE UNITED STATES

Freshwater Availability and Use

Peter H. Gleick

Introduction

The United States is relatively well-endowed with water—absolute scarcity has never been the most significant water challenge the nation has faced. Rather, the most difficult challenges have been associated with regional disparities in water availability, climatic variability and the seasonality of the hydrologic cycle, worsening water quality, and increasingly, controversies over management strategies and policies. All of these issues are addressed in this book. But the first steps in sustainable water management are to understand both our national endowment of water and how we have chosen to develop and use that resource. Both of these are critical but poorly understood components of US water resources. The vast size of the country, coupled with the tremendous geological, geophysical, and hydrological variations across the landscape, complicate any description or characterization of the nation's current water availability or use. And even though improvements in knowledge in these areas are vitally needed, we discuss here some basic characteristics that determine many of the nation's current and future water challenges.

Freshwater Availability

How much freshwater is available from the hydrologic cycle, on a renewable basis, in the United States? We have no precise estimate. Remarkably, comprehensive, long-term, and reliable data on total freshwater availability in the United States are not available.

According to the US Geological Survey (USGS), which is responsible for evaluating, monitoring, and reporting on US water resources, the annual renewable water resources of the United States, including Alaska and Hawaii, total around 3,070 cubic kilometers per year, or around 2 trillion billion gallons per day of renewable freshwater, but this assessment is an old estimate and only a rough calculation (Gleick 2006).[1] Many of these water resources are isolated in unpopulated areas, unmeasured or monitored, used by natural ecosystems, or are otherwise inaccessible, and this figure should not be considered a measure of readily available or usable water.

Water is available in both stocks and flows. *Stocks* include groundwater, lakes, soil moisture, and small amounts of water in biomass and in rivers measured on an instantaneous, volumetric basis. *Flows* of water include rainfall, streamflow, and evaporation and are measured in water volumes per unit time. Figure 1.1 shows annual average precipitation in the continental United States. Precipitation is measured widely around the United States and is a key water "flow" parameter, but converting highly variable precipitation measurements into estimates of total water availability requires integrating data over a long period, and it is only one factor affecting water available for human use. Nevertheless, this figure offers a clear indication of the most significant characteristic of water availability nationwide: east of the center of the country is relatively well-endowed with rainfall; west of this line (approximately the 100th meridian), the country is relatively dry, with the exception of the Pacific Northwest and parts of northern California.

Another key hydrologic flow parameter, which integrates to some degree water available in precipitation less water lost to evaporation, is *runoff*. Figure 1.2 shows average runoff in the continental United States over the period 1951 to 2000. Similar to the rainfall map, this map shows the relative abundance of river runoff in the eastern and northwestern parts of the country and lower surface runoff in the western and southwestern United States. But again, converting the data in this figure to total water availability requires integrating it over each hydrologic basin. This is a difficult task.

A third major component of water availability in the United States is *groundwater*. Groundwater has both *stock* and *flow* components. The magnitude of total groundwater stocks can be quite substantial. But renewable flows of water into groundwater are typically far smaller. Thus, long-term sustainable use of groundwater requires avoiding pumping at rates that exceed natural recharge, which will ultimately deplete stocks. Although groundwater is less monitored and mapped than surface water is, information is available on major groundwater aquifers in the United States (see figure 1.3). The map in figure 1.3 shows these aquifers, though without information on total renewable water available from them. Long-term systematic measurement of water withdrawals and groundwater levels would be required to determine total groundwater use. As the USGS (2002) has noted, "To have national or even regional significance, indices of ground-water levels have to be based on repeated observations at relatively large numbers of observation wells located in a wide range of representative hydrogeological environments." Few such measurements are available because no nationwide, systematic groundwater monitoring program exists (USGS 2002).

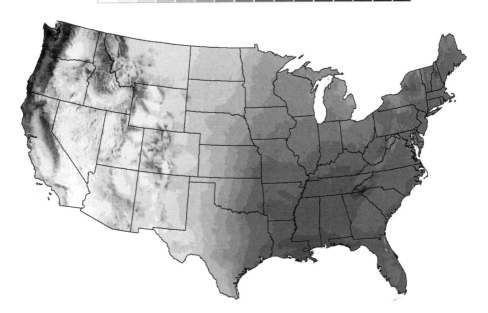

FIGURE 1.1. Annual average precipitation
Source: Pacific Institute (2011).

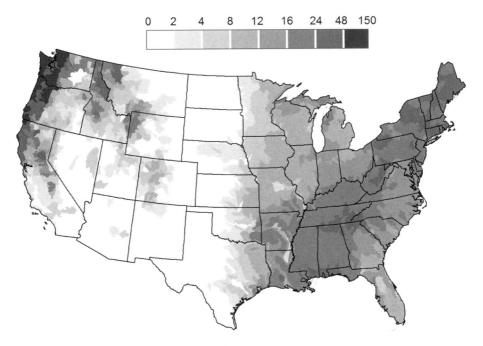

FIGURE 1.2. Average runoff, covering the period 1951–2000
Source: Pacific Institute (2011).

Because of these serious data limitations and gaps on US water availability, Congress passed Public Law 111–11 (2009), which directs the USGS to prepare a National Water Availability and Use Assessment Program—a National Water Census. This work is now at least partly underway, and long overdue, and it may substantially increase our understanding of the nation's water endowment.

Each of these maps, on precipitation, runoff, and groundwater aquifers, provides incomplete information on total water availability in the United States, which varies dramatically from year to year and region to region, but together they give a sense of the remarkable variability in hydrologic conditions in the continental United States. At any given time, some region in the United States is likely to be experiencing unusually dry conditions; others may be experiencing high flows or even flooding. While definitions of *drought* are varied, the US General Accounting Office released an assessment of the long-term vulnerability of US water resources to shortages, including an analysis of the current vulnerability to drought (see figure 1.4) (GAO 2003). As this map shows, hydrologic regions in the western part of the country are more likely to experience drought, but all regions are vulnerable. For example, in 2007–2008, the southeastern United States, including Georgia, experienced a severe drought that caused significant economic disruption and worsened regional tensions over water allocation and use. A few years earlier, in 2002, drought was particularly severe in much of the western United States, as well as parts of the eastern United States (figures 1.5). Overall, large portions of 30 states experienced moderate to extreme drought, resulting in estimated damages in excess of $11.4 billion (NCDC 2002, NOAA 2008).[2] Beyond the direct impacts, the drought also exacerbated wildfires, doubling the average

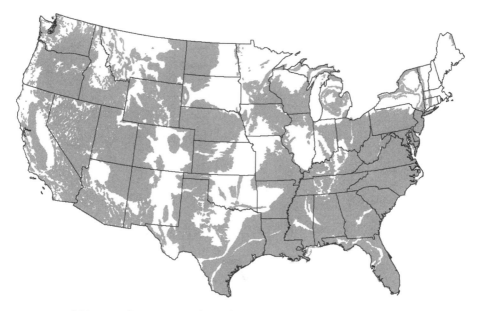

FIGURE 1.3. Major groundwater reservoirs (in gray)
Source: Pacific Institute (2011).

annual amount of forest area consumed by wildfires (Associated Press 2002). In 2011, Texas experienced unprecedented drought conditions that are likely to extend into 2012.

Another critical issue related to national water availability is how climatic changes will affect the hydrologic cycle. Substantial scientific evidence clearly links changes in climate with changes in precipitation patterns, storm frequency and intensity, snowfall and snowmelt dynamics, evaporation rates, and more. Some changes are already being observed in the hydrologic record, including especially changes in snow conditions, temperature and evaporation rates, and some precipitation and streamflow intensities; even more significant changes are anticipated in the future. As climate changes accelerate and as our understanding of hydroclimatology continues to improve, new estimates about national and regional water availability will have to be factored into water policy choices and decisions in order to improve future water management. A recent nationwide study that examined the sustainability of changing water demands and supply under future climate change scenarios found that 70 percent of counties in the United States may be at moderate to extreme risk of water demand outstripping supply by 2050 (NRDC 2010) (figure 1.6). These issues are explored in far more detail in chapter 10: Climate and Water.

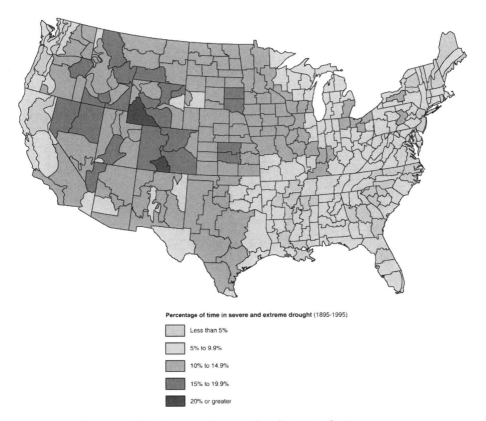

Percentage of time in severe and extreme drought (1895-1995)

Less than 5%

5% to 9.9%

10% to 14.9%

15% to 19.9%

20% or greater

FIGURE 1.4. Percentage of time in severe and extreme drought nationwide, 1895–1995
Source: GAO (2003), p. 16.

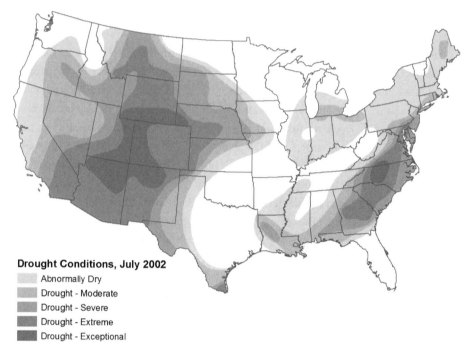

Drought Conditions, July 2002
- Abnormally Dry
- Drought - Moderate
- Drought - Severe
- Drought - Extreme
- Drought - Exceptional

FIGURE 1.5. Palmer hydrological drought index, July 2002
Source: Pacific Institute (2011).

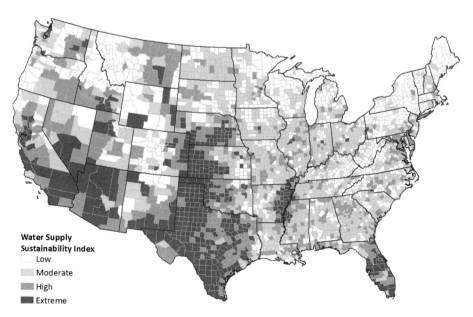

Water Supply Sustainability Index
- Low
- Moderate
- High
- Extreme

FIGURE 1.6. Water supply sustainability index (2050)
Source: NRDC (2010).

Freshwater Use

The relative abundance or scarcity of water is of general interest to hydrologists and other water scientists. Yet, from a policy perspective or from the point of view of the public, it is only important in the context of water demand and the ability to satisfy water demands within natural limits: Is enough water available to satisfy human demands at a given time and a given place without destroying ecological goods and services that we also value?

Water is used in the United States for a wide variety of purposes, from the relatively modest amounts of water used for domestic and residential use to much larger withdrawals and consumption for irrigated agriculture and the generation of energy. Water use in the United States greatly increased in the 20th century due to population growth and expanding economic and industrial activity. The growth in demand put increasingly more pressure on the nation's fixed water supplies, leading to increased diversion and manipulation of surface water resources and substantial withdrawals of groundwater supplies.

Accompanying the growing demand for water has been a massive investment in water-related infrastructure, including dams, aqueducts, irrigation systems, and municipal water purification and wastewater collection and treatment systems. For example, the 20th century witnessed one of the most remarkable expansions in storage capacity behind large dams of anywhere in the world (the Soviet Union saw a similar kind of expansion during this period, and China is undergoing such an expansion now). But as more dams were built in the United States, and more of the nation's rivers controlled, it has become increasingly difficult to find new water supplies that are economically, politically, and environmentally acceptable. This change is clearly shown in figure 1.7, which plots the cumulative reservoir storage capacity for all US dams. Storage capacity increased exponentially in the middle of the 20th century but has now leveled off, with very few, small additions in the past few decades. In some watersheds, we are now running up against "peak water" constraints of three different kinds: peak renewable, peak nonrenewable, and peak ecological water (see box 1.1, Peak Water) (Gleick and Palaniappan 2010). In particular, some rivers are now completely (or even over-) allocated (e.g., the Colorado River, the Klamath River)—all flows in an average year are assigned to one user or another.

In some regions, aquifers are being pumped faster than they can recharge. As noted, many rivers are being diverted to the maximum extent possible. Therefore, environmental flows that satisfy ecosystem health and provide a variety of ecosystem services are no longer available at adequate levels. To add to these concerns, existing infrastructures, including dams, distribution systems, and treatment plants, are sometimes deteriorating faster than they are being maintained. An era of dam building may be replaced by an era of dam decommissioning (see chapter 6: Protecting Freshwater Ecosystems, for a description of the decommissioning of the Elwha Dam).

BOX 1.1

PEAK WATER: THREE DIFFERENT FORMS OF "PEAK WATER"

Peak Renewable Water

A significant fraction of the total human use of water comes from renewable water resources taken from rainfall, rivers, streams, and groundwater basins. *Peak renewable water* refers to the limit on total renewable flows of water that can be withdrawn from a system. In theory, peak renewable water is 100 percent of the renewable supply, which may vary substantially over time due to natural hydrologic variability. In practice, actual peak renewable withdrawals may be far less than 100 percent of available supply due to economic, environmental, or political constraints.

Peak Nonrenewable Water

In some regions, water demands are satisfied with nonrenewable sources, such as groundwater aquifers with very slow recharge rates or overpumped groundwater systems that lose their ability to be recharged due to compaction or other physical changes in the basin. When the use of water from a groundwater aquifer far exceeds the natural recharge rate, stocks are quickly depleted. Similarly, when aquifers become contaminated with pollutants, a renewable aquifer can become nonrenewable. *Peak nonrenewable withdrawals* refers to the production of water above natural recharge rates, followed by increasing cost or difficulty in production, followed by a peak and then diminishing withdrawals and use. Peak nonrenewable water is most similar to the concept of "peak oil," which is more familiar to many (Hubbert 1956).

Peak Ecological Water

For many watersheds, a more immediate and serious concern than "running out" of water is exceeding a level of use that causes serious or irreversible ecological damage. At some point, increasing withdrawals or use of water can lead to a loss of ecological services greater than the value provided by using that water. After this point—called *peak ecological water*—additional increases in the human use of water lead to ecological disruptions greater than the value that this increased water provides to humans.

Source: Gleick and Palaniappan (2010).

Changing Trends in National Water Use

In part due to growing limits on overall water availability, it is vital that there be greater attention paid to water use. Unfortunately, like water availability, national data on water use are limited and incomplete, complicating current assessments and future projections. The most consistent and comprehensive data on water use are those from the USGS's national water-use studies, conducted every five years since the middle of the 20th century. These data provide a snapshot of trends in water use, withdrawals, consumption, and regional changes. During much of the 20th century, water withdrawals outpaced population growth, as indicated by continued increases in per capita demand (figure 1.8)

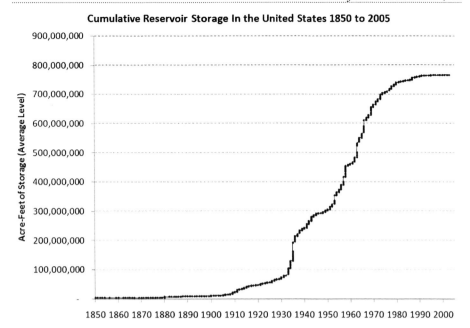

FIGURE 1.7. Cumulative reservoir storage in the United States, 1850–2005 (in acre-feet of storage)
Source: Pacific Institute analysis, from USGS (2006).

for the first seven decades of the century. As shown in figure 1.9, rising water demand was largely driven by the expansion of irrigated agriculture and continued increases in industrial use, especially for thermoelectric generation. This trend, however, largely reversed in the mid- to late 1970s, and total water use actually declined while the population and economy continued to grow (figure 1.10). Water use in the United States roughly doubled between 1950 and 1980, but then began to decrease. Average water use peaked in 1980 at approximately 370 billion gallons per day; current use is roughly 340 billion gallons per day (Hutson et al. 2004, Kenny et al. 2009). Overall, between 1975 and 2005, total water use in the United States has declined, yet population increased by 39 percent and gross domestic product increased by 159 percent. In 1975, Americans used an average of 1,940 gallons for every person each day. By 2005, water use was down to 1,380 gallons per person per day. If each American still used 1,940 gallons per day, our total water demand would be an additional 6,060 billion gallons per year, a volume equal to the annual flow of more than 12 new Colorado Rivers—or enough water for everyone in California, New York, Florida, Texas, Illinois, and Michigan.

These observed changes in water use demonstrate that the old assumption that total water use is inextricably tied to population and economic growth is false. This stabilization of water demand is a result of several factors, including efficiency improvements, federal regulations on wastewater discharge, and the transition from a water-intensive manufacturing economy to a less water-intensive service economy. The net result of these

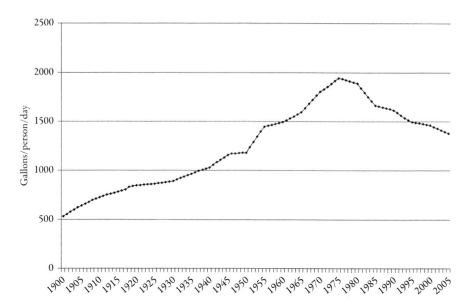

FIGURE 1.8. Per capita water use (gallons per person per day), 1900–2005

Source: Population data from U.S. Department of Commerce (2000, 2007). Water use data from Kenny et al. (2009) and previous US water-use assessments.

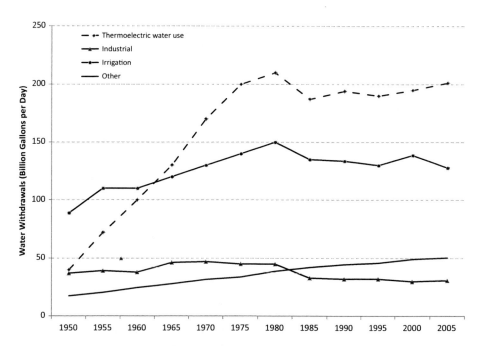

FIGURE 1.9. Water withdrawals in the United States, by major use, 1950–2000

Source: Based on data from Kenny et al. (2009).

factors is to reduce the nation's per capita water use to the level it was in the 1950s—a remarkable change away from the assumption of ever-increasing demand for water.

The Importance of Irrigated Agriculture

In 2000, irrigation accounted for 65 percent of all freshwater withdrawals excluding thermoelectric power, and an even greater share of consumptive use from developed water systems (Hutson et al. 2004). Agriculture accounts for approximately 80 percent of consumptive water use in the United States, and up to 90 percent in some western states (Aillery 2004). When the additional water that agriculture consumes directly from rainfall is factored in, it is apparent that this single sector has enormous impacts on overall water demand and supplies. Conversely, even modest improvements in agricultural water efficiency can have far-reaching effects. In the past decade, farmers have been able to irrigate approximately the same amount of acreage while reducing total applied water by about 6 million acre-feet (6 percent), largely through the increased utilization of sprinkler and drip systems, rather than water-intensive gravity flow systems, and through changes in cropping patterns, soil moisture management, and water-reuse systems (USDA 2008a, 2008b, 2003a, 2003b).

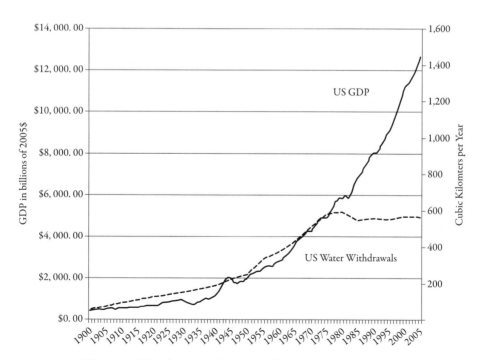

FIGURE I.10. US water withdrawals and gross domestic product, 1900–2005
Source: Based on data from Johnston and Williamson (2002), Kenny et al. (2009).

Why Have Water Use Dynamics Changed in the United States?

Water use in the United States is driven by many factors, including population size and distribution, the structure of economic activity, subsidies, commodity and water prices, water technologies, and laws and institutions that encourage or discourage water use. No comprehensive assessment has been done of the relative role of each of these in altering water use over the past two decades, but certain key observations can be made. The two most important drivers of the recent reductions in total and per capita water use nationwide are improvements in the efficiency of water use and changes in the structure of the US economy toward less water-intensive industries and activities.

The efficiency of water use has dramatically increased over the past three decades through improvements in both technologies and processes. These improvements are the result of several factors, including the development of new technologies, federal regulatory policies, economic strategies, and combinations of these. The Clean Water Act, for example, established water-quality standards for water discharged into the environment, which encouraged dischargers to reduce the volume of wastewater generated as the cheapest way to cut pollution treatment costs. This led to a wide range of improvements in water-use efficiency for major industrial sectors. For example, the steel industry in the United States reduced its water use from an average of 200 tons of water to produce a ton of steel in the early part of the 20th century to around 20 tons of water per ton of steel by the 1980s after the implementation of the Clean Water Act (Gleick 2003).

Other federal laws also had important effects on water-use efficiency. The National Energy Policy Act of 1992 established national efficiency standards for toilets, urinals, kitchen and lavatory faucets, and showerheads manufactured after January 1, 1994 (see table 1.1). Later, legislation at both the federal and state levels established additional standards for products not included in the original act, including clothes washers, dishwashers, and a number of commercial products. In addition, the Environmental Protection Agency developed the WaterSense program, a voluntary labeling program modeled after the Energy Star program (table 1.1). Products bearing the WaterSense label are substantially more efficient than average water-using appliances.

Improvements in agricultural water-use efficiency also play an important role. As shown in figure 1.11, more irrigated acreage is served by efficient sprinklers and drip systems instead of less-efficient flood-irrigation technology, permitting increases in crop productivity per unit water applied.

Another major component of the shift away from exponential growth in water demand has been a leveling off of the expansion in irrigated agriculture and high-volume energy cooling systems. Total water withdrawals in the United States are dominated by these two uses, and constraints on water and land availability in the western United States, where irrigated agriculture dominates, have slowed and even reversed overall national water demand increases. Similarly, large volumes of water are withdrawn for power plant cooling, but the most water-intensive cooling systems (once-through cooling) are being

TABLE 1.1.

Efficiency Standards Established by Federal Legislation

Fixture/appliance	Federal standard (current and future)	Law	Effective date
Toilet	1.6 gpf	EPAct 1992	Jan. 1, 1994
Showerhead	2.5 gpm at 80 psi	EPAct 1992	Jan. 1, 1994
Faucet	≤2.2 gpm at 60 psi	EPAct 1992	Jan. 1, 1994
Clothes washer	≥MEF 1.26 ft³/kWh/ cycle, WF ≤ 9.5 gal/cy-cle/ft³		Jan. 1, 2011
Dishwasher (regular size)	≤355 kWh/yr and ≤6.5 gal/cycle	Energy Independence and Security Act of 2007	Jan. 1, 2010
Dishwasher (compact)	≤260 kWh/year, ≤4.5 gal/cycle	Energy Independence and Security Act of 2007	Jan. 1, 2010
Commercial toilet	1.6 gpf	EPAct 1992	Jan. 1, 1994
Urinal	1.0 gpf	EPAct 1992	Jan. 1, 1994
Commercial faucet	2.2 gpm at 60 psi	EPAct 1992	Jan. 1, 1994
Commercial faucet (public lavatory)	0.5 gpm at 60 psi	American Society of Mechanical Engineers standard	2005
Commercial prerinse spray valves	1.6 gpm	EPAct 2005	Jan. 1, 2006
Commercial ice makers	sliding scale, based on ice har-vest rate	EPAct 2005	Jan. 1, 2010
Commercial clothes washers	≥MEF 1.26 ft³/kWh/ cycle, WF ≤ 9.5 gal/cycle/ft³	EPAct 2005	Jan. 1, 2007

Note: EPAct = Energy Policy Act; gpf = gallons per foot; gpm = gallons per minute; psi = pounds per square inch; MEF = modified energy factor; WF = water factor.

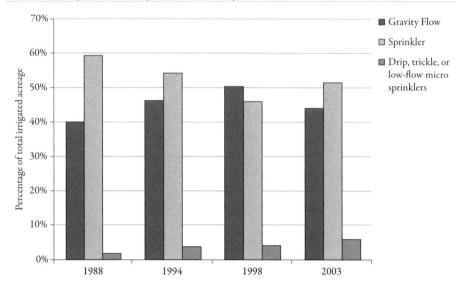

FIGURE 1.11. Irrigation methods by acreage in the United States in 1988, 1994, 1998, and 2003
Sources: USDA 1994, 1998, 2003a.

phased out to reduce their serious environmental consequences. Thus, while nationwide energy demands continue to rise, the total water required to satisfy these demands is actually decreasing. Finally, there has also been a structural shift in the industrial sector of the United States away from some water-intensive industries and toward less water-intensive goods and services, permitting total economic activity to continue to grow at a faster pace than water use. This has not been adequately analyzed, but it certainly plays a role.

Future Water Supply and Demand: The Science and Art of Water Use Projections

Making projections of future water use is a balance of science and art, given the uncertainties around population size, technology development, economic activity, and more. Though future water scarcity is widely acknowledged to be a significant concern for the United States, few studies have attempted to produce national scenarios of future water availability or shortage. In the second half of the 20th century, a series of large-scale projections of water use in the United States were attempted—table 1.2 summarizes national water projections from the early 1960s through 1990. One of the earliest national water projections was produced by the US Senate Select Committee on National Water Resources, chaired by Senator Robert S. Kerr (see Table 1.2 for a summary of major national water use forecasts). In 1960, this study forecast water supplies and use for 22 water resource regions of the United States to the year 2020 (US Senate 1961). A few years later, the US Water Resources Council was created by the Water Resources Planning Act of July 22, 1965, and the council completed its first national assessment in 1968 (US Water Resources Council 1968). The National Water Commission was established in September 1968 by Congress (PL 90-515, 82 Stat. 868, 42 USCA Sec. 1962a) to "review present and anticipated national water resource problems, making such projections of water requirements as may be necessary and identifying alternative ways of meeting these requirements."

In 1965, the USGS released another projection of water use (Piper 1965). In the early 1970s, the forecasts in the 1961 Senate Committee Print 32 were updated by Resources for the Future, a Washington research institute (Wollman and Bonem 1971). The National Water Commission issued final conclusions and recommendations to Congress and the president in June 1973 (US National Water Commission 1973).

A comprehensive 1999 Department of Agriculture national water report projected a 7 percent increase in total water withdrawals between 2000 and 2040, driven largely by a 41 percent increase in population (Brown 1999). Some of the earlier studies projected even larger increases, but in a clear indication of our inability to accurately project future resource use, almost all of these forecasts have been overestimates (see figure 1.12).

Differences in water-use projections of these reports can be traced to differences in assumptions about cooling water use for thermoelectric power generation, the extent to which the nation's water resources could be tapped, and different economic and population forecasts. In all these studies, water use was considered independent of water availability—the supply of water was implicitly assumed to be unlimited.

Even the earliest work on water forecasting acknowledged the limitations of making long-term projections:

- it would seem reasonable for many to question the usefulness of projections per se—because other factors (such as prices, technologies, and desired social objectives) are dominant in the real world or because they are so uncertain in the long run as to be undependable for decision (Thompson et al. 1971).
- the level of future demands for water is not inevitable but derives in large part from policy decisions within the control of society. Future demands for water cannot be forecast accurately by the simple extension of past trends (US National Water Commission 1973).
- A persistent tendency of water resources planning in the Nation's Capital and elsewhere has been the reliance upon single projections of water use into the future as a basis for forecasting water requirements. Such linear projections assume a continuation of present policies, and may lead to astronomical estimates of future water requirements (US National Water Commission 1973).
- It is therefore unrealistic, and in fact unwise, to attempt to forecast precise levels of future water use on the basis of past water use (US National Water Commission 1973).

TABLE 1.2.

Projections of Future Water Demand in the United States, by Year of Projection and Year the Forecast Was Made

	Year of forecast	Year of projection	km³/yr
Senate Select Committee	1961	2000	1,460
Water Resources Council	1968	2000	1,111
Water Resources Council	1968	2020	1,890
Wollman and Bonem	1971	2000	1,221
Wollman and Bonem	1971	1980	768
National Water Commission	1973	2000	815
National Water Commission	1973	2000	1,822
National Water Commission	1973	1980	768
Water Resources Council	1978	1985	614
Water Resources Council	1978	2000	619
USDA/Forest Service	1989	2000	633
USDA/Forest Service	1989	2010	696
USDA/Forest Service	1989	2020	758
USDA/Forest Service	1989	2030	814
USDA/Forest Service	1989	2040	867
Brown	1999	2020	576
Brown	1999	2040	599

Note: USDA = US Department of Agriculture.

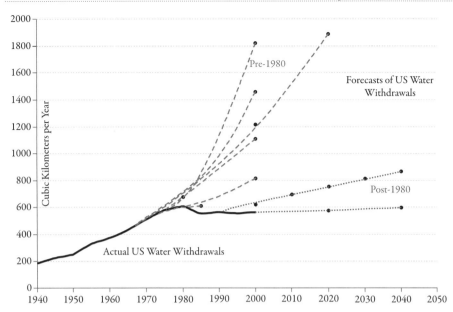

FIGURE 1.12. Actual US water withdrawals and projections of future use. The points indicate projections. The lines connect the points with the dates when the projections were made.

Even more important than these national estimates are regional projections. A growing number of regions are already, or will shortly become, vulnerable to long-term water shortages. A 2003 report from the Government Accountability Office included a survey of water managers from 47 of the 50 United States (not including Michigan, New Mexico, and California, all of which also have looming water scarcity or quality problems). Thirty-six of these water managers anticipated that their state would undergo a substantial degree of water shortage before 2013 even if normal, nondrought conditions occur. Forty-six of the state water managers predicted their states would have water shortages if drought conditions do occur (GAO 2003). Many of these shortages will occur in areas not traditionally associated with water constraints due to rising demands and changing climate.

Conclusions

The United States is well-endowed with freshwater, but the uneven distribution of water over both space and time has always posed management challenges. As the population and economy of the nation expanded throughout the 20th century, more regions of the country began to run up against absolute peak water limits to availability and use, including economic, political, and environmental constraints. Traditional solutions in the form of new large infrastructures (dams, aqueducts, and new groundwater withdrawals) are increasingly ineffective, costly, or simply physically unavailable. Water scarcity and quality problems are thus poised to become one of the most prominent natural resource challenges of the 21st century for the United States and the world, with consequences for economic, social, and environmental interests. Overconsumption and inefficient use of our water resources will lead to heightened competition among businesses, citizens needing to meet domestic and agricultural needs, and the environment. Long-term climatic changes threaten even greater water challenges. Successfully addressing water problems requires many things, but especially a comprehensive understanding of both the nature of the resource—where, when, and how much water is available, and of the nature of our water demand—where, when, and how water is used to satisfy our needs. A first step in sustainable management requires that we improve our understanding in both of these areas, and several chapters explore new supply and demand ideas. A second step, addressed throughout this book, is the need for water managers to begin to expand their thinking to encompass new approaches, tools, and communities in their efforts to satisfy our future water needs.

References

Aillery, M. 2004. "Briefing Room: Irrigation and Water Use." November 22, 2004. Economic Research Service, United States Department of Agriculture. http://www.ers.usda.gov/briefing/wateruse/.

Associated Press. 2002. "Science Confirms: USA's Summer Was Hot and Dry." *USA Today,* September 13. http://www.usatoday.com/weather/news/2002/2002-09-13-hot-dry-summer.htm.

Brown, T. C. 1999. *Past and Future Freshwater Use in the United States: A Technical Document Supporting the 2000 USDA Forest Service RPA Assessment.* General Technical Report RMRS-GTR-39. Fort Collins, CO: Rocky Mountain Research Station, Forest Service, United States Department of Agriculture. http://www.fs.fed.us/rm/pubs/rmrs_gtr039.pdf.

Gleick, P. H. 2003. "Water Use." *Annual Review of Environment and Resources* 28: 275–314.

———, ed. 2006. *The World's Water 2006–2007*. Vol. 5. New York: Island Press.

Gleick, P. H., and M. Palaniappan. 2010. "Peak Water: Conceptual and Practical Limits to Freshwater Withdrawal and Use." *Proceedings of the National Academy of Sciences* 107, no. 25: 11155–11162. www.pnas.org/cgi/doi/10.1073/pnas.1004812107.

Hubbert, M. K. 1956. "*Nuclear Energy and the Fossil Fuels.*" Spring Meeting of the Southern District. Division of Production. American Petroleum Institute. San Antonio, Texas: Shell Development Company. pp. 22–27. Available online: http://www.hubbertpeak.com/hubbert/1956/1956.pdf.

Hutson, S. S., N. L. Barber, J. F. Kenny, K. S. Linsey, D. S. Lumia, and M. A. Maupin. 2004. *Estimated Use of Water in the United States in 2000.* U.S. Geological Survey Circular 1268. Reston, VA: United States Department of the Interior, United States Geological Survey. http://pubs.usgs.gov/circ/2004/circ1268/pdf/circular1268.pdf.

Johnston, L. D., and S. H. Williamson. 2002. "The Annual Real and Nominal GDP for the United States, 1789–Present." April 2002. Economic History Serviceshttp://measuringworth.com/usgdp/.

Kenny, J. F., N. L. Barber, S. S. Hutson, K. S. Linsey, J. K. Lovelace, and M. A. Maupin. 2009. *Estimated Use of Water in the United States in 2005.* U.S. Geological Survey Circular 1344. Reston, VA: United States Geological Survey.

National Climate Data Center (NCDC). 2002. "Palmer Hydrological Drought Index: Long-Term (Hydrological Conditions)." July 2002. National Oceanic and Atmospheric Administration. http://www.ncdc.noaa.gov/img/climate/research/2002/ann/phd200207_pg.gif.

National Oceanic and Atmospheric Administration (NOAA). 2008. "Billion Dollar U.S. Weather Disasters." July 22, 2008. National Oceanic and Atmospheric Administration (NOAA) Satellite and Information Service. National Climatic Data Center. http://lwf.ncdc.noaa.gov/oa/reports/billionz.html.

Natural Resources Defense Council (NRDC). 2010. *Evaluating Sustainability of Projected Water Demands under Future Climate Change Scenarios.* July 2010. Prepared by Tetra Tech. New York: Natural Resources Defense Council. http://rd.tetratech.com/climatechange/projects/doc/Tetra_Tech_Climate_Report_2010_highres.pdf.

Piper, A. M. 1965. *Has the United States Enough Water?* U.S. Department of Interior, Geological Survey Water Supply Paper No. 1797. Washington DC: US Government Printing Office.

PRISM Climate Group. 2006. Precipitation: Annual Climatology (1971–2000). PRISM Group, Oregon State University. http://www.prism.oregonstate.edu/products/viewer.phtml?file=/pub/prism/us_30s/graphics/ppt/Normals/us_ppt_1971_2000.14.png&year=1971_2000&vartype=ppt&month=14&status=final.

Thompson, R. G., M. L. Hyatt, J. W. McFarland, and H. P. Young. 1971. *Forecasting Water Demands.* National Water Commission PB-206 491. Washington, DC: US Government Printing Office.

US Department of Agriculture/Forest Service. 1989. *RPA Assessment of the Forest and Rangeland Situation in the United States, 1989.* Forest Resource Report, No. 26. Washington, DC: US Department of Agriculture.

US Department of Agriculture (USDA). 1994. "Farm and Ranch Irrigation Survey. 1992 Census of Agriculture. Table 4." *Land Irrigated by Method of Water Distribution: 1994 and 1988.* Washington, DC: National Agricultural Statistics Service, US Department of Agriculture.

———. 1998. "Farm and Ranch Irrigation Survey. 1997 Census of Agriculture. Table 4." *Land Irrigated by Method of Water Distribution: 1998 and 1994.* Washington, DC: National Agricultural Statistics Service, US Department of Agriculture.

———. 2003a. "Farm and Ranch Irrigation Survey. 2002 Census of Agriculture. Table 4." *Land Irrigated by Method of Water Distribution: 2003 and 1998.* Washington, DC: National Agricultural Statistics Service, US Department of Agriculture.

———. 2003b. "Irrigation by Estimated Quantity of Water Applied: 2003 and 1998. Table 12." *Land Irrigated by Method of Water Distribution: 2003 and 1998.* Washington, DC: National Agricultural Statistics Service, US Department of Agriculture.

———. 2008a. "Farm and Ranch Irrigation Survey. 2007 Census of Agriculture. Table 4." *Land Irrigated by Method of Water Distribution: 2007 and 2003.* Washington, DC: National Agricultural Statistics Service, US Department of Agriculture.

———. 2008b. "Irrigation by Estimated Quantity of Water Applied: 2008 and 2003. Table 12." *Land Irrigated by Method of Water Distribution: 2007 and 2003.* Washington, DC: National Agricultural Statistics Service, US Department of Agriculture.

US Geological Survey (USGS). 2002. *Concepts for National Assessment of Water Availability and Use.* Circular 1223. Reston, VA: US Geological Survey, Department of the Interior. http://pubs.usgs.gov/circ/circ1223/html/p15–17.html

———. 2006. National Atlas GIS datalayer: Major Dams of the United States. http://nationalatlas.gov/mld/damsoox.html

US Government Accountability Office (GAO). 2003. *Freshwater Supply: States' View of How Federal Agencies Could Help Them Meet the Challenges of Expected Shortages.* GAO-03-514 July 9, 2003. Washington DC: US Government Accountability Office.

US National Water Commission. 1973. *New Directions in U.S. Water Policy: Summary, Conclusions, and Recommendations from the Final Report of the National Water Commission.* Washington, DC: US Government Printing Office.

US Senate Select Committee on National Water Resources. 1961. *Report of the Select Committee,* Senate Report No. 29. Washington, DC: US Government Printing Office. (Reporting on US Senate Select Committee on National Water Resources. 1960. *Water Supply and Demand.* Committee Print No. 32. Washington, DC: US Government Printing Office.)

US Water Resources Council. 1968. *The Nation's Water Resources Part 1, First National Water Assessment,* Washington, DC: US Government Printing Office.

———. 1978. *The Nation's Water Resources 1975–2000.* Washington, DC: US Government Printing Office.

Wollman, N., and G. W. Bonem. 1971. *Outlook for Water: Quality, Quantity, and National Growth.* Baltimore, MD: The Johns Hopkins Press, for Resources for the Future, Inc.

2

LEGAL AND INSTITUTIONAL FRAMEWORK

OF WATER MANAGEMENT

Juliet Christian-Smith and Lucy Allen

Introduction

At the turn of the twenty-first century, legal scholar Janet C. Neuman (2001) gave this assessment of the status of federal water policy in the United States:

> Here it is, the year 2001, and we still do not have a coherent federal water policy, in spite of repeated calls for action for more than half a century. Of course, hundreds of federal laws and regulations govern a plethora of water related programs and activities. . . . What is missing is a rational, consistent, comprehensive, and yet concise federal policy. . . . Considering that water is widely recognized to be the looming resource issue of this century, the lack of a clear and succinct federal policy is troubling.

Today, a decade later, this assessment still rings true. Whereas several nations have reformed their approach to water management in the 21st century (e.g., Australia, India, Russia, and the European Union), the United States continues to use a complex legal and administrative framework, based on a wide diversity of federal laws, regulations, and historical court rulings, to distribute authority over water between federal, tribal, state, and local governments.

This framework has been built up over two centuries and is based on the US Constitution, federal and state legislation, judicial decisions, common law, and even international treaties. For instance, the federal government has the authority to develop and manage navigation on interstate or international bodies of water used for commerce (derived from the Commerce Clause of the US Constitution), whereas authority over water allocation has traditionally been the purview of the states. Andreen and Jones (2008) describe the often confusing distinctions between federal, state, and local authority:

> While the EPA [Environmental Protection Agency] has primary authority over point source pollution, nonpoint source pollution is primarily left to the states. While the [Army] Corps tackles wetlands, the Fish and Wildlife Service is responsible for protecting endangered and threatened aquatic species. While the states regulate the allocation of water from our lakes and streams, our local governments are responsible for regulation of land use practices which often degrade the quality of our waters.

In addition to dispersed authorities, federal funding for water is split across 30 agencies and programs. Few of these agencies' central missions are related to water[1] and, therefore, no single agency is ultimately responsible for the combination of land and water use impacts that have led to the widespread poor condition of the nation's waterways (EPA 2006).

In addition, the ambiguity inherent in such a piecemeal approach to water management can cause conflict, particularly between users (e.g., environment, industry, and agriculture), in disaster situations (e.g., flood management in New Orleans and drought in California's Central Valley), and when the status quo is altered by individual pieces of legislation (e.g., a new species is listed under the Endangered Species Act or water quality does not meet Clean Water Act [CWA]-mandated levels). In these cases, different federal, tribal, and local entities with water-related responsibilities may find themselves overlapping or even opposing one another.

The fragmentation in authority and funding around water issues has been noted by many commissions and councils over the decades. After World War II, President Truman appointed the Hoover Commission to recommend improvements to federal programs. The commission recommended sweeping reorganizations of water agencies and the creation of interagency river basin commissions (Neuman 2001). In 1955, President Eisenhower's Advisory Committee on Water Resources Policy argued yet again for federal agency coordination, river basin committees, and an independent Board of Review and Coordinator of Water Resources that would report directly to the president. In 1973, the National Water Commission strongly urged greater integration of federal water-related programs, echoed by the Western Water Policy Review Advisory Committee (1998). In addition, many water-resource experts have argued for years that a more explicit national water policy is needed (Rogers 1993; Neuman 2001; Leshy 2009). More recently, several cross-sector coalitions have submitted recommendations to the president and/or Congress that emphasize the need for a more coordinated federal approach to water policy (e.g., the Johnson Foundation Freshwater Summit 2010; American Society of

Civil Engineers, the American Water Resources Association, and the National Wildlife Federation 2008).

These calls for greater coordination come as communities face new challenges in meeting water-quality standards and ensuring that safe drinking water is available for all. In many cases, the resolution of these problems requires smart state and local action. But national policies and actions are also needed, as is leadership at the national level, particularly as we begin to understand the wide-reaching impacts that climate change will have on the timing, reliability, and quality of water supplies throughout the nation (see chapter 10: Water and Climate; Pachauri and Reisinger 2007; Trenberth et al. 2007; Bates et al. 2008). As legal scholars have pointed out, "No body of law, including water law, should remain rigid in the face of significant changes in physical or social conditions" (Adler 2011). Water policy will have to adapt quickly to changing climatic conditions and do so in a coordinated fashion, reflecting the hydrologic connectivity of our nation's water resources. Such comprehensive action will be a challenge under the current, fragmented system. But federal involvement in water management is needed and appropriate where federal water is provided, where states are in legal conflict, and where unsustainable water uses threaten the nation's economic productivity, environmental integrity, or international security.

Federal Authority over Water Resources

Two separate questions arise over the scope of federal jurisdiction over water resources: its constitutional authority over water bodies, and its responsibilities mandated by legislation. Federal authority over fresh water is largely derived from two clauses in the Constitution—the Commerce Clause, which permits federal regulation of water that may affect interstate commerce ("navigable waters"), and the Property Clause, which permits the federal government to regulate water for the beneficial use of its property, for instance, US Forest Service lands (GAO 2003). In addition, the so-called spending power of Congress granted by the Constitution provides an important basis for federal action (*United States v. Gerlach Live Stock Co.*, 339 U.S. 725 [1950]). The question of which water bodies the federal government has authority to regulate has centered largely around the definition of the term *navigable waters*, particularly with regard to the CWA. Table 2.1 provides a partial evolution of the federal government's authority to regulate and manage freshwater.

Numerous federal laws also relate, at least peripherally, to water, of which seven are particularly important in directing federal water-related activities: the Water Resources Development omnibus legislation, the CWA, the Safe Drinking Water Act, the Reclamation Act, the Federal Power Act, the National Environmental Policy Act, and the Endangered Species Act (see the appendix for a summary of each). These statutes give certain federal agencies authority over a collectively wide range of water-related activities, including construction of flood control and hydroelectric dams, irrigation projects, discharge of pollutants, and protection of habitat and ecosystems. Despite the complex

TABLE 2.1.

Partial Evolution of Federal Authority over Water Bodies

1787　US Constitution gives Congress authority over interstate commerce (article I, section 8, clause 3) and gives the US court authority over maritime matters (article III, section 2).

1824　*Gibbons v. Ogden.* Supreme Court finds that under the Commerce Clause, Congress also has authority over *navigable interstate waters.*

1871　*The Steamer Daniel Ball v. U.S. Supreme Court* includes *tidal waters and nontidal, navigable-in-fact waters* in definition of *navigable waters* over which Congress has jurisdiction.

1874　*U.S. v. The Steamer Montello.* Supreme Court further defines *navigable* to include *bodies of water that were previously capable of interstate transport.*

1899　1899 Rivers and Harbors Act outlaws pollution discharges into navigable waters and their tributaries.

1921　*Economy Light and Power Company v. U.S.* Supreme Court clarifies Montello decision to give *navigable water* legal status to *water bodies which were once, but are no longer navigable* (known as the "rule of indelible navigability").

1940　*U.S. v. Appalachian Electric Power Company.* Supreme Court finds that the term *navigable* includes both naturally navigable waters and *those which are navigable after "reasonable improvements,"* regardless of whether these improvements were authorized by Congress.

1950　*U.S. v. Gerlach Live Stock Co.* Supreme Court clearly establishes federal government's broad power under the spending clause to fund water projects and legislate generally in the area of water.

1968　US Army Corps of Engineers (USACE) begins to apply permitting regulations to *waters up to the mean high tide line for tidal and up to ordinary high tide mark for nontidal waters,* including many wetlands that were not previously regulated.

1970　USACE defines scope of permitting under the Refuse Act to *include tributaries of navigable waters.*

1972　The CWA is passed, institutionalizing federal protection of water quality for *navigable waters*—defined in the act as "the waters of the United States, including the territorial seas."

1973　EPA promulgates regulations further defining the jurisdictional scope of CWA to include: (*1*) *all navigable waters of the United States;* (*2*) *tributaries of navigable waters of the United States;* (*3*) *interstate waters;* (*4*) *intrastate lakes, rivers, and streams which are utilized by interstate travelers for recreational or other purposes;* (*5*) *intrastate lakes, rivers, and streams from which fish or shellfish are taken and sold in interstate commerce;* (*6*) *intrastate lakes, rivers, and streams which are utilized for industrial purposes by industries in interstate commerce.*

TABLE 2.1 *(continued)*

Partial Evolution of Federal Authority over Water Bodies

1973   *Natural Resources Defense Council v. Callaway.* Court broadens a restrictive USACE definition of the scope of the CWA and rules that Congress intended that federal jurisdiction over the nation's water is as broad as could be interpreted under the CWA.

USACE promulgates new regulations (finalized in 1977), in which *navigable waters* were defined as including: *(1) navigable coastal waters subject to the ebb and flow of the tide; (2) all coastal wetlands, mudflats, swamps, and similar areas that are contiguous or adjacent to other navigable waters; (3) rivers, lakes, streams, and artificial water bodies that are navigable waters of the United States; (4) artificially created channels used for recreational or other navigational purposes that are connected to other navigable waters; (5) tributaries to navigable waters; (6) interstate waters; (7) intrastate lakes, rivers, and streams that are used by interstate recreational travelers for the removal of fish sold in commerce, for interstate industrial commercial purposes, or for the production of agricultural commodities sold in commerce; (8) freshwater wetlands that are contiguous or adjacent to other navigable waters; and (9) other waters that the District Engineer determines necessitate regulation for protection of water quality.*

1985   *U.S. v. Riverside Bayview Homes, Inc.* Supreme Court affirms the legality of the USACE's and EPA's assertions that CWA jurisdiction includes all wetlands adjacent to navigable or interstate waters and their tributaries, citing the interconnected nature of aquatic systems.

1986,   Migratory Bird Rule. Following uneven implementation of the CWA, the result-
1988   ing hearings before the Senate Committee on Environment and Public Works, and guidance from EPA General Counsel Francis Blake, the EPA and USACE establish, through regulatory preambles, the Migratory Bird Rule, which asserts that CWA jurisdiction extends to waters which: *(1) are or would be used as habitat by birds protected by Migratory Bird treaties; (2) are or would be used as habitat by other migratory birds or which cross state lines; (3) are or would be used as habitat for endangered species; or (4) are used to irrigate crops sold in interstate commerce.*

2001   *SWANCC v. USACE.* Supreme Court holds that the *presence of migratory birds is not a sufficient basis for applying CWA to isolated intrastate* water bodies.

2006   *Rapanos v. U.S.* Plurality of the court focused on "relatively permanent" water bodies and adjacent wetlands as jurisdictional.

2008   EPA publishes clarification on CWA jurisdiction following the *Rapanos* case.

This guidance, like the ruling, focused on permanence and adjacency to navigable waters. Although it was meant to clarify for the USACE and the EPA what waters came under their jurisdiction, widespread uncertainty remained after the guidance was issued.

responsibilities that these laws create, they have never undergone comprehensive review and integration. In the following section, we examine this piecemeal approach to federal water policy, describe the many different agencies involved in water management, and, finally, discuss the administration of established legal authorities—demonstrating how agency administration can affect policy outcomes.

Evolution of a Fragmented Federal Water Policy

The scope of federal water-related responsibilities has gradually evolved through nearly 150 years of litigation, legislation, and changing public priorities. In the 19th century, federal involvement in water resources was primarily confined to surveying, funding, and constructing projects to facilitate navigation. The Rivers and Harbors Act of 1899 authorized the Army Corps of Engineers to regulate most obstructions to navigation, the first *regulatory* responsibilities of the Army Corps. In the 20th century, subsequent acts extended the mandates of the Army Corps and other federal agencies to include flood control, construction and management of irrigation projects, surface water quality, drinking water safety, and protection of endangered species.

Direct federal responsibilities over water management are now shared across approximately 30 agencies in 10 different departments, plus numerous independent agencies, councils, commissions, and offices. These responsibilities range widely (table 2.2). For example, the US Bureau of Reclamation and the Army Corps construct, operate, and manage large water facilities and infrastructure (GAO 2003). The Forest Service, Bureau of Land Management, Fish and Wildlife Service, and National Park Service manage the waters within the lands for which they are responsible. The US Geological Survey (USGS) collects water-related data, analyzes water use, and is the locus of water science activities (GAO 2003). The Environmental Protection Agency (EPA) is primarily responsible for overseeing implementation of the nation's two water-quality statutes, the CWA and the Safe Drinking Water Act. The Food and Drug Administration is responsible for regulating bottled water in interstate commerce; and National Oceanic and Atmospheric Administration and National Aeronautics and Space Administration play important roles in water-related satellite observations and monitoring for storms, droughts, and other extreme events. Furthermore, agencies that do not have direct responsibilities over water also influence its use and management. For example, energy policies can have large impacts on water use and quality.

Budgets and Funding

The federal budget is decided by the president and Congress through a process laid-out in the Congressional Budget Act of 1974. The process begins with the president proposing a budget and recommending funding levels for individual program accounts. This budget is then sent to Congress, which must pass a budget

TABLE 2.2.

Major Water-Related Federal Activities

Role	Institution with primary responsibility
Building, operating, and maintaining dams and distribution infrastructure	USACE, Bureau of Reclamation
Administering surface water-quality and environmental protection laws	EPA
Administering drinking water safety standards (including for bottled water)	EPA, Food and Drug Administration
Assisting in the development and implementation of water-management agreements and treaties	Congress
Acting as trustee for federal and tribal water rights	Department of Interior
Data collection and sharing	USGS, Council on Environmental Quality
Preservation and restoration of aquatic ecosystems	Fish and Wildlife Service, National Marine Fisheries Service

Source: Adapted from GAO (2003).

resolution—a document stating how much the government will spend in each of 19 spending categories and how much revenue the government will collect. Many (but not all) federal water-related institutions have their budgets decided through this political process. Therefore, agency budgets can vary greatly over time with changing administrative priorities. For example, the EPA enforcement budget dropped 39 percent between 1980 and 1983, reflecting the Reagan administration's desire to reduce regulatory costs for businesses (Andreen 2007). Andreen argues that in addition to reducing the resources available, such drops in funding send strong signals to agencies about how they should carry out their mandate. One highranking official stated, after the EPA cuts in the 1980s, that:

> People got scared that their reputation among Congress was that they were heavy handed and beat up on the little guys. This created a tough environment for [EPA] enforcement to be aggressive. The Agency's reaction was to be cautious not to do anything that would get it negative publicity (Andreen 2007).

Other water-related agencies, such as the Army Corps, receive funding through specific bills that must be periodically passed by Congress. The Army Corps' water-related projects are funded through Water Resources Development Acts that are normally passed every two years by Congress and that allocate funding to specific projects. Because their

TABLE 2.3.

Federal Water-Related Agency Budgets (in Millions of 2011$)

	Budget authority, dollars in millions (appropriations reported where marked with *)				
	FY 2007	FY 2008	FY 2009	FY 2010 (estimated)	FY 2011 (estimated)
Department of Agriculture					
Farm Service Agency	4,392[a]	3,401[b]	16,069[c]	14,805[c]	14,220[c]
Economic Research Service	80[a]	80[b]	82[c]	83[c]	87[c]
Natural Resources Conservation Service	2,803[a]	3,479[b]	3,575[c]	3,931[c]	3,993[c]
Forest Service	6,119[a]	6,423[b]	7,316[c]	6,213[c]	6,145[c]
Rural Utilities Service	-2,213[a]	798[b]	4,598[c]	701[c]	643[c]
Department of Commerce					
Economic Development Administration	301[d]	797[e]	461[f]	296[f]	286[f]
National Oceanic and Atmospheric Administration	4,483[d]	4,442[e]	5,518[f]	4,951[f]	5,708[f]
Department of Defense					
Army Corps of Engineers— Civil Works	7,539[g]	9,366[g]	17,085[g]	5,477[g]	4,855[g]
Department of Health and Human Services					
Centers for Disease Control and Prevention	6,508[h]	6,366[i]	6,870[j]	6,511[j]	6,342[j]
Food and Drug Administration	1,684[h]	1,929[i]	2,124[j]	2,389[j]	2,510[j]
Department of Homeland Security					
Coast Guard	9,153[k]	8,890[l]	9,913[m]	10,224[m]	10,078[m]
Federal Emergency Management Agency	4,892[k]	5,680[l]	6,150[m]	6,256[m]	6,527[m]
Department of Housing and Urban Development					
Community Planning and Development	7,839[n]	10,864[n]	15,004[o]	8,667[o]	8,425[o]
Department of Interior					
Bureau of Land Management	1,496[p]	1,270[q]	1,629[r]	1,329[r]	1,314[r]

TABLE 2.3. (*continued*)

Federal Water-Related Agency Budgets (in Millions of 2011$)

	Budget authority, dollars in millions (appropriations reported where marked with *)				
	FY 2007	FY 2008	FY 2009	FY 2010 (estimated)	FY 2011 (estimated)
Bureau of Indian Affairs	2,578[p]	2,529[q]	3,077[r]	4,810[r]	2,706[r]
Office of Surface Mining Reclamation and Enforcement	438[p]	630[q]	605[r]	711[r]	606[r]
Bureau of Reclamation	1,216[p]	1,389	2,178[r]	1,222[r]	1,232[r]
Fish and Wildlife Service	2,335[p]	2,482[q]	2,796[r]	2,792[r]	2,873[r]
USGS	1,067[p]	1,039[q]	1,222[r]	1,124[r]	1,134[r]
National Park Service	2,863[p]	2,958[q]	3,779[r]	3,186[r]	3,147[r]
Department of Justice					
Environment and Natural Resources Division*	102[s]	102[t]	106[u]	111[u]	119[u]
Department of Labor					
Occupational Safety and Health Administration	521[v]	501[w]	536[x]	565[x]	573[x]
Department of State					
Oceans, International Environment, and Scientific Affairs Bureau	29[y]	19[z]	50[aa]	181[aa]	129[aa]
US Agency for International Development (administrative expenses)*	792[y]	799[z]	952[aa]	1,676[aa]	1,704[aa]
Department of Transportation					
Maritime Administration	465[bb]	616[cc]	685[dd]	601[dd]	528[dd]
St. Lawrence Seaway Development Corporation	17[bb]	18[cc]	35[dd]	33[dd]	33[dd]
Pipeline and Hazardous Materials Safety Administration	143[bb]	158[cc]	117[dd]	125[dd]	141[dd]
Executive Office of the President					
Council on Environmental Quality and Office of Environmental Quality	3[ee]	3[ff]	3[gg]	3[gg]	3[gg]
Office of Management and Budget	82[ee]	80[ff]	91[gg]	94[gg]	93[gg]

(*continued*)

TABLE 2.3. (*continued*)

Federal Water-Related Agency Budgets (in Millions of 2011$)

	Budget authority, dollars in millions (appropriations reported where marked with *)				
	FY 2007	FY 2008	FY 2009	FY 2010 (estimated)	FY 2011 (estimated)
Office of Science and Technology Policy	6[ee]	7[ff]	5[gg]	7[gg]	7[gg]
Independent Agencies					
Environmental Protection Agency	8,060[g]	7,615[g]	15,197[g]	10,305[g]	9,875[g]
The Surface Transportation Board	27[hh]	26[ii]	27[gg]	28[gg]	25[gg]
Tennessee Valley Authority	-458[jj]	115[jj]	232[gg]	1,122[gg]	719[gg]
Appalachian Regional Commission	70[jj]	75[jj]	77[gg]	77[gg]	76[gg]
Federal Maritime Commission	21[jj]	23[jj]	24[gg]	24[gg]	25[gg]
Congress					
Congressional Budget Office	37[kk]	38[ll]	47[gg]	45[gg]	47[gg]
Congressional Research Service	108[kk]	105[ll]	110[gg]	113[gg]	120[gg]
Bilateral Commissions					
(US-Canada) International Joint Commission*	6[mm]	7[nn]	8[oo]	8[oo]	8[oo]
(US-Mexico) International Boundary and Water Commission*	36[mm]	160[nn]	305[oo]	76[oo]	74[oo]
Total	75,643	85,282	128,658	100,872	97,130

Note: List of agencies adapted from Rogers (1993).

Sources:

a. http://www.obpa.usda.gov/budsum/FY09budsum.pdf
b. http://www.obpa.usda.gov/budsum/FY10budsum.pdf
c. http://www.obpa.usda.gov/budsum/FY11budsum.pdf
d. http://www.osec.doc.gov/bmi/budget/FY2009BIB.html
e. http://www.osec.doc.gov/bmi/BUDGET/10BIB/BA-OUTLAYS.pdf
f. http://www.osec.doc.gov/bmi/BUDGET/11BIB/BA-OUTLAYS.pdf
g. http://www.gpoaccess.gov/usbudget/fy11/pdf/hist.pdf
h. http://www.hhs.gov/budget/09budget/2009BudgetInBrief.pdf
i. http://www.hhs.gov/asrt/ob/docbudget/2010budgetinbrief.pdf
j. http://dhhs.gov/asfr/ob/docbudget/2011budgetinbrief.pdf
k. http://www.dhs.gov/xlibrary/assets/budget_bib-fy2009.pdf

TABLE 2.3. (*continued*)

Federal Water-Related Agency Budgets (in Millions of 2011$)

l. http://www.gpoaccess.gov/usbudget/fy10/pdf/hist.pdf

m. http://www.dhs.gov/xlibrary/assets/budget_bib_fy2011.pdf

n. http://www.hud.gov/offices/cfo/reports/2009/cjs/introduction.pdf

o. http://hud.gov/budgetsummary2011/budget-authority-by-prog.pdf

p. http://www.doi.gov/budget/2009/09Hilites/A001.pdf

q. http://www.doi.gov/budget/2010/10Hilites/A001.pdf

r. http://www.doi.gov/budget/2011/11Hilites/A001.pdf

s. http://www.usdoj.gov/jmd/2009summary/pdf/fy2009-bud-sum.pdf

t. http://www.usdoj.gov/jmd/2010summary/pdf/summary-bud-authority.pdf

u. http://www.justice.gov/jmd/2011summary/html/budget-authority-appropriation.htm

v. http://web.archive.org/web/20090825161150/http://www.whitehouse.gov/omb/budget/fy2009/pdf/appendix/lab.pdf

w. http://web.archive.org/web/20100114024338/http://www.whitehouse.gov/omb/budget/fy2010/assets/lab.pdf

x. http://www.gpoaccess.gov/usbudget/fy11/index.html

y. http://www.usaid.gov/policy/budget/cbj2009/101416.pdf

z. http://www.state.gov/documents/organization/124295.pdf

aa. http://www.gpoaccess.gov/usbudget/fy11/pdf/budget/state.pdf

bb. http://www.dot.gov/bib2009/pdf/bib2009.pdf

cc. http://www.dot.gov/budget/2010/bib2010.htm

dd. http://www.dot.gov/budget/2011/

ee. http://web.archive.org/web/20100209114937/http://www.whitehouse.gov/omb/budget/fy2009/pdf/ appendix/eop.pdf

ff. http://web.archive.org/web/20100114024235/http://www.whitehouse.gov/omb/budget/fy2010/assets/ eop.pdf.

gg. http://www.gpoaccess.gov/usbudget/fy11/index.html.

hh. http://www.dot.gov/bib2009/pdf/bib2009.pdf.

ii. http://www.dot.gov/budget/2010/bib2010.htm.

jj. http://web.archive.org/web/20090825161106/http://www.whitehouse.gov/omb/budget/fy2009/pdf/ appendix/oia.pdf.

kk. http://www.gpo.gov/fdsys/pkg/BUDGET-2009-APP/pdf/BUDGET-2009-APP-1-3.pdf.

ll. http://web.archive.org/web/20100114024620/http://www.whitehouse.gov/omb/budget/fy2010/assets/leg.pdf.

mm. http://www.state.gov/documents/organization/100033.pdf.

nn. http://www.state.gov/documents/organization/122511.pdf.

oo. http://www.state.gov/documents/organization/137844.pdf.

budgets are decided at the project level by Congress, the water-related work of the Army Corps has a large amount of Congressional oversight and is particularly influenced by changing political tides.

The federal budget authority for those agencies that are most involved in water policy and management are presented in table 2.3. These data were collected largely from departmental budgets. There are multiple ways in which to report budgets; here they are reported in terms of *budget authority*, or the amount of money that Congress allows an agency to commit to spend. It should be noted that in some cases, the actual amount of money spent (the *outlay*) may be significantly higher or lower than the budget authority. However, whereas outlays are important for understanding actual monetary flows at the federal level, budget authority gives a good indication of the importance that the president and Congress place on different roles of the government because it reflects their approval of spending for various priorities.

Calculating the federal water-related budget based on agency budgets, as is done in table 2.1, overestimates water-related spending—for some agencies significantly—because some agencies spend very little funding and staff time on water-related responsibilities. For example, the US Coast Guard plays a minor role in freshwater management through their responsibilities for navigational safety of inland waters. Still, even using this overestimate, only between about 2 percent and 3 percent of the federal budget has been devoted to water-related activities each of the past 5 years—allocated among the over 30 federal entities.

A lower-boundary estimate for federal water-related spending can be made by summing the categories of "water resources" and "water transportation" from federal budget documents categorized by function (EOP 2010). These provide a low estimate because they do not include all water-related spending, such as water-related programs of the EPA or Fish and Wildlife Service. Together, these categories comprised between 0.4 percent and 0.7 percent of the total budget authority in the past 5 years ($15.7 million to $28.9 million) (EOP 2010).

The federal water-related institutions that have had the largest average budget over the past 5 years are the Farm Service Agency, the Army Corps, the US Coast Guard, the Office of Community Planning and Development, and the EPA. Not all of these agencies, however, spend a significant portion of their budget on freshwater-related activities. As mentioned previously, only a small percentage of the US Coast Guard's work is related to freshwater. The water-related programs of the Farm Service Agency are the Emergency Conservation Program, which provides emergency funding and technical assistance to farmers for increasing water-use efficiency in severe droughts, and the Source Water Protection Program, which encourages prevention of pollution of drinking water supplies. The Emergency Conservation Program makes up a varying portion of the overall Farm Service Agency budget, between $0 and about $200 million in the last 5 years, whereas the Source Water Protection Program has a consistently small budget of $4 to $5 million per year out of an overall Farm Service Agency budget of $3,000 to $15,000 million. Thus, a small percentage of the Farm Service Agency's budget is spent on programs targeted toward water. The Office of Community Planning and Development assists in community development through helping provide safe homes and living environments and expanding economic opportunity. Some of their programs provide grants for community development, which can be used for water-related infrastructure such as water and wastewater treatment plants (OCDP 2011).

The Army Corps, on the other hand, is an agency with a mission primarily related to water resources, including to: "1) Facilitate commercial navigation; 2) reduce the risk of damage from floods and storms; and 3) restore aquatic ecosystems" (USACE 2009). Even though the EPA works on a range of environmental issues, a significant portion of its resources are allocated toward water-related programs. The EPA organizes its budget by goal area; since 2007, "Clean and Safe Drinking Water" has been allocated a low of 33 percent of net programs costs in 2008 and a high of 55 percent of net program costs in 2010 (EPA 2007, 2008, 2011).

Authority versus Administration

Although the legislation described in the previous section gives a wide array of federal agencies authority over the nation's freshwater resources, the actual administration of legislation is selective and, often, subject to political influence. All three branches of government can affect the administration of water policy: the executive branch appoints the directors of federal agencies, the legislative branch authorizes funds, and the judicial branch defines the scope of jurisdiction. Herein, we describe how the funding, enforcement, and scope of authority over water issues affect policy implementation. We use the CWA as an example.

The distribution of funding for water-related programs and agencies is one way in which legislative officials can affect the administration of environmental laws—as is evidenced by the preceding example regarding cuts to the EPA's budget under the Reagan administration. More recently, a Government Accountability Office report found that, taking inflation into account, the EPA's total enforcement funding dropped 8 percent from 1997 to 2006 (GAO 2007). During the same period, EPA grants to states to implement environmental programs required by federal laws such as the CWA dropped 9 percent when adjusted for inflation. These funding cuts occurred when state and EPA responsibilities under the CWA grew due to new regulations, and both state and federal officials reported difficulty in meeting their responsibilities.

Another way to weaken the effectiveness of environmental legislation is to cripple enforcement activities. Enforcement of environmental statutes can vary considerably depending on the political environment, largely because of the lack of transparency around EPA enforcement activity and sensitivity of enforcement staff to signals from their superiors regarding how strictly laws should be enforced (Kuehn 1994; Mintz 2004; Andreen 2007). This is clearly evident in the irregular enforcement of statutes, such as the CWA, administered by the EPA. The CWA gives the EPA some flexibility in how the law is enforced by authorizing—but not requiring—the EPA to refer civil violators to the Department of Justice (figure 2.1). The more serious *criminal* violations, on the other hand, carry established penalties that the EPA must enforce.

In his review of CWA enforcement, Andreen (2007) demonstrates that the EPA uses this flexibility, and he identifies various periods during which enforcement was relaxed. For instance, when new Republican leadership entered both houses of Congress after the 1994 election, the desire to cut "big government" led to civil penalty referrals being halved between 1994 and 1995 (Andreen 2007).

At the same time that funding and enforcement of the CWA was declining, the extent of federal jurisdiction over water quality was being constrained. The CWA's stated goal

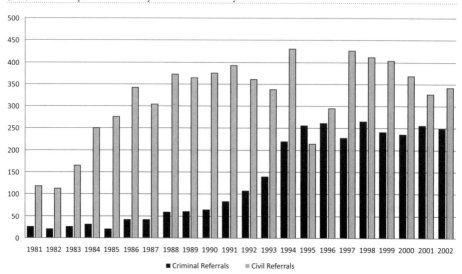

FIGURE 2.1. US Environmental Protection Agency criminal and civil referrals to the Department of Justice, 1981–2002

Note: These data include criminal and civil referrals related to violations of any environmental statute administered by the EPA (not only the Clean Water Act).

Source: Enforcement Accomplishment Reports (EPA 1990, 2003).

is to restore and maintain "the Nation's waters" (CWA, 33 U.S.C. §1251). Historically, the geographic scope of the CWA was interpreted quite broadly (H.R. Rep. No. 92-911, at 131, quoted in Downing, Winer, and Wood 2003); however, recent court cases have narrowed federal jurisdiction substantially.

In addition to litigation challenging the scope of federal jurisdiction, the influence of case law has changed administration of the act over time. The CWA prohibits discharge of any pollutants into *navigable waters*, defined as "the waters of the United States, including the territorial seas" (CWA, 33 U.S.C. §1362). Congress was reluctant to further define the term for "fear that any interpretation would be read narrowly" (H.R. Rep. No. 92-911, at 131, quoted in Downing, Winer, and Wood 2003). As a result, determining what exactly falls under navigable waters has been the source of much confusion.

In 2001, the court ruled that the presence of migratory birds did not qualify waters as "water of the United States," in *Solid Waste Agency of Northern Cook County v. U.S. Army Corps of Engineers (SWANCC v. USACE)*, 531 U.S. 159 (2001). Previously, the presence of migratory birds qualified a body of water to be regulated under the CWA, according to EPA general counsel guidance and case law, as millions of dollars are spent annually on hunting and observing these birds, and, therefore, they affect interstate commerce (Downing, Winer, and Wood 2003). Even more recently, in *Rapanos v. United States*, 547 U.S. 715 (2006), the court ruled, through a plurality rather than majority, that the phrase *waters of the United States* was limited to waters that are "relatively permanent, standing or continuously flowing bodies of water," and to wetlands or non-navigable, nonpermanent tributaries that have a "significant nexus" with a traditional navigable water (USACE and EPA 2008).

The ambiguity surrounding the *Rapanos* ruling, and the legal standards it required for determining what are or are not waters of the United States resulted in a significant obstacle to enforcement of the CWA. According to an EPA memorandum, between July 2006 and March 2008, there were over 300 cases in which enforcement actions were not pursued because of jurisdictional uncertainty and the burdensome data collection requirements for determining a "significant nexus" (GAO 2008). In addition to these enforcement problems, the ruling also obstructs the achievement of the goals of the CWA as it eliminates or jeopardizes CWA protection in a significant portion of the nation's water bodies: the EPA estimates that 59 percent of stream length in the United States is composed of nonpermanent streams (Grumbles 2005). This ambiguity will have to be addressed by future legislation or court decisions.

States' Authority over Water Resources

The federal government has primacy in matters concerning navigation, international treaty negotiations, federal water development projects, and water uses associated with federal lands and other property, and it has a stake in the national regulation of pollution and protection of natural resources, pursuant to the federal legislation summarized in the preceding section. However, rights to use water are allocated according to state and local laws, unless Congress intervenes (Getches 2009).

Most water rights are grounded in state constitutions and statutes, adjudicated by state courts, and administered by state agencies (Goldfarb 1988). States tend to have wide-ranging power to determine surface and groundwater allocation and management structures. Legal frameworks to allocate water among the 50 states vary widely, reflecting the unique histories, cultures, economies, and physical characteristics of different regions. Common state water allocation structures for surface water and groundwater resources are discussed and compared in the following sections.

Surface Water

Initially, water was allocated in the United States via a system of *riparian rights*. Riparian rights developed from English common law and tie water rights to property ownership, allowing property owners adjacent to a water course to use/divert water as they see fit without harming those downstream. They are limited rights that are reduced proportionally in times of shortage. Although this system worked relatively well in the eastern United States (and continues today), a separate approach—the *prior appropriation doctrine*— was adopted in the western United States to meet the unique needs of water users in arid climates, particularly nonlandowners who were interested in diverting water for mining, industry, and agriculture. The prior appropriation doctrine typically allocates water rights on a first-come, first-serve basis—often referred to as "first in time, first in right."

TABLE 2.4.

Framework of Western Surface Water Law

Legal framework	State
Pure prior appropriation	Alaska, Arizona, Colorado, Idaho, Montana, Nevada, New Mexico, Utah, and Wyoming
Riparian → appropriation (formerly a riparian system that became an appropriative system)	Kansas, North Dakota, South Dakota, Oregon, Texas, and Washington
Mixed riparian-appropriation	California, Nebraska, and Oklahoma

Source: Beck and Kelley (2009).

The prior appropriation doctrine differs from riparian rights in several important ways. First, mere ownership of land confers no rights to divert water under a prior appropriation system. Second, a user acquires an appropriative right by taking water from a natural stream and applying it to a *beneficial use*. Individual states define beneficial use differently, but usually include water stored and used for domestic and industrial water supply, irrigation, mining, hydropower, commercial navigation and transportation, recreation, and, in far fewer cases, the in situ support of ecosystems and wildlife.[2] Finally, the date when the user first applied the water to a beneficial use or first applied for an appropriative right determines the priority of use. When water runs short, junior appropriators must yield to senior appropriators. But, because appropriative rights are based on use, if a right is not being exercised for a statutorily defined number of years, it is subject to forfeiture in most prior appropriation states, leading to the maxim "use it or lose it." This can provide a strong disincentive for appropriators to conserve water.[3]

The vast majority of western states now allocate water purely based on the doctrine of prior appropriation, although some states that initially had a riparian rights system continue to recognize riparian uses that existed before the changeover (see table 2.4). Three western states—California, Nebraska, and Oklahoma—still allow riparian landowners to assert new uses superior to those with appropriative rights under some circumstances.

Riparian rights are recognized in the eastern states (table 2.5). Though, about half of eastern states have adopted water-use permitting systems, called *regulated riparianism*, that allow nonriparian land owners to acquire water rights to apply to a reasonable use[4] (Beck and Kelley 2009). These systems are based on riparian principles but permits can allow water to be applied to nonriparian land, can be issued for a limited time period, and can be conditioned on the protection of public values (Beck and Kelley 2009).

In addition to the common methods of allocating water already mentioned, there are also:

- *Federally reserved rights:* water rights necessary to meet the purposes for which federal lands and Native American reservations were originally set aside (see chapter 4: Tribes and Water);

TABLE 2.5.

Framework of Eastern Surface Water Law

Legal framework	State
Pure riparianism	New Hampshire, Vermont, Rhode Island, West Virginia, Ohio, Tennessee, Missouri, and Louisiana
Regulated riparianism	Alabama, Arkansas, Connecticut, Delaware, New York, New Jersey, Maryland, Illinois, Indiana, Iowa, Kentucky, Massachusetts, Pennsylvania, Mississippi, Minnesota, North Carolina, South Carolina, Georgia, Florida, Virginia, and Wisconsin

Source: Beck and Kelley (2009).

- *Pueblo rights:* rights derived from Spanish law and based on the needs of a settlement to serve its inhabitants. These rights expand with growth of the municipality;
- *Prescriptive rights:* public rights that are acquired from private property through use; and
- Numerous compacts, federal laws, court decisions and decrees, and regulatory guidelines (for example, a combination of these manages the Colorado River, referred to as the "law of the river").

Overall, the complexity of these systems makes it difficult to efficiently regulate water or to adapt to changing circumstances.

Groundwater

Groundwater law and rights are also extremely complex. Several overarching doctrines govern groundwater use, including absolute ownership, reasonable use, correlative rights, and prior appropriation. The absolute ownership doctrine, which survives most strongly in Indiana, Maine, and Texas, confers an unlimited right to withdraw groundwater by the overlying land owner. In other words, in these states, overlying landowners can pump groundwater without any legal liability to not harm existing uses (Getches 2009). Reasonable use, common in the eastern states, is similar to absolute ownership except that waste is prohibited and water must be used on overlying land unless it can be transported without injuring other overlying owners (Goldfarb 1988). Although called *reasonable use*, this doctrine imposes few restrictions on the nature and amount of groundwater use on overlying land. Neither absolute ownership nor the reasonable use doctrine consider the total demand on the aquifer or offer remedies for harm due to groundwater overdraft. However, there are approaches that consider total water demand, such as Section 858 of the *Restatement of Torts* (second edition). Section 858 states that a groundwater user may withdraw water unless other users are unreasonably affected by a lowered water table or reduced pressure, the user exceeds his or her share of the total annual supply, or the amount withdrawn affects surface supplies. Section 858 has been explicitly adopted in Michigan, Ohio, and Wisconsin, and a similar concept appears in the groundwater law of Arkansas, Florida, Nebraska, New Jersey, and Missouri (Goldfarb 1988). In addition, under the correlative rights doctrine, landowners are each entitled to a reasonable share of the total groundwater supply, commonly based on the amount of overlying acreage. California, Nebraska, and Tennessee recognize correlative groundwater rights. Finally, when the doctrine of prior appropriation is applied to groundwater, junior groundwater users can be held liable for harm caused to more senior users (Getches 2009).

One of the most obvious disincentives for the efficient use of groundwater is that, despite these legal frameworks, there is little to no monitoring and many states do not require reporting groundwater use, so there can be no substantive enforcement of statutes that set limits on pumping or require reasonable use. Increasingly, rising energy costs (which increase the price to pump water out of the ground) along with groundwater overdraft illustrate the need for more comprehensive and effective groundwater management. Some states have created statewide water management systems in response. In New Mexico, the statewide management system emphasizes basin-wide adjudications; in Nebraska, groundwater pumping is regulated through natural resources districts; and in Kansas, local residents form groundwater management districts and apply their own standards for preventing overdraft (Goldfarb 1988). The lack of comprehensive groundwater law or management, however, has led some regions to suffer from unsustainable groundwater overdraft (see next section).

A CASE STUDY OF THE OGALLALA AQUIFER

The Ogallala Aquifer is located in the Great Plains region of the United States and is one of the world's largest aquifers. Spreading beneath eight states and part of a ninth (South Dakota, Wyoming, Colorado, Kansas, New Mexico, Oklahoma, New Mexico, Texas, and nearly all of Nebraska), the Ogallala lies under 174,000 square miles and reaches up to 1,300 feet in depth (figure 2.2). Water from the Ogallala aquifer accounts for 30 percent of groundwater used for irrigation in America (Guru and Horne 2000). Groundwater declines began in parts of the aquifer soon after the beginning of extensive groundwater irrigation. By 1980, groundwater levels in parts of Texas, Oklahoma, and southwestern Kansas had declined by more than 100 feet (Luckey, Gutenag, and Weeks 1981). In response, the USGS began monitoring annual groundwater level changes in 1988 (McGuire 2007). Based on these data, the USGS estimates that total water storage declined by about 253 million acre-feet (312 km³) or 9 percent since substantial irrigation began in the 1950s (McGuire 2007).

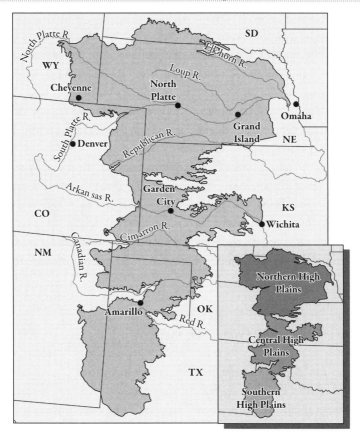

FIGURE 2.2. Geographic extent of Ogallala Aquifer
Source: Peck (2007).

Extractions from the aquifer allowed large-scale irrigation in the arid Great Plains, an area previously considered unfit for agricultural activities (Peterson, Marsh, and Williams 2003). Water in the aquifer was so abundant that many used the water without discrimination, in large part encouraged by the lack of groundwater management and oversight. Today, 94 percent of the water pumped from the aquifer is used to irrigate primarily corn, wheat, and cotton (Guru and Horne 2000). Agriculture accounts for a large portion of employment and the overall economy in the Great Plains. Unfortunately, the increased pumping of the aquifer has led to severe groundwater overdraft —water outputs from the aquifer are approximately 10 times greater than the natural recharge (Guru and Horne 2000). Due to the aquifer's slow rate of recharge, the aquifer has been depleted to the point where it is uncertain whether it will be able to meet human demand in the next decade. The resulting scarcity of water could severely damage the basis of the Great Plains economy through higher pumping costs, lower overall agricultural production, and deficient soil and planting conditions.

The problems caused by groundwater overdraft are largely a result of mismanagement or a lack of management. The overall groundwater levels and quality were unregulated for many years. The 1970s brought about several attempts to manage pumping from the Ogallala; however, these measures were inconsistently applied in different states. For instance, in Oklahoma, legislation was passed to allow the state to regulate total groundwater withdrawals. Permits were required and maximum yield regulations were set in place (Wickersham 1980). However, in the neighboring state of Texas, overlying landowners have unlimited rights to groundwater (Wickersham 1980).

Given the biophysical qualities of groundwater, cones of depression (or areas where groundwater is being extracted quickly) will actually draw water from other parts of the aquifer. Thus, sustainable management in one area will have little impact if other areas continue to mine groundwater. The interconnected nature of shared groundwater resources requires comprehensive management across overlying lands. Despite this hydrologic reality, the Ogallala aquifer continues to lack a comprehensive management strategy.

Legal Hurdles to Sustainable Water Management

State water law can, as previously mentioned, serve as a disincentive to sustainable water management practices such as conservation and efficiency. The Environmental Law Institute recently examined the structure of water rights in western states and identified significant legal hurdles to water conservation embedded within the doctrine of prior appropriation, and the institute offered several ways for states to overcome them. Chief among these hurdles were: (1) the risk of forfeiture (or the "use it or lose it" principle), and (2) burdensome and time-consuming procedures for transferring a water right or changing its use (Schempp 2009).

The doctrine of prior appropriation includes rules about water right abandonment and forfeiture due to nonuse, which were put in place to discourage speculation. Because not fully using a water right can be grounds for losing the right to the unused portion, these rules encourage use at historic levels and, thus, discourage water conservation. In addition, few states allow the transfer of conserved water to other users or change of its use to other purposes, limiting what can be done with the conserved water to avoid forfeiture and abandonment.

The doctrine of prior appropriation also emphasizes the protection of existing water rights, which often results in extensive review procedures for changing the purpose of use, place of use, and point of diversion as well as transferring the right to another user. The cost of such a process can price out small changes and transactions, and the time required can make quick responses impossible.

Some states have implemented strategies to overcome these hurdles, including through significant reforms in state water law. These reforms include: (1) defining water conservation as a beneficial use or exempting activities that conserve water from forfeiture or abandonment provisions, and (2) accelerating the transfer and change-of-use processes to allow more flexibility. It is critical that state water law support, rather than stymie, sustainable water management. There are also opportunities for federal actions that can both reduce these hurdles and strengthen effective water management at all levels.

Federal Engagement in Sustainable Water Management

The federal government has, at times, engaged states to improve their management of surface and groundwater resources. Federal engagement offers a variety of advantages, it can bring greater resources to bear, it can focus on transboundary issues that involve more than one state or nation, and it can help to ensure that federal laws are being upheld by the states. In the following section, we describe two cases where federal engagement has led to better planning and more comprehensive efforts to address water-resource management challenges.

A CASE STUDY OF THE CHESAPEAKE BAY

The Chesapeake Bay area is home to 16 million people; it supports over 3,600 species of plants, provides a resting place for many species of migratory birds, supplies 500 million pounds of seafood products every year, and is a crucial economic, recreational, educational, and cultural resource. However, in the last half a century, the bay has suffered from increasing pollution, the collapse of many of its fisheries, and large-scale habitat loss (Fraites and Flanigan 1993). In response to worsening conditions, in the early 1980s, Maryland Senator Charles Mathias sponsored a five-year, congressionally-funded study analyzing the bay's ecology. In 1983, as a result of the study, Maryland, Pennsylvania, Virginia, the District of Columbia, the EPA (as administrator of the CWA), and the Chesapeake Bay Commission signed the Chesapeake Bay Agreement, which formally established the Chesapeake Bay Program. The program defines formal agreements on restoration goals and policy directives, which are meant to inform state and federal laws.

In 2000, the program set goals for Chesapeake restoration through 2010, aiming to restore and protect habitats, fisheries, and the larger aquatic ecosystem by improving water quality, promoting sound land use practices, and encouraging individual and community stewardship of the bay's resources. However, most of the restoration plans were voluntary and there was been little success in meeting quantitative goals to reduce contaminants entering the bay (Fahrenthold 2006). In response, President Obama issued an executive order in 2009 for the protection and restoration of the Chesapeake Bay, as the efforts of the past 25 years were not showing sufficient progress in restoring the health of the bay and its watershed. The order states:

Restoration of the health of the Chesapeake Bay will require a renewed commitment to controlling pollution from all sources as well as protecting and restoring habitat and living resources, conserving lands, and improving management of natural resources, all of which contribute to improved water quality and ecosystem health. The Federal Government should lead this effort. Executive departments and agencies working in collaboration, can use their expertise and resources to contribute significantly to improving the health of the Chesapeake Bay. Progress in restoring the Chesapeake Bay also will depend on the support of State and local governments, the enterprise of the private sector, and the stewardship provided to the Chesapeake Bay by all the people who make this region their home.

The executive order established a Federal Leadership Committee—composed of representatives from the EPA and the departments of Agriculture, Commerce, Defense, Homeland Security, Interior, and Transportation—and charged it with developing a coordinated strategy to protect the nation's largest estuarine ecosystem. Responding to that charge, the committee developed goals and actions described in the Strategy for Protecting and Restoring the Chesapeake Bay in 2010, identifying the specific activities that agencies will undertake. The action plan is organized into four goal areas ("restore water quality," "recover habitat," "sustain fish and wildlife," and "conserve land and increase public access") and four supporting strategy sections ("expand citizen stewardship," "develop environmental markets," "respond to climate change," and "strengthen science"). In 2011, the federal government released its plan to finance each goal and strategy. In total, more than $490 million is targeted in Fiscal Year (FY) 2011 toward meeting the outcomes and goals set forth in the strategy, contingent on appropriations by Congress (table 2.6).

Today, several departments of the federal government are working together with state and local agencies to implement the action plan. In 2012, the Federal Leadership Committee reported progress on many fronts, including expanding data collection to better assess progress toward improved water quality, opening 148 stream miles for fish passage, and providing technical and financial assistance to agricultural producers to reduce the amount of sediment and nutrients entering the Bay (Federal Leadership Committee for the Chesapeake Bay 2012). While restoration of the Bay is a long-term effort, the federal government has played an important role in setting targets and bringing resources to bear to help achieve them.

A CASE STUDY OF ARIZONA'S GROUNDWATER MANAGEMENT CODE

In the late 1970s, after decades of overexploiting Arizona's groundwater resources, President Carter's administration told Arizona policy makers that no allocations of Central Arizona Project water (Arizona's primary surface water supply) would be made until passage of a comprehensive groundwater code. In 1980, Arizona passed their historic Groundwater Management Code, demonstrating how the federal government influences states to conform to federal policy (Smith 1985).

TABLE 2.6.

FY 2011 Funding Proposed in the President's Budget for Chesapeake Bay Projects

Department agency	Water quality goal	Habitat goal	Fish and wildlife goal	Land conservation and public access goal	Citizen steward-ship	Environ-mental markets	Climate Change	Science	Total
Dept. of Agriculture total	31,775,000	8,745,000	205,000	10,470,000	1,340,000	220,000	553,000	270,000	153,578,000
Forest Service	435,000	745,000	205,000	120,000	1,340,000	20,000	553,000	270,000	3,688,000
National Resources Conservation Service	131,340,000	8,000,000	—	10,350,000	—	20,000	—	—	149,740,000
Office of Emergency Management	—	—	—	—	—	150,000	—	—	150,000
Dept. of Commerce/National Oceanic and Atmospheric Administration	2,255,000	1,995,000	6,885,250	15,000	450,000	—	1,252,000	6,494,000	19,346,250
Dept. of Defense total	6,733,062	501,013	5,200,000	4,700,000	—	—	300,000	—	17,434,075
Services	6,723,062	—	—	4,700,000	—	—	—	—	11,423,062
USACE	10,000	501,013	5,200,000	—	—	—	300,000	—	6,011,013
Dept. of Interior total	5,061,250	7,600,087	2,907,892	18,611,298	5,087,791	—	1,924,561	1,623,339	42,817,218
Fish and Wildlife Service	482,264	7,115,363	2,282,171	2,390,292	2,891,184	—	—	—	15,161,274
National Park Service	—	298,700	120,369	15,822,006	2,196,607	—	290,958	441,000	19,169,640
USGS	4,578,986	186,024	505,352	400,000	—	—	1,633,603	1,182,339	8,486,304
Dept. of Transportation	175,000	95,000	—	8,231,000	—	—	—	—	8,501,000
EPA	237,295,566	—	—	565,920	2,105,000	150,000	75,000	4,689,866	248,873,881
Total	383,294,878	18,936,100	15,198,142	42,594,218	8,952,791	370,000	4,104,561	13,077,205	490,550,424

Source: Federal Leadership Committee for the Chesapeake Bay (2010).

The code has three specific goals: to control overdraft, to provide a means to allocate the state's limited groundwater most efficiently, and to augment Arizona's groundwater through water supply development. To respond to severe overdraft, the code created *active management areas*—currently Tucson, Phoenix, Prescott, Pinal, and Santa Cruz. In these five areas, the Groundwater Management Code restructured water rights, required water budgets, prohibited irrigation of new agricultural lands, created a comprehensive system of conservation targets updated every decade, developed a program requiring developers to demonstrate a 100-year ensured water supply for new growth, and required groundwater users to meter wells and report on annual water withdrawal and use. In addition to the Active Management Areas, the code also established *"irrigation nonexpansion areas"* throughout the state.

Implementation of Arizona's Groundwater Management Code has been difficult. A recent evaluation of the code found that access to data limits the effectiveness of the management guidelines, particularly in creating accurate water budgets (Megdal, Smith, and Lien 2008).[5] More consistent, detailed, and regularly updated information about water inflows and outflows in the Active Management Areas will be needed to comply with the intent of the Groundwater Management Code. In addition, the code does not recognize the interconnection of surface water and groundwater, and in many ways, it has incentivized the increased use of surface water supplies. Nevertheless, the code is one of the only examples of comprehensive groundwater management. Interviews with individuals involved with the passage of the 1980 Arizona Groundwater Management Act indicate that it is unlikely that the code would have been produced without significant federal pressure (Smith 1985).

There are several avenues for federal intervention to improve groundwater management elsewhere. Many federal water projects are designed at least in part to mitigate the effects of overdrafting (e.g., California's Central Valley Project); Arizona's experience with the Central Arizona Project provides some evidence that as a quid pro quo for access to federally developed water, improved groundwater management can be required. In addition, the federal government has a clear interest in maintaining an agricultural economy and avoiding economic disruption. In cases where groundwater depletion threatens agricultural productivity and sustainability, there is reasonable cause for federal involvement. Finally, water is necessary for many aspects of energy production and development, including mining, processing, transportation, refining, and conversion to other forms of energy (see chapter 9: Water and Energy). Therefore, there is a growing federal interest in the management of water resources that may affect energy production.

Rethinking the Federal Role in Water Policy

Even though some have suggested that the federal government has the constitutional authority to nationalize water management, such a solution is neither politically feasible nor desirable (Leshy 2009). Instead, it remains appropriate for the federal government to provide comprehensive policies to ensure that our nation's public water resources are adequately protected from pollution and overexploitation, used efficiently, and managed in a way to ensure continued national and economic security. Indeed, Neuman (2001) argues that a federal water policy is needed for the 21st century for three primary reasons: (1) water is an interstate resource with crucial importance to the nation's health and economy, (2) that nation's waters are under severe and increasing stress, and (3) the federal government currently spends tens of billions of dollars on water-related programs with insufficient policy guidance to ensure that it is money well spent.

Similarly, we argue that there is an appropriate and necessary role for the federal government in water management where the federal government provides water, in legal conflicts between states, and when the nation's economic, environmental, or security interests are threatened by unsustainable management and use. We also suggest several federal actions that could improve water law and legislation:

A National Strategy to Address Major Threats to Water Resources

The Office of Science and Technology Policy's Committee on Environment, Natural Resources, and Sustainability should be tasked with developing a national strategy for ensuring the long-term sustainability of our nation's water resources. Such a strategy would: (1) define a protocol to assess existing pressures and potential threats to interstate surface and groundwater resources, and (2) recommend amendments, new legislation, or improved administrative approaches to reduce nonpoint source pollution and manage interstate groundwater basins. These two issues are widely regarded as major threats to our water resources and are linked as more than half of the nation's drinking water comes from groundwater, "a source that is easily contaminated by indiscriminate and largely unregulated discharges of pollutants, and once contaminated, is very difficult to clean up" (Rogers 1993).

Revived River Basin Commissions and River Basin Management Plans

Increasingly, state and tribal water resource professionals, scientists, and are turning to watershed management as a means for achieving greater results from their programs (National Research Council 1999). The federal government once had several active river basin commissions, yet they were eliminated by Executive Order 12319 (issued by President Reagan in 1981). River basin commissions were first devised by the Hoover Commission on the Reorganization of the Executive Branch and were supported in recommendations of the Cooke Commission, the Presidential Advisory Committee on Water Resources Policy, the National Water Commission, and the Western Water Policy Review Advisory Committee (Neuman 2010).

Given increasing tensions over water and the 21st century challenges identified herein, the US river basin commissions could be reinstituted as a rational locus for organizing water management responsibilities and prioritizing key projects and programs to address major threats. These commissions could be tasked with developing river basin management plans that then become a gateway for federal funding. For example, grants for improved water management that are now dispersed through separate agencies and programs, such as the Farm Service Agency, the EPA, and State Revolving Loans, could instead include scoring criteria that prioritizes projects developed through comprehensive river basin management plans.

A National Water Commission to Guide River Basin Plans and Review Water-Related Budgets

In addition, numerous studies have recommended a national water commission or council that reports directly to the president (Rogers 1993). We agree, and recommend the commission be composed of diverse, nonfederal experts representing a broad range of disciplines, including leaders of the environmental justice movement. The commission's first task should be to develop guidelines and requirements to ensure that river basin management plans are scientifically rigorous and participatory, identifying key threats and stressors to the basin's water resources and prioritizing projects to address those threats. The council's responsibilities would also include reviewing all water-related budgets and making recommendations for key priorities. This review would provide a much needed analysis of gaps and overlaps in existing water-related programs.

Conclusions

Water management operates at federal, state, and local scales, with a great deal of heterogeneity within each. There is no one-size-fits-all management of this highly diverse resource. Although essentially a local resource, water has the unique ability to link the local to the nonlocal: water connects us to those above and below us in a watershed, transcending political boundaries and demanding attention to the larger implications of local actions. Even though unique hydrologic, economic, and cultural characteristics demand state- and local-level decision making, it has been recognized since the earliest days of the nation that federal efforts are needed to ensure that water quality and quantity are maintained for all citizens, interstate commerce is fairly regulated, and multistate watersheds are appropriately managed.

It is past time for an integrated and comprehensive national water strategy. Though many water issues will remain local, to be resolved by community participation and regional efforts, our national government can play a more effective role. The following chapters describe, in more detail, persistent and emerging water challenges and the appropriate role for the federal government to play in addressing those challenges in a coordinated, comprehensive manner.

References

Adler, R. 2011. "Rethinking Water Law in a Changing Climate." In: *Global Warming: A Reader*. Edited by W. H. Rodgers, xx–xx. Durham, NC: Carolina Academic Press.

American Society of Civil Engineers, the American Water Resources Association, and the National Wildlife Federation. 2008. "Fourth National Water Policy Dialogue." Dialogue, American Society of Civil Engineers, the American Water Resources Association, and the National Wildlife Federation, Washington, DC. http://www.waterresourcescoalition.org/files/pdf/FourthNationalWaterPolicyDialogueComplete.pdf.

Andreen, W. L. 2007. "Motivating Enforcement: Institutional Culture and the Clean Water Act." *Pace Environmental Law Review* 24: 67.

Andreen, W. L., and S. C. Jones. 2008. *The Clean Water Act: A Blueprint for Reform*. Washington DC: Center for Progressive Reform. http://www.progressivereform.org/articles/CW_Blueprint_802.pdf.

Bates, B. C., Z. W. Kundzewicz, S. Wu, and J. P. Palutikof, eds. 2008. *Climate Change and Water*. Intergovernmental Panel on Climate Change Technical Paper VI. Geneva: IPCC Secretariat.

Beck, R., and A. Kelley, eds. 2009. *Waters and Water Rights*. New Providence, NJ: Lexis-Nexis.

Downing, D. M., C. Winer, and L. D. Wood. 2003. "Navigating through Clean Water Act Jurisdiction: A Legal Review." *Wetlands* 23 (3): 475–493.

Executive Office of the President of the United States (EOP). 2010. "Table 32-1: Policy Budget Authority by Function, Category, and Program." Excel table. http://www.gpoaccess.gov/usbudget/fy11/fct.html.

Fahrenthold, D. A. 2006. "Bay Program Ready to Study Less, Work More." *Washington Post*, September 26.

Federal Leadership Committee for the Chesapeake Bay. 2010. "Fiscal Year 2011 Action Plan." http://executiveorder.chesapeakebay.net/file.axd?file=2010%2F9%2FChesapeake+EO+Action+Plan+FY2011.pdf.

———. 2012. "Executive Order 13508 Progress Report: Strategy for Protecting and Restoring the Chesapeake Bay Watershed, FY2011." Public Review Draft. http://executiveorder.chesapeakebay.net/file.axd?file=2012%2f3%2fChes_Bay_Progress_Report_2011_05Mar12.pdf

Fraites, E. L., and F. H. Flanigan. 1993. "Perspectives on the Role of the Citizen in Chesapeake Bay Restoration." In) *Water Resources Administration in the United States*. Edited by M. Reuss, 105–118. East Lansing, MI: American Water Resources Association.

Getches, D. H. 2009. *Water Law in a Nutshell*. 4th ed. St. Paul, MN: Thomson/West.

Goldfarb, W. 1988. *Water Law*. Chelsea, MI: Lewis Publishers.

Government Accountability Office (GAO). 2003. *Freshwater Supply: States' View of How Federal Agencies Could Help Them Meet the Challenges of Expected Shortages*. GAO-03-514. Washington, DC: Government Accountability Office. http://www.gao.gov/new.items/d03514.pdf.

———. 2007. *Environmental Enforcement: EPA-State Enforcement Partnership Has Improved, but EPA's Oversight Needs Further Enhancement*. GAO-07-883. Washington, DC: Government Accountability Office.

———. 2008. *Environmental Enforcement: EPA Needs to Improve the Accuracy and Transparency of Measures Used to Report on Program Effectiveness*. GAO-08-111R. Washington, DC: Government Accountability Office.

Grumbles, Benjamin H. 2005. Benjamin H. Grumbles, Assistant Administrator, EPA, to Ms. Jeanne Christie, Executive Director, Association of State Wetland Managers, January 9, 2005. Association of State Wetland Managers. http://www.aswm.org/fwp/letterbg.pdf.

Guru, M., and J. Horne. 2000. *The Ogallala Aquifer*. Portreau, OK: The Kerr Center for Sustainable Agriculture. http://www.kerrcenter.com/publications/ogallala_aquifer.pdf.

Johnson Foundation Freshwater Summit. 2010. "Charting New Waters: A Call to Action to Address U.S. Freshwater Challenges." Web page. http://www.johnsonfdn.org/chartingnewwaters.

Kuehn, R. R. 1994. "Remedying the Unequal Enforcement of Environmental Laws." *St. Johns Legal Comment* 9: 625–668.

Leshy, J. 2009. "Notes on a Progressive National Water Policy." *Harvard Law and Policy Review* 3 (1): 133–159.

Luckey, R. R., E. D. Gutentag, and J. B. Weeks. 1981. *Water-Level and Saturated-Thickness Changes, Predevelopment to 1980, in the High Plains Aquifer in Parts of Colorado, Kansas, Nebraska, New Mexico, Oklahoma, South Dakota, Texas, and Wyoming*. U.S. Geological Survey Hydrologic Investigations Atlas, HA-652. Reston, VA: USGS National Center. (2 sheets, scale 1:2,500,000.) http://pubs.er.usgs.gov/usgspubs/ha/ha652.

McGuire, V. L. 2007. *Water-Level Changes in the High Plains Aquifer, Predevelopment to 2005 and 2003 to 2005*. U.S. Geological Survey Scientific Investigations Report, SIR 2006–5324. VA: USGS National Center. http://pubs.usgs.gov/sir/2006/5324/.

Megdal, S., Z. A. Smith, and A. M. Lien. 2008. *Evolution and Evaluation of the Active Management Area Management Plans*. Final Report, University of Arizona. Tucson, AZ: Water Resources Research Center.

Mintz, J. A. 2004. "'Treading Water': A Preliminary Assessment of EPA Enforcement during the Bush II Administration." *Environmental Law Reporter* 34: 10933–19353. http://www.environmentalintegrity.org/pdf/publications/ERL_Article.pdf.

National Research Council. 1999. *New Strategies For America's Watersheds*. Committee on Watershed Management, Water Science and Technology Board. Washington, DC: National Academy Press.

Neuman, J. 2001. "Adaptive Management: How Water Law Needs to Change." *Environmental Law Reporter* 31: 11432–11437.

Office of Community Development and Planning (OCDP). 2011. CPD Appropriations Budget. http://www.hud.gov/offices/cpd/about/budget/.

Pachauri, R. K., and A. Reisinger, eds. 2007. *Climate Change 2007: Synthesis Report. Contribution of Working Groups I, II, and III to the Fourth Assessment Report of the Intergovernmental Panel on Climate Change*. Geneva: IPCC Secretariat.

Peck, J. 2007. "Groundwater Management in the High Plains Aquifer in the USA: Legal Problems and Innovations." In *The Agricultural Groundwater Revolution: Opportunities and Threats to Development*. Edited by M. Giordano and K. G. Villholth, 296–319. Cambridge, MA: CAB International.

Peterson, J. M., T. L. Marsh, and J. R. Williams. 2003. "Conserving the Ogallala Aquifer: Efficiency, Equity, and Moral Motives." *Choices* 1: 15–18.

Rogers, P. 1993. *America's Water: Federal Roles and Responsibilities*. Cambridge, MA: The MIT Press.

Schempp, A. 2009. *Western Water in the 21st Century Policies and Programs that Stretch Supplies in a Prior Appropriation World*. Washington, DC: Environmental Law Institute.

Smith, Z. A. 1985. "Federal Intervention in the Management of Groundwater Resources: Past Efforts and Future Prospects." *Publius: The Journal of Federalism* 15 (1): 145–159.

Trenberth, K. E., P. D. Jones, P. Ambenje, R. Bojariu, D. Easterling, A. Klein Tank, D. Parker, et al. 2007. "Observations: Surface and Atmospheric Climate Change." In *Climate Change 2007: The Physical Science Basis. Contribution of Working Group I to the Fourth Assessment Report of the Intergovernmental Panel on Climate Change*. Edited by S. Solomon, D. Qin, M. Manning, Z. Chen, M. Marquis, K. B. Averyt, M. Tignor, and H. L. Miller, 236–336. Cambridge: Cambridge University Press.

US Army Corps of Engineers (USACE). 2009. "Corps of Engineers—Civil Works." Office of Management and Budget. http://m.whitehouse.gov/sites/default/files/omb/assets/omb/budget/fy2009/corps.html.

US Army Corps of Engineers (USACE) and US Environmental Protection Agency (EPA). 2008. "Clean Water Act Jurisdiction following the U.S. Supreme Court's Decision *in Rapanos v. United States* & *Carabell v. United States*." Memorandum, US Army Corps of Engineers and US Environmental Protection Agency, Washington, DC. http://www.usace.army.mil/CECW/Documents/cecwo/reg/cwa_guide/cwa_juris_2dec08.pdf.

US Environmental Protection Agency (EPA). 1990. *FY 1989 Enforcement Accomplishments Report*. Washington, DC: Enforcement and Compliance Monitoring. http://www.epa.gov/compliance/resources/reports/accomplishments/oeca/fy88accomp-rpt.pdf.

———. 2003. *Environmental Results through Smart Enforcement, Fiscal Year 2002 Enforcement and Compliance Assurance Accomplishments Report*. Washington, DC: Office of Enforcement and Compliance Assurance. http://www.epa.gov/compliance/resources/reports/accomplishments/oeca/fy02accomplishment.pdf.

———. 2006. *Wadeable Streams Assessment: A Collaborative Survey of the Nation's Streams*. EPA 841-B-06-002. Washington, DC: EPA Office of Research and Development, Office of Water. www.epa.gov/owow/streamsurvey.

———. 2007. *Fiscal Year 2007 Performance and Accountability Report: Highlights*. Washington, DC: US Environmental Protection Agency. http://www.epa.gov/planandbudget/archive.html.

———. *Fiscal Year 2008 Performance and Accountability Report: Highlights*. Washington, DC: US Environmental Protection Agency. http://www.epa.gov/planandbudget/archive.html.

———. 2011. *Fiscal Year 2010 Agency Financial Report*. Washington, DC: US Environmental Protection Agency. http://www.epa.gov/ocfo/perf_report/FY_2010_EPA_AFR.pdf.

Western Water Policy Review Advisory Committee. 1998. *Water in the West: Challenges for the Next Century*. Springfield, VA: National Technical Information Service.

Wickersham, G. 1980. 'Groundwater Management in the High Plains." *Ground Water* 18 (3): 286–90.

Water is life. The People's Water Board advocates for
access, protection, and conservation of water. We believe
water is a human right and all people should have access
to clean and affordable water. Water is a commons that
should be held in the public trust free of privatization.
The People's Water Board promotes awareness of the
interconnectedness of all people and resources.
—*Mission of the People's Water Board of Detroit, Michigan*

3

WATER AND ENVIRONMENTAL JUSTICE

Amy Vanderwarker

Introduction

The United States has remarkable water systems, developed over two centuries of technological, institutional, and economic advances. Yet the benefits of those systems have not been felt equally across regions, communities, or populations. And the adverse consequences of inadequate water quality or quantity, and the lack of responsiveness of some water institutions to community input and participation, have helped contribute to the growing environmental justice (EJ) effort to reform water policies based on respect and justice for all, free from discrimination, bias, or inequity. In communities from Detroit to New Orleans, the inner city to the tribal areas, efforts to understand and address EJ issues around water are beginning to take shape.

Environmental justice research documents disproportionate environmental burdens facing low-income communities and communities of color, ranging from high concentrations of hazardous facilities to contaminated groundwater from agricultural activities. Environmental justice contextualizes the environmental conditions that threaten the physical, social, economic, or environmental health and well-being of these communities within overall patterns of racism, classism, and other forms of discrimination in the US economy, government, and society in general. Water justice is one piece of a larger vision for EJ. Concepts of the "soft path for water" and of water justice demand that all communities be able to access and manage water for beneficial uses, including drinking, waste removal, cultural and spiritual practices, reliance on the wildlife it sustains, and enjoyment for recreational purposes (EJCW 2005).

Recent experience in Detroit offers an example of both the challenges and innovative solutions associated with inequities in water policy and management. Frustrated by a series of water shutoffs, threats of privatization, and a closed and unresponsive water board, residents from across Detroit formed a People's Water Board to shadow the governing Board of Water Commissioners of the municipal water supplier, the Detroit Water and Sewage Department. The demands of the People's Water Board include a citywide water affordability plan, public control of water services, and more transparent water decision making (People's Water Board 2009). These kinds of organizing efforts in Detroit, a predominantly African American city with high rates of poverty and unemployment, exemplify growing community responses to water injustices, especially the chronic lack of access to safe, clean, affordable water in some low-income communities and communities of color.

This chapter draws on concepts that EJ advocates and organizers from across the country have long used to demand healthy, clean places to live, work, and play as a framework to explore water-specific EJ issues in federal policy and to identify needed policy changes. We explore some of the most severe and well-documented examples of water injustices and their underlying causes, with recommendations to better incorporate EJ into federal water policy. Indigenous water issues are addressed separately (see chapter 4: Tribes and Water), however, any consideration of water injustices must highlight both the historical legacy of indigenous water struggles and the imperative need to address current indigenous water concerns.

The Environmental Justice Movement

> Environmental Justice affirms the sacredness of Mother Earth, ecological unity and the interdependence of all species, and the right to be free from ecological destruction. Environmental Justice demands that public policy be based on mutual respect and justice for all peoples, free from any form of discrimination or bias.
>
> —*First and Second Principles of Environmental Justice*

Many communities have struggled to protect their natural resources and quality of life for years, but the modern EJ movement emerged from several currents of social justice activism in the 1970s. It gained momentum from grassroots struggles around the country to protect community lands and people from pollutants. The movement expands the definition of the environment to include where people live, work, and play. In doing so, it challenges mainstream environmentalism to move beyond ecological protection and address the broad hazards that low-income communities and communities of color face (Cole and Foster 2001).

The EJ movement challenges the exclusive nature of environmental decision making. For example, decisions about where to build a dam have historically been made without any input from those who would be most affected by the proposal—such as the people displaced by flooding or the people whose water would be dammed. To counter this pattern, the EJ movement has worked to ensure the voices of those most affected by environmental decisions are involved in a transparent decision-making process (Di Chiro 1996).

In 1991, the First National People of Color Environmental Leadership Summit authored the *17 Principles of Environmental Justice,* which remain foundational today. The principles outline three major concepts of EJ: no community should bear a disproportionate burden of environmental hazards, all communities should have access to environmental benefits, and decision-making processes need to be transparent and include community voices.

Many early EJ struggles revolved around battles to prevent the siting of toxic facilities, ranging from refineries to hazardous waste facilities, in low-income communities and communities of color (Cole and Foster 2001). Water issues were and continue to be a piece of many fights, but rarely has a comprehensive EJ analysis applied directly to water problems and the range of agencies involved in water management.

Mounting pressure on both state and national governments resulted in the creation of a federal-level policy infrastructure to incorporate EJ into environmental decision making. In 1992, the federal Environmental Protection Agency (EPA) created an Office of Environmental Justice and in 1993 established a National Environmental Justice Advisory Committee (NEJAC) to provide independent advice and analysis from stakeholders on EJ issues (EPA 2010b). In 1994, President Clinton signed Executive Order 12898, directing agencies receiving federal funding to address the disproportionate environmental impacts of their policies and programs on low-income communities and communities of color. The executive order also established an Interagency Working Group on Environmental Justice, bringing together representatives from 12 federal agencies to integrate EJ into federal programs, including agencies with water jurisdiction.

Environmental Justice and Federal Water Policy

All federal agencies involved in national water policy, no matter their diversity or jurisdiction, are encompassed within the executive order on EJ. As was noted in chapter 2: Legal and Institutional Framework of Water Management, "federal water policy" includes the literally dozens of agencies, laws, Congressional committees, and regulations designed to manage water resources in the United States. It includes sweeping pieces of legislation such as the Safe Drinking Water Act (SDWA) and the Clean Water Act (CWA), as well as water provisions within legislation as diverse as that governing the Department of Agriculture and the Resource Conservation and Recovery Act, which manages hazardous waste disposal. The Bureau of Reclamation and the Army Corps of Engineers build and operate large-scale, publicly funded water projects, which develop water resources for irrigation, domestic supplies to urban areas, and hydropower. With the exception of the Army Corps, all have been represented within the Interagency Working Group on Environmental Justice.

Federal environmental policy, including water policy, has struggled to fully institutionalize EJ, despite the strong guidance of NEJAC. Independent studies by the National Academy of Public Administration, the US Commission on Civil Rights, and the Office of the Inspector General have all reached similar conclusions: EJ "has not yet been integrated fully into the agency's core mission or its staff functions" (NAPA 2001) and "federal agencies have not established accountability and performance outcomes for programs and activities" (USCCR 2003, 8). As result, there has been little effective or comprehensive implementation of EJ policies (OIG 2006).

The history of federal water policy has created a particular set of EJ issues. Federal water policy has prioritized use of water for economic purposes, primarily through large-scale water developments, such as dams, irrigation, and flood control, and in doing so, has overlooked a range of impacts on specific communities and the environment (Steinberg 1993). A heavy reliance and emphasis on "engineering" solutions to water problems, such as dams, has emphasized technological skills rather than community voices or local consequences (Espeland 1998; Donahue and Johnston 1998). Correspondingly, water decisions, whether at a local or federal level, have been exclusive and opaque (EJCW 2005;Ingram, Whiteley, and Perry 2008). Consequently, as water scholars Helen Ingram, John Whitely, and Richard Perry note, "many water developments fail to satisfy the basic distributional equity and environmental justice tenet that no groups, particularly the disadvantaged, should be made worse off . . . because of water policies" (2008, 16).

Documenting Environmental Injustices

The poor and especially the nonwhite poor bear a disproportionate burden of exposure to suboptimal, unhealthy environmental conditions in the United States.

—Evans and Kantrowitz *(2002)*

In the past several decades, there have been hundreds of studies investigating the correlations between race, income, and environmental burdens.[1] Literature reviews reveal overwhelming evidence that backs up what many communities long suspected: Race and class matter in the distribution of environmental burdens. Toxic waste sites and facilities that release toxic emissions are more likely to be sited in low-income neighborhoods, with primarily nonwhite residents (Bullard et al. 2007; Fricker and Hengarten 2001; Rowan and Fridgen 2003). Health in the United States is inextricably linked to race and class. Lower-income communities and communities of color have higher rates of a vast array of diseases ranging from asthma to lead poisoning to higher rates of mortality (Evans and Kantrowitz 2002; Brulle and Pellow 2006; Gee and Payne-Sturges 2004; Quintero-Somaini and Quirindongo 2004; Williams and Collins 1995). An analysis of California health data suggested that about 250,000 Californians sometimes go without water due to insufficient supply or are exposed to contaminated water, and that many of these residents "reside in rural, economically disadvantaged communities" (Wilber 2003; Moore and Matalon 2011).

As a result, low-income communities and communities of color may experience the cumulative impacts of exposure to a wide variety of contaminants or disproportionate lack of access to resources. According to NEJAC, the idea of cumulative risks and impacts is the "matrix of physical, chemical, biological, social and cultural factors which result in certain communities and sub-populations being more susceptible to environmental toxins, being more exposed to toxins, or having compromised ability to cope with and/or recover from such exposure" (NEJAC 2004, i).

There are many barriers to achieving change for EJ in communities. More affluent communities have an array of privileges that help ensure healthier environments, including more political influence and resources to fight unwanted environmental hazards (Brulle and Pellow 2006). An Institute of Medicine report on EJ and public health found that "there are identifiable communities of concern that experience a certain type of double jeopardy in the sense that they (1) experience higher levels of exposure to environmental stressors in terms of both frequency and magnitude and (2) are less able to deal with these hazards as a result of limited knowledge of exposures and disenfranchisement in the political process" (Committee on Environmental Justice 1999, 6).

These problems extend to water resources. Water injustices within federal water policy include:

- Instances where low-income communities and communities of color are disproportionately burdened by water hazards, ranging from lack of clean drinking water to higher exposure to fish contamination;
- Legacies of discrimination in land-use planning and housing that perpetuate water inequities, such as exposure to lead contamination in drinking water;
- Inequalities in the enforcement of water-specific policies and regulations;
- Gaps in existing regulations around water policy and a lack of regulations around critical water justice issues;
- Cumulative risks and impacts to low-income communities and communities of color that are overlooked;
- Community voices and water needs that have been excluded from federal water policy.

Regional studies and stories from across the country document the water struggles of low-income communities and communities of color and demonstrate that there is much progress to be made before water justice is achieved in the United States. Accurate data on water quality and water use do not exist in many places and is not comprehensively collected nationwide (see chapter 1). There is also a lack of data comparing water issues in the context of race and income. For example, the US Census once collected information on individual sources of drinking water, but the question is no longer asked, making it difficult to assess questions of inequitable access to water (GWTF 2007).

LACK OF ACCESS TO SAFE, CLEAN DRINKING WATER AND WASTEWATER SERVICES

There is a widespread assumption that safe, affordable water for drinking and household use is available to all residents in the United States—indeed UN estimates of urban populations with access to safe water or sanitation often assume 100 percent coverage in the United States. The reality is that some low-income communities and communities of color lack access to water for the most basic human needs. This lack of access to clean, safe drinking water can be caused by contamination in the water or because of a lack of adequate drinking water and wastewater infrastructure, such as old or nonexistent plumbing.

DRINKING WATER CONTAMINATION

> Without water we can't live, but we have nitrates. There is no money put into communities for certain things. Either the community doesn't have enough money to fix the problem or agencies don't really care about it.
>
> —Jessica Sanchez, *resident of East Orosi, California*

Jessica Sanchez lives in East Orosi, a small predominantly low-income, Latino town in California's agricultural heartland, the San Joaquin Valley. The groundwater that is the source of drinking water in East Orosi has been contaminated with nitrates, a result of fertilizer application at large farms and confined animal facilities (Harter 2009). Nitrates can cause death in infants, reproductive problems, and have been linked to cancer (Moore and Matalon 2011).

The federal Safe Drinking Water Act requires all drinking water to meet health standards set by the EPA, but violations occur regularly. In one year alone, the water of nearly one-third of all people drinking water from a public system had a health violation (EPA 2009c). Over the last five years, more than 49 million people were served by water systems that reported instances of contaminants exceeding federal health limits (Duhigg 2009c). This leads to widespread, but poorly quantified and hard to measure, health impacts. By one estimate, there are 16.4 million gastrointestinal illnesses caused by contaminated drinking water each year (Messner et al. 2006).

Low-income communities and communities of color often face the most severe and persistent drinking water contamination (Evans and Kantrowitz 2002). Sixty-one percent of drinking water systems on Native American reservations had health violations or other significant reporting violations in 2006, compared with 27 percent of all public systems in the United States (EPA 2009c). One study found that levels of both nitrate and coliform on two reservations in Nebraska were significantly higher than both regional and national averages (McGinnis and Davis 2001). Another report linked high levels of industrial contaminants in the drinking water of Latino residents in Tucson, Arizona, to abnormally high rates of adult cancer and neurological disorders in newborns (Pinderhughes 1996). In the Appalachia region of West Virginia, the drinking water supply of low-income communities has been contaminated with coal slurry injections containing a host of toxic chemicals (Sludge Safety Project 2009).

Lead is a metal found in natural deposits, but it is commonly used in a variety of household products, old paints and household plumbing materials, and water service lines. The greatest exposure to lead comes from swallowing or breathing in lead paint chips and dust, but lead in drinking water is also a health risk. A prohibition on lead in plumbing materials has been in effect since 1986, but an old infrastructure can contaminate drinking water with lead. Drinking water can contribute over 20 percent of lead poisoning in children (EPA 2004), and low-income, African American, and Latino children consistently have disproportionately high levels of lead in their blood (EPA 2000).

LACK OF ACCESS TO ADEQUATE INFRASTRUCTURE FOR THE POOR

> We're like a hole in the doughnut with regard to sewer, garbage pickup and street lighting.... We want a voice in political affairs and we want the services that are afforded to everyone around us. We're trying to get communities that have been neglected for 100 years brought up to date, up to code, up to 21st-century standards.
>
> —Maurice Holland, *Midway Community Association, North Carolina (qtd. in UNCCR 2006)*

In small towns like Midway, North Carolina, African American residents live with the vestiges of Jim Crow segregation and lack of basic services such as sewer systems (Parnell et al. 2004). Residents in the small, rural African American community struggle with sewage overflows while nearby, white, affluent communities are developed as major tourism destinations (UNCCR 2006). Researchers in North Carolina found that "discriminatory zoning ordinances and land-use regulations continue to be used to deny African Americans access to basic services and political voice in critical community and economic development decisions" (Johnson et al. 2004, 3).

While many people often take the pipes that bring water to their fingertips for granted, literally hundreds of thousands of houses across the country lack complete plumbing, many in impoverished rural areas (Gasteyer and Vaswami 2004). The 2007 American Housing Survey indicates that 1.1 percent of all housing units lack some aspect of indoor plumbing, rising to 2.3 percent for houses below the poverty level. Over 3 percent of households experienced a water stoppage at some point in the year (US Census 2008).

Numerous studies have shown that these problems are higher among low-income communities and communities of color. One study shows that African Americans are more than twice as likely and Hispanics are more than three times as likely as non-Hispanic whites to live in homes with incomplete plumbing (Mather 2004). Nearly 12 percent of Native Americans on reservations and 30 percent of Alaska Natives lack plumbing (EPA 2001b). Rural African American households are three times as likely as other rural households to lack plumbing (George, Pinder, and Singleton 2004). In rural subdivisions, called *colonias,* along the 2,000-mile border between the United States and Mexico, just about one-quarter of all residents lack treated water and 44 percent of the houses do not have wastewater plumbing (FRBD nd). Residents are overwhelmingly Latino, of Mexican descent, and immigrants. About one-third of these residents live below the poverty level and average incomes are as low as $5,000 per year in some areas (FRBD nd).

Discrimination in zoning and construction has denied low-income communities and communities of color basic infrastructure such as sewers and wastewater (Lichter et al. 2007; Troesken 2002; WERA 2002; Anderson 2008). *Colonias,* both along the border and in agricultural areas, rural African American communities, and Native American reservations illustrate a material form of racial discrimination (Snipp 1996). And these same isolated rural areas are most likely to lack basic water and wastewater services (Snipp 1996).

Access to, and the scale of, water financing is also often inequitable. Water distribution systems are generally financed and constructed at a local level, with some federal support, but such funding (primarily in the form of loans and grants for infrastructure construction) has a series of barriers for low-income water systems (discussed in the next section) and has traditionally failed to address the underlying persistence of water problems in low-income communities and communities of color.

WHO PAYS AND WHO IS LEFT OUT: EQUITY IN WATER FINANCING AND FUNDING

Despite the clear evidence that many people in the United States still lack basic water infrastructure, federal appropriations for water projects have been steadily declining since the mid-1960s (Cody and Carter 2009). Drinking water and wastewater systems throughout the country, not just those serving low-income communities and communities of color, are facing funding needs estimated between $334.8 and $504 billion over the next 20 years to maintain the current drinking water systems and replace outdated infrastructure (EPA 2009a). In the face of an already glaring gap in services for low-income communities and communities of color, this looming need threatens to exacerbate the existing inequities in both access and funding.

SMALL SYSTEMS IN NEED

Ninety-four percent of water systems in the country are small water systems, serving fewer than 3,300 connections (EPA 2009c). Small systems generally have higher rates of health violations and infrastructure costs per person served. In 2005, small systems had

93 percent of all health violations, with one violation per 80 persons served, versus one violation per 196,204 persons served in very large systems (Imperial 1999).

According to the Congressional Research Service, the "EPA and states have documented the difficulties many small systems face in meetings SDWA [Safe Drinking Water Act] rules, and more fundamentally, in ensuring the quality of their water supplies. Major problems include deteriorated infrastructure . . . diseconomies of scale; and limited technical and managerial capacities" (Teimann 2006, 15). Because of these barriers, small water systems also have three times the per-household infrastructure need of large systems (EPA 1999a).

These systems have largely failed to receive the benefits of federal environmental programs established to help drinking water systems comply with health standards, primarily through the Safe Drinking Water State Revolving Fund, and to a lesser extent, the Clean Water State Revolving Fund. Federal and state grant or low-interest loan programs are extremely hard to obtain because of extensive engineering and reporting requirements, and often small systems "are characterized by narrow or weak tax bases, limited or no access to capital markets, lower relative household incomes, and higher per capita needs" (Copeland 2010, 7). Even when grants and loans can be obtained, the cost of installing and operating a new treatment system may put a large cost burden on a low-income community because of the small number of people to share the costs (NDWAC 2003).

Compounding this lack of resources is the failure of states to use provisions within the Safe Drinking Water State Revolving Fund that would assist small communities. The federal government allows states to use up to 30 percent of capitalization grants to provide loan subsidies for low-income communities, but most states have used only a fraction of this. State are also empowered to forgive the principal of a safe drinking water loan, but according to the EPA, since 1996, only 16 states have done so, totaling less than 3 percent of all loan funds awarded (Copeland and Tiemann 2008). Also, the EPA has failed to set aside authorized funds for technical assistance to small systems (Tiemann 2009). Another study documented the inequitable distribution of the Clean Water State Revolving Fund for wastewater systems: low-income, minority communities were statistically less likely to receive construction grants (Imperial 1999). Federally recognized tribes, which face chronic drinking water and infrastructure issues, are prohibited from receiving more than 1.5 percent of all available funding under the CWA and SDWA, despite the well-documented need in these areas (EJESC 2009).

AGRICULTURE AND INEQUALITY

Agriculture is the largest water user in the nation, and one of the largest sources of water contamination (EPA 2005; chapter 8: Water and Agriculture). The western United States produces the vast majority of the country's crops, but this production would be impossible without large-scale water developments that move water from rivers to farmlands, often across great distances. The federal Bureau of Reclamation maintains and operates publicly funded infrastructure, such as aqueducts, dams, and pumping stations, and delivers subsidized irrigation water to farms that do not naturally have enough rainfall to sustain production. These subsidies have enabled, and are a critical support for, large-scale, corporate agriculture (Reisner 1993). In 2009, the Associated Press found that the Bureau of Reclamation gave out more than $687 million in subsidies over two years to hundreds of farmers in California and Arizona (Burke 2009). "Although water subsidies originally may have possessed a legitimate social purpose, that purpose largely has been outlived. Instead of the intended small family farmers receiving the benefits, much of the subsidies now go to large growers and corporations" (Candee 1989, 657–658).

Federal water policy supports large-scale agriculture, but for the most part, agribusinesses are not held responsible for the impacts of their farming practices (Kimbrell 2002). This includes the impacts on local water resources, ranging from the flooding of rivers to create dams for irrigation to the contamination of streams and drinking water wells throughout rural areas (Woefle-Erskine 2007; Duhigg 2009b). Even though the federal government spends billions on water, energy, and crop subsidies, it does not authorize enough money to help provide safe drinking water to small systems in the same agricultural areas. In some areas of California, farms receive federally subsidized irrigation water piped from hundreds of miles away, while low-income communities next door cannot drink their tap water due to agricultural contamination (Scott 2010).

In studies from California to the Great Plains to the southern states, the communities next to highly profitable farming enterprises often struggle with high rates of unemployment, poverty, and a lack of basic water and wastewater services (Carter 2010; MacCannell 1983; Preston and Bailey 2003). In a study of 13 midwestern agricultural states, with nearly 3 million people, researchers found that rural development funding, which goes to projects such as water and wastewater infrastructure, was about $53 per capita, whereas the top 20 farm subsidy recipients received on average over $1 million in federal payments (Bailey and Preston 2007). Though this is an imperfect comparison, it provides a sense of the scale and nature of inequitable federal subsidies.

It is not just federal subsidies that keep large-scale farming afloat; low-wage labor is also a fixture of industrialized agriculture (Kimbrell 2002). According to the Occupational Health and Safety Act of 1970, employers are required to provide proper sanitation, including drinking water, for farm workers in the fields. However, many studies show that farm workers face a lack of clean, safe water in both the fields where they work and the housing that is provided and maintained by farm operations (Vela-Acosta, Bigelow, and Buchan 2002). Testing of drinking water wells for migrant farm workers in Colorado found they contained high rates of nitrates (EPA 2009b). In Washington County, Oregon, which seasonally employs 8,000 migrant farm workers, 40 percent of all migrant farm worker housing lacked access to drinking water (McCauley et al. 2001). In another example, almost half the water supply of migrant farm workers in North Carolina contained bacterial contamination (Cieslski, Handzel, and Sobsey 1991). Federal water subsidies are thus being provided to companies that cannot or will not provide basic water and wastewater services for their employees or in their employee housing, in violation of federal labor laws.

The connections between federal water and agricultural policy extend from the Bureau of Reclamation to the Department of Agriculture to the powerful lobbying interests that ensure regular reauthorization of federal subsidies (Reisner 1993). Even though agriculture is a critical piece of local economies and the nation's food security, the larger environmental and social costs of our current system of industrialized agriculture must be reconsidered if there is a true commitment to water justice.

AFFORDABILITY

> If you don't pay your water bills, they cut off your water, and don't give you an opportunity to appeal. Then they transfer the bills above $100 to property tax rolls for collection. If you can't pay, your house can be foreclosed. . . . People lose their homes, business and can even lose their children.
>
> —Maureen Taylor, *Michigan Welfare Rights Organization (qtd. in NCLC 2006)*

After over 40,000 families had their water shut off in one year, the Michigan Welfare Rights Organization launched a campaign to create a citywide plan to ensure affordable water for Detroit's low-income residents. For low-income households, affordability is a question of both the economic burden a water bill places on a resident and whether that resident is being forced to displace other essential services to provide the basic need of water. The EPA defines water service *affordability* as 2.5 percent of Median Household Income (MHI). As long as water bills do not exceed 2.5 percent of MHI, water service is considered affordable. However, the MHI obscures many of the large discrepancies in the range of incomes in an area, or the geographic distribution of differing incomes. Although, on average, people can be paying less than 2.5 percent of their income on water bills, low-income households may be paying a much higher percentage. The percentage of MHI spent on a water bill also may not encompass all the water-related costs that a household may bear. For example, if household members must purchase bottled water because their water is contaminated, the actual amount they are paying is much higher.

The economic crisis that began in 2009 sharpened the types of affordability issues that Detroit faced. Reports of water shutoffs have become more common as utilities have been raising rates, becoming more aggressive in collecting overdue water bills, and shutting off accounts as their investments have fallen due to the recession (Smith 2008; DePalma 2007; Canfield 2010). Utilities in Chicago saw a 70 percent increase in the number of delinquent water bills in 2008 and implemented rate increases of 15 percent each year for the next three years (Cottrell 2008). The rising rate of foreclosures has impacted renters; for example, in Oakland, California, many low-income tenants faced abrupt utility shutoffs as their landlords faced foreclosure in the wake of massive mortgage defaults (Grady 2008).

Despite the limitations of this measure, recent data has shown that the number of houses whose water and wastewater bills exceeded EPA's designated affordability criteria is growing. From 2002 to 2004, the number of bills for water and wastewater services in major cities that exceeded the EPA's affordability criteria rose from 3 to 7 percent (Brandt 2004). The Congressional Budget Office predicts that between 10 and 20 percent of households may be spending more than 4 percent of household income on water by 2019 (CBO 2002). For more information on a community campaign to ensure equitable access to affordable water, see the case study of Michigan Welfare Rights Organization in chapter 7: Municipal Water Use.

Another indicator of affordability is how much people spend on water as compared to other services or needs. In general, low-income residents spend a higher percent of their household income on water than wealthier residents do (Morello-Frosch et al. 2009). As many as one in five households face difficulties meeting "essential needs" over the course of a year, and the most common difficulty is paying utility bills (Bauman 2003).

There are no federal programs to assist low-income residents in covering their water bill, such as the ones that exist for telephone and energy usage. It is left to the discretion of the utility to create such a program. A survey of large utilities found that only 8 percent had a subsidy, or "lifeline" rate (Raucher 2004). Given this lack of a safety net, the rising cost of drinking water is also a rising threat to the water security of low-income communities.

URBANIZATION: LEGACIES OF DISCRIMINATION IN LAND-USE PLANNING
PERPETUATE WATER INJUSTICES

> When I was a little girl, because our wetlands were of good quality, we would get all excited to run out and play. Turkey Creek had a cultural significance—we couldn't use the beaches because they were segregated. We used the creek for fishing and swimming and baptizing. But then development started coming, and it ruined the quality of our wetlands, and there was flooding in our streets and homes and churches.
>
> —Rose Johnson, *Turkey Creek resident and activist (Johnson, pers. comm. 2010)*

North Gulfport and the neighboring community of Turkey Creek, Mississippi, were founded by emancipated slaves. The entire area is a flood zone, and African American residents were relegated to the edges of the wetlands along Turkey Creek. Residents long used the creek for recreation, as nearby beaches were segregated. The creek slowly became contaminated as industries such as DuPont Chemical moved into the area and urban sprawl devoured the creek's wetlands and increased flooding in the homes of nearby residents (Ray 2004). The wetlands would absorb water and prevent flooding, but as they were paved over, flooding worsened. Today, residents are fighting to create a greenway along Turkey Creek.

Urbanization—the process of urban growth—has led to a drastic increase in the amount of land covered by impervious surfaces, such as concrete. These surfaces generate much larger quantities of water running off streets than the nonurbanized landscapes they replace. This runoff picks up the many chemicals and heavy metals that exist in urban areas, including pesticides, oil and grease, bacteria, and trash, and is one of the largest sources of water contamination today (EPA 2010a). Exacerbating runoff are combined sewage overflows, or CSOs, which are sewer systems built to carry both sewage and stormwater in the same pipes. These systems overflow when there is lots of rain or snow and discharge directly into nearby water bodies, carrying many pollutants that affect health, including bacteria, viruses, and floating trash (EPA 2001a).

Widespread water issues with urbanization have been caused, in large part, by the overwhelming disconnect between land-use planning policies and water planning. As the Government Accountability Office notes, "most states and localities do not comprehensively assess the impacts of different land uses on water quality and develop strategies to mitigate any adverse effects" (GAO 2001, 6).

The disconnect between land-use planning and water management maps onto legacies of discriminatory planning. Land-use planning and zoning practices determine what land uses are allowed where, including residential housing and industrial facility sites. From *redlining* practices, which deliberately excluded people of color from living in certain neighborhoods, to federal housing policies that encouraged suburban development at the expense of urban city centers, land use and zoning decisions have facilitated the concentration of low-income communities and communities of color in impoverished areas and near toxic facilities (NAPA 2003). Ultimately, land-use planning and zoning have "segregated communities along the lines of race and class" and led to "the creation of an urban underclass that is denied access to mainstream opportunities" (Wilson, Hutson, and Mujahid 2008, 212).

Today, this "urban underclass" is often especially susceptible to the water-related problems of urbanization, ranging from overflowing CSOs to seasonal flooding (EJCW 2005). Case studies from communities such as Turkey Creek; West Philadelphia (Spirn 2005); Bayview Hunters Point in San Francisco (EJCW 2005); Columbia Sloughs in Portland, Oregon (Stroud 1999); Anacostia River in Washington (Williams 2001); Gary, Indiana (Hurley 1988); and Sun Valley in Los Angeles (TreePeople 2009) attest to the complex ways the low-income communities and communities of color come to live in areas with high rates of contamination, storm and wastewater overflows, or increased risks of flooding.

Most urban runoff prevention programs are run at the state level and are voluntary. EPA efforts to regulate national stormwater permitting programs have been slow and ineffective (GAO 2007). There are few incentives and resources for local governments to tackle the issue independently.

When cities do take action to address the impacts of urbanization, it can have EJ implications. In several cities, municipal plans to address CSOs have called for the construction of large wastewater treatment plants to be located in low-income communities and communities of color (Lane and Heath 2009). For more on one community's struggle to ensure an equitable CSO treatment plan, please see chapter 5: Water Quality.

The combination of discriminatory land-use patterns and the impacts of urbanization means that water issues in a low-income community or community of color may be easily overlooked. Whereas many of the water-related impacts of urbanization are related to local planning and permitting decisions, it is also local-level planning that has influenced the concentration of low-income communities and communities of color into marginal urban geographies. As the EPA takes an increased role in addressing the disconnect between water and land-use planning policy, it must also address the historical and living legacies of discrimination that affect communities today.

Bearing the Burden: Low-income Communities and Communities of Color Pay for Industrial Development

One of the most important contributions of the EJ movement has been demonstrating how the costs of pollution that impact low-income communities and communities of color are not factored into traditional environmental decision making. Federal water policies around industrial discharge show how the environmental costs of industrial development are displaced onto these communities.

CONTAMINATED FISH

Studies from around the country have shown that many communities of color have some of the highest rates of fish consumption, ranging from Native American and Alaskan Natives to African Americans to Latinos to Asian and Asian American populations (OEHHA 2001; Corburn 2002; EHC 2005; Shilling 2009; Silka nd; Williams et al. 2000; AMAP 2009). The EPA has found low-income communities consume significantly higher amounts of both cooked and uncooked fish (EPA 2002). Studies in Pennsylvania and South Carolina demonstrate that African American anglers consume up to four times the amount of fish as white anglers do (Weintraub and Birnbaum 2008). Another study in Indiana found significantly higher daily average fish consumption rates among anglers of color versus white anglers (Williams et al. 2000). In one survey from California's Sacramento–San Joaquin Delta, 86 percent of Hmong women, 75 percent of Cambodian women, 58 percent of Vietnamese, and 57 percent of Filipino women surveyed ate sport fish versus 30 percent of white women (Silver et al. 2007).

Many fish today are contaminated by pollutants that bioaccumulate in their flesh after being released into the water. Common contaminants include mercury from historic gold mining, ongoing mercury depositions from coal plants, and chemicals called persistent organic pollutants used in a variety of manufacturing processes.

The policy response to fish contamination has been one of *risk avoidance,* which allocates the responsibility for addressing risks to those who bear the risks (O'Neill 2007). The EPA issues fish advisories to provide guidance on safe levels of consumption for contaminated fish. In areas with high levels of contamination in specific fish species, they recommend replacing or reducing consumption. Under the CWA, all facilities are required to obtain permits that specify the quality of water they will discharge; this is the National Pollutant Discharge Elimination System. Under the CWA's Total Maximum Daily Load program, the EPA can limit the total amount of contaminants in a particular water body. But instead of using these tools to create pollution limits in waterways with documented subsistence fishing, the EPA ultimately places the burden of protection on low-income communities, communities of color, and other fish consumers (O'Neill 2007).

Risk avoidance also simply fails at its policy objectives when it comes to low-income communities and communities of color. Many communities have found that fish advisories are difficult to understand or are not language-appropriate (Silka nd; EJCW 2005). The fish advisories are often based on recreational angler levels of consumption, rather than subsistence rates (Shilling 2009).

As the NEJAC explains, "For many communities of color, low-income communities, tribes, and other indigenous peoples, there are no real alternatives to eating and using fish, aquatic plants, and wildlife. For many members of these groups it is entirely impractical to 'switch' to 'substitutes' when the fish and other resources on which they rely have become contaminated. There are numerous and often insurmountable obstacles to seeking alternatives (e.g., fishing 'elsewhere,' throwing back 'undesirable' species of fish, adopting different preparation methods, or substituting beef, chicken or tofu)." The "cost" of widespread fish contamination, caused by private companies and government facilities, thus disproportionately is borne by low-income communities and communities of color (Gauna, O'Neill, and Rechtschaffen 2005).

LACK OF ACCESS TO WATER FOR RECREATIONAL OPPORTUNITIES

> We all grew up in Chelsea and we didn't realize we had a river. You can't see it, you can't touch it, there are no viewpoints—just huge industries up and down the waterfront. We started to question why are all these industries in Chelsea? It became clear to us that it was because we are a low-income community of color.
>
> —Roseann Bongiovanni, *Chelsea Creek Action Group*

Chelsea Creek runs into the Boston Harbor through East Boston and Chelsea, both working-class neighborhoods with large immigrant communities. An EPA investigation in partnership with community groups found that Chelsea and East Boston have significantly less access to green space than elsewhere in Boston. Working with local and national agencies, companies, and residents, community groups such as the Chelsea Creek Action Group cleaned up and redeveloped an old industrial site into the Condor Street Urban Wild Park, and they are now working to create an entire Chelsea Riverway for local residents to access the waterfront (NOAH 2006).

Disparities in distribution of open spaces have been well documented. Low-income communities often have less access to open spaces and recreational opportunities than do more affluent communities (Timperio et al. 2007; Harnick 2006; Kibel 2007). In a report mapping race, income, and park access in Los Angeles, the City Project found that the communities that had the worst access to parks were the largely nonwhite and poor communities of Central and South Los Angeles (Garcia and White 2006). Along many industrialized waterfronts, the adjacent low-income and predominately minority communities are effectively cut off from the waterfront; in the low-income, predominately Latino and African American industrial shipping area of South Bronx, New York City, the Hunts Point area has six miles of waterfront, and only 200 feet of waterfront recreation access (Sustainable South Bronx 2008). Research from around the country demonstrates that a lack of recreational opportunities translates into increased health problems, ranging from high rates of obesity, type II diabetes, and other diseases among low-income communities and communities of color (Wilson, Hutson, and Mujahid 2008).

Natural spaces can promote physical and psychological health (Giles-Corti et al. 2005; Garcia and White 2006), and increasingly, EJ activists are working to secure access to healthy creeks and water-based recreational opportunities as a means of creating positive changes in their communities (Miller 2009). Even though many of the patterns of industrial development along waterways trace back to local land-use planning decisions and ordinances, the federal government can play a proactive role in not only creating strict CWA permits for industrial facilities and thus limiting pollution, but also in identifying and supporting watershed restoration projects in low-income communities and communities of color.

ENERGY PRODUCTION AND WATER INJUSTICES

> There was a sludge dam holding nine billion gallons of toxic substances right above where we lived. I also watched the March Fork stream get poisoned three miles above the intake valve for the town of Sylvester, West Virginia. If we're poisoning our drinking water, we have to ask what kind of people are we?
>
> —Judy Bonds, *Coal River Mountain Watch, West Virginia (qtd. in Smecker 2009)*

Community organizations such as Coal River Mountain Watch and Ohio Valley Environmental Coalition have been working to stop the impacts of coal mining in Appalachia for years. Efforts to secure tighter water restrictions on coal mining practices face two huge barriers: the power of corporate lobbying interests, and the country's reliance on coal for electricity (Duhigg 2009c). The work and challenges of the Ohio Valley Environmental Coalition exemplify the struggle many low-income communities and communities of color face in trying to address the impacts of energy production on water resources.

Energy production and water are highly interdependent (Feeley et al. 2005). Energy production is the second largest user of water in the United States, and virtually every type and phase of production requires water, from the mining of fossil fuels to the cooling water used in power plants to the transport of coal. This can lead to the depletion of local water sources. Not only is energy production water-intensive, it is water-polluting, especially fossil fuel plants, which dump large quantities of contaminated water used in the production process into local ecosystems (Clean Air Task Force and The Land and Water Fund of the Rockies 2003).

The EJ impacts of energy production are clear. In New Mexico, Navajo drinking water wells have been contaminated by uranium mines (EPA 2008). Throughout the West, indigenous communities have been displaced from ancestral rivers and their subsistence lifestyles destroyed for hydropower dam construction (Woefle-Erskine 2007). On the Cheyenne reservation in Wyoming, coal bed methane extraction contaminates vast quantities of groundwater (Small 2005). A new rush to access natural gas using a water-intensive method called *hydraulic fracturing* (or "fracking") has resulted in such high levels of methane that drinking water is actually flammable in some communities throughout the Northeast (Duncan 2010).

Energy policy, dispersed through a variety of federal agencies, has not worked in tandem with water policy (Gleick 2009). As calls for more integrated water and energy policy become prevalent, addressing the long-standing impacts of energy production on low-income communities and communities of color is an important starting place.

CLIMATE CHANGE AND WATER INJUSTICES

> New Orleans has been made the ground zero of climate change.
>
> —Dr. Myra Lewis, *Deep South Center for Environmental Justice*

The experience of Hurricane Katrina revealed the connections between climate change, EJ, and management of our water resources. As Dr. Myra Lewis, assistant director at the Deep South Center for Environmental Justice, explains, "New Orleans always had intense environmental justice issues and contamination. Katrina reset our agenda. It was a monumental failure of every level of government that was supposed to be protecting our interests." Katrina revealed how a confluence of geographic, social, and political factors that created a situation in which low-income communities and communities of color in New Orleans were disproportionately affected by the disaster (Smith 2006).

Climate change will worsen some of the existing inequalities outlined in this chapter (Pastor et al. 2006). For a broader discussion of climate change impacts on water resources see chapter 10: Water and Climate. In the example of Hurricane Katrina, the numerous contaminated sites and facilities near low-income communities and communities of color in Louisiana created a public health threat as flooding waters were polluted by toxic materials (Bullard and Wright 2009). For subsistence communities relying on fish and other aquatic life for income, changing water temperatures and flows will drastically reduce these sources of livelihoods (FAO 2008). In agricultural areas, changing growing conditions may increase the use of fertilizer and pesticides, risking increased contamination in rural places where small, low-income communities already struggle with polluted ground and surface water (Fougères 2007). Alaskan Native communities already face accelerated erosion due to melting sea ice and heavy wave activity; 31 villages are facing relocation (GAO 2009).

There are two main policy responses to climate change—mitigation and adaptation. Mitigation reduces the emissions of greenhouse gases, which drive climate change. Adaptation refers to adjustments in the built environment, lifestyles, and management practices to new climate conditions. A community's ability to both mitigate and adapt to the wide-ranging impacts of climate change is influenced by their vulnerability, which depends on many factors, including income, race, class, gender, and ethnic dynamics, but also hinges on the "basic provision of health care, the livability of places, overall indicators of quality of life, and accessibility to lifelines (goods, services, emergency response personnel), capital, and political representation" (Cutter 2006, 121). Many low-income communities and communities of color will experience the impacts of climate change most acutely because they are the most vulnerable (Morello-Frosch et al. 2009).

Given this reality, from an EJ perspective, the federal government's first step should be strong measures to reduce greenhouse gas emissions, which are linked to water management in several critical ways. Water management itself is energy-intensive. Water and wastewater systems account for at least 4 percent of the nation's energy use (EPRI 2002), although some experts believe this number could be considerably higher. Energy costs are a major proportion of the total utility operating costs with some estimates indicating that electricity is 80 percent of the cost of water provision (WRRC 2010). For example, in both Arizona and California, the single largest users of electricity are massive water infrastructure projects that bring water supplies to cities such as Tucson and Los Angeles (WRRC 2010). Additionally, energy use in our homes, businesses, and institutions to pump, heat, and treat water may be four times greater than that for the provision of water and wastewater systems (CEC 2005).

Other proposals to curb greenhouse gas emissions perpetuate water injustices. Hydropower is often framed as a "clean" way of generating energy and reducing carbon emissions from use of fossil fuels, but large dams can contribute to water contamination, severely disrupt the local ecosystem, and displace communities or community resources

(Leslie 2008). Large-scale ethanol production, proposed as a "bio-fuel" to reduce fossil fuel dependence, has led to a host of water problems and threatened small farmers around the globe (Hauter 2008). Environmental justice advocates fear proposals such as creating markets for carbon trading will exacerbate the already existing pollution in low-income communities and communities of color (Shepard and Corbin-Mark 2009).

With a predicted increase in severe weather events, how the federal government prepares and assists communities after water-related disasters is a crucial EJ issue. "Many minorities and the poor have had greater difficulties recovering from disasters due to less insurance, lower incomes, fewer savings, more unemployment, less access to communication channels and information, and the intensification of existing poverty" (Pastor et al. 2006, 23). Vulnerability is compounded by disparities in government disaster preparedness, aid, relief, and recovery. These range from the basic failure to provide assistance, to disaster materials issued in inappropriate languages, cultural stereotypes and racism in service provision, and unequal distribution of disaster relief and recovery assistance from local, state, and national agencies (Heberger et al. 2009; Pastor et al. 2006).

Ultimately, for many EJ activists, moving forward means moving away from a dependence on fossil fuels. The Environmental Justice Leadership Forum on Climate Change, an alliance of EJ organizations working to impact the development of climate change policy in the United States, calls for "a national goal supported by legislatively dedicated resources to transition us from the fossil fuel economy to the green, clean renewable energy economy by 2020" (Shepard and Corbin-Mark 2009).

Underlying Causes of Water Injustices

Climate change has heightened the sense of urgency to address water injustices. However, any potential solutions for both water management issues and climate change will not be adequate if they fail to address some of the underlying inequalities in federal water policy that link the various water injustices outlined in this chapter.

INEQUALITIES IN ENVIRONMENTAL REGULATION AND ENFORCEMENT

A driving force behind much of the EJ movement has been the reality that environmental regulations are not equitably enforced. Biases in government regulation and enforcement have failed to ensure that low-income communities and communities of color receive the same environmental protections that more affluent, white areas do (Bullard 2001). In an exhaustive report examining penalties applied by the EPA, researchers found that penalties under the Resource Conservation and Recovery Act are up to 500 percent higher in white communities than in communities of color for comparable violations (Lavelle and Coyle 1992). For example, petroleum refineries along the Mississippi River, surrounded by predominantly African American communities, tend to receive smaller fines than refineries in white, affluent communities do (Lynch, Stretesky, and Burns 2004).

The CWA is the EPA's main tool to keep water bodies free of pollution, yet illegal wastewater discharges have been routinely identified as a problem (Leavitt 2007) and enforcement of the act in low-income communities and communities of color is not evenhanded. A recent lawsuit by African American residents in Texas documented consistent pollution of their drinking water by local oil companies, despite clean-up efforts in neighboring, white areas (Hoffman 2007). In Dickinson, Tennessee, a county landfill is sited in the one African American community in the area, and the local well water has been poisoned by leaking hazardous materials. Even though city and county officials knew of the contamination, they continued permitting landfill operations. Additionally, they provided notification and treatment to nearby white families, but not to African American residents (Bullard et al. 2007).

Another example is the National Priority List created under the Superfund Program to identify and clean up sites with hazardous contamination. One study demonstrated that it took 20 percent longer for Superfund sites in low-income communities and communities of color to be listed and that penalties for pollution in white communities were 46 percent higher than in nonwhite communities (Lavelle and Coyle 1992). Another showed that the more people of color there are in an area, the less likely it is to receive Superfund protection (Anderton, Oakes, and Egan 1997; Hird 1993). Yet another shows that a 10 percent higher Native American population lowers the chance of being listed by a shocking 80 percent, and a 10 percent higher level of poverty decreases listing chances by 31 percent (O'Neil 2007).

An important mechanism at the federal level for low-income communities and communities of color is filing complaints with the Office of Civil Rights (OCR) under Title VI of the Civil Rights Act of 1964, which prohibits any agency that receives federal funding from discrimination in services (Ringquist and Clark 1999). A recent court case, however, highlights the failure of the federal government to respond to EJ complaints. In 2003, the community group Rosemere Neighborhood Association, based in Vancouver, Washington, filed a Title VI complaint with the OCR against the City of Vancouver, Washington. Rosemere alleged that Vancouver failed to use EPA funds to address long-standing problems in 17 low-income and minority neighborhoods, including inadequate sewer services and other standard amenities found in more affluent areas.

Over the course of six years, the organization faced retaliation by the City of Vancouver and was forced to file a second civil rights claim. Finally, in 2009, the Ninth Court Circuit of Appeals found that the OCR had failed to respond to Rosemere's complaints, which "bloomed into a consistent pattern of delay by the EPA." The court noted "that Rosemere's experience before the EPA appears, sadly and unfortunately, typical of those who appeal to OCR to remedy civil rights violations" (*Rosemere Neighborhood Association v. United States Environmental Protection Agency*, 581 F. 3d 1169, 9th Cir. 2009, 13510).

OVERLOOKING LARGE SOURCES OF CONTAMINATION

Efforts to regulate nonpoint source contamination have not effectively addressed the root causes of the contamination or they overlook large sources. For example, the wastes from large animal facilities are technically subject to water-quality permits by the CWA, but these only apply if the facilities discharge into surface waters. This regulatory loophole has effectively left hundreds of thousands of facilities entirely unregulated (GAO 2008). Even compliance and enforcement of regulations that do exist have been acknowledged by the EPA to be insufficient; as of 2008, less than one-third of eligible facilities even had permits (Copeland 2010). Nonpoint source contamination (originating from a variety of sources), such as agricultural runoff or animal feedlots, is largely exempt from CWA regulation (ELI 2000; see also chapter 5: Water Quality).

> The pork industry came to eastern North Carolina because we are black, poor, rural and have no political clout. The farms permitted seepage of waste into groundwater from their cesspools. The wells here were constructed over 50 years earlier. They were open for all kinds of contamination.
> —Gary Grant, *Executive Director of Concerned Citizens for Tillery*

The injustices within water management are not simply the result of unequal enforcement of existing regulations, but also are due to a lack of policies or regulations in place that address the chronic water issues faced by low-income communities and communities of color. Concerned Citizens for Tillery in North Carolina have been fighting the industrial hog industry for the past decade. Hogs now outnumber residents of the state, and hog farming has been linked to elevated rates of nitrates in nearby wells (Marks 2001). After partnering for a study with professors at the University of North Carolina, the citizens' group found that areas with lower incomes and more African American residents had the highest numbers of hog farms (Wing, Cole, and Grant 2000). Subsequent studies found similar conditions in the Mississippi hog industry (Wilson et al. 2002).

Agricultural and animal facility runoff can lead to high rates of nitrates in groundwater (Harter 2009). The EPA has a drinking water standard for nitrates, but its regulation of nutrients in both drinking water and surface water has been found to be "inadequate at both a statewide and national scale" by State-EPA Nutrient Innovations Task Group (SENITG 2009). This type of gap results in severe health and quality-of-life risks for residents in Tillery and many other communities throughout the United States (Duhigg 2009b).

GROUNDWATER PROTECTION: A GLARING GAP

Over half of US residents rely on groundwater for some part of their drinking water (GWTF 2007), but the quality of groundwater is increasingly found to be degraded. There are many sources of contamination, and the contaminants vary widely across geographic regions, but some of the main sources are a combination of industrial discharges, hazardous facilities such as waste sites, farming operations, and runoff (EPA 1999b).

Rural, private well owners are acutely at risk of drinking water contamination. Over 43 million people, mostly in rural areas, rely exclusively on groundwater from private, domestic wells (DeSimone, Hamilton, and Gilliom 2009). Incomes in rural areas are anywhere from 15 to 30 percent lower, and poverty rates 30 to 40 percent higher, than in nonmetropolitan areas (Rubin 2001). A recent US Geological Survey study found that 20 percent of private wells sampled contained at least one contaminant at levels of concern to human health (DeSimone, Hamilton, and Gilliom 2009), but private wells are not regulated by the Safe Drinking Water Act.

Instead of an overarching federal vision for groundwater management, a fragmented array of federal laws touch on some aspect of groundwater protection or cleanup (GWPC 2006a; see also chapter 2: Legal and Institutional Framework of Water Management). This actually hinders comprehensive cleanup and assessment because most of these laws are built to address a separate environmental issue, rather than groundwater (Pye and Patrick 1983), and the regulations that do exist have large holes. For example, more than 50 percent of liquid hazardous waste produced in the United States is disposed of through underground wells. These wells are divided into five categories, known as *classes,* and regulated under the Safe Drinking Water Act, but there are serious deficiencies in the regulatory program. Class V wells are the most numerous, with over 1.5 million in the country, but only one-fifth have permits (GWPC 2006b). As the Groundwater Protection Council explains, "Groundwater has too often been taken for granted and has suffered from a lack of emphasis on the part of local, state, and national leadership and a lack of funding for protection and research" (GWPC 2006, 4).

Complicating groundwater management are the multiple legal frameworks governing its use. Many of these doctrines rely on strong private property doctrines, which protect, to varying degrees, the rights of landowners with property overlying aquifers to pump groundwater (Ashley and Smith 2001). This makes groundwater quality and quantity impacts hard to control and ongoing monitoring very difficult.

Even when efforts to remediate contamination are taken, as the EPA's Groundwater Task Force noted, "Groundwater cleanup activities and decisions are often not prioritized in a manner that would result in addressing the most pressing needs or maximizing the public health benefit of monies spent" (GWTF 2007). The EPA's overall failure to more proactively manage groundwater thus compounds the already existing inequalities in water regulation in low-income communities and communities of color.

CUMULATIVE RISKS AND IMPACTS OVERLOOKED WITHIN FEDERAL WATER POLICY

Environmental justice activists have long pushed for a cumulative impacts model of protecting public health in environmental regulation (Bullard 2001), but two major components of water-quality regulation related to public health have failed to incorporate the basic elements of cumulative impacts: the formation of drinking water standards and the industrial permitting under the CWA (NAPA 2001). Neither process routinely includes the wide variety of contaminants that communities may be exposed to or the chemical interplay these contaminants may have (Gauna, O'Neill, and Rechtschaffen 2005). They also overlook the protection of vulnerable populations, such as children or pregnant women, even when contaminants are shown to be particularly harmful for these groups (EJCW 2005; NEJAC 2004).

Drinking water standards are set using cost-benefit analyses, which attempt to quantitatively assess the public health risks associated with a particular contaminant in comparison to the overall costs of fully cleaning up or regulating the contaminant (Foster 2002). As noted earlier, low-income communities and communities of color are more likely to live near polluting facilities, but these disparities are not addressed in traditional cost-benefit analyses. Environmental justice and law scholar Sheila Foster points out that this type of technical evaluation "violates most notions of equity and justice" because "many environmental issues, such as siting decisions, entail clearly different distributions of net benefits and costs (or risks), often along lines of geography, income, political power, and race" (Foster 2002, 468).

Theoretically, a cost-benefit analysis is an objective means of comparison. But the process for establishing drinking water standards has been beset by industry pressure. Lobbyists have been able to secure less stringent standards by using considerable private resources to argue that the costs of regulation are too expensive, as well as bankrolling studies to argue that the health threats of a particular contaminant are minimal (Duhigg 2009d; Corn 2009).

Water discharge permits required by the CWA are similarly drafted by staff who use technical methodologies and work with the polluter to create an amenable limit on discharges, rather than working with communities to identify needed protections (NAPA 2001). From an EJ perspective, these quantitative methods are a way of "managing, regulating, and distributing risks—instead of protecting public health and the environment in low income and people of color communities" (Bullard et al. 2007).

SUPPORTING THE SOCIAL, CULTURAL, AND ENVIRONMENTAL VALUE OF WATER

> Water rights are everything we have in our communities. They are part of our history and culture, part of our livelihood.
>
> —Janice Varela, *New Mexico Acequia Association*

Water has value that goes beyond economic production. It has cultural, spiritual, and social meanings (Donahue and Johnston 1998). But these values have few legal or political protections (Ingram, Whiteley, and Perry 2008; Espeland 1998), particularly in regards to water rights and increasingly, private values have crowded out these public ones. For example, the water-sharing customs of acequias, which hold water rights communally rather than privately, are integral to identity, survival, and sense of community in small, rural, Latino, and Native American towns throughout New Mexico. For more on water rights, please see chapter 2: Legal and Institutional Framework of Water Management.

Many EJ activists oppose privatization of water services because it threatens to infringe on this heritage and local water values and uses. Privatization commodifies what many communities feel is a common resource that should be protected for overall public use (Barlow and Clarke 2001). Furthermore, private takeover of water services has caused a host of negative impacts in low-income communities and communities of color, ranging from drastic rate increases and service shutoffs (Snitow, Kaufman, and Fox 2007; EJCW 2005). Other types of privatization are emerging throughout the country; new "water markets" are forming that allow entities with water rights to sell water from one area to another (Klein 2007). New water markets and privatization threaten to exacerbate existing water injustices as low-income communities and communities of color will not be able to access these markets (Gibler 2005). Providing water services to a low-income, rural community will not be profitable.

The failure to integrate social and cultural values is not solely the result of private involvement. Public water agencies have also often failed to protect these aspects of the public interest. While growing privatization of water infrastructure worldwide prompts questions about *justice* by directing our attention to issues such as unfair allocation and pricing and limited public access to decision making, we also know that historically, policy failures regarding water equity have as often been the result of misguided government decisions to dam rivers, divert water, and buy and sell water rights in order to better benefit the interests of the rich and powerful (Ingram, Feldman, and Whiteley 2008). The United States' dam-building boom reflects the ways that particular values can get lost in the calculus of federal water policy and the need to better incorporate and protect the social, environmental, and cultural values of water.

Recommendations for Federal Water Policy

Past water policy in the United States has often had adverse and inequitable consequences for low-income and communities of color. Although strategies to address these consequences are varied, one thing is clear: providing communities with a voice in water policy decisions—a key component in the soft path to water, and environmental issues broadly, is central to accepted principles of EJ (EJCW 2005). Whether it is breaking down barriers of discrimination that bar certain communities from basic water services, or incorporating information on the cumulative impacts of pollution in a community, or recognizing the cultural value of water, the issues faced by low-income communities and communities of color must be more carefully and explicitly integrated into federal water policy. The EJ movement has struggled to show agencies and decision makers the importance of an open and transparent decision-making process (Cole and Foster 2001; Di Chiro 1996). In order to begin addressing EJ in federal water policy, we must start by including the voices of those directly affected by the existing system of water management.

The following policy recommendations offer ways to address the current water injustices and, in doing so, create a more equitable, sustainable vision for federal water policy.

FULLY INTEGRATE ENVIRONMENTAL JUSTICE PRINCIPLES INTO FEDERAL WATER-RELATED PROGRAMS AND POLICIES

Many federal agencies, including the Environmental Protection Agency and Department of the Interior, already have the statutory ability to address the concerns raised by EJ communities in permitting, project review and construction, and financing activities related to water. There are guidance documents through the work of NEJAC and other efforts of the Office of Environmental Justice.

A more serious effort must be made to fully integrate EJ into federal water policy, using the benchmarks of measurable progress in eliminating disproportionate impacts in low-income communities and communities of color, as well as implementing a clear system of evaluation and accountability based on demonstrable results in a specified time frame. Some of the key elements of such an effort to integrate EJ into federal water policy include staff positions charged with EJ assessments. For instance, federal agency staff should assess the disproportionate impacts of any proposed project, policy, or permit, ranging from CWA National Pollutant Discharge Elimination System permits to Bureau of Reclamation dam operations. In addition, methods should be developed to incorporate noneconomic water uses, such as social and cultural activities, into proposed projects, policies, or permits. Finally, the federal government should reform water quality permits and programs, such as the Underground Injection Control and the Total Maximum Daily Load programs, to be based on numeric standard that are protective of the most sensitive populations.

SET PRIORITIES FOR ADDRESSING WATER-RELATED ENVIRONMENTAL JUSTICE ISSUES

Addressing EJ in federal water policy requires not only revising programs to include EJ principles moving forward, but also recognizing and proactively addressing current water injustices. Federal agencies with water management authority should ensure that their programs identify communities facing disproportionate water impacts and create concrete action plans within defined goals and time frames to address issues. Clean-up and remediation priorities should be based on disproportionate impacts to low-income communities and communities of color within programs such as the Resource Conservation and Recovery Act or Superfund remediation. Finally, when working with community groups to develop solutions to longstanding EJ and water issues, the technical expertise of federal agencies (National Fish and Wildlife Services, Army Corps, and others) should be used. These projects should use a collaborative, community-based framework to identify and implement needed actions.

COLLABORATE WITH STATE AND LOCAL GOVERNMENTS TO ADDRESS WATER-RELATED ENVIRONMENTAL JUSTICE ISSUES

Given the local nature of both EJ issues and water management, and the delegation of authority to state agencies implementing federal water legislation, federal agencies must participate in related state processes to ensure EJ is adequately addressed. This can include, but is not limited to, providing leadership in working with state and local governments as well as other stakeholders to identify and prioritize issues of water and EJ concern in a specified region and coordinating with state and local governments to ensure implementation of an enhanced, standard public participation process.

USE CUMULATIVE IMPACT ASSESSMENTS IN WATER PROJECT PLANNING AND PERMITTING CONSIDERATIONS

For any piece of federal water policy to effectively integrate EJ principles, it must use a cumulative risk and impact model in decision making. The EPA has created a *Framework for Cumulative Risk Assessment* and NEJAC has issued guidance on how to most effectively implement such a framework. Efforts should be undertaken within all federal agencies with water authority to implement the framework and NEJAC recommendations. This would include incorporating social, economic, cultural, and community health factors, particularly those involving vulnerability, into the EPA's and other water-related agencies' decision-making processes; assessing diverse types of discharges a facility emits and emissions from other adjacent polluters in permitting decisions; using diverse sources of information and expertise including that of communities that stand to be directly affected by the proposed project, program, or permit; and focusing on community-based approaches, particularly community-based participatory research and intervention.

MAKE WATER POLICY AND GOVERNANCE DECISIONS AND POLICIES MORE ACCESSIBLE AND RESPONSIVE TO COMMUNITY NEEDS

NEJAC has produced many guiding documents on how to ensure adequate and meaningful public participation, including the Model Plan for Public Participation. The EPA, Department of Interior, Department of Agriculture, Army Corps, and other agencies that are involved in water policy should ensure the core values expressed within the model plan strategies are part of their water-related activities and take proactive steps to ensure meaningful public participation, including providing documentation in languages other than English in areas where more than 10 percent of the impacted community speaks a language other than English; facilitating ongoing opportunities for direct interaction between agency heads and communities, allocating funding for staff positions trained and dedicated to community outreach, and facilitating collaborations; and choosing arrangements for community interactions to maximize effective participation, assessing factors such as meeting times, locations, and translation needs.

PROVIDE RESOURCES FOR COMMUNITY-BASED ORGANIZATIONS TO ADDRESS WATER ISSUES AND FACILITATE PUBLIC PARTICIPATION

Organizations in low-income communities and communities of color often lack the resources or capacity to effectively resolve ongoing water issues. Community-based organizations and technical assistance providers can play a central role in ensuring meaningful involvement of affected community residents in environmental decision making and resolving community-based issues/concerns. Federal agencies such as the EPA, Department of Agriculture, and Army Corps should build relationships and collaborate with community-based organizations to help bridge community needs and agency efforts to resolve water issues.

ESTABLISH AN INTERAGENCY GROUNDWATER PROTECTION AND OVERSIGHT PROGRAM

Groundwater management and clean-up is currently dispersed among a variety of federal laws and legislation, ranging from administration of the Underground Injection Control program within EPA's Office of Ground Water and Drinking Water to guidelines within the Resource Conservation and Recovery Act for disposal of hazardous waste near groundwater aquifers. This fragmented approach does not provide a comprehensive strategy for protection and management of groundwater. Steps to implement a comprehensive strategy for protection include improving data collection and assessment of threats and existing conditions within aquifers; providing support for interagency and state efforts to protect and manage groundwater; identifying critical EJ and groundwater issues; and allocating sufficient funding to ensure program maintenance.

IMPLEMENT NEW FEES AND STRICTER FINES ON DISCHARGERS UNDER THE CLEAN WATER ACT

The noneconomic costs of water discharges, ranging from the contamination of fish to the contamination of local water bodies, are often borne by low-income communities and communities of color. The EPA should use its statutory authority to fine dischargers that violate National Pollutant Discharge Elimination permits and work with state-delegated authorities to ensure state agencies also use their statutory authority to strictly enforce permit violations. Such fines can provide funding for water needs and deter future pollution.

RECOGNIZE THE HUMAN RIGHT TO WATER

The US Congress should pass legislation recognizing the human right to water, as recognized by the UN Human Rights Council in September 2010. Such legislation can lay the groundwork for a new ethic underlying water management across federal agencies and create an imperative for all federal government agencies to prioritize the provision of basic water resources for all Americans.

ADDRESS CRITICAL ENVIRONMENTAL JUSTICE ISSUES WITH APPROPRIATE FEDERAL WATER FUNDING

Addressing long-standing water injustices will require federal financial support. Programs such as the Clean Water State Revolving Fund, the Safe Drinking Water Revolving Fund, and the Department of Agriculture's Rural Loan and Grant program, should be required to prioritize funding and expand current programs specifically for low-income communities and communities of color to fund critical water supply, water quality, and wastewater projects. This can be accomplished through expanding existing set-asides dedicated to small and low-income communities, creating EJ prerequisites within programs that currently lack such standards, and reducing local match requirements for grants for small-system or low-income water projects.

A second aspect to equitable federal funding is ensuring that both direct grant and loan programs and subsidy programs are not worsening water injustices. This requires an assessment of federal subsidy programs and identification of communities eligible for subsidies. Entities receiving federal funding should be required to demonstrate collaboration with affected communities and ongoing efforts to address disproportionate impacts in order to continue receiving funding. This would apply to programs to both grant and loan programs such as Department of Agriculture's Environmental Quality Incentives Program, State Revolving Funds, but also Bureau of Reclamation agricultural water delivery programs such as California's Central Valley Project.

DIRECT FEDERAL WATER-RELATED CLIMATE CHANGE ADAPTION AND
MITIGATION PLANNING PROCESSES TO IDENTIFY AND PROTECT VULNERABLE
COMMUNITIES

Federal water policy must include efforts to reduce the rapidly growing risks of climate change for water resources and developed water systems. This includes broad efforts at all federally owned or operated infrastructure, with special attention to inequitable or disproportionately large impacts on vulnerable populations. This includes assessing water- and climate-related risks in EJ communities, particularly those risks related to flooding, water scarcity, quality threats, and sea-level rise, and developing adaptation plans with those communities.

References

Anderson, M. 2008. "Cities Inside Out: Race, Poverty and Exclusion at the Urban Fringe." *UCLA Law Review* 55: 1095–1160.

Anderton, D. L., J. M. Oakes, and K. L. Egan. 1997. "Environmental Equity in Superfund." *Evaluation Review* 21 (1): 3–26.

Arctic Monitoring and Assessment Programme. 2009. *AMAP Assessment 2009: Human Health in the Arctic*. Oslo: Arctic Monitoring and Assessment Programme.

Ashley, J. S., and Z. A. Smith. 2001. "Western Groundwater Wars." *Forum for Applied Research and Public Policy* 16. (1): 33-39.

Bailey, J. M., and K. Preston. 2007. *Swept Away: Chronic Hardship and Fresh Promise on the Rural Great Plains*. Lyons, NE: Center for Rural Affairs.

Barlow, M., and T. Clarke. 2002. *Blue Gold: The Fight to Stop the Corporate Theft of the World's Water*. New York: The New Press.

Bauman, K. J. 2003. *Extended Measures of Well-Being: Living Conditions in the United States: 1998*. Washington, DC: US Census Bureau.

Brandt, P. 2004. "Overview of Affordability Programs." USEPA Environmental Financial Advisory Board, Affordability Workshop. San Francisco: August 18, 2004.

Brulle, R. J., and D. N. Pellow. 2006. "Environmental Justice: Human Health and Environmental Inequalities." *Annual Review of Public Health* 3 (27): 1.

Bullard, R. D. 2001. "Environmental Justice in the 21st Century: Race Still Matters." *Phylon* 49: 151–171.

Bullard, R. D., P. Mohai, R. Saha, and B. Wright. 2007. *Toxic Waste and Race at Twenty: 1987–2007*. Cleveland, OH: The United Church of Christ.

Bullard, R. D., and B. Wright. 2009. "Race, Place and the Environment in Post-Katrina New Orleans." In *Race, Place and Environmental Justice after Hurricane Katrina: Struggles to Reclaim, Rebuild and Revitalize New Orleans and the Gulf Coast*. Edited by R. D. Bullard and B. Wright, 19–48. Philadelphia: Westview Press.

Burke, G. 2009. Large Subsides to Corporate Farms in West Depleting Vital Water Supplies. *The Arizona Daily Star*, April 15.

California Energy Commission (CEC). 2005. *2005 Integrated Energy Policy Report.* Report CEC-100-2005-007. Sacramento: California Energy Commission. http://www.energy.ca.gov/2005publications/CEC-100-2005-007/CEC-100-2005-007-CMF.PDF.

Candee, H. 1989. "The Broken Promise of Reclamation Reform." *Hastings Law Journal* 40: 657–685.

Canfield, C. 2010. "Water Bills Go up in down Economy as Usage Drops." *Inside Bay Area.* April 4.

Carter, L. G. 2010. "Reaping Riches in a Wretched Region: Subsidized Industrial Farming and Its Link to Perpetual Poverty." *Golden Gate University of Environmental Law Journal* 3 (1): 5–41.

Cieselski, S., T. Handzel, and M. Sobsey. 1991. "The Microbiologic Quality of Drinking Water in North Carolina Migrant Labor Camps." *American Journal of Public Health* 81: 762.

Clean Air Task Force and The Land and Water Fund of the Rockies. 2003. *The Last Straw: Water Use By Power Plants in the Arid West.* Hewlett Foundation Energy Series. San Francisco and Menlo Park: The Energy Foundation and The Hewlett Foundation.

Cody, B. A., and N. T. Carter. 2009. *35 Years of Water Policy: The 1973 National Water Commission and Present Challenges.* Washington, DC: Congressional Research Service.

Cole, L. W., and S. R. Foster. 2001. *From the Ground Up: Environmental Racism and the Rise of the Environmental Justice Movement.* New York: New York University Press.

Committee on Environmental Justice, Institute of Medicine. 1999. *Toward Environmental Justice: Research, Education, and Health Policy Needs.* Washington, DC: National Academy Press.

Congressional Budget Office (CBO). 2002. *Future Investment in Drinking Water and Wastewater Infrastructure.* Washington, DC: The Congress of the United States.

Copeland, C. 2010. *Water Quality Issues in the 111th Congress: Oversight and Implementation.* CRS Report R40098. Washington, DC: Congressional Research Service.

Copeland, C., and M. Tiemann. 2008. *Water Infrastructure Needs and Investment: Review and Analysis of Key Issues.* CRS Report RL31116. Washington, DC: Congressional Research Service.

Corburn, J. 2002. "Combining Community-Based Research and Local Knowledge to Confront Asthma and Subsistence-Fishing Hazards in Greenpoint/Williamsburg, Brooklyn, New York." *Environmental Health Perspectives* 110 (Suppl 2): 241–248.

Corn, D. 2009. Rocket (Fuel) Man. *Mother Jones,* February 13. http://motherjones.com/politics/2009/02/rocket-fuel-man.

Cottrell, M. 2008. "City Sees Sharp Rise in Unpaid Water Bills." *Chi-Town Daily News,* September 8.

Cutter, S. 2006. "The Geography of Social Vulnerability: Race, Class and Catastrophe." In: *Understanding Katrina: Perspectives from the Social Sciences.* Edited by D. A. Farber and J. Chen, 120–122. New York: Aspen Publishers.

DePalma, A. 2007. "City Keeping Water Rate From Rising." *New York Times,* December 7.

DeSimone, L. A., P. A. Hamilton, and R. J. Gilliom. 2009. *Quality of Water from Domestic Wells in Principal Aquifers of the United States, 1991–2004 – Overview of Major Findings.* USGS Circular 1332. Reston, VA: US Geological Survey.

Di Chiro, G. 1996. "Nature as Community: The Convergence of Environment and Social Justice." In *Uncommon Ground: Rethinking the Human Place in Nature.* Edited by W. Cronon, 298–320. New York: W. W. Norton.

Donahue, J. M., and B. R. Johnston. 1998. "Conclusion." In *Water, Culture, & Power: Local Struggles in a Global Context*. Edited by J. M. Donahue and B. R. Johnston, 339–346. Washington, DC: Island Press.

Duhigg, C. 2009a. "Cleansing the Air at the Expense of Waterways." *New York Times*, October 12.

———. 2009b. "Health Ills Abound as Farm Runoff Fouls Wells." *New York Times*, September 17.

———. 2009c. "Millions in US Drink Dirty Water, Records Show." *New York Times*, December 7.

———. 2009de. "That Tap Water Is Legal But May Be Unhealthy." *New York Times*, December 17.

Duncan, B. 2010. "Flammable Drinking Water? Why Gas Drilling in New York and Nearby States Could Become an Environmental Catastrophe." *AlterNet*, April 21. http://www.alternet.org/story/146540/.

Electric Power Research Institute (EPRI). 2002. *Water & Sustainability (Volume 3): U.S. Water Consumption for Power Production—The Next Half Century*. Report 1006786. Palo Alto: Electric Power Research Institute.

Environmental Health Coalition (EHC). 2005. *Survey of Fishers on Piers in San Diego Bay: Results and Conclusions*. National City, CA: Environmental Health Coalition. http://www.environmentalhealth.org/EHC_Misc_Archive/CBCPierFishersSurveyReport.htm.

Environmental Justice Coalition for Water (EJCW). 2005. *Thirsty for Justice: A People's Blueprint for California Water*. Oakland: Environmental Justice Coalition for Water.

Environmental Justice Executive Steering Committee (EJESC). 2009. "Environmental Justice at EPA—Transition Paper." Environmental Justice Executive Steering Committee, Washington, DC. http://environmentaljusticeblog.blogspot.com/2009/02/environmental-justice-at-epa-transition.html.

Environmental Law Institute (ELI). 2000. *Putting the Pieces Together: State Nonpoint Source Enforceable Mechanisms in Context*. Washington, DC: Environmental Law Institute.

Espeland, W. N. 1998. *The Struggle for Water: Politics, Rationality, and Identity in the American Southwest*. Chicago: University of Chicago Press.

Evans, G. W., and E. Kantrowitz. 2002. "Socioeconomic Status and Health: The Potential Role of Environmental Risk Exposure." *Annual Review of Public Health* 23: 303–331.

Federal Reserve Bank of Dallas (FRBD). nd. "Texas Colonias: A Thumbnail Sketch of the Conditions, Issues, Challenges and Opportunities." Federal Reserve Bank of Dallas. Accessed August 2, 2009. http://www.dallasfed.org/ca/pubs/colonias.html.

Feeley, T., J. Duda, L. Green, R. Kleinmann, J. Murphy, T. Ackman, and J. Hoffman. 2005. *Addressing the Critical Links Between Fossil Energy and Water*. Washington, DC: Department of Energy/Office of Fossil Energy's Water-Related Research, Development, and Demonstration Programs.

Food and Agriculture Organization of the United Nations (FAO). 2008. *Climate Change Adaptation and Mitigation in the Food and Agriculture Sector*. Technical Background Document from the Expert Consultation held on 5 to 7 March 2008. Rome: United Nations.

Foster, S. 2002. "Environmental Justice in an Era of Devolved Collaboration." *Harvard Environmental Law Review* 26: 459–498.

Fougères, D. 2007. "Climate Change, Environmental Justice, and Human Rights in California's Central Valley: A Case Study." Center for International Environmental Law, Washington, DC. http://www.ciel.org/Publications/Climate/CaseStudy_CentralValleyCA_Nov07.pdf.

Fricker, R. D., and N. W. Hengartner. 2001. "Environmental Equity and the Distribution of Toxic Release Inventory and Other Environmentally Undesirable Sites in Metropolitan New York City." *Environmental and Ecological Statistics* 8: 33–52.

García, R., and A. White. 2006. *Healthy Park, Schools, and Communities: Mapping Green Access and Equity for the Los Angeles Region.* Los Angeles: The City Project.

Gasteyer, S., and R. T. Vaswani. 2004. *Still Living without the Basics in the 21st Century: Analyzing the Availability of Water and Sanitation Services in the United States.* Washington, DC: Rural Community Assistance Partnership.

Gauna, E., C. A. O'Neill, and C. Rechtschaffen. 2005. *Environmental Justice: A Center for Progressive Regulation White Paper.* CPR White Paper 505. Washington, DC: Center for Progressive Reform. http://www.progressivereform.org/whitePapers.cfm.

Gee, G. C., and D. C. Payne-Sturges. 2004. "Environmental Health Disparities: A Framework Integrating Psychosocial and Environmental Concepts." *Environmental Health Perspectives* 112 (17): 1645–1653.

George, L., J. Pinder, and T. Singleton. 2004. *Race, Place, and Housing: Housing Conditions in Rural Minority Counties.* Washington, DC: Housing Assistance Council.

Gibler, J. 2005. *Water for People and Place: Moving Beyond Markets in California Water Policy.* Oakland: Public Citizen.

Giles-Corti, Billie., M. H. Broomhall, M. Knuiman, C. Collins, K. Douglas, K. Ng, A. Lange, et al. 2005. Increasing Walking: How Important Is Distance to, Attractiveness, and Size of Public Open Space?" *American Journal of Preventive Medicine* 28 (2S2): 169–176.

Gleick, P. 2009. "Testimony of Dr. Peter H. Gleick before the United States Senate Committee on Energy and Natural Resources on the Energy and Water Integration Act of 2009." Pacific Institute. http://pacinst.org/publications/testimony/.

Grady, B.2008. "Foreclosed Property Renters Won't Lose Water." *Oakland Tribune*, February 27.

Ground Water Protection Council. 2006a. *Ground Water Report to the Nation: A Call To Action.* Oklahoma City: Ground Water Protection Council.

———.2006b. *Ground Water and Underground Injection Control.* Oklahoma City: Ground Water Protection Council.

Ground Water Task Force (GWTF). 2007. *Recommendations from the EPA Ground Water Task Force.* EPA 500-R-07-001. Washington, DC: US Environmental Protection Agency.

Harnik, P. 2006. *The Excellent City Park System: What Makes It Great and How to Get There.* San Francisco, CA: The Trust for Public Land.

Harter, T. 2009. "Agricultural Impacts on Groundwater Nitrate." *Southwest Hydrology* 8 (4): 22–23, 35.

Hauter, W. 2008. "Agriculture's Big Thirst: How To Change the Way We Grow Our Food." In *Water Consciousness: How We All Have To Change To Protect Our Most Critical Resource.* Edited by T. Lohan, chap. 6. San Francisco, CA: AlterNet Books.

Heberger, M., H. Cooley, P. Herrera, P. Gleick, and E. Moore. 2009. *The Impacts of Sea-Level Rise on the California Coast.* Oakland: California Climate Change Center.

Hird, J. A. 1993. "Environmental Policy and Equity: The Case of Superfund." *Journal of Policy Analysis and Management* 12 (2): 323–343.

Hoffman, D. 2007. "Under Pressure from Citizens, EPA to Provide Water for Oil and Gas-polluted Rural Community." Sierra Club press release. http://texas.sierraclub.org/press/newsreleases/20070615.asp?AID=/20070614/BREAKINGNEWS/70614062.

Hurley, A. 1988. "The Social Biases of Environmental Change in Gary, Indiana, 1945–1980." *Environmental Review* 12 (4): 1–19.

Imperial, M. T. 1999. "Environmental Justice and Water Pollution Control: The Clean Water Act Construction Grants Program." *Public Works Management & Policy* 4 (2): 100–118.

Ingram, H., J. M. Whiteley, and R. Perry. 2008. "The Importance of Equity and the Limits of Efficiency in Water Resources." In *Water, Place and Equity*. Edited by J. M. Whiteley, H. Ingram, and R. Perry, 1–33. Boston: MIT Press.

Johnson, J. H., A. Parnell, A. M. Joyner, C. J. Christman, and B. Marsh. 2004. "Racial Apartheid in a Small North Carolina Town." *The Review of Black Political Economy* 31 (4): 89–107.

Kibel, Paul S. 2007. *Access to Parklands: Environmental Justice at Eastbay Parks*. San Francisco, CA: Golden Gate University School of Law.

Kimbrell, A. 2002. "Introduction." In *Fatal Harvest: The Tragedy of Industrial Agriculture*. Sausalito, CA: Foundation for Deep Ecology.

Klein, C. A. 2007. "Water Transfers: The Case against Transbasin Diversions in the Eastern States." *UCLA Journal of Environmental Law and Policy* 25: 249–282.

Lane, A., and T. Heath. 2009. *Environmental Racism in Syracuse, NY: A Case Study of Government's Failure to Protect an Endangered Waterway and a Neglected Community*. Syracuse, NY: Partnership for Onondaga Creek. http://www.onondagacreek.org/resources/presentations.

Lavelle, M. and M. Coyle. 1992. "Unequal Protection: The Racial Divide in Environmental Law." *The National Law Journal* 15 (3): S1–S12.

Leavitt, C. 2007. *Troubled Waters: An Analysis of 2005 Clean Water Act Compliance*. Washington, DC: US PIRG Education Fund.

Leslie, J. 2008. "The Age of Consequence: A Short History of Dams." In *Water Consciousness: How We All Have To Change To Protect Our Most Critical Resource*. Edited by T. Lohan, chap. 7. San Francisco: AlterNet Books.

Lichter, D. T., D. Parisi, S. M. Grice, and M. Taquino. 2007. "Municipal Underbounding: Annexation and Racial Exclusion in Small Southern Towns." *Rural Sociology* 72 (1): 47–68.

Lynch, M. J., P. B. Stretesky, and R. G. Burns. 2004. "Slippery Business: Race, Class and Legal Determinants of Penalties against Petroleum Refineries." *Journal of Black Studies* 34 (3): 421–440.

MacCannell, D. 1983. *Agribusiness and the Small Community. Background Paper to Technology, Public Policy and the Changing Structure of American Agriculture*. Washington, DC: US Office of Technology Assessment.

Marks, R. 2001. *Cesspools of Shame: How Factory Farm Lagoons and Sprayfields Threaten Environmental and Public Health*. New York: Natural Resource Defense Council.

Mather, M. 2004. *Housing and Commuting Patterns in Appalachia*. Washington, DC: Population Reference Bureau.

McCauley, L. A., M. Beltran, J. Phillips, and M. Lasarev, and D. Sticker. 2001. "The Oregon Migrant Farmworker Community: An Evolving Model for Participatory Research." *Environmental Health Perspectives Supplements* 109 (Suppl 3): 449–455.

McGinnis, S., and R. K. Davis. 2001. "Domestic Well Water Quality within Tribal Lands of Eastern Nebraska." *Environmental Geology* 41: 321–329.

Messner, M., S. Shaw, S. Regli, K. Rotert, V. Blank, and J. Soller. 2006. "An Approach for Developing a National Estimate of Waterborne Disease due to Drinking Water and a National Estimate Model Application." *Journal of Water and Health* 4 (Suppl 2): 201–240.

Miller, J. 2009. "Rebooting Urban Watersheds." *High Country News,* June 1. http://www.hcn.org/issues/41.10/rebooting-the-urban-watershed-movement.

Moore, E., and E. Matalon. 2011. *The Human Costs of Nitrate-Contaminated Drinking Water in the San Joaquin Valley.* Oakland, CA: Pacific Institute.

Morello-Frosch, R., M. Pastor, J. Sadd, and S. B. Shonkoff. 2009. *The Climate Gap: Inequalities in How Climate Change Hurts Americans & How to Close the Gap.* Los Angeles: USC Program for Environmental and Regional Equity.

National Academy of Public Administration (NAPA). 2001. *Environmental Justice in EPA Permitting: Reducing Pollution in High-Risk Communities Is Integral to the Agency's Mission.* Washington, DC: National Academy of Public Administration.

———.2003. *Addressing Community Concerns: How Environmental Justice Relates to Land Use Planning and Zoning.* Washington, DC: National Academy of Public Administration.

National Consumer Law Center, Consumer Federation of America, US Public Interest Research Groups and Consumers Union (NCLC). 2006. "Consumer Groups Comments to EPA's Proposed Revisions to the Existing National-Level Affordability Methodology for Small Drinking Water Systems Variances." Docket ID No. OW-2005-0005.

National Drinking Water Advisory Council (NDWAC). 2003. "Recommendations of the National Drinking Water Advisory Council to U.S. EPA on Its National Small Systems Affordability Criteria." Office of Water, US Environmental Protection Agency. http://www.epa.gov/ogwdw/ndwac/pdfs/report_ndwac_affordabilitywg_final_08-08-03.pdf.

National Environmental Justice Advisory Committee Cumulative Risks and Impacts Group (NEJAC). 2004. *Ensuring Risk Reduction in Communities with Multiple Stressors: Environmental Justice and Cumulative Risks/Impacts.* Washington, DC: US Environmental Protection Agency.

Neighborhood of Affordable Housing (NOAH). 2006. "Chelsea Creek Action Group." Neighborhood of Affordable Housing. http://www.noahcdc.org/cbe/ccrp.html.

Office of Environmental Health Hazard Assessment (OEHHA). 2001. *Chemicals in Fish: Consumption of Fish and Shellfish in California and the United States.* Oakland, CA: California Environmental Protection Agency.

Office of Inspector General (OIG). (2006). *EPA Needs to Conduct Environmental Justice Reviews of Its Programs, Policies, and Activities.* Report No. 2006-P-00034. Washington, DC: US Environmental Protection Agency.

O'Neil, S. G. 2007. "Superfund: Evaluating the Impact of Executive Order 12898." *Environmental Health Perspectives* 115 (4): 1087–1093.

O'Neill, C. 2007. "No Mud Pies: Risk Avoidance as Risk Regulation." *Vermont Law Review* 31: 273–354.

Parnell, A. M., A. M. Joyner, C. J. Christman, and D. P. Marsh. 2004. *The Persistence of Political Segregation: Racial Underbounding in North Carolina.* Mebane, NC: Cedar Grove Institute for Sustainable Communities.

Pastor, M., R. D. Bullard, J. K. Boyce, A. Fothergill, R. Morello-Frosch, and B. Wright. 2006. *In the Water of the Storm: Environment, Disaster, and Race after Katrina.* New York: Russell Sage Foundation.

People's Water Board. 2009. "People's Water Board Mission." People's Water Board. http://peopleswaterboard.blogspot.com/2009/06/peoples-water-board-mission.html.

Pinderhughes, R. 1996. "The Impact of Race on Environmental Quality: An Empirical and Theoretical Discussion." *Sociological Perspectives* 39 (2): 231–248.

Preston, M., and A. Bailey. 2003. "The Potential for High-performance Design Adoption in Retail Property Portfolios." *Corporate Social Responsibility and Environmental Management* 10 (3): 165–174.

Pye, V. I., and R. Patrick. 1983. "Ground Water Contamination in the United States." *Science* 221 (4612): 713–718.

Quintero-Somaini, A., and M. Quirindongo. 2004. *Hidden Danger: Environmental Health Threats in the Latino Community*. New York: Natural Resource Defense Council.

Raucher, R. 2004. "Affordability of Water Service: What Does It Mean? How Is It Measured? Why Does It Matter?" Paper presented at USEPA Environmental Financial Advisory Board, Affordability Workshop. San Francisco, August 18, 2004.

Ray, J. 2004. "Delta Defender: Stopping Developers with an 'African Drumbeat.'" *Sierra Magazine*. http://www.sierraclub.org/sierra/200405/profile_printable.asp.

Reisner, M. 1993. *Cadillac Desert: The American West and Its Disappearing Water*. New York: Penguin Books.

Ringquist, E. J. 2005. "Assessing Evidence of Environmental Inequities: A Meta-Analysis." *Journal of Policy Analysis and Management* 24 (2): 223–247.

Ringquist, E. J., and D. H. Clark. 1999. "Local Risks, States' Rights, and Federal Mandates: Remedying Environmental Inequities in the U.S. Federal System." *Publius* 29 (2): 73–93.

Rowan, G. T., and C. Fridgen. 2003. "Brownfields and Environmental Justice: The Threats and Challenges of Contamination." *Environmental Practice* 5: 58–61.

Rubin, S. J. 2001. *Economic Characteristics of Small Systems*. Rural Water Partnership Fund White Paper. Duncan, OK: National Rural Water Association.

Scott, J. 2010. "Nitrate Contamination Spreading in California Communities." *California Watch*, May 13. http://californiawatch.org/nitrate-contamination-spreading-california-communities.

Shepard, P. M., and C. Corbin-Mark. 2009. "Climate Justice." *Environmental Justice* 2 (4): 1–4.

Shilling, F. M. 2009. "Fishing for Justice or Just Fishing?" *Ecology Law Currents* 36: 205–211.

Silka, L. nd. "The Southeast Asian Environmental Justice Partnership: Citizens Revive a New England Mill Town River." *New Village Journal*. Accessed September 10, 2009. http://www.newvillage.net/Journal/Issue3/3silka.html.

Silver, E., J. Kaslow, D. Lee, S. Lee, M. L. Tan, E. Weis, and A. Ujihara. 2007. "Fish Consumption and Advisory Awareness Among Low-Income Women in California's Sacramento–San Joaquin Delta." *Environmental Research* 104 (3): 410–419.

Sludge Safety Project. 2009. "What Is Underground Coal Slurry Injection?" Sludge Safety Project. http://www.sludgesafety.org/coal_slurry_inj.html.

Small, Gail. 2005. "The Coal Wars: Northern Cheyenne Reservation, Lame Deer, Montana." *Voices from the Earth* 6 (1). http://www.sric.org/voices/2005/v6n1/coal_wars.html.

Smecker, F. J. 2009. "Coal Mine Laws Written in Blood: An Interview with Judy Bonds." May 27. Towards Freedom. http://towardfreedom.com/home/content/view/1593/1/.

Smith, N. 2006. "There's No Such Thing as a Natural Disaster." Understanding Katrina: Perspectives from the Social Sciences. http://understandingkatrina.ssrc.org/Smith/.

Smith, R. 2008. "More Utility Bills Go Unpaid: Consumers' Economic Struggles Spur More Power Shutoffs as Firms Step Up Collections." *Wall Street Journal*, November 3.

Snipp, C. M. 1996. "Understanding Race and Ethnicity in Rural America." *Rural Sociology* 61 (1): 125–142.

Snitow, A., D. Kaufman, and M. Fox. 2007. *Thirst: Fighting Corporate Theft of Our Water*. San Francisco: John Wiley and Sons, Inc.

Spirn, A. W. 2005. "Restoring Mill Creek: Landscape Literacy, Environmental Justice and City Planning and Design." *Landscape Research* 30 (3): 395–413.

State-EPA Nutrient Innovations Task Group (SENITG). 2009. *An Urgent Call to Action: Report of the State-EPA Nutrient Innovations Task Group*. Washington, DC: US Environmental Protection Agency.

Steinberg, T. 1993. "That World's Fair Feeling: Control of Water in 20th-Century America." *Technology and Culture* 34: 401–109.

Stroud, E. 1999. "Troubled Waters in Ecotopia: Environmental Racism in Portland, Oregon." *Radical History Review* 74: 65–95.

Sustainable South Bronx. 2008. "In My Backyard: A Profile of Hunts Point with Recommendations for Realizing Community Members' Vision for their Neighborhood." Sustainable South Bronx. http://www.warnkecc.com/wp-content/uploads/wcc_ssb_report_2408.pdf.

Szasz, A., and M. Meuser. 1997. "Environmental Inequalities: Literature Review and Proposals for New Directions in Research and Theory." *Current Sociology* 45 (3): 99–120.

Tiemann, M. 2006. *Safe Drinking Water Act: Issues in the 109th Congress*. Washington, DC: Congressional Research Service.

———. 2008. *Drinking Water State Revolving Fund (DWSRF): Program Overview and Issues*. Washington, DC: Congressional Research Service.

Timperio, A., K. Ball, J. Salmon, R. Roberts, and D. Crawford. 2007. "Is Availability of Public Open Space Equitable across Areas?" *Health & Place* 13 (2): 335–340.

TreePeople. 2009. "Sun Valley Watershed." TreePeople. http://www.treepeople.org/sun-valley-watershed.

Troesken, W. 2002. "The Limits of Jim Crow: Race and the Provision of Water and Sewerage Services in American Cities, 1880–1925." *Journal of Economic History* 62 (3): 734–772.

University of North Carolina Center for Civil Rights (UNCCR). 2006. *Invisible Fences: Municipal Underbounding in Southern Moore County*. Chapel Hill: UNC Center for Civil Rights.

US Census Bureau. 2008. *American Housing Survey for the United States: 2007*. Washington, DC: U.S. Government Printing Office.

US Commission in Civil Rights (USCCR). 2003. *Not in My Backyard: Executive Order 12,898 and Title VI as Tools for Achieving Environmental Justice*. Washington, DC: US Commission on Civil Rights.

———. 1999a. *National Characteristics of Drinking Water Systems Serving Populations Under 10,000*. Washington, DC: US Environmental Protection Agency.

———. 1999b. *Safe Water Drinking Act, Section 1429, Groundwater Report to Congress*. Washington, DC: US Environmental Protection Agency.

———. 2000. *America's Children and the Environment: A First View of Available Measures*. Washington, DC: US Environmental Protection Agency.

———. 2001a. "EPA Report to Congress: Implementation and Enforcement of the Combined Sewer Overflow Control Policy." Office of Water, US Environmental Protection Agency. http://cfpub.epa.gov/npdes/cso/cpolicy_report.cfm.

———. 2001b. *1999 Drinking Water Infrastructure Needs Survey*. Washington, DC: US Environmental Protection Agency.

———.2002. *Fish Consumption and Environmental Justice: A Report Developed from the National Environmental Justice Advisory Council*. Washington, DC: Washington: US Environmental Protection Agency.

———. 2004. *Lead and Copper Rule: A Quick Reference Guide for Schools and Child Care Facilities That are Regulated Under the Safe Drinking Water Act*. Washington, DC: US Environmental Protection Agency.

———.2005. *Protecting Water from Agricultural Runoff*. EPA 941-F-05-001. Washington, DC: US Environmental Protection Agency. http://www.epa.gov/owow/nps/Ag_Runoff_Fact_Sheet.pdf.

———. 2008. *Health and Environmental Impacts of Uranium Contamination in the Navajo Nation: Five Year Plan*. Washington, DC: US Environmental Protection Agency. http://www.epa.gov/region9/superfund/navajo-nation/pdf/NN-5-Year-Plan-June-12.pdf.

———. 2009a. *Drinking Water Infrastructure Needs Survey and Assessment: Fourth Report to Congress*. Washington, DC: US Environmental Protection Agency.

———.2009b. "Migrant Farm Worker Drinking Water: Safe at the Well?" US Environmental Protection Agency. http://www.epa.gov/Region8/ej/mfw.html.

———. 2009c. *2006: Public Water System Compliance Report*. Washington, DC: US Environmental Protection Agency. http://cfpub.epa.gov/compliance/resources/reports/accomplishment/sdwa/.

———. 2010a. "Basic Information: What Is Nonpoint Source Pollution?" US Environmental Protection Agency. http://www.epa.gov/nps/whatis.html.

———. 2010b. "Environmental Justice Factsheet." US Environmental Protection Agency. http://www.epa.gov/compliance/ej/nejac/index.html.

US Government Accountability Office (GAO). 2001. *GAO 02-12 Environmental Protection: Federal Incentives that Could Help Promote Land Use that Protects Air and Water Quality*. Washington, DC: US General Accountability Office.

———.2007. *GAO-07-479 Clean Water: Further Implementation and Better Cost Data Needed To Determine Impact of EPA's Storm Water Program On Communities*. Washington, DC: US General Accountability Office.

———. 2008. *GAO-08-1177T Concentrated Animal Feeding Operations: EPA Needs More Information and a Clearly Defined Strategy To Protect Air and Water Quality*. Washington, DC: US General Accountability Office.

———.2009. *GAO-09-551 Alaska Native Villages: Limited Progress Has Been Made on Relocating Villages Threatened by Flooding and Erosion*. Washington, DC: US Government Accountability Office.

Vela-Acosta, M. S., P. Bigelow, and R. Buchan. 2002. "Assessment of Occupational Health and Safety Risks of Farmworkers in Colorado." *American Journal of Industrial Medicine Supplement* 42 (S2): 19–27.

Water Resources Research Center. 2010. *The Water-Energy Nexus. Arroyo*. Tucson: University of Arizona.

Weintraub, M., and L. S. Birnbaum. 2008. "Catfish Consumption as a Contributor to Elevated PCB Levels in a Non-Hispanic Black Subpopulation." *Environmental Research* 107 (3):412–417.

West End Revitalization Association. 2002. *Failing Septic Systems and Contaminated Well Waters: African-American Communities in Mebane, North Carolina*. Mebane, NC: West End Revitalization Association.

Wilber, M. 2003. *Californians without Safe Water*. Sacramento: California Department of Water Resources, Statewide Planning Office.

Williams, B. 2001. "A River Runs through Us." *American Anthropologist* 103 (2): 409–431.

Williams, D. R., and C. Collins. 1995. "US Socioeconomic and Racial Difference in Health: Patterns and Explanations." *Annual Review of Sociology* 21: 349–386.

Williams, R. L., J. T. O'Leary, A. L. Sheaffer, and D. Mason. 2000. *An Examination of Fish Consumption by Indiana Recreational Anglers: An On-Site Survey*. Technical Report 99-D-HDFW-2. West Lafayette, IN: Purdue University.

Wilson, S. M., F. Howell, S. Wing, and M. Sobsey. 2002. "Environmental Injustice and the Mississippi Hog Industry." *Environmental Health Perspectives* 110 (Suppl 2): 195–201.

Wilson, S., M. Hutson, and M. Mujahid. 2008. "How Planning and Zoning Contribute to Inequitable Development, Neighborhood Health, and Environmental Injustice." *Environmental Justice* 1 (4): 211–216.

Wing, S., D. Cole, and G. Grant. 2000. "Environmental Injustice in North Carolina's Hog Industry." *Environmental Health Perspectives* 108: 225–231.

Woefle-Erskine, C. 2007. "Who Needs Dams?" In *Dam Nation: Dispatches from the Water Underground*. Edited by C. Woelfle-Erskine, J. O. Cole, and L. Allen, 1–416. New York: Soft Skull Press.

4

TRIBES AND WATER

Kate A. Berry

Introduction

A long-standing and still unresolved federal water problem is how to address the rights and access of contemporary American Indian tribal governments and communities to freshwater. This chapter examines major issues that tribes face concerning water.[1] It begins with the recognition that tribes face different circumstances than all other ethnic and racial groups in the United States, and this affects tribal water governance. Tribes have a unique political (and legal) relationship with the federal government; they are sovereign within a framework of other sovereigns who often compete with one another. Three water challenges that many tribes face are considered in detail: water rights and administration, energy and water, and water quality governance. Progress toward resolving these challenges was slow during the 20th century when tribes were either ignored or sidelined in discussions around water policy. The chapter begins with a discussion of the dimensions of sovereignty as it relates to the tribes, states, and the federal government and concludes with suggestions on an approach to 21st-century federal policy on tribal water matters.

The experience of the Lummi Indian Nation, in the state of Washington, offers some insights into the unresolved challenges facing many Native American communities. In response to a long-standing water dispute with the state of Washington, the Lummi Indian Nation distributed the 23-page *Call to Action* in 1995. The document encouraged tribes and their allies to lobby Congress and the administration to prevent tribal funding reductions buried in an appropriation bill. The funding cuts were proposed by Senator Gorton, who actively opposed many aspects of tribal sovereignty, particularly anything related to water governance, fisheries management, or jurisdiction over land on the Lummi reservation, initially as an attorney in private practice and later as an elected senator from Washington. A letter from Henry Cagey, then-chair of the Lummi's Business Council, described not only to the Lummi's dilemma but introduced many of the contemporary water issues that tribes across the western United States continue to face:

> As water becomes scarce throughout the West, many tribes have found themselves competing for water with non-Indians on their reservations. In order to resolve water conflicts, determination of the treaty-reserved water right must take place. In a long-standing conflict on the Lummi Reservation, the state has claimed authority to allocate reservation groundwater to non-tribal users until the Lummi Nation quantifies its reserved water rights. This has led to salt water intrusion and depletion in reservation aquifers, impairing the tribe's salmon hatchery program and our efforts to develop our economy and provide badly needed housing for our people. In 1990, the tribe offered to consolidate all non-tribal systems with the larger Lummi system and provide water for their existing and future homes. Most of the non-tribal groups refused, and thus the Lummi government decided to quantify the tribal right, seeking negotiations outside of litigation. Negotiations have just begun (Cagey 1995).

With their tribal self-determination being tested, the Lummi engaged in several types of actions—public outreach, litigation, negotiation, and legislative lobbying. In these forums, they drew connections between various types of problems, each related to water matters in its own way—exerting tribal sovereignty versus living with nontribal neighbors, connections between groundwater use and surface water quality, and economic impacts as they relate to environmental protection. Part of the difficulty facing the Lummi is uncertainty over how decisions affecting their water (and more generally, their sovereignty) are made and who makes them.

Who Makes Decisions and How are They Made? Tribal Sovereignty within the US Federalist System

Political order within the United States is widely recognized as being unusual because it is neither a strong federal state nor an interstate confederation but something in between (Deudney 1996). Pisani (1992) argued that the American populace, particularly during the 19th century, embraced the shared power and decentralization inherent in US federalism, reinforced by belief that it embodied a natural law that transcended the state itself. On the one hand, individual states assert full sovereignty based on the authority inherent in their constitutions. As noted in "Federalist Paper no. 39," "each state, in ratifying the [federal] Constitution, is considered a sovereign body independent of all others, and only to be bound by its own voluntary act" (Hamilton, Madison, and Jay 1999, 212). Another interpretation of the sovereignty of individual states is based on the premise that the federal government possesses only those powers granted by the Constitution (Powell 2002). As such, sovereignty for individual states within the federalist system serves the goal of devolving power from the center to the people (Powell 2002).

Nonetheless, there are certainly limits to the sovereignty of states within the federal system (Althouse 1987). States within the United States, for example, cannot sign treaties with governments outside the United States, nor can they regulate commerce with tribes—those powers are limited by the Commerce Clause of the US Constitution (see chapter 2: Legal and Institutional Framework of Water Management). Thus, the sovereignty of individual states in this federalist system is bounded or partial.

The same can be said of tribal sovereignty. The terms *domestic sovereign* and *quasi-sovereign* are frequently used as qualifiers because of limitations placed on tribal sovereignty. But measured sovereignty is true for all entities: for states and the federal government, as well as tribes in the United States. Given the dynamics within which sovereignty arises and is articulated, it must be qualified and bounded (Berry 2006a).

Despite these limits, tribes have made great strides in asserting their rights as sovereigns. Consider, for example, the active court systems of many tribal governments as well as their police forces, social service agencies, transportation planning, educational institutions, and water-management agencies. Many American Indian tribes see sovereignty and self-determination as fundamental to interpreting their past and preparing for their future. This is not to suggest that all is settled and things are progressing smoothly for tribal sovereignty in the United States. State governments, in particular, have historically served as active opponents of tribes, and, even today, many states continue to challenge tribal sovereignty. In the past couple decades, for example, the US Supreme Court has made decisions on a number of major lawsuits, in which states were pitted against native groups or tribes over issues of sovereignty and jurisdiction. These include a decision in 1993 about the rights to regulate hunting and fishing, a 1996 decision about dispute resolution between states and tribes over reservation gaming, a 1997 decision about whether a tribe or a state owned submerged lands under a lake, and a decision in 2000 regarding the water rights allocated to tribes relative to the allocations of individual states.[2] The very existence of these cases and the fact these conflicts are being adjudicated by the highest court in the nation underscores the adaptability of sovereignty and its connection with tribal governance initiatives. Sovereignty cannot be standardized because it is dynamic. Nowhere is this more evident than in water matters, for which tribes and states alike exert their sovereign capacities and interests.

Access to Water: Tribal Water Rights in Context

Many creation myths, from diverse communities around the world, revolve around water.[3] The Arapaho's creation myth tells of the earth covered by floodwaters. One lonely Arapaho man stood on a mountain peak weeping and the Creator called to a dove to find him a home. The dove searched but could not find any dry place for a home, so a turtle dived into the waters and came up with mud, reporting that the earth was under the water. The Creator commanded the waters to flow away (Hannum 1992).

Originally from the Great Lakes area, the Northern Arapaho are now on the Wind River Reservation in western Wyoming, along with their traditional enemies, the Eastern Shoshone. The Shoshone were granted rights to the Wind River Reservation under a treaty in 1868; a decade later, the Arapaho were moved by the US Army onto the reservation, where they have resided ever since. Since that time, the boundaries of the reservation have changed through a series of land cessions and restorations, but both tribes remain on the Wind River Reservation. The reservation supports abundant water on lands ranging from 12,500-foot alpine areas to 4,500-foot arable valley bottoms (Hannum 1992). Both tribes worked to secure water rights to the Wind River and the Big Horn River, into which the Wind River flows. As with many other tribes today in the western United States, the Shoshone and Arapaho tribes have long been in conflict with local and state governments and ranchers who were allocated water rights under the prior appropriation doctrine (for a description of water rights law, see chapter 2. Despite traditional differences between the Eastern Shoshone and Northern Arapaho people, the tribes came together to secure water rights for the places both valued on the reservation. Substantive political organization and legal will was involved, as the tribes had to work closely with representatives from the federal government, state government, and local ranching organizations.

In 1985, after years of litigation, a court decree awarded the Wind River tribes over a half-million acre-feet of senior water rights to the Big Horn River and Wind River (Hannum 1992). Exerting their powers as a sovereign government, the tribes appointed the Wind River Water Resource Control Board, which developed a water code. The code was agreed on by both tribal councils in 1990. Under the terms of the water code, the tribes issued a permit for instream flows for their reservation and dedicated about 16 percent of the tribes' overall water rights entitlements to instream flows to enhance conditions for fisheries and ensure flows through the reservation. In 1992, the Wyoming Supreme Court ruled against the tribes, preventing them from using water for instream flows and disallowing the Wind River Water Resources Control Board from administering either state or tribal water rights within the reservation (Hannum 1992; Willis-Friday 1992). Since that decision, the state of Wyoming and the tribes have continued discussion over these issues. Although the tribes were not ultimately successful in fully asserting their administrative powers over water, they did secure reserved water rights for the reservation. This chain of events enhanced the tribes' institutional capacity, exerted tribal governance over water matters, and advanced tribal sovereignty.

The award of water rights to the Wind River tribes was made possible through a judicial decision made over a century ago. The 1908 US Supreme Court case *Winter v. the United States* has become a landmark for all subsequent water allocation that involves tribal governance and western states. The *Winters* case, as it has come to be known, involved a dispute over waters of the Milk River in northern Montana between the Gros Ventre and the Assiniboine Indians of the Fort Belknap Indian Reservation and settlers who had arrived during the waning years of the 19th century after the tribal land base had been diminished. In 1905, the US Bureau of Indian Affairs, who had developed irrigation on the reservation, requested the US Department of Justice take action against the settlers to ensure an adequate supply of water for crops on the tribe's reservations. In its capacity as trustee for the tribes, the Department of Justice filed suit in US District Court on behalf of the Fort Belknap. The federal government and the tribes of the Fort Belknap Reservation not only won this case, but they prevailed in subsequent appeals in the 9th Circuit Court and the US Supreme Court. The decision of the US Supreme Court in this case forms the foundation of the reserved water right (or Winters) doctrine that is used to this day as guide to allocating waters between tribal governments and water users in western states.

Over the past century, other litigation has crafted the findings from this case into a legal doctrine that recognizes the means by which tribes have access to water. The essential elements of the Winters or reserved water rights doctrine are:

- whether explicitly stated or not, treaties and agreements made between the United States and Indian tribes imply a reservation of both land and water, in order to make the land habitable;
- the basis for a reserved water right claim is to meet the purpose of the reservation, as set forth in congressional treaty, executive order, or federal statute;
- reserved water rights are based on federal laws rather than state laws;
- unlike the prior appropriation system of water allocation adopted by many western states, reserved rights are reserved indefinitely;
- the amount of a reserved right is based on a determination of the resources available on the reservation, regardless of how many people historically or currently reside on the reservation;
- the priority to use water (or the "seniority" of the water right) is generally based on the date when the reservation was established, although certain rights extend back to the distant past ("time immemorial");
- in the years since the Winters decision, in addition to federally designated Indian reservations, other federal reservations of land have also been granted reserved water rights, such as military reservations or national parks.

The reserved rights doctrine has provided tribes with the legal basis to claim water rights, often with higher priorities than competing water rights granted under state law. As a result, tribal governments are often well positioned to negotiate settlements over water rights (McCool 2002). For the past three decades, tribes have negotiated with states over water rights and the result has been a dizzying array of negotiated water-right agreements, which more often than not become incorporated into ongoing litigation (water-right adjudications) and often are congressionally approved. Starting in 1978 with the Ak-Chin Indian Water Rights Settlement Act, congressional approval of tribal water-rights settlements continues today as water-rights settlements for the White Mountain Apache Tribe and the Pueblos of Taos, Nambe, Pojoaque, San Ildefonso, and Tesuque were signed into law in December 2010.

An advantage for tribes to pursue negotiations linked with litigation and/or congressional action is the possibility of clarifying and defining distinct water rights as well as securing funding from a variety of sources, including federal, state, or private entities. This may facilitate the actual use of water by tribes rather than simply having abstract water rights. One of the largest challenges in what McCool (2002) calls the "second treaty era" will be for tribes to develop options on how they choose to use water. It will also be important to establish tribal authority to administer water within reservations. Even though the Wind River tribes were prohibited from changing water uses and administering water on their reservation by the Wyoming Supreme Court, federal policy and case law could resecure these dimensions of tribal water governance.

With a long history of litigating state-tribal conflicts over water and little statutory guidance from Congress, tribal water rights have been shaped by case law and more recently by water-rights settlements. Litigation remains the primary means tribes use to ensure their proprietary rights to water remain intact as well as to exercise governance over reservation waters. Often tribes end up in multiple court cases— sometimes as plaintiffs, sometimes as defendants—and litigate over many decades to protect their water rights and assert their jurisdiction over matters of water allocation. Such is the situation with the Pyramid Lake Paiute Tribe of Indians who have participated in a few negotiated settlements and been in dozens of water-rights court cases over many decades. In addition to having a Water Resources Division within the tribal government, Pyramid Lake hires its own outside legal counsel specifically for water issues. The tribe prevailed in the most recent case, in which the US 9th Circuit Court of Appeals ruled on the allocation of groundwater that supports the tribe's senior water rights granted under a court decree in 1944 (*United States of America & Pyramid Lake Tribe v Orr Ditch Co., Nevada State Engineer & Tri Water and Sewer* 2010). Negotiated settlements, litigation, and specific congressional actions addressing individual or groups of tribes are likely to continue as the way to resolve tribal water-right matters.

Demands for Energy: Mining, Sustainable Energy, and Water in Indian Country

There are strong and growing links between water and energy challenges in Indian Country. Tribal lands hold considerable renewable and nonrenewable energy potential. In 2003, the Department of Energy estimated tribal lands held 890 million barrels of oil and natural gas liquids as well as 5.6 trillion cubic feet of natural gas

(Miles 2006), and it is estimated that tribal lands hold the potential to produce 10 percent of the country's renewable energy. Tribes face numerous issues at the nexus of energy production and water management. Extraction of nonrenewable resources through mining of coal, uranium, as well as other hard rock mining (along with their processing) influences the ability of tribes to protect, use, and govern water. The most significant water issues associated with mining that confront tribes are mine dewatering, aquifer contamination, and surface water contamination. Hydropower energy production has also been an issue for some tribes. Despite the energy resources on reservation lands, 14 percent of homes on Native American reservations are still without electricity as compared to the nationwide average of 1.2 percent (National Wildlife Federation 2010).

In the 20th century, energy and water issues on tribal lands focused on the extraction of traditional energy sources, especially coal, natural gas, and uranium. These issues posed serious competing challenges: some tribes saw tapping local energy resources as a way out of poverty; others feared the environmental and cultural damages that result from resource extraction. The intensity of poverty and unemployment in some areas directly conflicts with the intensity of commitment to the land and the spiritual values of many of the tribes. Finding ways of resolving these conflicts in the coming decades in a way that protects water, and other resources, will be critical.

As mining or excavation begins, it is often necessary to remove massive amounts of water, which in turns draws down groundwater in the surrounding aquifer. This dewatering occurs with many types of mining, including coal bed methane production. In order for gas to be released from the coal, the partial pressure must be reduced, which is accomplished by removing water from the coal bed. Large amounts of water, sometimes saline, are produced from coal bed methane wells, especially in the early stages of production. As the production of methane increases, it becomes harder and harder to implement environmentally acceptable water disposal options that are also economically feasible. As a result, water may be simply discharged on the surface if it is not too saline or otherwise contaminated, or it may be injected into the ground where the quality of the injected water is worse than that of the surrounding resource (USGS 1997).

Dewatering also influences surface water because of the hydrologic connection between groundwater and surface water. Such was the case for a lake that the Zuni Pueblo fought to protect against dewatering caused by a coal mine. In the 1990s, the Zuni, with assistance from native and environmental organizations, successfully blocked the coal mine. Effects on surface water through mine dewatering have also been associated with gold mining in central Nevada. In 2009, the 9th Circuit Court of Appeals heard a case brought by the South Fork and Te-Moak Bands of Western Shoshone and the Timbisha Shoshone Tribe along with native and environmental organizations against the Department of Interior's Bureau of Land Management (BLM). The tribes alleged that the permitting process for a major gold mine development violated their religious rights as well as failed to adequately address the hydrologic and environmental consequences of mine dewatering. The court ruled that the BLM did not adequately address the hydrologic connection that would affect surface waters:

> the EIS states that BLM has identified fifty perennial springs and one perennial creek that are the most likely to dry up, though among these it is impossible to "conclusively identify specific springs and seeps that would or would not be impacted." That these individual harms are somewhat uncertain due to BLM's limited understanding of the hydrologic features of the area does not relieve BLM of the responsibility under NEPA to discuss mitigation of reasonably likely impacts at the outset. . . . Even if the discussion must necessarily be tentative or contingent, NEPA requires that the agency give some sense of whether the drying up of these water resources could be avoided (*Shoshone Tribes v. US Dept of Interior* 2009).

In this recent case, the Shoshone tribes succeeded in drawing attention to the potential loss and need to mitigate the effects on numerous springs and a stream that would result from dewatering associated with mining.

Tribes have also confronted groundwater contamination as a result of energy and mineral exploration. The Spokane Tribe, Pueblo of Acoma, Navajo (Diné) Nation, and Havasupai Tribe have each opposed mining operations that threaten to contaminate aquifers with highly radioactive elements associated with many types of human cancer, kidney damage, and birth defects. The reservation for the Havasupai Tribe is downstream and on the south side of the Grand Canyon. After an uranium mining boom in northern Arizona during the 1980s, abandoned and poorly tended mines released tons of sediments with uranium during flash flood events down Kanab Creek and the Little Colorado River and into the Grand Canyon. The Havasupai, People of the Blue-Green Water, consider themselves to be guardians of the Grand Canyon and its waters. They are concerned about the effects of uranium mining on the Grand Canyon and have disputed the proposed Canyon Uranium Mine because of the potential contamination of groundwater around a sacred site, Red Butte, as well as in the Grand Canyon itself. In response, a bill HR 644 Grand Canyon Watersheds Protection Act was introduced to withdraw certain lands in and around the Grand Canyon from entry and patent under federal mining laws. In the summer of 2009, the House Subcommittee on National Parks, Forests, and Public Lands held a hearing in which a single witness entered testimony, a geologist from the US Geological Survey who supported the uranium mine operations and denied any negative impacts from contemporary uranium mining practices. According to Dr. Karen Wenrich, "to use the sins of a 60-year old uranium mining legacy to punish mining in a different district, which has clearly demonstrated safe clean mining practices, is like the past punishing of the Navajo Tribe by moving them eastward to Texas because of the sins of a few renegade Apaches"(HR 644 hearing 2009). Since this hearing, no further action has been taken on the bill and the Havasupai Tribe continues to oppose the uranium mining operation.

Stream contamination in association with uranium mining has also posed problems for tribes. In 1979, after the closure of a uranium mine near Church Rock, New Mexico, a dam broke sending 11,000 tons of radioactive mill wastes and 90,000,000 gallons of contaminated liquids into the Rio Puerco River. The Navajo Nation still cannot use the waters of the river. The Church Rock disaster is considered to be the largest accidental release of radioactive material in US history (Ali 2003). Coal bed methane mining also can contaminate streams by discharging water with high levels of ammonia, selenium, boron, iron, radium, and fluoride, as well as the most significant problem, sodium salts. Sodium levels in the discharged water may render it unsuitable for irrigation and the increased sodium bicarbonate levels can be lethal to fish and aquatic and riparian vegetation. One well can produce 12 to 20 gallons of water per minute or 17,000 to 29,000 gallons per day of contaminated water that requires disposal (Montana Wildlife Federation 2002). The Crow tribal government is currently considering coal bed methane production in the southeast corner of the reservation. The Crow government has long been active in energy production, leasing reservation coal reserves to Westmoreland Resources Inc. since 1974 and recently establishing other arrangements with Australian Energy Co. for coal slurry production and with Ursa Major to extract natural gas from wells 850 to 1,200 feet in depth (Brown 2008; Olp 2009).

Northern Cheyenne Reservation exemplifies the dilemma some tribes face, wedged between economic hardships, increasing pressures to develop energy resources, and the losses such extraction would mean for their water, land, and people. The intensity of poverty and lack of economic opportunities influence all tribal governance decisions on the Northern Cheyenne. Eighty percent of reservation residents are unemployed (Keen 2009). Whereas some tribal members argue that the tribal government should develop operations for coal and coal bed methane mining on the reservation, the tribe has thus far opted for environmental protection. The Northern Cheyenne started by leveraging the Clean Air Act to require air pollution scrubbers on an adjacent coal-fired power plant, the largest in Montana. Then the tribe voided Reagan-era leases for coal on the reservation and cancelled many allotments of subsurface mineral rights in order to centralize tribal ownership of these rights so they would not be bought out by mining corporations (Struckman and Ring 2003). The majority of tribal members have rejected coal and coal bed methane mining due to fear of groundwater and surface water pollution that could threaten drinking water, irrigation supplies, and water for ceremonial practices. Recently the Northern Cheyenne Tribe sued the Montana Department of Environmental Quality in the Montana Supreme Court. In a unanimous decision, the court agreed with the tribe, ruling that the state violated the Clean Water Act by failing to require a coal bed methane operator to treat groundwater extracted at the mining site before discharging it into the Tongue River (*Northern Cheyenne Tribe, Tongue River Water Users Association, and Northern Plains Resource Council v Montana Department of Environmental Quality and Fidelity Exploration & Production Co.* 2010). Some Northern Cheyenne tribal members look to the potential for renewable energy development, in the form of solar and wind power on the reservation; however, the economic returns to the tribe would not likely be as great as with extractive mining (Struckman and Ring 2003).

One renewable energy system with direct impacts on water and with a long history on tribal lands has been the development of hydropower, especially in the Pacific Northwest. This development has involved the construction of hundreds of massive dams and thousands of smaller ones, with a wide range of ecological impacts (see chapter 6: Protecting Freshwater Ecosystems). Hydropower generation can block fish passage, kill young fish heading downstream to the ocean, alter stream temperatures, flood spawning grounds, and increase pollution loads. As our understanding of these impacts has improved, efforts in recent years have turned to ecosystem restoration and even dam removal—key features of a 21st-century water policy. For the federal government, new efforts to reduce the impacts of past federal hydropower projects may include both dam reoperation and dam removal. The Nez Perce, for example, in the headwaters of the Columbia–Snake River Basin, have experienced cultural losses associated with major declines in salmon and other cold water anadromous fish due to the development of massive dams along the rivers. As a result of the massive fisheries disruptions in the Pacific Northwest, the Nez Perce and other tribes in the Columbia River Intertribal Fisheries Council, have called for the dismantling of four hydropower dams on the Snake River (Berry, Grossman, and Pawiki 2006).

To the south, the Klamath Basin Tribal Water Quality Work Group, which includes Yurok, Karuk, and Hoopa Valley tribes, has researched the Iron Gate and Copco reservoirs on the Klamath River in California. The work group found blue-green algae species growing in these reservoirs creates water quality problems downstream to the river's mouth. This contamination continues to pose threats to ceremonial and recreational use of the river (Klamath Basin Tribal Water Quality Work Group 2008). In addition, the tribes are concerned about the detrimental effect of dams on the natural hydrograph of the river and the resulting negative impacts to salmon. The tribes recommend management of the dam and river to better mimic a natural hydrograph that will enhance fluvial processes, flush parasites and disease organisms out of salmon habitat, and help transport young fish to the ocean. The Karuk and Yurok tribes are signatories to the Klamath Hydroelectric Settlement Agreement and related Klamath Basin Restoration Agreement, intended to restore a more natural river system. The Hoopa Valley Tribe has chosen to not sign the agreements.

More attention is also being paid to other sorts of renewable energy resources, including solar, geothermal, biofuels, and wind energy production. In each of the sources, water is involved, to a greater or lesser degree, in the process of extraction or energy production. It remains to be seen what sorts of water-related challenges renewable energy development will pose for tribes and how tribes will address these challenges and create new opportunities for themselves.

In 2005, the George W. Bush administration's interest in maximizing energy development on reservations resulted in legislation that provided tribal governments with new authority over their energy futures. The Indian Tribal Energy Development and Self-Determination Act of 2005 allows tribal governments to directly negotiate contracts on their own behalf with public or private energy developers for leases of less than 30 years (or for oil and gas, 10 years) as long as the tribe has been approved by the Department of Interior for a Tribal Energy Resource Agreement. For tribes with a Tribal Energy Resource Agreement approval this is a more efficient process, allowing them to determine the positive and negative impacts a lease would have on their own reservation, and it reduces inherent conflicts of interests between tribes and the federal government (Miles 2005/2006). However, while seemingly facilitating tribal governance, the legislation is controversial. Many tribal governments simply do not have sufficient resources to complete thorough assessments that will allow them to make informed decisions. Moreover, unless the federal government continues to support such assessments, they may be relinquishing their trust responsibilities to protect the reservation (Miles 2005/2006). Thus, some view this legislation as increasing tribal self-determination, and others see the dangers of a diminished federal role (Shipps and May 2007).

Although new federal legislation encourages greater governance capacities for tribes in the area of energy production, many things have not changed about the energy–water connection for tribes. Tribes still face tough choices about mining and energy extraction between economic development, on the one hand, and protection of people and the environment, including sustaining surface water and groundwater, on the other hand. Neighboring tribes, such as the Crow and Northern Cheyenne, have taken different positions on these matters, but neither way offers a panacea. The legislation of 2005 will likely change this situation only in minor ways and threats to tribal water from mining and energy production remain. In April 2010, for example, the Arizona legislature passed a bill to expedite the permitting and review process for mining within the state. Among other things, the legislation eliminates the need for mining companies to get state permits that ensure mining discharges will not adversely affect groundwater (Davis 2010). Key elements of Arizona's Groundwater Management Act that restrict transport of groundwater have also recently been relaxed (see chapter 2: Legal and Institutional Framework of Water Management). The Inter-Tribal Council of Arizona opposed the bill on environmental grounds and asked Arizona Governor Jan Brewer to veto it. Nonetheless, the governor signed it and the bill became law in May 2010.

Despite the difficulties that tribes have faced, there is room for hope that these issues will be addressed in the coming years. Old approaches in new combinations may offer better alternatives, whereas new approaches may be good prospects too. Litigation will continue to be a significant tool that tribes use to protect both their water and governance capacities. Negotiated settlements, which have proven remarkably versatile and popular for tribal water-rights agreements, may prove to have potential in the energy arena as well. Creative alliances—in business ventures, in resistance to projects, in settlement discussions—are promising as well. For example, some tribal governments have chosen to partner with nongovernmental organizations that support native rights but also with environmental or agricultural water organizations. Finally, new forms of energy production on the horizon will present novel opportunities as well as new challenges.

Clean Water: Tribal Water Quality Governance

In October 1992, the Pueblo of Isleta became the first tribe in the nation to receive regulatory approval from the Environmental Protection Agency (EPA) to administer their own water-quality standard program under Sections 518 and 303 of the Clean Water Act (CWA). Two months later, Isleta put into effect their tribal water-quality code for the Rio Grande River and other streams on the reservation, which included 13 general water-quality standards (e.g., turbidity, pH, dissolved oxygen), over 100 standards on toxic substances (e.g., arsenic, dieldrin, and selenium), and various other measures that protect surface water quality. Not long afterward, Isleta's water-quality standards were enforced as part of the permitting process for effluent releases from a municipal wastewater treatment facility upstream of the reservation, despite the fact that the standards for some constituents were more stringent than the state of New Mexico's were. The city of Albuquerque sued, challenging the tribal standards and the EPA's authority in approving the standards. After losing their lawsuit and going through a change in city administration, Albuquerque along with the state of New Mexico took a different tact. Negotiations led to a settlement agreement in 1994 between the Pueblo, the EPA, and the state of New Mexico that worked out the details of Albuquerque's wastewater facility permit. In turn, the city agreed to help fund research on water quality in the Rio Grande River (Gover, Stetson, and Wilson 1995).

Since the CWA was amended in 1987, tribes can be "treated as states" (TAS) for the governance of water quality. The EPA determines TAS status and approves standards and other water-quality measures, just as they do for states. To date, 48 tribes have been approved to administer their own water-quality standards program and 41 have had specific tribal water codes approved by EPA, as shown in table 4.1. A few tribes have also been approved to develop point-source management programs or permitting processes and many have received funding for developing water pollution control programs or for research on lake or stream quality.

This is a marked increase in tribal capacity to govern water quality, particularly in light of the two decades from 1975 to 1996 when an order from the Department of Interior prevented the majority of tribal governments from enacting their own water codes (McCool 2002). As it worked out, Isleta Pueblo was unaffected by the prohibition as was the Navajo Nation, which early on developed "a comprehensive and sophisticated water code designed to 'provide for a permanent homeland . . . ; to protect the health, the welfare and the economic security . . . ; [and] to develop, manage and preserve the water resources of the Navajo Nation'" (McCool 2002, 185 quoting the Navajo Tribal Code). Tribes with successful programs have often shared their experiences. Moreover, there are a variety

TABLE 4.1.

Indian Tribal Approvals for EPA Water Quality Standards

Tribe	Date found eligible to administer a WQS program	Date initial WQS approved by EPA
Pueblo of Isleta (NM)	October 13, 1992	December 24, 1992
Pueblo of Sandia (NM)	December 24, 1992	August 10, 1993
Ohkay Owingeh (NM) (formerly the Pueblo of San Juan)	May 12, 1993	September 16, 1993
Puyallup Tribe of Indians (WA)	May 25, 1994	October 31, 1994
Seminole Tribe, Big Cypress Reservation (FL)	June 1, 1994	September 26, 1997
Seminole Tribe, Brighton Reservation (FL)	June 1, 1994	November 18, 1998
Miccosukee Tribe (FL)	December 20, 1994	May 25, 1999
Miccosukee Tribe, Miccosukee Reserve Area (FL)	December 20, 1994	March 15, 2001
Confederated Salish and Kootenai Tribes of the Flathead Reservation (MT)	March 1, 1995	March 18, 1996
Confederated Tribes of the Chehalis Reservation (WA)	March 7, 1995	February 3, 1997
Pueblo of Santa Clara (NM)	July 19, 1995	July 19, 1995
Pueblo of Picuris (NM)	August 7, 1995	August 7, 1995
Pueblo of Nambe (NM)	August 18, 1995	August 18, 1995
Mole Lake Band of the Lake Superior Tribe of Chippewa Indians (WI)	September 29, 1995	January 22, 1996
Pueblo of Pojoaque (NM)	March 21, 1996	March 21, 1996
Tulalip Tribes (WA)	May 9, 1996	
Fond du Lac Band of Chippewa (MN)	May 16, 1996	December 27, 2001
Hoopa Valley Tribe	May 17, 1996	September 11, 2002
Grand Portage Band of Chippewa (MN)	July 16, 1996	November 2, 2005
Assiniboine and Sioux Tribes of the Fort Peck Indian Reservation (MT)	August 29, 1996	April 25, 2000
White Mountain Apache Tribe (AZ)	February 3, 1997	September 27, 2001
Pueblo of Tesuque (NM)	April 29, 1997	April 29, 1997

Table 4.1 (*continued*)

Tribe	Date found eligible to administer a WQS program	Date initial WQS approved by EPA
Confederated Tribes of the Warm Springs Reservation (OR)	May 25, 1999	September 28, 2001
Pueblo of Acoma (NM)	April 17, 2001	April 17, 2001
Confederated Tribes of Umatilla (OR)	April 30, 2001	October 18, 2001
Spokane Tribe of Indians (WA)	July 23, 2002	April 22, 2003
St. Regis Band of Mohawk Indians NY)	October 16, 2002	September 14, 2007
Kalispel Indian Community (WA)	November 4, 2002	June 24, 2004
Port Gamble S'Klallam (WA)	September 24, 2003	September 27, 2005
Makah Indian Nation (WA)	December 23, 2003	September 29, 2006
Hualapai Indian Tribe (AZ)	July 22, 2004	September 17, 2004
Pawnee Nation (OK)	November 4, 2004	
Coeur D'Alene Tribe (ID)	August 5, 2005	
Ute Mountain Ute (CO)	September 26, 2005	October 19, 2011
Big Pine Band of Owens Valley (CA)	October 24, 2005	January 18, 2006
Pueblo of Taos (NM)	December 8, 2005	June 19, 2006
Navajo Nation (AZ, NM, UT)	January 20, 2006	April 11, 2006
Paiute-Shoshone Indians of the Bishop Community (CA)	April 11, 2006	August 15, 2008
Northern Cheyenne (MT)	August 11, 2006	
Twenty-Nine Palms (CA)	October 26, 2006	
Pyramid Lake Paiute (NV)	January 30, 2007	December 19, 2008
Lummi Tribe (WA)	March 5, 2007	September 30, 2008
Lac du Flambeau Band of Chippewa (WI)	April 8, 2008	September 17, 2010
Swinomish Indian Tribal Community (WA)	April 18, 2008	
Hopi Tribe (AZ)	April 23, 2008	July 8, 2008
Shoshone-Bannock Tribes (ID)	September 5, 2008	
Bad River Band of Lake Superior Chippewa (WI)	June 26, 2009	September 21, 2011
Confederated Tribes of the Colville Reservation (WA)	Not applicable	Promulgated June 7, 1989

Note: WQS = water-quality standards.
Source: EPA (2011).

of regional intertribal organizations dedicated to assisting tribes with water-quality governance, such as Mni-Sose Inter-tribal Water Rights Coalition (focused on tribes in the Missouri River Basin), Inter-tribal Environmental Council (with membership from Oklahoma-based tribes as well as Texas and New Mexico), and the Water Commission of the Inter-tribal Council of California.

There have been successes in tribal water-quality governance. For example, the Confederated Salish and Kootenai Tribes of the Flathead Reservation formed a water-management division in 1989 and were granted TAS status in spring of 1995. One year later, their tribal water code was approved. A decade later, the tribes enacted a refined water-quality program, which rivals many state programs. The tribal government's Water Division now has programs in water management, water-rights administration, dam safety, and geographic information systems. In addition to formal codes and procedures, the Flathead Reservation tribal government also uses informal practices of culturally specific decision making (CSKT Natural Resource Department 2006; Sanders 2010). A 1998 case brought by the state of Montana against the Confederated Salish and Kootenai Tribes questioned the extent of the tribes' jurisdiction. In this case, the US 9th Circuit Court of Appeals ruled for the tribe. Their decision established that, under TAS of the Clean Water Act, tribes have regulatory authority over all lands and people within the reservation and the EPA should take this into account when reviewing TAS applications (De Young and Scott 2000).

Despite a statute that acknowledges tribes as capable governments, growing EPA administrative support, the positive governance experiences of some tribes, emerging intertribal resources, and some favorable outcomes in litigation, challenges remain on many fronts. Today fewer than 10 percent of all federally recognized tribes have EPA designation as TAS for administering their water-quality programs. Porter (2007) suggests that reasons for the lack of tribal participation include: threats of litigation by states because of different standards; perception by tribes that TAS threatens their sovereignty; lack of funding and infrastructure to develop and implement water-quality programs; and differences in cultural concepts about water. Moreover, resistance off the reservation may be a significant deterrent.

Frequently, western states oppose the increased governance capacity of tribes over water especially because states have fought bitterly to maintain control over water, not only with tribes but with the federal government and other states. A telling example of this is the Pawnee Nation of Oklahoma, which was granted TAS status by the EPA for its water-quality program in 2004 but still has not received endorsement for a water-quality program because of obstacles put in place by the state and the state's congressional delegation. In response to granting TAS to the Pawnee Nation, litigation was filed by the state of Oklahoma challenging the EPA's approval process. In addition, an Oklahoma senator who served as the chair of the Senate Environmental and Public Works Committee proposed an investigation of the EPA's handling of TAS approvals throughout the state. Finally, a "midnight rider" was added to an unrelated transportation bill (whose language had already been agreed on by the House and Senate) that prevents the EPA from approving TAS for tribes in Oklahoma, unless the state agrees to it and enters into a cooperative agreement to jointly administer the program (Sanders 2010). This provision further dilutes the capacity of tribes to effectively manage and govern water quality.

Such fierce sentiments against tribal governance over water quality are often based on longstanding sovereignty and jurisdictional debates between states and tribes. Yet some tribes believe their best recourse is to negotiate with the surrounding state(s). The Shoshone-Bannock Tribe of the Fort Hall Reservation was approved for TAS in the fall of 2008. Within a month, the tribe had entered into an intergovernmental cooperation agreement with the state of Idaho and the EPA. This agreement encourages sharing technical information on water quality and developing a mutual review process of water-quality standards by both the tribe and state.

One of the key ingredients necessary to build effective water-quality management in Indian Country remains the same today as in 1994 when Gover, Stetson, and Williams (1994) recommended that Congress set aside additional funds for tribes to manage reservation water quality. Today the EPA only makes available up to 3 percent of its general water-quality funds for tribes. Moreover, there are major areas that remain unfunded. Another issue is challenging the efforts of those in Congress and elsewhere who would undermine TAS as well as tribal water governance more generally. In terms of policy recommendations for tribes themselves, Sanders (2010) offers ideas for moving forward on these issues in the coming years:

- sustain stable and capable tribal institutions and policies;
- adopt fair and effective dispute resolution mechanisms;
- increase the cultural legitimacy of tribal governance institutions among tribal members; and
- work toward long-term governance objectives without neglecting more immediate political and legal realities.

Conclusions

Water management issues in Indian tribal areas are influenced by a wide range of federal water policies. There are opportunities to move toward solutions in the coming years, but new efforts will be needed. Tribal water governance does not rely heavily on statutory law and with a few notable exceptions (such as the TAS provision of the 1987 CWA and the Tribal Energy Resource Act of 2005), there has been little use of federal statues to craft tribal water governance. More has been done to guide tribal governance structures in federal administrative agencies than in Congress. After regulatory rule making, litigation and the resulting case law remains the most common approach to policy making.

Whereas negotiated settlement agreements have been on the rise for tribal water issues and often involve Congress as a final approval, the political dynamics are such that Congress is unlikely to deliver a comprehensive and coherent policy that effectively resolves the myriad of tribal water issues. A soft path approach to water management, however, requires far stronger commitments to work with tribal communities in transparent ways.

The lack of congressional influence has both positive and negative effects for tribes. On the one hand, tribes have more freedom to choose the ways they want to exert sovereignty and put governance of water into practice. It also permits different solutions to evolve for the wide variety of environmental and social contexts that the over 500 federally recognized tribes find themselves in. On the other hand, tribes are more likely to find sustained funding and resources through congressional actions than elsewhere. Moreover, the lack of overarching statutory guidance has made it easier for those who promote antitribal legislation on particular issues in a secretive fashion. With allies "on the Hill," as well as in federal regulatory agencies, tribes should seek opportunities for congressional action on tribal water initiatives. Continuing to cultivate tribal policy advocates in Congress and elsewhere may help in incrementally working toward broader-based federal legislation on tribal water matters. In addition, it is important that Congress provides adequate federal funds for tribal water governance.

For this to happen effectively, however, more needs to be done to educate policy makers and the public at large about tribal water issues. Given that policy makers and the public generally have little knowledge about contemporary tribal matters or even understand basic differences between tribes, this would be a significant undertaking. Moreover, policy makers and the public know little about water matters and would benefit from education aimed at improving understandings about tribal water issues and governance. A rigorous educational initiative that tackles both water and tribal matters could unlock unforeseen dividends.

Finally, alliances and partnerships that tribes have developed offer the potential for advancing tribal water objectives. Despite the resource dispossession and cultural domination experienced by American Indians, the breadth, depth, and variety of recent partnerships that involve tribes is remarkable. Grossman (2005) underscores the significance of such cooperative alliances on environmental issues between tribes and nontribal peoples and organizations. Such alliances may provide networks, expertise, and even possible funding sources to support tribal self-determination and improved water governance in the coming years, and they may offer insights into improved water management and community engagement—characteristics of a soft path approach—for the country as a whole.

Acknowledgments

I greatly appreciate the assistance of Kathryn Mann who provided background research used in this chapter.

References

Ali, S. H. 2003. *Mining, the Environment, and Indigenous Development Conflicts*, Tucson: University of Arizona Press.

Althouse, A. 1987. "How To Build a Separate Sphere: Federal Courts and State Power." *Harvard Law Review* 100 (4): 1485–1538.

Berry, K. 2006a. "Scaling Sovereignty: Conflicts over Sovereign Immunity and Water Rights Policies for American Indian Tribes." Paper presented at GECOREV International Symposium on the Environment, Versailles, France, June 26, 2006.

———. 2006b. "Water in the Life of American Indians." In *Velka Kniha O Vode (Great Book of Water)*. Edited by Josip Kleczek. Prague, Czech Republic: Academia Press (Czech Academy of Sciences) (published in Czech language only).

Berry, K., Z. Grossman, and H. M. Pawiki. 2006. "Native Americans." In *Contemporary Ethnic Geographies of America*. Edited by I. M. Miyares and C. A. Airriess, 51–70. Lanham, MD: Rowman & Littlefield Publishers.

Brown, M. 2008. "Crow Tribe Strikes Deal for $7B Coal Project." *News from Indian Country*, August 8.

Cagey, H. 1995. "Letter." In *Lummi Indian Nation. 1995. A Call to Action: Funding Reduction to Indian Tribes, FY 96 Appropriations*. Bellingham, WA: Lummi Indian Nation.

Confederated Salish and Kootenai Tribes of the Flathead Reservation, Natural Resources Department, Water Quality Program (CSKT). 2006. *Surface Water Quality Standards and Antidegradation Policy*. Pablo, MT: CSKT. http://www.cskt.org/tr/docs/epa_wqs-antidegradationpolicy.pdf.

Davis, T. 2010. "Enviros, Tribes Urge Veto of State Mine Bill." *Arizona Daily Star*, April 30.

De Young, T., and W. C. Scott. 2000. "Environmental Protection in Indian Country." *Natural Resources and Environment* 15: 20.

Deudney, D. 1996. "Binding Sovereigns: Authorities, Structures, and Geopolitics in Philadelphian Systems." In *State Sovereignty as Social Construct*. Edited by T. J. Biersteker and C. Weber, 190–239. Cambridge: Cambridge University Press.

Gover, Stetson, and Williams, P. C. 1995. *Survey of Tribal Actions to Protect Water Quality and the Implementation of the Clean Water Act*. Washington, DC: National Indian Policy Center, George Washington University.

Grossman, Z. 2005. "Unlikely Alliances: Treaty Conflicts and Environmental Cooperation between Native American and Rural White Communities." *American Indian Culture and Research Journal* 29 (4): 21–43.

Hamilton, A., J. Madison, and J. Jay. 1999. *The Federalist Papers*. Edited by C. Rossiter. New York: Penguin Putnam.

Hannum, E. 1992. "Administration of Reserved and Non-Reserved Water Rights on an Indian Reservation: Post-Adjudication Questions on the Big Horn River." *Natural Resources Journal* 32: 681–704.

HR 644 Hearing. 2009. "Grand Canyon Watersheds Protection Act of 2009. House Committee on Natural Resources, Subcommittee on National Parks, Forests, and Public Lands. July 21, 2009." *Congressional Quarterly* Congressional Testimony.

Keen, J. 2009. "For Indian Tribes, Economic Needs Collide with Tradition." *USA Today*, March 3.

Klamath Basin Tribal Water Quality Work Group. 2008. "Dam Relicensing and Tribal Water Quality Plans." Klamath Basin Tribal Water Quality Work Group. http://www.klamathwater-quality.com/dam_location.html.

Miles, A. S. 2005/2006. "Tribal Energy Resource Agreements: Tools for Achieving Energy Development and Tribal Self-Sufficiency or an Abdication of Federal Environmental and Trust Responsibilities?" *American Indian Law Review* 30 (2): 461–476.

McCool, D. 2002. *Native Waters: Contemporary Indian Water Settlements and the Second Treaty Era*. Tucson: University of Arizona.

Montana Wildlife Federation. 2002. "Coal Bed Methane: Short Term Boom, Long Term Bust." *Issues and Answers*, August 2002-25. Helena, MT: Montana Wildlife Federation. http://cf.nwf.org/wildlife/pdfs/coalbedmethane.pdf.

National Wildlife Federation. 2010. *The New Energy Future in Indian Country: Confronting Climate Change, Creating Jobs, and Conserving Nature*. Report Confronting Climate Change Report, March 23. Boulder, CO: Rocky Mountain Regional Center, National Wildlife Federation.

Northern Cheyenne Tribe, Tongue River Water Users Association, and Northern Plains Resource Council v Montana Department of Environmental Quality and Fidelity Exploration & Production Co. 2010 MT 111, May 18, 2010, DA 09-0131.

Olp, S. 2009. "Crow Tribe Begins Producing Natural Gas." *Billings Gazette*, August 6.

Pisani, D. J. 1992. "Water Law and Localism in the West." *Halcyon* 14: 33–114.

Porter, K. S. 2007. "Good Alliances Make Good Neighbors: The Case for Tribal-State-Federal Watershed Partnerships." *Cornell Journal of Law and Public Policy* 16: 495–538.

Powell, H. J. 2002. *A Community Built on Words: the Constitution in History and Politics*. Chicago: University of Chicago.

Sanders, M. 2010. "Indian Law: Clean Water in Indian Country: The Risks (and Rewards) of Being Treated in the Same Manner as a State." *William Mitchell Law Review* 36: 533–564.

Shipps, T. H., and David S. M. 2007. "Tribal Energy Resource Agreements: A Step toward Self-Determination." *Natural Resources and Environment* 22: 55–57.

South Fork Band Council of Western Shoshone of Nevada; Te-Moak Tribe of Western Shoshone Indians of Nevada; Timbisha Shoshone Tribe; Western Shoshone Defense Project; Great Basin Resource Watch, Plaintiffs-Appellants, v.US Department of the Interior, US Bureau of Land Management, Defendant-Appellees, and Barrick Cortez, Inc., Defendant-intervenor-Appellee. 588 F.3d 718; 2009 U.S. App. LEXIS 26329.

Struckman, B., and R. Ring. 2003. "A Breath of Fresh Air." *High Country News*, January 20.

US Environmental Protection Agency (EPA). 2011. "Indian Tribal Approvals." US Environmental Protection Agency. http://water.epa.gov/scitech/swguidance/standards/wqslibrary/approvtable.cfm.

US Geological Survey (USGS). 1997. *Coalbed Methane—An Untapped Energy Resource and an Environmental Concern*. Energy Resource Surveys Program, USGS Fact Sheet FS-019-97. Reston, VA: US Geological Survey.

United States of America & Pyramid Lake Paiute Tribe of Indians v Orr Water Ditch Co, Nevada State Engineer & Tri Water and Sewer Co. 2010. 9th Circuit Court of Appeals April 7, 2010, 07-17001.

Willis-Friday, B. 1992. "Tribal Water Subject to State Law." *Wind River News* 15 (23): 1.

5

WATER QUALITY

Lucy Allen

Introduction

The United States should be justifiably proud of the improvement over the past century in the safety of drinking water and the reduction in the types and amounts of pollution discharged untreated into rivers, lakes, and streams. Rivers are no longer catching fire, as they did in the 1960s, from huge quantities of industrial wastes. Thousands of people no longer die every year from water-related diseases such as cholera, dysentery, and typhoid. Most Americans have access to highly reliable, safe, and remarkably inexpensive water from their taps for drinking, as well as for flushing toilets, providing safe and reliable sanitation.

Despite these improvements, the nation still faces serious threats to water quality. And the benefits of our efforts to improve water quality have not been equitably distributed. Communities in California's Tulare County, for example, have gone decades without tap water that is safe to drink (Moore et al. 2011). Fertilizer application in this intensively farmed county, as well as manure from dairy farms and leaking septic tanks, have caused heavy nitrate pollution of the groundwater—the primary source of drinking water for most people in the county (Harter and Lund 2012). High levels of pesticides and other contaminants have also been found in local groundwater. As a result of this contamination, one-fifth of public water systems in Tulare County do not meet federal health-based drinking water standards (Firestone and DeAnda nd). Additionally, 40 percent of private wells that have been tested have nitrate concentrations exceeding health-based standards and 75 percent have at least one contaminant exceeding health-based standards (CWC Web site). Nitrates have numerous adverse health impacts and are particularly dangerous for infants, causing *blue baby syndrome*, or a loss of ability for their blood to carry oxygen, which can be fatal. In adults, possible health effects of long-term exposure include pregnancy complications, hypotension, spleen disease, and cancers of the throat, bladder, and prostate (Manassaram, Backer, and Moll 2006; Firestone 2009; ATSDR 2007). Exposure to contaminated water is uneven;low-income Latino communities within Tulare are more likely to have unsafe drinking water than are non-Latino communities (Moore et al. 2011).

The case of groundwater contamination in Tulare County highlights one of most significant water quality challenges in the nation—the need to provide safe and affordable drinking water to all. But it is only one of a wide range of water-quality concerns facing us. Urban runoff, pollution caused by agricultural pesticides and fertilizers, direct industrial discharges, mining, modification of river flows, deposition of air pollution, and a multitude of other practices and processes all contribute to poor water quality and its associated environmental harm and adverse health effects States are required by law to assess the quality of their water bodies every two years and to determine which ones are *impaired*—defined to mean that they are not clean enough for their "designated uses," which can include, for example, recreation or providing fish and wildlife habitat. These state assessments do not necessarily accurately represent nationwide water quality because states do not monitor all, or even a representative set, of water bodies. However, they are one of the most comprehensive inventories and offer insight into trends over time and the extent and causes of water pollution, showing it to be a widespread problem. The 2006 assessment (the most recent year for which complete data are available) found that over 40 percent of the surveyed river and stream miles, and nearly 60 percent of lake acres surveyed were not clean enough to support desired uses (EPA 2009c) (see figure 5.1 for data on impaired waters over time). The Environmental Protection Agency (EPA) has also conducted statistical surveys of streams, rivers, lakes, ponds, and reservoirs in order to gain a better understanding of the state of these resources nationwide; a statistical survey of wetlands is planned. The Wadeable Streams Assessment (discussed further in chapter 6: Protecting Freshwater Ecosystems) found that only 30 percent of the nation's small streams support healthy biological communities. For lakes, ponds, and reservoirs, 56 percent are in good biological condition, and one in five have high levels of nitrogen and phosphorus, making them more likely to have poor biological health (EPA 2010c).

In addition to this national inventory, studies conducted by the US Geological Survey document and characterize surface water and groundwater pollution. For example, a study on pesticides in water found the presence of at least one pesticide in every stream tested (Gilliom and Hamilton 2006), while another study found that:

> contaminants from nonpoint and point sources continue to affect our streams and ground water in parts of every study unit . . . contamination of streams and ground water is widespread in agricultural and urban areas, and is characterized by complex mixtures of nutrients, trace elements, pesticides, VOCs, and their chemical breakdown products (Hamilton, Miller, and Myers 2004, 2).

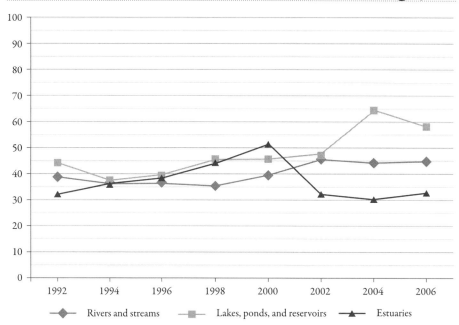

FIGURE 5.1. Percentage of assessed waters found to be *impaired*, or of inadequate quality to support designated uses, in biennial reports to Congress

Source: Based on data from National Water Quality Report to Congress, 1994–2004, and Water Quality Assessment and Total Maximum Daily Loads Information (ATTAINS).

Drinking water quality and environmental water quality are regulated separately; in some states, these regulations are even administered by separate agencies. But the health of our environment has a direct impact on the overall quality of our drinking water systems. Drinking water regulations tend to focus on *treating* water to make it safe to drink, but preventing pollutants from entering the water in the first place—known as *source water protection*—is often a more cost-effective way to provide water that is safe to drink. Cost-effectiveness is crucial in increasing the overall safety of drinking water in the nation, as it is most often the small drinking water systems with few ratepayers that are unable to provide safe water. When the water supply in Burlington, North Carolina, became contaminated with the agricultural pesticide atrazine, the city chose to pursue source water protection rather than treatment. The pollution was traced to its source, and the city provided farmers with subsidies to assist them in shifting to alternate pesticides and pest control practices. This cost the city around $30,000 total in lab analyses and subsidies to farmers, compared with an estimated cost of $108,000 a year to treat the water to remove atrazine (NC Division of Water Quality 2002). Studies have shown that in the case of groundwater, preventing contamination is on average 30 to 40 (and up to 200) times cheaper than dealing with the subsequent consequences of contaminated groundwater (EPA 2003). Despite this, more than 84 percent of all water systems report at least one potential source of contamination within two miles of their water intake or well (EPA 1999a).

Federal Water Quality Laws

The federal government has long played a central role in identifying water quality threats and in developing and implementing laws to protect water quality. This role began with a primary focus on improving and maintaining navigability of interstate waterways and has expanded and evolved over the past century because of the massive inefficiencies of having separate water-quality standards, laws, and regulations for 50 states. A brief summary of the major components of these laws is provided herein.

The Water Pollution Control Act of 1948 and Amendments

In 1948, Congress enacted the Federal Water Pollution Control Act in recognition of the threat to public health and welfare from contaminated water. The act's objectives are to enhance the quality and value of our water resources and to establish a national policy for the prevention, control and abatement of water pollution (33 U.S.C. §1251). The Federal Water Pollution Control Act and subsequent amendments set out the basic legal authority for federal regulation of water quality. In 1956, the Water Pollution Control Act Amendments strengthened enforcement provisions by providing for an abatement suit at the request of a state pollution control agency. If threats to public health were involved, the federal government could act without waiting for state consent. The federal role was further expanded under the Water Quality Act of 1965, which provided for the setting of federal water-quality standards. The Clean Water Restoration Act of 1966 authorized $100 per day fine on a polluter who failed to submit a required report. The Water Quality Improvement Act of 1970 established a state certification procedure to prevent degradation of water below a certain quality.

Despite the improvements achieved by each amendment to the original act, the result of this sporadic legislation was a hodgepodge of law. Eleven reorganizations and restructurings of federal agency responsibility compounded the difficulty of effectively implementing the law. To solve these problems, as part of a wave of national environmental laws passed in the late 1960s and early 1970s, a major revision was undertaken by Congress, leading to the Clean Water Act in 1972.

The Clean Water Act

The Clean Water Act (CWA) was the most sweeping amendment to the Federal Water Pollution Control Act of 1948 and is now the primary law protecting surface water quality in the United States. The act set the ambitious objective of "restoring and maintaining the chemical, physical and biological integrity of the Nation's waters" and was adopted by Congress in 1972 over the veto of President Nixon. Pollution of groundwater is *not* directly addressed by the CWA (nor is it addressed in a comprehensive way by any other federal law).

The CWA led to tremendous progress in tackling the major sources of water pollution of its day—direct discharges of pollution into bodies of water, for example, by wastewater treatment plants or factories. The CWA achieved this through a two-pronged approach to water-quality improvement: permitting of direct discharges to water bodies (point-source pollution), and the requirement that all bodies of water be clean enough to support designated uses. The permitting program, called the National Pollutant Discharge Elimination System (NPDES), requires that all direct discharges into water bodies be covered by a permit and regulates the amounts and types of pollutants that can be released. Support of designated uses is the CWA's measuring stick for water quality: If designated uses are supported, quality is considered to be good; if they are not, the body of water is deemed *impaired*. This means that there are not standard pollutant levels that are applied to every water body; instead, states define unique water-quality parameters for each designated use. When a water body is considered impaired, a Total Maximum Daily Load (TMDL) program is implemented, which is intended to bring the water body back into compliance with its quality goals (or maintain such goals, to the extent that the water body is already in compliance).[1] Under this program, the amount of each type of pollutant that can be discharged while maintaining good water quality is calculated and this amount is then allocated among the various pollution sources in the watershed. Whereas the EPA is legislatively responsible for administering the provisions of the CWA, primary enforcement authority ("primacy") can be designated by the EPA to individual states to assist the EPA in executing its responsibilities. Therefore, administration of the CWA is both a federal and a state responsibility.

Domestic uses of water—for drinking, cooking, and cleaning—require particularly high water quality in order to protect human health (see chapter 7: Municipal Water Use, for more on drinking water systems). Because of this, water is usually treated before it is distributed to the public for domestic uses, and all public drinking water must comply with the standards and provisions contained in the Safe Drinking Water Act (SDWA) and the associated EPA regulations. Many US water suppliers have been using water-treatment methods such as filtration and the addition of chlorine since the early 1900s, but it was not until the enactment of the SDWA in 1974 that US public drinking water was comprehensively and consistently regulated. Under the SDWA, the EPA sets concentration limits for contaminants in drinking water (or, in some cases, specifies "treatment techniques" for certain kinds of contaminants for which concentration limits are impractical). Public drinking water systems[2] must comply with these standards and with monitoring and reporting requirements, including a requirement that they provide consumers with an annual report of test results and promptly notify the public when certain contaminant levels are exceeded. The SDWA focuses primarily on treatment and disinfection to achieve compliance with standards, but any means that ensures compliance, including protecting sources of drinking water, is acceptable. Amendments to the act in 1996 sought to take a more comprehensive approach by mandating a one-time drinking water source water assessment, improving operator training, and requiring an annual "right to know" report and other public notification and awareness efforts. Additionally, the SDWA contains the only federal regulation of groundwater by regulating the underground injection of various wastes. As with the CWA, the SDWA allows states to obtain primacy and assist the EPA in carrying out its legislated responsibilities.

Surface and groundwater

Water pollution is commonly characterized as originating from either point or nonpoint sources (see table 5.1). *Point-source pollution* comes from direct discharges into waters from factory pipes, sewers, or other discernible outlets, whereas *nonpoint-source pollution* is caused by water moving over or through the ground and picking up contaminants from different sources, then transporting them into water bodies in a diffuse manner. Deposition of contaminants from the air can also be a significant contributor to poor water quality in some areas (EPA 2001).

Remaining point-source pollution challenges

Point-source pollution (or direct discharges from a pipe) was once the leading source of water pollution in the United States, but has been significantly reduced in the last several decades. Yet despite almost 40 years of CWA regulation, over 850 billion gallons of untreated sewage (from storm drainage and domestic, industrial, and commercial sewers) are discharged into surface waters annually (EPA 2004) (see box 5.1), and 230 million pounds of toxic chemicals were released into waterways in 2007 alone (Dutzik, Crowell, and Rumpler 2009).

TABLE 5.1.

Examples of Point and Nonpoint Sources of Pollution and Associated Contaminants

Source	Contaminants
Point-source pollution	
Commercial and industrial	Heavy metals, volatile organic compounds, petroleum hydrocarbons, other chemical compounds, biodegradable organic materials
Sewage overflow	Nutrients, pathogens, biodegradable organic materials
Concentrated feed lots	Nutrients, sediment, pathogens
Nonpoint-source pollution	
Agriculture	Nutrients (e.g., from fertilizers or manure), sediment, pesticides, pathogens
Urban runoff/ stormwater	Oil, trash, sediment, metals
Forestry	Sediment, nutrients

BOX 5.1.

A CASE STUDY OF THE COMMUNITY IMPACTS OF COMBINED SEWER
OVERFLOW ABATEMENT PROJECTS IN SYRACUSE, NEW YORK

The siting of combined sewer wastewater treatment plants in minority neighborhoods of Syracuse, New York, has ignited a community movement advocating for
better alternatives, including the use of green infrastructure to reduce stormwater
volumes. The community has argued that low-income communities of color bear
disproportionate environmental and health impacts associated with wastewater
treatment plants. The dispute has centered around a large, chlorine-based sewage
treatment facility in the Southside neighborhood, known as the Midland Plant.

Combined sewer systems collect stormwater runoff, domestic sewage, and industrial wastewater into one system where it is treated before being discharged into
the environment. During wet weather, these systems can be overwhelmed by the
volume of stormwater, in which case they may overflow at predesignated locations.
These overflow events are called combined sewer overflows, or CSOs. Because
CSOs release raw sewage into the environment, they pose environmental and public
health risks (EPA 2004). Combined sewer overflows are regulated under the CWA,
and communities must take actions to prevent them.

In the late 1980s, Onondaga County was sued over water pollution caused by
CSOs. Original plans to mitigate these overflows called for nine treatment facilities throughout the city to store and treat CSO pollution. A decade later, these
proposals were altered to instead feature smaller treatment centers that did not use
chlorine in the predominantly white and affluent Northside community while constructing large, chlorine-based plants in the low-income, predominantly African
American Southside neighborhood (POC 2006). Dozens of families were evicted
in order to construct the Midland plant, and the plant raised concerns about potential environmental and health impacts associated with the plant's chlorinated discharge (Lane and Heath 2007). In addition, the local community feels that having
a wastewater treatment plant in their neighborhood is stigmatizing (POC 2009).

In response to these concerns, Southside community members and other concerned citizens organized themselves as the Partnership for Onondaga Creek
(POC). Since its establishment, POC has advocated for more equitable and safer
CSO abatement projects—namely, the use of green infrastructure to promote
stormwater infiltration combined with storage infrastructure.

Despite POC's work, Onondaga County continued with its plans for the Midland plant, while cancelling $3 million earmarked for Southside community devel-
opment. However, POC did successfully get the county to modify its design plans
to be less harmful to nearby communities. Additionally, POC was able to stop three
additional wastewater treatment plants from being built; instead, the county is implementing a combination of storage and green infrastructure, such as installation
of rain gardens and permeable pavement, and green roofs (POC 2009). Although
costs are uncertain, the county has calculated that this will cost 10–20 percent less
than construction of the previously planned treatment plants.

Facilities that discharge wastewater into surface water bodies must operate under permits required by the NPDES and comply with restrictions and monitoring requirements. Despite some progress, the NPDES program has not completely eliminated discharges or even put all polluting industries on a trajectory toward achieving that goal. Some observers suggest that this is largely due to the failure to set rigorous pollution control standards in all cases and to update those standards as frequently as needed (Andreen and Jones 2008 and Adler, Landerman, and Cameron 1993) (see table 5.2). The NPDES permits contain limits on the amount of individual pollutants that can be discharged based on what is achievable with current treatment technologies. This type of technology-based limit on pollution was originally intended to help reach a zero discharge goal, or as close to that as possible, by requiring increasingly stringent effluent limits as new technology emerged. The CWA states:

TABLE 5.2.

Dates of Original Effluent Limitation Guidelines and Most Recent Amendments for the Top 10 Polluting Industries (as Measured by Toxic Waste Pound Equivalents Reported in EPA's Toxic Releases Inventory)

Rank	Point-source category	Total toxic weighted pound equivalents	Original ELG date	Last amended	Notes
1	Steam electric power generating	20,916,337	1983	1983	Effluent guideline rulemaking currently underway.
2	Pulp, paper and paperboard	3,186,823	1998	2002	Detailed study performed; conclusions in 2006 Final ELG Plan.
3	Fertilizer manufacturing	1,099,509	1974	1995	
4	Organic chemicals, plastics and synthetic fibers	987,968	1987	1993	Detailed study of vinyl chloride manufacturers, coal tar manufacturers, and facilities generating aniline-bearing wastewaters was done in the 2004 ELG Plan. Effluent guideline rulemaking is currently underway for dioxin discharges from chlorinated hydrocarbon manufacturers.

(continued)

TABLE 5.2. (*continued*)

Rank	Point-source category	Total toxic weighted pound equivalents	Original ELG date	Last amended	Notes
5	Petroleum refining	574,262	1982	1985	Detailed study performed; conclusions in 2004 Final ELG Plan.
6	Inorganic chemicals Manufacturing	448,181	1982	1984	Effluent guideline rulemaking currently underway for dioxin discharges from chlor-alkali facilities.
7	Nonferrous metals manufacturing	381,632	1984	1990	
8	Ore mining and dressing	228,892	1982	1988	Preliminary study performed, conclusions will be published in 2010 Final ELG Plan.
9	Pesticide chemicals	204,810	1978	2007	The 2007 rule modified some testing procedures. The last major changes occurred in 1996.
10	Nonferrous metals forming and metal powders	128,077	1985	1985	It has not been substantively updated since 1985. There have been correction notices issued.

Note: Effluent limitation guidelines are reviewed by EPA each year.

Source: Code of Federal Regulations, Title 40: Protection of Environment and EPA (2008a).

it is the national policy that a major research and demonstration effort be made to develop technology necessary to eliminate the discharge of pollutants into the navigable waters, wasters of the contiguous zone, and oceans (33 U.S.C. §1251 (a)).

Additionally, the approach was meant to encourage the development of new technologies by giving them a guaranteed market (Andreen and Jones 2008).

The creation of new standards has been slow, and many are now outdated. For example, half of the effluent limitation guidelines for the top 10 most-polluting industries (listed in Table 5.2) have not been substantively updated in the past 20 years, and only 2 have been updated in the past 10 years. As Shepherdson, Odefey, and Baer (2005) point out with regard to the petroleum refining industry (which has not been updated since 1985):

It beggars the imagination to believe, as the [Environmental Protection] Agency would have the American people do, that during twenty years of astonishingly rapid technological development, neither the petroleum refining industry nor EPA could identify more effective and economically feasible pollution control measures than those adopted in 1985 (8).

The same could be said of the other high-polluting industries for which regulations are outdated. Conventional pollutants—or those pollutants that can be treated in a conventional wastewater treatment plant, such as fecal coliform, organic material, and suspended solids—have similarly outdated standards. These pollutants were originally regulated fairly loosely, as a baseline, with the intention of implementing more stringent standards later. In reality, almost all of the updated standards are the same as the original baseline (Andreen and Jones 2008).

Weak enforcement of CWA regulations also contributes to the failure to solve water-quality challenges. Violations of NPDES permits are pervasive. Of the approximately 7,000 major permitted facilities across the United States, 57 percent exceeded their permit limits at least once in 2005,[3] and many exceeded their permits more than once. In fact, over 600 facilities exceeded their permits in half of their monthly reporting periods, and 81 facilities exceeded their permits in every monthly reporting period in 2005. Furthermore, exceedances are often large—on average, permit limits were exceeded by 263 percent (Leavitt 2007). In addition to these major facilities, there are also 80,000 minor facilities holding NPDES permits. Given that these minor facilities are inspected far less often than the major facilities are, it is likely that their rate of noncompliance is even higher than that of major facilities (Andreen and Jones 2008).

Tackling Polluted Runoff: The Nonpoint-Source Challenge

In contrast to the clear, enforceable regulation of point-source pollution, the CWA's regulation of nonpoint sources is weak and in some cases unenforceable. As a result, whereas point sources of pollution were the major concern when the CWA was passed, a majority of water pollution today is from nonpoint sources (EPA 2009a). Urban and agricultural landscapes both contribute to nonpoint pollution. Stormwater running over urban and suburban landscapes and into water bodies carries with it contaminants including metals, sediments, pesticides, oil and grease, pathogens, and trash. In a natural setting, water from precipitation typically encounters rough terrain along with water absorbing flora, which slows the movement of the water and allows it to slowly seep into the ground, allowing some contaminants to be naturally filtered out. In most urban settings, on the other hand, water moves rapidly over paved surfaces, picking up any pollutants on these surfaces. Typically, much of this contaminated water is discharged directly into a water body. Agricultural runoff can also be contaminated with pesticides, fertilizers, sediments, pathogens, salts, and metals. Overgrazing and erosion of stream banks, plowing too often or at the wrong time, and excessive or poorly timed application of irrigation water, pesticides, and fertilizers increase water-quality impacts of farms (EPA 2005).

The CWA's strongest tools for regulating polluted runoff are the NPDES permit process and certain actions aimed at reducing polluted runoff from urban stormwater sewers and some construction and industrial sites (EPA 2008c). However, these requirements are generally weak. All medium and small cities are required to implement a stormwater management program that satisfies the following "minimum control measures": public education and outreach, public participation or involvement, illicit discharge detection and elimination, construction site runoff control, postconstruction runoff control, and pollution prevention (see figure 5.2). Although these help to reduce pollution, they do not address the full range of sources of pollution (e.g., smaller construction sites, agricultural runoff). Furthermore, many of these categories such as public education and outreach are difficult to enforce and have widely variable degrees of effectiveness depending on how well they are implemented.

Other sections of the CWA contain even weaker nonpoint-source pollution controls. States are required to identify water bodies impaired by nonpoint sources of pollution and develop best management plans to reduce this pollution (CWA, Section 319).

FIGURE 5.2. Storm drain signs such as this one are one public education strategy that can be used for stormwater control minimum control measures
Photo courtesy of NOAA (2008).

However, these plans are not required to contain mandatory approaches, and, instead, many state plans contain only voluntary measures. As a result, these state plans have been largely unsuccessful (Andreen and Jones 2008). Additionally, the EPA has little control over the contents of these plans and lacks the authority to take action when states fail to do so, as it can with other sections of the CWA (Andreen and Jones 2008). Currently,

---

BOX 5.2.
NEW WATER-QUALITY SOLUTIONS: LOW IMPACT DEVELOPMENT

Low-impact development (LID) is a stormwater management approach that can help to minimize the negative effects of urban and suburban land use on water quality and the natural hydrology of a watershed. This is done primarily through the use of vegetation and permeable surfaces to allow infiltration of water into the ground, thereby reducing the quantity of potentially polluted runoff and allowing natural filtration through the soil to enhance water quality. A wide variety of specific strategies and practices are encompassed by the LID approach, including permeable streets and sidewalks, "green" roofs, and vegetated medians or swales that allow water to infiltrate into soils rather than flow directly into sewers. Facilities that filter stormwater through vegetation and soil have been shown to reduce total suspended solids, organic pollutants and oils, and heavy metals by at least 90 percent (EPA 1999c).

Some regions have made significant progress in designing and implementing innovative stormwater management solutions. In 2007, the Portland City Council adopted a Green Streets Resolution that promotes LID policies to reduce the amount of polluted runoff and waste from sewer overflows that enter rivers and streams. These policies have a number of additional benefits, such as helping to recharge groundwater and increasing urban green space (City of Portland, Oregon 2009). The city has also amended its code and construction practices to facilitate these policies, codifying "downspout disconnections" that reduce stormwater flows into the city's combined sewer system by infiltrating or treating runoff on-site (Portland City Code Chapter 17. 37) and has incorporated green street facilities into all City of Portland–funded development, redevelopment, or enhancement projects as required by the city's Stormwater Management Manual.

Urban land is constantly being redeveloped. By one estimate, 42 percent of urban land in the United States will be redeveloped by 2030, suggesting that there are many opportunities for implementing LID (Brookings Institute 2004, cited by CRSDCWP & NRC 2008). Additionally, LID is typically less costly than traditional stormwater management techniques, which require construction and maintenance of infrastructure, including curbs, gutters, and underground pipes (EPA 2007). For waters that are a source of drinking water, it could also result in savings on water treatment costs. Still, many barriers to LID still exist. These include lack of technical knowledge regarding LID strategies, zoning requirements, and stormwater management regulations that require stormwater to be concentrated and removed from roadways as quickly as possible.

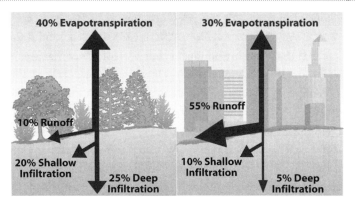

FIGURE 5.3. Relationship between impervious cover and evaporation, runoff, and infiltration in rural (a) and urban (b) areas

Images courtesy of EPA.

the only leverage the EPA has over these state plans is to deny funding if they are found to be inadequate; from a practical standpoint, however, denying states funding is only likely to make the problem worse (Andreen and Jones 2008). Nonpoint-source pollution can also be addressed through the CWA's TMDL programs, which are required for water bodies that do not have adequate quality for their designated uses—but again, these lack enforceable requirements for nonpoint-source pollution (Adler 2001). As a way to strengthen their efforts to control nonpoint sources, the EPA has recently proposed the development and implementation of "reasonable assurance guidelines" for reduction in nonpoint sources of pollution identified in TMDLs (EPA 2010a).

Regulation of nonpoint-source pollution is inherently more difficult than that of point-source pollution. It can be difficult to trace pollutants to the polluter, multiple small contributions are harder to collect and treat than large industrial or urban sources, and decentralized, dispersed treatment of numerous discharges is often not possible. On the other hand, there are solutions to some nonpoint-source pollution that are technologically simple (Andreen and Jones 2008; Houck 2002). Implementation of best management practices can reduce polluted runoff substantially, while also having peripheral benefits like aquifer recharge. In urban areas, this can include controlling runoff by rethinking construction approaches and increasing pervious surfaces and vegetation (see box 5.2 and figures 5.3 for more details). Nutrient and pesticide management plans, improving irrigation and water use efficiency, and keeping livestock away from streams are examples of agricultural best management practices to reduce dispersed water quality threats.

Inadequate Scope of Water-Quality Regulations

The jurisdiction of the CWA has expanded and contracted over the years as the act's mandate has been interpreted and administered during changing political and judicial conditions. Recently, many headwater and ephemeral streams and wetlands have lost

CWA protections, through a series of cases including *Solid Waste Agency of Northern Cook County v. US Army Corps of Engineers (SWANCC v. USACE)* and *Rapanos v. United States*. Chapter 2: Legal and Institutional Framework of Water Management includes a thorough discussion of the changing administration and scope of the CWA. The CWA also contains a number of exemptions. For example, the CWA specifically exempts "agricultural stormwater discharges and return flows from irrigation" from its definition of a point source (33 U.S.C. § 1362(14)).

Additionally, as stated previously, the CWA does not apply (for the most part) to groundwater. The narrow groundwater protections in the SDWA—which consist of regulation of direct injections into the ground—do not address many threats to groundwater quality, including failing septic systems and farm and other runoff that leaches into the groundwater over time. Ground and surface waters are routinely treated as separate, disconnected entities in both water-quality and -quantity regulations, despite the clear scientific understanding that they are closely intertwined.

Finally, there are too many exemptions even to the SDWA's meager groundwater-quality protections. For example, hydraulic fracturing, an increasingly prevalent technique used to release natural gas trapped in underground shale formations by injecting water, chemicals, and sand to fracture the rock and the release the gas, is exempted from the SDWA in the 2005 Energy Policy Act. This means that federal laws do not require companies using hydraulic fracturing to obtain permits, undergo monitoring, or disclose the complex chemical compositions of the fluids they are using (Wiseman 2009; Berkowitz 2009). This exemption was made based on a highly criticized 2004 EPA report on hydraulic fracturing impacts on groundwater, which concluded that it was a "minimal threat" (Manuel 2010; Wiseman 2009). Indeed, from the limited information on chemicals used in hydraulic fracturing that is available, either through voluntary disclosure or in states that require disclosure, we know that chemicals that can potentially cause respiratory problems or harm to the nervous and reproductive systems are used (Berkowitz 2009). Though there is a dearth of good research on the connections between groundwater contamination and hydraulic fracturing, a growing body of circumstantial evidence and the limited monitoring that has been done increasingly reveals contamination of wells by hydraulic fracturing activities (PDEP 2009; Lustgarten 2008). The EPA has initiated additional research into its effects on groundwater (EPA 2010b).

Challenges for Enforcement: Monitoring and Data Insufficiencies

Sustainable management of water quality cannot be done without adequate information and monitoring of the quality of the nation's surface water and groundwater. Yet such monitoring has been inadequate. In the words of former assistant administrator for water at the EPA, Tracy Mehan, we have collected years of data of all types and sources, yet today we cannot describe, in a scientifically defensible way, the quality of our water. Moreover, we cannot quantify the progress we have made to date in cleaning those waters, nor where we need to go to fix remaining problems (Mehan 2006, 7).

Only around 20 percent of total stream miles in the United States are monitored in any two-year period (table 5.3). Although monitoring of other water bodies is better, the number of areas assessed has declined markedly over the last two decades. Nearly 74 percent of estuaries were monitored in 1992, but by 2006, this number had declined to 26 percent. Wetlands have been especially poorly monitored, with only 2 percent monitored in 2006. Furthermore, waters studied are not a representative sample of all waters in a state. Monitoring of groundwater quality is not required and is not done regularly or comprehensively. And the number of contaminants monitored is insufficient, given our growing understanding of the health and environmental consequences of the growing numbers of compounds and chemicals found in water.

Our failure to adequately monitor surface and groundwater quality prevents us, in many cases, from identifying whether existing programs are effective and if new programs are needed. The TMDL process, for example, which is meant to rehabilitate impaired waters, depends on first identifying which waters are impaired, and then again identifying when these waters are in good condition. One study on the TMDL delisting process, for example, states that "in many cases, determination of impairment was based on insufficient water-quality information" (Keller and Cavallaro 2007). This lack of sufficient water-quality information can result in a lack of accountability in the TMDL process, as impaired water bodies may be inappropriately delisted in order to avoid the TMDL requirements. For example, New York state delisted Onondaga Creek and other tributaries to Onondaga Lake during plans to clean up that lake, claiming that there was inadequate data to justify their listing (ONCN 2008). Delisting allowed the state and Onondaga County to avoid establishing TMDL programs to clean up the creeks, despite the fact that the creek water quality was so poor that in some places it was hazardous for people to even come into contact with it (ONCN 2008). The Onondaga Nation successfully fought to have these tributaries relisted, after conducting studies with a local organization to document the poor quality of the tributaries (ONCN 2008). The EPA has recently proposed—as part of a larger clean water strategy—to start the National Aquatic Resource Surveys to help remedy the lack of good water-quality data.

Drinking Water Quality

The drinking water that Americans receive from their taps is among the safest in the world and is protected by some of the most complex and costly regulations mandated by the EPA. Yet, as described earlier, not all Americans have access to or can afford safe

TABLE 5.3.

Waters Assessed in EPA's National Water Quality Inventory

	1992	1994	1996	1998	2000	2002	2004	2006
Rivers, streams, creeks								
Miles assessed	642,881	615,806	693,905	842,426	699,946	695,540	563,955	717,504
Percent of total	18	17	19	23	19	19	16	20
Lakes, ponds, reservoirs								
Acres assessed	18,300,000	17,134,153	16,819,769	17,390,370	17,339,080	15,022,000	16,230,384	14,819,217
Percent of total	46	42	42	42	43	37	39	35
Estuaries (bays and estuaries in 2002)								
Square miles assessed	27,227	26,847	28,819	28,687	31,062	30,446	25,399	23,207
Percent of total	74	78	72	32	36	35	28	26
Wetlands								
Acres assessed	11,080,000	8,310,000	8,405,875	9,831,988	8,282,133	1,300,000	1,789,464	1,855,771
Percent of total	4a	3	3	4	8	1	2	2

a Many states were still developing standards for wetlands; therefore, we could not monitor them.

Source: National Water Quality Report to Congress, 1994–2004, and Water Quality Assessment and Total Maximum Daily Loads Information (ATTAINS).

drinking water. With an ever-growing number of chemicals being introduced into the environment without the necessary research on their potential health and ecological impacts, there is growing uncertainty and concern about drinking water quality.

Unequal Distribution of Safe Drinking Water

Even though the United States commonly reports 100 percent access to safe water and sanitation in international water surveys, there is a small, but not insignificant number of people who lack such services (Wescoat, Headington, and Theobald 2007). For example, 0.64 percent of the US population, representing 1.7 million people, lack indoor plumbing (RCAP 2004). Others lack access to safe drinking water because it is not affordable in their communities—8,000 people on average have their water temporarily shut off in Denver each year due to nonpayment of bills, for example (Wescoat, Headington, and Theobald 2007). Additionally, the *quality* of tap water varies between communities. Examples from across the country demonstrate that some already disadvantaged communities receive tap water that is less safe than the water that other communities receive (see chapter 3: Water and Environmental Justice). These communities—which are typically small drinking water systems, rural communities dependent on unprotected wells, and communities on tribal lands—often lack the resources necessary to provide high-quality drinking water.

Even given the limited data we collect on water quality and violations of the SDWA, there is strong evidence that tap water in rural areas tends to be less safe than that supplied in urban areas. People in rural areas typically receive their water either from a small public drinking water system or from private wells. On average, small systems supply water of much poorer quality than do large systems (see figure 5.4). For example, the smallest class of water systems (serving 25–500 people) have 28 times more water quality violations, per person, than the average for systems of all sizes, and more than 500 times more than the large systems serving more than 10,000 people (EPA 1999a; EPA-OIG 2004).

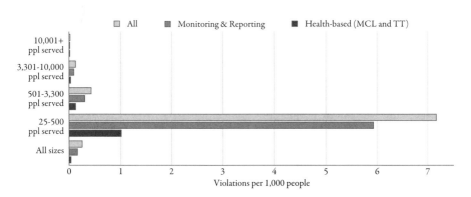

FIGURE 5.4. Safe Drinking Water Act violations by type of violation and by water system size
MCL = maximum containment level; TT = treatment technology.
Source: Based on data from EPA (1999a).

Private wells serve as the drinking water source for nearly 15 percent of the nation's population (about 43 million people) (DeSimone, Hamilton, and Gilliom 2009). A recent US Geological Survey study found that 20 percent of private wells sampled contained at least one contaminant at levels of concern to human health (compared to 6 percent in public water systems) and nearly half failed to meet voluntary parameters for aesthetic quality (e.g., odor, taste, color) (DeSimone, Hamilton, and Gilliom 2009). Contaminants found in the study included a mix of natural and human-produced materials, including nitrates, radon, pesticides, solvents, disinfection by-products, and chemicals from gasoline. Despite the greater risk of contamination of private wells, they remain unregulated under the SDWA, and no federal laws exist that require treatment or monitoring of water from private wells.

Access to safe drinking water varies across communities of different economic and ethnic compositions as well. According to a US Census report from 1995, just over 20 percent of American Indians living on reservations with 500 or more households had complete plumbing (Bureau of the Census 1995). Public water systems on American Indian lands consistently report more SDWA violations than those not in Indian country; in 2005, 69 percent of water systems on American Indian lands reported health-based or significant reporting violations (compared to 27 percent nationwide), and 12 percent reported health-based violations (compared to 7 percent nationwide) (EPA-OECA 2008). In Texan *colonias* (rural subdivisions along the US/Mexico border), where roughly half of the population is of Hispanic origin, 24 percent of households use untreated water for drinking and cooking (HAC 2005). In comparison, less than 1 percent of the total US population did not have access to clean drinking water in 2000 (RCAP 2004). Additionally, public notifications of violations of SDWA standards do not need to be in all languages spoken in an affected community, resulting in a lack of adequate communication about the safety of drinking water to those who do not speak English well.

Economics of Safe Drinking Water for Small Systems

Many small drinking water systems are not in compliance with the SDWA because they lack adequate funds to build or upgrade treatment systems, train and pay a system operator, and pay for ongoing maintenance and operation of treatment technologies. The SDWA requires that contaminant standards be set at a level that is "feasible" for systems to achieve; however, this determination is generally based on the costs to systems serving 50,000 people or more (Tiemann 2007). For small systems, serving fewer people, complying with some standards comes at a higher cost per person.

There are several mechanisms for assisting small water systems financially. The primary one is the Drinking Water State Revolving Fund, which provides EPA-funded grants to states for eligible projects. Under the 1996 SDWA amendments, states are required to make 15 percent of their annual grant available to water systems serving 10,000 people or fewer.[4] Current levels of funding for the State Revolving Loan Fund, however, are not sufficient to cover the comprehensive upgrading of small water systems that is needed. Further, the provision of technical assistance to these communities through traditional service providers such as the National Environmental Services Center, Rural Community Assistance Partnership, and National Rural Water Association is becoming increasingly limited as the EPA struggles with increasing demands on its budget (G. Iwan, director, National Environmental Services Center, pers. comm. 2010).

The SDWA contains two mechanisms for providing flexibility to water systems in complying with the act: exemptions and variances. These flexibility mechanisms are based on ability to pay for treatment standards under the SDWA and, thus, are used most often by small systems. Although some argue that they are essential for small systems to be able to provide affordable drinking water, others see them as unjust, as they permit some systems to provide lower quality drinking water. Regional consolidation of water systems is another tactic that has been proposed. Such an approach allows small systems to pool resources, thereby decreasing costs (Holmes 2006). Additionally, a mechanism for spreading cost of compliance more evenly across the nation would make stricter regulations affordable for smaller systems.

Inadequacy of Standards

The EPA develops enforceable contaminant concentration limits (standards) through a three-step process:

1. Identification and study of contaminants present in drinking water supplies at concentrations that potentially threaten human health
2. Determination of whether or not to regulate each contaminant studied
3. Establishment of a concentration limit, called a maximum contaminant level (EPA 2006a).

To help prioritize regulation of the many contaminants present in drinking water, every five years, the EPA publishes a list of contaminants that pose a potential health threat and are known, or anticipated, to be in drinking water systems. These contaminants are then studied to determine whether they require regulation. Contaminants may also be considered for regulation at the direction of Congress. The decision of whether to regulate a contaminant is based on the potential for it to cause adverse health effects, the frequency and level of occurrence of the contaminant in public drinking water systems, and whether there is a "meaningful opportunity" to reduce public health risks through regulation. After a decision is made to regulate a contaminant, the EPA must decide at what concentration to set the standard. First, the EPA determines a *maximum contaminant level goal*—the concentration at which the contaminant does not pose known or expected health risks. This limit, however, is not enforceable. The EPA then establishes an enforceable limit, called the *maximum contaminant level*,[5] that takes into account the cost and feasibility of treatment, which is enforceable.

Unregulated Contaminants and Mixtures

Increasingly, diverse and complicated mixes of synthetic chemicals are being detected in treated drinking water, including pesticides, pharmaceuticals, fragrance compounds, and flame retardants (Stackelberg et al. 2004; Blomquist et al. 2001). Increased detection is a result of both more advanced testing mechanisms that allow for detection of lower concentration levels as well as increased occurrence of chemicals in drinking water. Each year, around 700 new chemicals are introduced into the environment, and over 800,000 chemicals are now registered for use in the United States (GAO 2009). Many of these chemicals end up in drinking water—through leaks during their manufacture, storage, or transport, or through their normal use—and conventional approaches for treating drinking water (i.e., coagulation, sedimentation, filtration, and chemical disinfection) are often ineffective at removing synthetic chemicals (Ternes et al. 2002; Westerhoff et al. 2005).

Large numbers of contaminants that can now be detected in water are not regulated under the SDWA. A study by the Environmental Working Group found over 300 different pollutants in samples of tap water across the nation (EWG 2005), whereas the SDWA regulates 91 contaminants. The fact that there are unregulated chemicals in drinking water does not in itself mean that drinking water is unsafe. The concentrations may be so low that they do not affect human health, or the human health effects of exposure may be negligible. But our understanding of the health effects of many of these chemicals at chronic low levels is still poor. A growing numbers of studies suggest that even trace amounts of some chemicals found in water supplies and drinking water can have biological effects, particularly those that disrupt hormone functioning that have been observed to cause reproductive and other effects in aquatic organisms (Hayes et al. 2002; Panter, Thompson, and Sumpter 1998; Routledge et al. 1998; Langlois et al. 2010; Rahman, Yanful, and Jasim 2009).

Furthermore, contaminated drinking water often contains more than one chemical, and a growing body of literature suggests that mixtures of chemicals can have biological effects that single chemicals do not (Hayes et al. 2006; Jaeger, Carlson, and Porter 1999; Rajapakse, Ong, and Kortenkamp 2001; Rajapakse, Silva, and Kortenkamp 2002; Silva, Rajapakse, and Kortenkamp 2002; Kortenkamp 2007; Kortenkamp et al. 2007). In a review of studies on combined effects of chemicals, Kortenkamp et al. (2007, 106) write,

> The widely held view that mixtures of dissimilarly acting chemicals are "safe" at levels below NOAELs [no observable adverse effect levels] is not supported by empirical evidence. We show that this view is also based on the erroneous

assumption that NOAELs can be equated with zero-effect levels. Thus, on the basis of published evidence, it is difficult to rule out the possibility of mixture effects from low-dose multiple exposures.

Perhaps most significantly, a study of the combined effects of pesticides and nitrates in concentrations at which they occur in groundwater found that if mice drank this water, "endocrine, immune, and behavior changes occurred due to doses of mixtures, but rarely due to single compounds at the same concentrations" (Jaeger, Carlson, and Porter 1999, 133). Despite this, standards are not required to (and generally do not) take into account the combined effects of chemicals mixtures, despite the mounting evidence that levels of contaminants that are safe when isolated become unsafe in combination with certain other chemicals (Monosson and Draggan 2010). The EPA has recently proposed addressing contaminants as groups to enhance drinking water protection and for cost-effectiveness, but progress toward this goal has been slow.

These studies indicate that our current suite of drinking water standards may not address all health concerns related to drinking water; they also highlight the failure of scientific studies on the health impacts of chemicals to keep pace with the introduction of new chemicals. The large number of new chemicals introduced every year, and limited requirements for companies to test their toxicity, puts a large burden of developing toxicity and risk data on the EPA or academics (GAO 2005). Unlike in the European Union or Canada, chemical companies are not required to develop data on basic toxicological and health effects, unless the EPA promulgates a rule specifically requiring a company to conduct tests (GAO 2005). A recent review by the Government Accountability Office found that, largely as a result of this system, "EPA lacks adequate scientific information on the toxicity of many chemicals" (GAO 2009, 4).

Non-Health-Based Factors

In order for a contaminant to be regulated, the SDWA requires that the regulation, "in the sole judgment of the [EPA] administrator," offers a "meaningful opportunity for health risk reduction for persons served by public water systems." This puts powerful discretion in deciding whether or not to regulate contaminants into the hands of single person. For example, the preliminary regulatory decision on perchlorate (a component of jet fuel) determined that regulation would not provide a "meaningful opportunity" to protect human health, based on the fact that "in over 99 percent of public drinking water systems, perchlorate was not at levels of public health concern" (EPA 2008b, 1). Still, this decision means that almost 1 million people will continue to be exposed to perchlorate levels exceeding the level at which the EPA considers it to be a health concern (the health reference level) (EPA 2008a). Furthermore, despite stating that "in deciding whether to regulate perchlorate, EPA focused attention on the most sensitive subpopulation, a pregnant woman and her fetus," they also estimated that "about 16,000 pregnant women (with a high end estimate of 28,000) could be exposed at levels exceeding the health reference level at any given time" (EPA 2008a, 60, 277).

Once the decision is made that a federal standard is needed for a contaminant, a standard level must then be set. This process allows for further consideration of non-health-based factors—specifically, it requires a cost-benefit analysis to determine if the benefits justify the costs, in other words, if the cost of removing the contaminant to a certain concentration is worth the impact of doing so on human health. In order to be effective, laws must take into account the feasibility of what they are trying to achieve. Still, in the case of drinking water standards, which exist to protect public health, applying a cost-benefit analysis raises ethical questions. In a paper on this subject, Ackerman (2007, 2) writes,

> Suppose that studies showed that the benefits exceeded the costs for child labor, or for selling the national parks to developers, or for selling votes on election day. It is not only that these activities are illegal; if they were up for debate, few people would propose that cost-benefit analysis was the right way to make the decisions about such issues. That is, there are matters of rights and morality that are not subject to cost-benefit analysis, nor to market decisions.

One of the failures of cost-benefit analyses in this area is the known inability to comprehensively assess, in economic terms, all of the factors. While the costs of water treatment can be calculated fairly accurately, the benefits of treatment are much more difficult to quantify (Ackerman 2007). For example, in the case of radon, the quantifiable benefits of treating for radon were considered to be the reduced incidence of fatal and nonfatal cancers. To quantify the benefits of reducing fatal cancer, the *value of a statistical life* was used. Estimating the value of a statistical life is done by "inferring individuals' implicit tradeoffs between small changes in mortality risk and monetary compensation," and in the cost-benefit analysis used for radon, was estimated to be between $700,000 (1997$) and $16.3 million (1997$), with a best estimate of $5.8 million (1997$) (EPA 1999b, 9563). To quantify benefits of nonfatal cancer, the "willingness to pay" (based on surveys) to avoid chronic bronchitis and nonfatal lung and stomach cancers was used. These are, at best, surrogates for true costs.

Regulation is required to consider the most vulnerable populations, but the discretion allowed in setting contaminant standards inevitably affects vulnerable populations disproportionately, because they can be sickened by lower levels of contaminants than the general population. Vulnerable populations include children, the elderly, and those with compromised immune systems, such as people undergoing chemotherapy. A recent study suggests that standards for microbial contaminants may not be strict enough to protect the elderly, who tend to be less tolerant to pathogens (Colford et al. 2009).

Challenges for Enforcement: Monitoring and Reporting

In addition to weaknesses in the regulatory process, there are serious problems with enforcement of existing regulations. Widespread monitoring and reporting (M/R) violations raises questions about the actual safety of some drinking water. The SDWA requires states and tribes to report drinking water system compliance through the Public Water Supply Supervision program. As a part of this program, public water systems submit lab tests of their water to states or tribes, which then review the lab test results, identify violations, and report these violations to the EPA. The information generated as a part of this program helps gauge the effectiveness of the current regulatory program and informs the public of the quality of their drinking water.

There is a high rate of *significant M/R violations*, defined as, "with rare exceptions . . . when no samples are taken or no results are reported during a compliance period" (EPA 2006b, 2). Since 1996, between 20 percent and 27 percent of systems report a significant violation of either a health-based or M/R standard (see figure 5.5). These violations are reported together, because the EPA notes that, "if a system did not monitor the quality of its water, it is impossible to know if it has violated a health-based requirement" (EPA 2009b, 5).

Furthermore, there is significant underreporting of violations. Data on drinking water quality must be passed from the water system to the state to the EPA. In many cases, states are not reporting violations to the EPA, or the EPA is unable to ensure data transfer into the national computerized Safe Drinking Water Information System, resulting in incomplete data in the EPA's database. A review of EPA's database from 1996 to 1998 showed that only 40 percent of all health-based violations and 9 percent of all

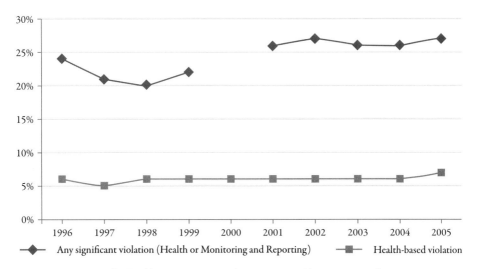

FIGURE 5.5. Reported US public water systems violations over time, by percentage of systems

Note: Gaps in data reflect gaps in data reported in these reports, as metrics for reporting changed over time.
Source: Based on data from National Public Water System Compliance Reports (EPA 2009b).

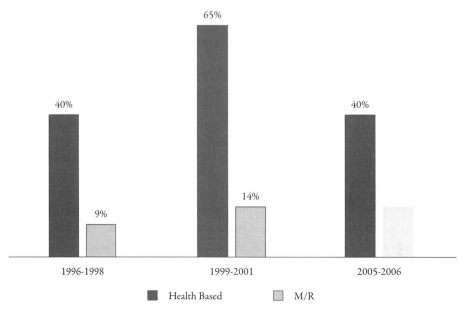

FIGURE 5.6. Completeness of EPA Safe Drinking Water Act violations data
Source: Based on data from EPA-OIG (2004).

M/R violations that were in state's records were recorded in the EPA's database. Data quality was shown to improve between 1999 and 2001, but between 2005 and 2006, the percentage of health-based violations recorded was back down to 40 percent (see figure 5.6). The M/R data quality for this year was unknown, but it was estimated to be worse than that for health-based violations (EPA 2008d).

Due to these known data discrepancies, the EPA Office of Inspector General determined that the EPA consistently overstates the safety of drinking water, when the safety of drinking water is to a large extent unknown (EPA-OIG 2004). In addition to obscuring the safety of public drinking water, poor monitoring and reporting of data limits the EPA's ability to effectively direct limited resources to protect human health. Improving both the collection and reporting of water-quality data should be a top priority in the drinking water program.

Developing a 21st-Century Water-Quality Policy

Collectively, the flaws and limitations in the design, monitoring, and enforcement of the current US water-quality regulation result in uncertainty about the true quality of some of the nation's drinking water and exposure to unregulated pollutants with unknown health effects. They also inequitably distribute both the costs and benefits of water-quality pollution, with the costs of pollution primarily borne by the public rather than by the polluters.

Great progress has been made in cleaning up contaminated waters, but much more needs to be done at the federal level. Among the major challenges are providing adequate resources to update old or inadequate regulations, improving or using different financial tools for helping smaller systems, and adopting better approaches for monitoring and enforcing standards. It also entails a broader perspective on protecting the nation's waters, moving toward more comprehensive planning that recognizes the importance of clean surface water and groundwater for environmental, human health, and other uses. Pollution prevention is a key part of this new approach. Additionally, the lack of reliable water-quality data must be addressed in order to better monitor progress or identify problems. The specific recommendations that follow outline our vision for reinvigorating the federal role in water-quality regulation in the United States.

Recommendations

INTEGRATE REGULATION OF DRINKING AND SURFACE WATER QUALITY

Whereas the goals of providing safe drinking water and having clean water in our lakes and rivers may have once seemed separate, we now understand that clean source waters are important for safe drinking water. The EPA should conduct a review of where implementation and enforcement of the CWA and the SDWA can be integrated to provide greater operational efficiency. For example, new chemicals having adverse health effects that have the real potential to contaminate drinking water supplies should be prohibited from being disposed of through NPDES-permitted discharge. Furthermore, restructuring the EPA to integrate the wastewater and drinking water offices into a single program would assist the EPA in appropriately prioritizing the public health elements of water-quality protection and in providing resource assistance to small disadvantaged communities. In the case of groundwater protections, federal legislation should be enacted that would adequately address and protect all drinking water sources.

IMPROVE SURFACE AND GROUNDWATER QUALITY
Strengthen controls on nonpoint-source pollution

Polluted runoff is now the leading type of water pollution in the United States; however, the CWA has not been used to require that the states effectively regulate this type of pollution. The solutions to nonpoint-source pollution are often technologically simple and include slowing down and promoting infiltration of stormwater in urban areas, and various nutrient and other management practices in agriculture. The CWA should be updated to make best management practices for control of nonpoint-source pollution mandatory and enforceable, beyond those required in the NPDES Stormwater Program. One way of doing this is through the "reasonable assurance guidelines" that the EPA has proposed regarding TMDL pollution reduction plans. State nonpoint-source pollution (section 319) management plans should also contain mandatory (rather than voluntary) application of best management practices.

Strengthen controls on point-source pollution.

The CWA mandated pollution limits that were tied to technologies so that these limits would become increasingly stringent as new technologies emerged. In reality, new limits have not kept pace with technological advances. Controls on point sources of pollution should be tightened to better reflect the CWA's goal of zero discharge of pollutants. Technology standards should be reviewed and aggressively updated to reflect current best available technologies and encourage innovation.

Enforce NPDES permits more strictly.

NPDES permits are currently violated by a high percentage of permitted facilities. The EPA should enforce these permits more strictly by levying financial penalties that are sufficiently large to make polluting no longer a viable cost of doing business and by rescinding or denying renewal of permits to repeat violators.

Promote green infrastructure

Green infrastructure, such as green roofs, vegetative swales, and permeable pavement, can help reduce polluted runoff that ends up in water bodies and reduce combined sewer overflows. It also has peripheral benefits such as groundwater recharge and city beautification. These types of solutions should be further developed and promoted. The EPA recently proposed a shift toward including solutions with multiple water-quality benefits, including these types of green infrastructure.

Increase scientifically defensible monitoring of surface water quality

In order to effectively address the remaining water-quality problems, we must have reliable and complete data to inform water-management decisions, including time-series data to establish baselines, seasonality, and longer-term trends. Even though states are the primary bodies responsible for data collection, the federal government needs to provide sufficient funding for monitoring and to hold states accountable for adequate data collection.

IMPROVE DRINKING WATER SAFETY

Increase research on health impacts of drinking water contaminants and update more quickly the Safe Drinking Water Act's regulations to make them more protective of human health

The first step in making sure that drinking water standards are protective of human health is to understand the health impacts of the contaminants that are in our water. Increased research must be conducted on these contaminants and could be funded by fees on companies that introduce new chemicals. These studies should include synergistic and additive effects of common mixtures of chemicals. This science should be relied on when creating standards that prioritize protection of human health but do not create overly stringent regulations that place economic hardship on small systems. Additionally, the EPA must use this information to update drinking water standards in a more timely manner, taking into account health effects of chemical mixtures.

Integrate equality of access to safe drinking water into the Safe Drinking Water Act's mandate

Safe drinking water is now recognized as a basic human right, and the federal government must show leadership in working to ensure access to safe drinking water to communities of all types and sizes. The EPA should prioritize efforts to decrease disparities in the quality of water provided to different communities, particularly between large and small systems and between systems on tribal and other lands.

Additionally, an effective mechanism for providing financing to systems unable to meet water-quality standards needs to be adopted, through grants, loans, subsidies, fees, or other approaches. This recognizes that the current system of offering loans that cannot be repaid by disadvantaged communities is an ineffective mechanism to achieve SDWA compliance. Additionally, further research on cost-effective treatment technologies for small systems should be funded and conducted, similar to the EPA's recent proposal to foster development of new treatment technologies and to treat chemical mixtures for more cost-effective protection of human health.

Improve enforcement of monitoring and reporting violations under the Safe Drinking Water Act

Without complete and reliable information on water quality, it is impossible to know the safety of drinking water being provided by drinking water systems. For this reason, monitoring and reporting violations should be considered to be as severe as health-based violations, and the EPA should prioritize improvement of the data quality that they receive from states. Monitoring and reporting requirements should also be reviewed for simplification and economy. Current complexity of monitoring and reporting should be reduced where violations are being incurred based only on technicalities and not on health concerns.

References

Ackerman, F. 2007. "High-Risk Economics: Gambling on Cost-Benefit Analysis for Arsenic Standards." Comment, Global Development and Environment Institute, Medford, MA. http://ase.tufts.edu/gdae/publications/articles_reports/arsenic-final.pdf.

Adler, R. 2001. "Controlling nonpoint source water pollution: Is help on the way (from the courts or EPA)?" Environmental Law Reporter 31: 10270–10282.

Adler, R., J. C. Landerman, and D. M. Cameron. 1993. *The Clean Water Act 20 Years Later*. Washington, DC: Island Press.

Agency for Toxic Substances and Disease Registry (ATSDR). 2007. "Case Studies in Environmental Medicine (CSEM) Nitrate/Nitrite Toxicity What Are the Physiological Effects of Exposure to Nitrates/Nitrites?" Agency for Toxic Substances and Disease Registry. http://www.atsdr.cdc.gov/csem/csem.asp?csem=9&po=8.

Andreen, W., and S. C. Jones. 2008. *The Clean Water Act: A Blueprint for Reform*. Center for Progressive Reform, White Paper 802. Washington DC: Center for Progressive Reform. http://www.progressivereform.org/cleanWater.cfm.

Berkowitz, M. 2009. *Toxic Chemicals on Tap: How Natural Gas Drilling Threatens Drinking Water*. Boston: Environment America Research and Policy Center.

Blomquist, J. D., J. M. Denis, J. L. Cowles, J. A. Hetrick, R. D. Jones, and N. B. Birchfield. 2001. *Pesticides in Selected Water-Supply Reservoirs and Finished Drinking Water, 1999–2000: Summary of Results from a Pilot Monitoring Program*. Open-File Report 01–456. Baltimore, MD: US Geological Survey. http://md.water.usgs.gov/nawqa/OFR_01-456.pdf.

Brookings Institute. 2004. "Toward a New Metropolis: The Opportunity To Rebuild America. Arthur C. Nelson, Virginia Polytechnic Institute and State University." Discussion paper prepared for The Brookings Institution Metropolitan Policy Program, Washington DC.

Bureau of the Census. 1995. *Housing of American Indians on Reservations—Plumbing. Statistical Brief*. SB 95-9. Washington, DC: US Department of Commerce. http://www.census.gov/apsd/www/statbrief/sb95_9.pdf.

City of Portland, Oregon. 2009. "Portland Green Streets Program." Portland Bureau of Environmental Services. http://www.portlandonline.com/bes/index.cfm?c=44407.

Code of Federal Regulations, Title 40: Protection of Environment and EPA. 2008a.

Colford, J. M., J. F. Hilton, C. C. Wright, B. F. Arnold, S. Saha, T. J. Wade, J. Scott, and J. N. S. Eisenberg. 2009. "The Sonoma Water Evaluation Trial: A Randomized Drinking Water Intervention Trial to Reduce Gastrointestinal Illness in Older Adults." *American Journal of Public Health* 99 (11): 1988–1995.

Committee on Reducing Stormwater Discharge Contributions to Water Pollution and National Research Council (CRSDCWP & NRC). 2008. *Urban Stormwater Management in the United States*. Washington, DC: The National Academies Press. http://www.nap.edu/catalog.php?record_id=12465.

Community Water Center (CWC). 2011. Community Water Center Web site. Accessed December 28, 2011. http://www.communitywatercenter.org/.

DeSimone, L. A., P. A. Hamilton, and R. J. Gilliom. 2009. *Quality of Water from Domestic Wells in Principal Aquifers of the United States, 1991–2004—Overview of Major Findings*. US Geological Survey Circular 1332. Reston, VA: US Geological Survey. http://pubs.usgs.gov/circ/circ1332/.

Dutzik, T., P. Crowell, and J. Rumpler. 2009. "Wasting our Waterways: Toxic Industrial Pollution and the Unfulfilled Promise of the Clean Water Act." Environment America Research and Policy Center. http://cdn.publicinterestnetwork.org/assets/b818d52cb8d5ba4c6530431f800bfb66/Wasting-Our-Waterways-vAM.pdf.

Environmental Working Group (EWG). 2005. "A National Assessment of Tap Water Quality." Environmental Working Group. http://www.ewg.org/tap-water/fullreport.

Firestone, L. 2009. *Guide to Community Drinking Water Advocacy*. Visalia, CA: Community Water Center.

Firestone, L., and S. DeAnda. nd. *Nitrate Contamination in Central Valley Communities*. Visalia, CA: Community Water Center.http://www.communitywatercenter.org/files/PDFs/RB_nitrate_presentation.pdf.

Gilliom, R., and P. A. Hamilton, 2006. *Pesticides in the Nation's Streams and Ground Water, 1992–2001: A Summary*. Reston, VA: US Geological Survey. http://pubs.usgs.gov/circ/2004/1265/.

Hamilton, P. A., T. L. Miller, and D.N. Myers. 2004. *Water Quality in the Nation's Streams and Aquifers: Overview of Selected Findings, 1991–2001*. US Geological Circular 1265. Reston, VA: US Geological Survey. http://pubs.usgs.gov/circ/2004/1265/.

Harter, T. and J. Lund. 2012. Addressing Nitrate in California's Drinking Water with a Focus on Tulare Lake Basin and Salinas Valley Groundwater. Report to the State Water Resources Control Bard to the Legislature. University of California, Davis.

Hayes, T. B., P. Case, S. Chui, D. Chung, C. Haefele, K. M. Lee, V. P. Mai, Y. Marjuoa, J. Parker, and M. Tsui. 2006. "Pesticide Mixtures, Endocrine Disruption, and Amphibian Declines: Are We Underestimating the Impact?" *Environmental Health Perspectives* 114 (suppl 1): 40–50.

Hayes, T. B., A. Collins, M. Lee, M. Mendoza, N. Noriega, A. A. Stuart, and A. Vonk. 2002. "Hermaphroditic, Demasculinized Frogs after Exposure to the Herbicide Atrazine at Low Ecologically Relevant Doses." *Proceedings of the National Academy of Sciences USA* 99: 5476–5480.

Holmes, M. 2006. "Regionalization of Rural Water Systems in New Mexico." *Southwest Hydrology*, September/October 18–19, 34. http://www.swhydro.arizona.edu/archive/V5_N5/feature2.pdf.

Houck, O. 2002. *The Clean Water Act TMDL Program: Law, Policy, and Implementation*. Washington, DC: Environmental Law Institute.

Housing Assistance Council (HAC). 2005. *Housing in the Colonias*. Washington DC: Housing Assistance Council. http://www.ruralhome.org/storage/documents/colonias_infosheet.pdf.

Jaeger, J. W., I. H. Carlson, and W. P. Porter. 1999. "Endocrine, Immune, and Behavioral Effects of Aldicarb (Carbamate), Atrazine (Triazine), and Nitrate (Fertilizer) Mixtures at Groundwater Concentrations." *Toxicology and Industrial Health* 15 (1–2): 133–151.

Keller, A. A., and L. Cavallaro. 2007. "Assessing the U.S. Clean Water Act 303(d) Listing Process for Determining Impairment of a Waterbody." *Journal of Environmental Management* 86 (4): 699–711.

Kortenkamp, A. 2007. "Ten Years of Mixing Cocktails: A Review of Combination Effects of Endocrine-Disrupting Chemicals." *Environmental Health Perspectives* 115 (S-1): 98–105. doi: 10.1289/ehp.9357.

Kortenkamp, A., M. Faust, M. Scholze, and T. Backhaus. 2007. "Low-Level Exposure to Multiple Chemicals: Reason for Human Health Concerns?" *Environmental Health Perspectives* 115 (S-1): 106–114. doi: 10.1289/ehp.9358.

Lane, A., and T. Heath. 2007. "Environmental Racism in Syracuse, NY: A Case Study of a Government's Failure to Protect an Endangered Waterway and a Neglected Community." Paper presented at The State of Environmental Justice in America 2007 conference, Howard University Law School, Washington, DC, March 29–31, 2007. http://www.onondagacreek.org/sites/default/files/presentations/howardpaper.pdf.

Langlois, V. S., A. C. Carew, B. D. Pauli, M. G. Wade, G. M. Cooke, and V. L. Trudeau. 2010. "Low Levels of the Herbicide Atrazine Alter Sex Ratios and Reduce Metamorphic Success in Rana pipiens Tadpoles Raised in Outdoor Mesocosms." *Environmental Health Perspectives* 118 (4): 552–557.

Leavitt, C. 2007. *Troubled Waters: An Analysis of 2005 Clean Water Act Compliance*. Washington, DC: US Public Interest Research Group Education Fund. http://www.environmentalifornia.org/reports/clean-water/clean-water-program-reports/troubled-waters-an-analysis-of-2005-clean-water-act-compliance.

Lustgarten, A. 2008. "Buried Secrets: Is Natural Gas Drilling Endangering U.S. Water Supplies?" *ProPublica*, November 13. http://www.propublica.org/article/buried-secrets-is-natural-gas-drilling-endangering-us-water-supplies-1113.

Manassaram, D. M., L. C. Backer, and D. M. Moll. 2006. "A Review of Nitrates in Drinking Water: Maternal Exposure and Adverse Reproductive and Developmental Outcomes." *Environmental Health Perspectives* 114 (3): 320–327.

Manuel, J. 2010. "EPA Tackles Fracking." *Environmental Health Perspectives* 118: a199–a199. doi:10.1289/ehp.118-a199.

Mehan, G. T. 2006. "Water Monitoring in the Age of Information." Paper presented at: New Jersey Water Monitoring and Assessment Technical Workshop, Columbus, New Jersey, April 20, 2006. http://www.state.nj.us/dep/wms/Mehan.pdf.

Monosson, E., and S. Draggan. 2010. "Regulation of Toxic Chemicals." Encyclopedia of Earth. http://www.eoearth.org/article/Regulation_of_toxic_chemicals.

Moore, E., E. Matalon, C. Balazs, J. Clary, L. Firestone, S. De Anda, and M. Guzman. 2011. "The Human Costs of Nitrate-contaminated Drinking Water in the San Joaquin Valley." Oakland, CA: Pacific Institute.

National Oceanic and Atmospheric Administration (NOAA). 2008. "Nonpoint Source Pollution: Urban and Suburban Areas." US Department of Commerce, National Oceanic and Atmospheric Administration. http://oceanservice.noaa.gov/education/kits/pollution/05areas.html.

National Water Quality Report to Congress, 1994–2004, and Water Quality Assessment and Total Maximum Daily Loads Information (ATTAINS). Online database. http://www.epa.gov/waters/ir/

Natural Resources Conservation Service (NRCS). nd. "Manure Management," Natural Resources Conservation Service. http://photogallery.nrcs.usda.gov.

North Carolina Division of Water Quality. 2002. "Local Source Water Protection Pays." *Streamlines: A Newsletter for North Carolina Water Supply Watershed Administrators* 6 (2): 1–4. http://h2o.enr.state.nc.us/wswp/SL/v6i2.pdf.

Onondaga Nations Communication Newsletter (ONCN). 2008. "Onondaga Creek." Onondaga Nation: People of the Hills. http://www.onondaganation.org/news/2008/2008_0322.html.

Panter, G. H., R. S. Thompson, and J. P. Sumpter. 1998. "Adverse Reproductive Effects in Male Fathead Minnows (Pimephales promelas) Exposed to Environmentally Relevant Concentrations of the Natural Oestrogens, Oestradiol and Oestrone." *Aquatic Toxicology* 42: 243–253.

Partnership for Onondaga Creek (POC). 2006. "Study in Environmental Racism." Partnership for Onondaga Creek. http://www.onondagacreek.org/resources/research/study-environmental-racism.

———. 2009. "Partnership for Onondaga Creek Declares Victory after 10 Years of Advocacy: Judge Amends ACJ to Scrap Sewage Plants and Include Green Infrastructure."

Pennsylvania Department of Environmental Protection (PDEP). 2009. "DEP Identifies Responsibility for Bradford Township Gas Migration/Water Supply Problems." Press release. Pennsylvania Department of Environmental Protection. http://www.portal.state.pa.us/portal/server.pt/community/newsroom/14287?id=2198&typeid=1.

Rahman, M. F., E. K. Yanful, and S. Y. Jasim. 2009. "Endocrine Disrupting Compounds (EDCs) and Pharmaceuticals and Personal Care Products (PPCPs) in the Aquatic Environment: Implications for the Drinking Water Industry and Global Environmental Health. *Journal of Water and Health* 7 (2): 224–243.

Rajapakse, N., D. Ong, and A. Kortenkamp. 2001. "Defining the Impact of Weakly Estrogenic Chemicals on the Action of Steroidal Estrogens." *Toxicological Sciences* 60: 296–304.

Rajapakse, N., El. Silva, and A. Kortenkamp. 2002. "Combining Xenoestrogens at Levels below Individual No-Observed-Effect Concentrations Dramatically Enhances Steroid Hormone Action." *Environmental Health Perspectives* 110 (9): 917–921.

Routledge, E. J., D. Sheahan, C. Desbrow, G. C. Brighty, M. Waldock, and J. P. Sumpter. 1998. "Identification of Estrogenic Chemicals in STW Effluent. 2. In Vivo Responses in Trout and Roach." *Environmental Toxicology and Chemical* 32: 1559–1565.

Rural Community Assistance Partnership (RCAP). 2004. *Still Living without the Basics in the 21st Century*. Washington, DC: Rural Community Assistance Partnership. http://www.rcap. org/stilllivingwithoutbasics.

Shepherdson, M., J. Odefey, and K. Baer. 2005. "Comments of the Natural Resource Defense Council, Waterkeeper Alliance, and American Rivers on U.S. EPA Preliminary Effluent Guidelines Program Plan for 2006, 70 Fed. Reg. 51042." Regulations.gov. http://www.regulations. gov/#!documentDetail;D=EPA-HQ-OW-2004-0032-1090.

Silva, E., N. Rajapakse, and A. Kortenkamp. 2002. "Something from 'nothing'—eight weak estrogenic chemicals combined at concentrations below NOECs produce significant mixture effects." *Environmental Science and Technology* 36 (9): 179A–180A.

Stackelberg, P., E. Furlong, M. Meyer, S. Zaugg, A. Henderson, and D. Reissman. 2004. "Persistence of Pharmaceutical Compounds and Other Organic Wastewater Contaminants in a Conventional Drinking-Water Treatment Plant." *Science of the Total Environment* 329 (1–3): 99–113.

Ternes, T. A., M. Meisenheimer, D. McDowell, F. Sacher, H.-J. Brauch, B. Haist-Gulde, G. Preuss, U. Wilme, and N. Zulei-Seibert. 2002. "Removal of Pharmaceuticals during Drinking Water Treatment." *Environmental Science and Technology* 36 (17): 3855–3863.

Tiemann, M. 2007. "Arsenic in Drinking Water: Regulatory Developments and Issues." CRS Report for Congress, Congressional Research Service, Library of Congress, Washington, DC. http://www.fas.org/sgp/crs/misc/RS20672.pdf.

US Environmental Protection Agency (EPA). 1999a. *National Characteristics of Drinking Water Systems Serving Populations Under 10,000*. EPA 816-R-99-010. Washington, DC: Environmental Protection Agency, Office of Water. http://www.epa.gov/ogwdw/smallsystems/pdfs/ smallsys.pdf.

———. (1999b). "Radon in Drinking Water Health Risk Reduction and Cost Analysis; Notice." *Federal Register* 64 (38): 9560–9599. http://www.epa.gov/safewater/radon/hrrcafr.pdf.

———. (1999c). *Storm Water Technology Fact Sheet: Bioretention*. EPA 832-F-99-012. Washington, DC: Environmental Protection Agency, Office of Water. http://www.epa.gov/owmitnet/ mtb/biortn.pdf.

———. (2001). *Frequently Asked Questions about Atmospheric Deposition: A Handbook for Watershed Managers*. Washington, DC: Environmental Protection Agency.

———. 2003. *Introduction to EPA'S Drinking Water Source Protection Programs*. Washington, DC: Environmental Protection Agency, Drinking Water Academy. http://www.epa.gov/ watertrain/pdf/swp.pdf.

————. 2004. *Report to Congress on the Impacts and Control of CSOs and SSOs.* Washington, DC: Environmental Protection Agency, Office of Water. http://cfpub.epa.gov/npdes/cso/cpolicy_report2004.cfm.

————. 2005. *Protecting Water from Agricultural Runoff.* EPA 941-F-05-001. Washington, DC: Environmental Protection Agency. http://www.epa.gov/owow/nps/Ag_Runoff_Fact_Sheet.pdf.

————. 2006a. *Setting Standards for Safe Drinking Water.* Washington, DC: Environmental Protection Agency. http://permanent.access.gpo.gov/lps21800/www.epa.gov/safewater/standard/setting.html.

————. 2006b. *2004 National Public Water Systems Compliance Report.* EPA 305-R-06-001. Washington, DC: Environmental Protection Agency, Office of Enforcement and Compliance Assurance.http://www.epa.gov/compliance/resources/reports/accomplishments/sdwasdwacom2004.pdf.

————. (2007). *Fact Sheet: Reducing Stormwater Costs through Low Impact Development (LID) Strategies and Practices.* EPA 841-F-07-006. Washington, DC: Environmental Protection Agency, Office of Water. http://www.epa.gov/owow/nps/lid/costs07/factsheet.html.

————. 2008a. *Drinking Water: Preliminary Regulatory Determination on Perchlorate.* Washington, DC: Environmental Protection Agency, Office of Water.

————.2008b. *Fact Sheet: Preliminary Regulatory Determination for Perchlorate.* EPA 815-F-08-009. Washington, DC: Environmental Protection Agency, Office of Water. http://www.epa.gov/ogwdw000/ccl/pdfs/reg_determine2/fs_ccl2-reg2_perchlorate.pdf.

————. 2008c. *National Pollutant Discharge Elimination System: Stormwater Basic Information.* Washington, DC: Environmental Protection Agency, Office of Water.

————. 2008d. *Population Served by Community Water Systems with No Reported Violations of Health-Based Standards.* Washington, DC: Environmental Protection Agency, Office of Water. http://cfpub.epa.gov/eroe/index.cfm?fuseaction=detail.viewPDF&ch=47&lShowInd=0&subtop=203&lv=list.listByChapter&r=216626.

————. 2009a. "About Smart Growth." Environmental Protection Agency. http://www.epa.gov/dced/about_sg.htm.

————. 2009b. *2006 National Public Water Systems Compliance Report.* EPA-K-09-002. Washington, DC: Environmental Protection Agency, Office of Enforcement and Compliance Assurance. http://www.epa.gov/compliance/resources/reports/accomplishments/sdwa/sdwacom2006.pdf.

————. 2009c. *Watershed Assessment, Tracking and Environmental Results: National Summary of State Information.* Washington, DC: Environmental Protection Agency. http://iaspub.epa.gov/waters10/attains_nation_cy.control.

————. 2010a. "Coming Together for Clean Water." Public Discussion Draft, Environmental Protection Agency, Washington, DC.

————. 2010b. "EPA Initiates Hydraulic Fracturing Study: Agency seeks input from Science Advisory Board." News release, Environmental Protection Agency, Washington, DC. http://yosemite.epa.gov/opa/admpress.nsf/e77fdd4f5afd88a3852576b3005a604f/ba591ee790c58d30852576ea004ee3ad!OpenDocument.

————. 2010c. *National Lakes Assessment A Collaborative Survey of the Nation's Lakes.* Washington, DC: Environmental Protection Agency. http://water.epa.gov/type/lakes/upload/nla_newlowres_fullrpt.pdf.

US Environmental Protection Agency—Office of Enforcement and Compliance Assurance (EPA-OECA). 2008. *Providing Safe Drinking Water in America: 2005 National Public Water Systems Compliance Report.* Washington, DC: Environmental Protection Agency, Office of Enforcement and Compliance Assurance.

US Environmental Protection Agency—Office of Inspector General (EPA-OIG). 2004. *EPA Claims to Meet Drinking Water Goals Despite Persistent Data Quality Shortcomings.* Washington, DC: Environmental Protection Agency, Office of Inspector General. http://www.epa.gov/oigearth/reports/2004/20040305-2004-P-0008.pdf.

US Government Accountability Office (GAO). 2005. *Chemical Regulation: Approaches in the United States, Canada, and the European Union.* GAO-06-217R. Washington, DC: US Government Accountability Office. http://www.gao.gov/new.items/d06217r.pdf.

———. 2009. *Chemical Regulation: Observations on Improving the Toxic Substances Control Act.* GAO-10-292T. Washington, DC: US Government Accountability Office. http://www.gao.gov/new.items/d10292t.pdf.

Wescoat, J. L., L. Headington, and R. Theobald. 2007. "Water and Poverty in the United States." *Geoforum* 38: 801–814.

Westerhoff, P., Y. Yoon, S. Snyder, and E. Wert. 2005. "Fate of Endocrine-Disruptor, Pharmaceutical, and Personal Care Product Chemicals during Simulated Drinking Water Treatment Processes." *Environmental Science and Technology* 39 (17): 6649–6663.

Wiseman, H. 2009. "Untested Waters: The Rise of Hydraulic Fracturing in Oil and Gas Production and the Need to Revisit Regulation." *Fordham Environmental Law Review* 115: 115–195.

6

PROTECTING FRESHWATER ECOSYSTEMS

Juliet Christian-Smith and Lucy Allen

Introduction

In the 20th century, national water policies focused on building infrastructure and institutions for the purposes of satisfying human demands for water, controlling the vagaries of natural climatic variability including floods and droughts, generating power, providing recreational opportunities, and more. Ecosystem values and conditions were rarely considered or made an explicit part of water-policy decisions. The consequence has been serious degradation and destruction of the nation's ecological heritage.

Freshwater ecosystems—including floodplains, wetlands, rivers, and estuaries, as well as the flora and fauna they sustain—provide a wide range of services of tremendous value to society, from mitigating floods, to recharging aquifers, to enhancing water quality (Costanza et al. 1997). Despite their economic and inherent values, human activities are causing the rapid decline of freshwater ecosystems. According to one study, freshwater species in North America are becoming extinct at rates similar to those in tropical rainforests, which are widely regarded as among the most stressed ecosystems on earth (Ricciardi and Rasmussen 1999).

The soft path approach to water management acknowledges the vital role of healthy ecosystems in water management and accordingly recognizes them as legitimate users of water resources (Brooks, Brandes, and Gurman 2009). This book envisions a national water strategy for the 21st century that incorporates the soft path approach, including the maintenance and restoration of ecosystems as management objectives. This strategy must explicitly include improving our understanding of freshwater ecosystems and their value, policies for protecting remaining ecosystems, and strategies for improving degraded ones. This chapter explores the management of our nation's freshwater ecosystems, providing an overview of threats to US aquatic environments, the health of the nation's water sources, a brief review of existing legal protections, and a summary of growing efforts to protect and restore freshwater ecosystems.

Background

For much of the last 200 years, freshwater management in the United States has consisted primarily of draining, channeling, damming, and diverting water out of our nation's rivers while dumping untreated or poorly treated industrial waste and sewage into them. These practices have seriously damaged water quality and aquatic ecosystems. Beginning in the 1960s, newspapers around the nation chronicled massive fish kills with headlines that read, "Mystery Fish Kill Clogs Bay Waters" (Graves 1963); "Huge Fish Kill Blamed on Chemical Dumping" (*Los Angeles Times* 1970); and "A California Fish Kill Causes Pollution Worry" (*New York Times* 1968). As early as the late-19th century and continuing through the 1960s, reports document fires fueled by accumulated oil and debris on rivers in eastern industrial centers, including the Patapsco River, which discharged into the Baltimore Harbor, the Buffalo River in upstate New York, the Rouge River in Michigan, and Cleveland's Cuyahoga River. The infamous Cuyahoga burned over a half dozen times before a 1969 fire received national attention as a potent symbol of environmental destruction. The polluted river became a testament to the need for a new approach to resource management and is often cited as a catalyst for the passage of the federal Clean Water Act (CWA) in 1972 (Adler 2002).

Since the passage of the CWA, there has been significant progress in improving our nation's water *quality*, particularly in reducing point-source pollution, or pollution originating from a discrete source, such as a factory pipe or sewage treatment plant (see chapter 2: Legal and Institutional Framework of Water Management). However, aquatic ecosystems continue to decline, in large part due to water-use and land-use decisions that do not consider freshwater ecosystems and instream flows. Progress in reducing non-point-source pollution, or more dispersed effluent from farms and city streets, has been limited (see chapter 5: Water Quality). And growing concentrations of contaminants continue to impair water quality. At the same time, more and more watersheds are being physically modified with large dams or reservoirs, channelization, flood control levees, and significant water withdrawals.

Historically, states and local governments have overseen decisions surrounding water allocation. As they have divvied up the nation's freshwater supply and built dams and diversions, they have dramatically altered the size and timing of flows in the majority of US river basins (Poff et al. 2007). This, along with growing human water demands and increasing extreme weather events, has contributed to the widespread degradation of aquatic ecosystems, leading to significant declines in the populations of aquatic species and of terrestrial species that require aquatic ecosystems for some part of their life cycle (Richter et al. 1996). Today, there is a growing recognition that protecting key parts of the natural flow regime is critical to maintaining the ecological integrity of freshwater and riparian ecosystems (Richter et al. 1996; Poff et al. 1997; Lytle and Poff 2004; Arthington et al. 2006).

The State of Aquatic Ecosystems in the United States

Despite federal legislation designed to protect freshwater ecosystems and significant reductions in point-source pollution due to the CWA, recent assessments offer a grim appraisal of the health of the nation's aquatic systems. In an assessment of all freshwater and diadromous fish in the United States, Canada, and Mexico, the American Fisheries Society found that 39 percent of described species are either endangered, threatened, vulnerable, or extinct (Jelks et al. 2008).[1] The assessment reveals a large increase in the number of imperiled fish species over the last two decades and shows that little progress has been made in terms of conserving imperiled species. For instance, of those fish species identified as endangered, threatened, or vulnerable in 1989, 89 percent were found to have the same or worse conservation status in the recent assessment. The main threats to fish species identified in the study were invasive (nonindigenous) species and habitat degradation (Jelks et al. 2008).

In addition to this assessment of fish species, the Environmental Protection Agency's Environmental Monitoring and Assessment Program (EMAP) and Wadeable Streams Assessment (WSA) monitor and assess the ecological condition of the nation's waters based on measures called *indices of biotic integrity*. The EMAP effort covers 12 western states,[2] and the WSA program is nationwide, but both assessment efforts are constrained by limited access to some waterways, low budgets, and sampling restrictions. Indices of biotic integrity analyze key characteristics of aquatic communities, such as the composition and relative abundance of key groups of animals (e.g., fish and invertebrates) and plants (e.g., periphyton or algae). Because some organisms are more sensitive to pollution or hydrologic changes than others are, information on the abundance of the various types of organisms can indicate whether a stream is healthy or disturbed.[3] These new assessment programs mark a departure from the past as they specifically examine the biology of streams and rivers, not just their chemical constituents (Karr 1991). EMAP and WSA also examine the sources of disturbances that contribute to poor ecological condition, such as chemical stressors, physical habitat stressors, and biological stressors. Based on both fish and macroinvertebrate indices, EMAP finds that more than a quarter of the stream network in the 12 western states is "very disturbed" (figure 6.1), demonstrating poor ecological conditions (EPA 2006). The sources of these disturbances were found to be the result of riparian land uses (47 percent of stream length), non-native fishes (34 percent of stream length), high nitrogen levels (27 percent of stream length), and changes to the sediment regime (26 percent of stream length).

Data samples for the WSA were collected at nearly 1,400 random sites across the nation using uniform protocols and a statistical sampling method. Results indicate that 42 percent of the nation's total stream length is considered to be in poor condition. Major stream stressors were similar to those identified by EMAP: high nitrogen levels (32 percent), riparian disturbance (26 percent), and streambed instability (25 percent) are top

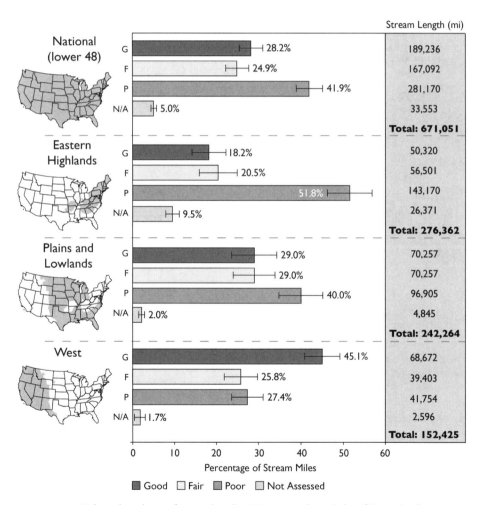

FIGURE 6.1. Biological condition of streams based on Macroinvertebrate Index of Biotic Condition

Note: The Macroinvertebrate Index combines metrics of benthic community structure and function into a single index for each region. The thresholds for defining good, fair, and poor condition were developed for each of the nine WSA eco-regions based on condition at the least-disturbed reference sites.*Source:* EPA (2006).

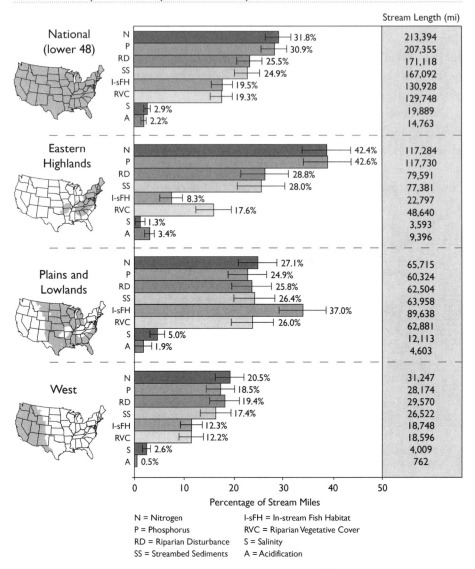

FIGURE 6.2. Proportion of stream length ranked as "poor" in terms of different stressors
Source: EPA (2006).

stressors nationwide (figure 6.2). In the plains and lowlands, the number one stressor is the absence of instream fish habitat (37 percent). Thus, key stressors that threaten the biological and physical integrity of aquatic ecosystems are surrounding land and water uses and physical alterations to waterways.

Increased water extraction along with the construction of massive infrastructure, including dams and reservoirs designed to store water for human use, have altered both the timing and volume of water flows for aquatic systems. The human demand for water in the United States more than doubled between 1950 and 1985, though since 1985, demand has flattened even though total population grew by more than 20 percent (figure 6.3). A growing understanding of aquatic ecology (and common sense) suggests that the aquatic ecosystems, from macroinvertebrates to fish, require a certain quantity and quality of water in order to function and remain healthy (Richter et al. 1996; Poff et al. 1997; Lytle and Poff 2004; Arthington et al. 2006).

There are several federal laws and statutes that give the federal government responsibility and authority to act to protect aquatic ecosystems. These include the Commerce Clause of the Constitution, the CWA, the Wild and Scenic River Act, and the Endangered Species Act (ESA). Each of these tools offers different approaches to address ecosystem challenges, but none have been used consistently or effectively.

The Commerce Clause of the Constitution has been interpreted by the Supreme Court to provide federal authority over *"navigable waters,"* including protection of recreational fishing and waterfowl hunting. The stated purpose of the CWA of 1972 (described in detail in chapter 5: Water Quality) is broadly to "restore and maintain the chemical, physical, and biological integrity of the Nation's water" (CWA, 33 U.S.C. Title 1 §101), while the Wild and Scenic Rivers Act of 1968 protects individual rivers: "selected rivers of the Nation, which with their immediate environments, possess outstandingly remarkable scenic, recreational, geologic, fish and wildlife, historical, cultural or other similar values, shall be preserved in free-flowing condition, and that they and their immediate environments shall be protected for the benefit and enjoyment of present and future generations" (Wild and Scenic River Act, 16 U.S.C. 1273).The ESA is the primary legal instrument used to protect instream flows for ecological benefits.

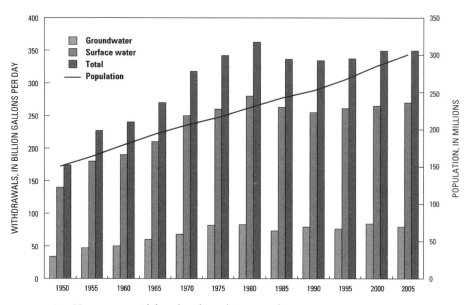

FIGURE 6.3. Human water withdrawals and population growth, 1950–2005
Source: Based on data from Kenny et al. (2009).

The ESA gives the federal government the authority to protect and recover species that it identifies as threatened or endangered by extinction. For aquatic species, this authority can include requiring minimum instream flows, water-quality protections, or fish passage at dams.

The power of the ESA, both generally and in protecting aquatic ecosystems, became evident when, in the late 1970s the presence of the endangered snail darter slowed the construction of a dam. The federal Tennessee Valley Authority was forced to postpone the completion of Tellico Dam after the Supreme Court ruled the congressional intent of passing the ESA, and specifically section 7, was to put the protection of endangered species above even legitimate missions and functions of federal agencies. In recent years, ESA requirements have led to restricting irrigation water sent to farmers in the Klamath River Valley, operational changes at the Grand Coulee Dam, pressure to breach four major dams on the Snake River, and modest restrictions on water exports from California's Sacramento–San Joaquin River Delta to farms and cities in Southern California (*Natural Resources Defense Council et al. v. Kempthorne* 2007).

The priority given to the ESA has made it arguably the single most powerful environmental law in terms of protecting instream flows, and it is frequently cited in litigation to protect ecosystems that support endangered species. However, the ESA's extensive authority also invites frequent attempts to weaken it through litigation, proposed amendments, and adopted regulations. To confront our 21st-century water challenges, we must both improve the enforcement of existing laws and create new avenues for the federal government to protect and restore the physical, chemical, and biological integrity of our nation's waterways. With scientists now in wide agreement that restoring more natural flow processes to rivers is essential to safeguard aquatic ecosystems (Maunder and Hindley 2005; Poff et al. 1997; Postel and Richter 2003), there are a variety of new policy solutions that address freshwater ecosystem protection.

Potential Solutions

IMPROVED DATA AND INFORMATION

Collecting instream flow and other basic hydrologic data

Information about both natural hydrologic conditions and human uses of water are critical knowledge gaps. Even though the United States leads much of the rest of the world in monitoring basic river flows and water uses, water data collection and dissemination remain grossly inadequate, and inadequate data collection and monitoring of river flows and water uses in the United States poses an enormous barrier to any kind of rational water management. Without these data, it is difficult to make informed decisions and set appropriate policies to satisfy both human and ecosystem needs.

The US Geological Survey (USGS) began measuring the flow in the nation's rivers in 1889 using stream gauges. These data are used to guide many water- and land-use planning decisions. For example, hydrologists routinely use this information to develop rainfall-runoff relationships, return intervals, flood forecasts, and drought risks. Engineers use these data to design flood- and drought-protection systems. Stream gauge information has become even more important in terms of documenting changing runoff patterns associated with climate change.

Figure 6.4 shows the number of active USGS continuous record stream gauges in operation from 1901 through 2009. The number of gauges rose steadily from 1901 for nearly 7 decades, reaching a peak number in operation in 1968 of 8,326 active stream gauges. From 1968 until 1981, the number of active stream gauges fell slightly to about 7,831 stream gauges, then the number declined rapidly to under 7,000 stream gauges by 1984, where it stayed relatively stable for nearly 15 years until 1998 when the number of active stream gauges started increasing again to about 7,872 stream gauges by 2008 (USGS 2011).

Long-term stream gauge information is critical for sound water- and land-use planning decisions and for the detection of trends, the effects of land use and water use, and for identifying longer-term climatic changes. Federal support for these data collections systems must be sustained to ensure that data are continuously collected, archived, and made available to scientists and the public. Unfortunately, large numbers of long-term gauges are being lost. Figure 6.5 shows the number of USGS stream gauges discontinued each year from 1988 through 2009 that had at least 30 years of streamflow records when

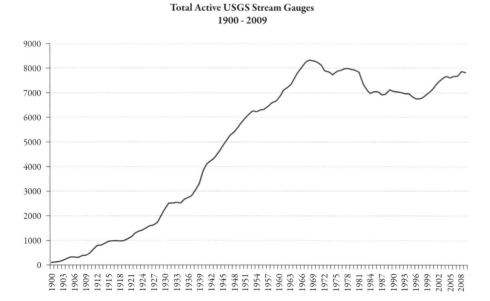

FIGURE 6.4. Total active USGS stream gauges, 1900–2009

Source: Based on data from USGS (2010).

they were shut down. The loss of long-term stream gauges is quite variable through time and is directly related to federal funding. The graph shows, for example, a temporary increase in support for the national stream gauge program in 2001. More recently, however, the rate of loss has approached the higher levels of previous years—nearly 100 long-record stream gauges were discontinued in 2009 (USGS 2011). It is critical that Congress ensure adequate, long-term funding for stream gauges.

LEGISLATIVE APPROACHES

Ecosystems and the Clean Water Act

The administration of the CWA has focused primarily on reducing point-source and, to a lesser extent, nonpoint-source pollution (see chapter 5: Water Quality for a detailed discussion of the act). To the extent that aquatic ecosystems depend on water that is not polluted with chemical contaminants, the CWA has played a role in their protection. However, recent assessments have identified physical alterations to waterways, riparian land uses, non-native aquatic species, and changes to the sediment regime as primary contributors to the decline of aquatic ecosystems (EPA 2006; Jelks et al. 2008). These types of threats are rarely regulated under the CWA. As others have noted, "it is time for the EPA to revisit its virtually exclusive focus on chemical impairments to our aquatic ecosystems" (Adler 2003, 1).

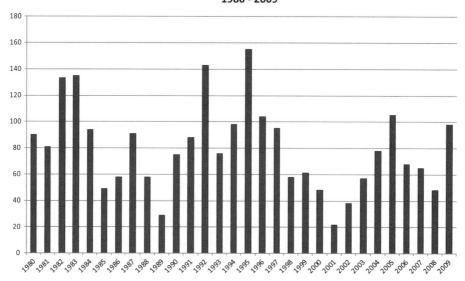

FIGURE 6.5. Number of stream gauges with 30 or more years of records discontinued
Source: Based on data from USGS (2009).

Despite the limited role that it has played to date, the CWA's text indicates the potential for the law to be used far more broadly to protect aquatic ecosystems (Adler 2003). The law's stated objective includes restoration and maintenance of the biological integrity of the nation's waters. Additionally, the way in which the law defines *pollution* encompasses a range of human activities not limited to the discharge of contaminants; pollution is defined as the "the man-made or man-induced alteration of the chemical, physical, biological, and radiological integrity of water" (CWA, 33 U.S.C. §502). In a review of the Total Maximum Daily Load program of the CWA, the National Research Council stressed the need to incorporate this broad definition of pollution into the act's administration (National Research Council 2001).

Some states have adopted biological standards to help determine whether ecosystems are being protected and to trigger other actions under the law such as discharge permit denials and development of permit standards. However, states are not required to develop and use such criteria and few have fully developed biological criteria in place. Fulfilling the law's mandate of protecting aquatic ecosystems would likely require administrative changes as well as amendments (Adler 2003). For example, under its current authority, the Environmental Protection Agency could require all states to develop and use biological criteria. An amendment that has been proposed that would better address some of the threats to ecosystems, for example, is to make it explicit in the text of the law that waters that have been impaired due to hydrologic modifications must be addressed by Total Maximum Daily Load programs (Andreen and Jones 2008).

Establishing state instream flow programs

All states west of the 100th meridian and a growing number of eastern states have implemented some type of instream flow rights or requirements. A 2005 Nature Conservancy survey evaluated state and federal efforts for state instream flow programs. The results reveal that the programs vary in their scope and effectiveness, yet have several common challenges, especially financial challenges. Programs within state fish and wildlife agencies were reported most likely to be underfunded or not funded at all. As a result, these agencies lack the staff necessary to participate in or inform the legal and regulatory processes that affect river flows (Mathews 2006). To be more effective, agencies require greater capacity, including additional staff, increased training, increased data collection, and funding for water-rights and/or land-acquisition programs.

Another challenge is that fish and wildlife agency programs most often have no regulatory authority over one of the most critical habitat components for aquatic organisms: water (Mathews 2006). This highlights the overarching issue of deference to state water allocation structures, which directly impacts available water and instream flows. In many western river systems, states have overallocated available water supplies. Though clearly detrimental to the health of aquatic ecosystems, the federal government rarely intervenes, even in the most extreme cases where federal statutes are being violated. Survey respondents report that monitoring and enforcement are extremely difficult in any basin where disputes over water diversions, water rights, monitoring, and enforcement have not been resolved by a process known as *adjudication*.

Respondents also reported that they were hindered by the political decision-making process, which is often time-consuming and revolves around the validity of instream flow models and methods. This, Mathews (2006) argues, not only puts the burden of proof on public rather than private interests, but also stalls even incremental progress toward the protection of instream flows. For example, in Georgia, low-flow protections have long been considered inadequate to protect ecosystems, and, in 1995, the state's Wildlife Resources Division recommended more protective standards (Evans and England 1995). These recommendations were initially rejected: "A major concern was that the policies recommended by the group were not sufficiently based upon site-specific scientific research conducted within the rivers and streams in the State" (Caldwell 2005, 2). Then, in 2001, after a severe drought, the state adopted the recommendations as an interim instream flow policy. To date the interim policy has not been finalized or updated.

Through a federal-state partnership, the federal government (under the auspices of the Fish and Wildlife Service) should create an Environmental Flow Program that offers the assistance needed to establish environmental flows for all major river systems in the United States. States would maintain primary authority over water rights and allocation by retaining the autonomy to choose how to achieve appropriate flow levels. The Environmental Flow Program would provide a clearinghouse of information and technical assistance to help address the common challenges that states face in setting and enforcing instream flows, including using scientifically defensible methods for setting instream flows and creating adequate measurement programs to monitor flows. Federal funds are currently available to states through the Fish and Wildlife Service; these funds should be directed toward the development and implementation of action plans to achieve environmental flows.[4] This will help target these grants toward coordinated, ecosystem-oriented projects rather than the current piecemeal system. In addition, where endangered species are present, states can apply to the Cooperative Endangered Species Conservation Fund.[5]

Designating Wild and Scenic Rivers

In 1968, the Wild and Scenic Rivers Act was passed into law. At the time, the legislation included eight rivers; today the Wild and Scenic Rivers System includes more than 200 rivers. The act has several provisions to protect instream flows, including a direct ban on dams and other projects licensed under the Federal Power Act that would have a "direct and adverse" effect on the river's free-flowing character, water quality, or outstanding values. In addition, Wild and Scenic Rivers undergo a multistakeholder planning process to create a management plan. The act also indicates the availability of federal water rights necessary to accomplish the purposes of the act (reserved rights).

BOX 6.1.

OREGON AND NEBRASKA'S INSTREAM FLOW PROGRAMS

Oregon has the oldest instream flow programs of any state; legislation allowing for the establishment of minimum flows was first passed in 1955. Nearly 550 flows were set under this law, but the program was largely ineffective because the state had the discretion to not enforce the minimum flows (Neuman, Squier, and Achterman 2006; B. Hunter, staff attorney, Oregon Water Watch, pers. comm. October 20, 2010). The minimum streamflow program was essentially replaced in 1987 by the enactment of Oregon's landmark Instream Water Right Act (ORS 537.332 to 537.360), which converted all established minimum flows into instream rights to be held in trust by the state. The instream rights maintained the original priority date and were given the same legal status as other water rights. In addition, the Instream Water Right Act defined instream uses as beneficial uses and authorized the Oregon Department of Fish and Wildlife, the Oregon Department of Environmental Quality, and Oregon State Parks and Recreation Department to apply for instream water rights to support fish and wildlife, ecological values, recreation, scenic attraction, navigation, and pollution abatement.

A major challenge for instream flow protection in Oregon is that instream water rights are often junior to other rights. In most Oregon rivers, all of a river's flow and sometimes more than a river's average annual flow, was appropriated well before 1955 and certainly before 1987 (B. Hunter, pers. comm. October 20, 2010). To address this issue, the Oregon Instream Water Right Act included provisions that allow for the transfer by purchase, lease, or gift of out-of-stream senior water rights to instream water rights with the priority date of the original water right. Under this provision, some 300 instream leases, transfers, and allocations have restored a total flow of approximately 1,700 cubic feet per second. Of these, 61 transfers accounting for 285 cubic feet per second are permanent, and more than 70 percent of these transfers are senior rights that predate 1909 (OWRD 2009). Enforcement is an additional challenge. Staff and financial resources are required to monitor streamflows and regulate junior water users to meet the flows, and protection of instream flows is not always a priority for the state. In addition, the actual measurement of water diversions is required for only 8 percent of combined surface and groundwater rights holders as of 2003 (Pilz 2006). The lack of monitoring is one of the main hurdles in protecting streamflows nationwide.

In comparison, Nebraska's instream flow legislation is among the most narrow and restrictive of all state instream flow laws, while also arguably more scientifically defensible. The negative effects of water pumping and diversions in Nebraska became obvious in 1976, when segments of 21 streams in the northeastern part of the state went totally dry (Zuerlein 2007). Legislation was passed in 1984 authorizing Nebraska's Department of Game and Parks to appropriate water rights for instream flows. Water can be appropriated by the Department of Game and Parks for fish and wildlife or recreational uses, but several conditions must be met to ensure that an instream appropriation has a clear public benefit. First, appropriations can be for an amount no greater than is necessary for the specified use, and this amount must be quantified by studies before the Department of Game and Parks applies for water rights. In the case of Platte River and Long Pine Creek, habitat simulation models were used to simulate a relationship between streamflow and physical habitat for various life stages of a species. Additionally, there must be enough unappropriated water available for the minimum needs of the use at the time of the application. Finally, unlike many other states, a cost-benefit analysis must be conducted and appropriations must be reviewed every 15 years to ensure they continue to be in the public interest.

The major successes and challenges of Nebraska's instream flow program stand in contrast to Oregon's program. Unlike Oregon's approach of acquiring instream rights regardless of addressing a specific ecosystem need, Nebraska has used more scientifically defensible, habitat-based methods to determine instream flow quantities and timing. However, implementation of Nebraska's program has been very limited, largely because of the rigor and expense of the required process. As of 2008, only about 2 percent (247 miles) of Nebraska's rivers and streams have been protected under the act (Zellmer 2006). Additionally, although individuals are permitted to change the purpose of their water rights to instream flow, the implications of doing so are unclear, and many fear that their water rights may be permanently lost if dedicated to instream flow (Zellmer 2006).

Wild and Scenic River designation under the Wild and Scenic River Act have proven to have a wide variety of benefits for instream flows and beyond. According to a report by American Rivers (McGrath 2009), the Deschutes Wild and Scenic River management plan provided a forum for 17 agencies to coordinate their monitoring efforts. In addition, the leverage provided by Wild and Scenic River designation helped the Forest Service and the county to adopt a coordinated bioengineering approach to streambed restoration.

More generally, Wild and Scenic River designations have been found to bring greater public awareness and appreciation of local river systems (McGrath 2009). Often the designation leads to increased funding for river protection, restoration, and management. For example, the Skagit River in Oregon was designated a Wild and Scenic River in 1978, and this played a key role in attracting more funding for land-acquisition and restoration projects and increasing public awareness about the special nature of the Skagit system (McGrath 2009).

Clearly, the Wild and Scenic River designation provides greater protection of instream flows and can lead to a variety of additional benefits. However, the designation requires approval by Congress, a state legislature, or the secretary of the Interior if requested by the governor of the state concerned. There are several rivers currently under study for potential designation: Eight Mile River in Connecticut; Lower Farmington River and Salmon Brook in Massachusetts; and the Missiquoi and Trout Rivers in Vermont. However, there are hundreds, if not thousands, of river segments in the United States still eligible for designation. In order for these waterways to be protected, the secretary of the

Interior could make a concerted effort to work with governors in states with particularly valuable river systems to bring them under the act.

Improving interstate compacts

Political boundaries and watershed boundaries rarely coincide, leading to growing political disputes over water management. In the continental United States, 48 states share hundreds of watersheds. In the 20th century, political disputes among the states over water were infrequent. By the end of the century, however, new conflicts flared between Alabama, Georgia, and Florida over the Apalachicola-Chattahoochee-Flint River system; between the states that share the Ogallala Aquifer in the Great Plains; and between Oregon and California over the Klamath River, to name a few.

Today, there are almost 20 interstate compacts in force in the United States. These compacts are often necessary to address disputes over water boundaries and uses and a number of them offer instream flow protections. When such disputes cannot be resolved by the states themselves, federal involvement may be necessary. Many states with transboundary waters have chosen to enter into compacts, ratified by Congress or the Supreme Court. For example, the Great Lakes–St. Lawrence River Basin Water Resources Compact, commonly known as the Great Lakes Compact, is intended to provide a forum and process with which these separate entities can collaborate to sustainably manage their shared water resources. The compact is composed of eight states (Illinois, Indiana, Michigan, Minnesota, New York, Ohio, Pennsylvania, and Wisconsin), and two Canadian provinces (Ontario and Quebec). Initially voluntary and nonbinding, at the turn of the 21st century, the Great Lakes governors and premiers of Ontario and Quebec signed "Annex 1" to the original 1985 Great Lakes Charter, which agreed to establish a legally binding agreement for management of basin waters.

The new compact is intended to develop management plans for the basin and implement ways to solve the problems related to water resources in the basin. Stipulations include a ban of diversions outside the basin and a regulatory standard that prohibits individual withdrawals of more than 100,000 gallons per day. The compact is responsible for ensuring that policy decisions on water management are informed by the best scientific data possible. The compact has been widely supported and lauded for providing a sustainable and collaborative approach to managing shared water resources. Many argue that this style of management provides much better opportunity to address concerns of sustainability.

Interstate compacts are an important governance framework for shared water resources. In many cases, conflicts will worsen in the coming decades due to rising demands on increasingly uncertain freshwater supplies. There are several regions where conflict is already apparent, such as the Ogalla High Plains Aquifer (see chapter 2: Legal and Institutional Framework of Water Management) and the Apalachicola–Chattahoochee–Flint River Basin (see chapter 8: Water and Agriculture). In these instances, and many others, federal leadership would be particularly useful to encourage more sustainable water management planning. The federal government could take a much more active role in coordinating and enforcing interstate compacts around shared water resources, as it did in the creation of the Chesapeake Bay Commission (see chapter 2: Legal and Institutional Framework of Water Management).

ECONOMIC TOOLS AND FINANCIAL INCENTIVES
Water pricing

The price of water can have an important impact on its use. The federal government sets the price for water delivered via federal water projects. Given that the Bureau of Reclamation provides water to one out of every five farmers in the western United States, this rate-setting authority can have widespread implications. At the turn of the 20th century, the Bureau of Reclamation was created to build water projects that were to be repaid without interest, establishing an enormous indirect subsidy and contributing to extremely low water prices for many bureau water users (see chapter 8: Water and Agriculture for a more detailed discussion).

One of the bureau's most extensive water projects is the Central Valley Project, which dams water in Northern California and transports it through a series of pumps and canals to drier Southern California. Although the project allowed irrigated agriculture to thrive, it came at a cost. According to the Bureau of Reclamation, Central Valley Project operations caused populations of many native fish species to decline significantly and it is estimated that flood control projects and land-use conversions destroyed 95 percent of the wetland habitats that existed in the Central Valley at statehood (USBR 2005).

At the end of the 20th century, the Central Valley Project Improvement Act was passed by Congress, which amended previous legislation to include fish and wildlife protection, restoration, enhancement, and mitigation as purposes having equal priority with power generation and irrigation and domestic water supply. In addition, the act specifically directed the bureau to reformulate its water-rate structures to encourage water conservation through tiered prices that increase with greater water use. Finally, the act created a restoration fund financed by Central Valley Project water and energy costs.

In the 21st century, many more federal water projects should reformulate their water-rate structures to encourage water conservation and efficiency. In addition, the federal government should consider a public goods surcharge on federal water and energy users to reinvest in restoration, particularly where federal water projects have led to the destruction of critical habitats for aquatic species and to species declines or extinction.

Water markets and transfers

In the last two decades, market-based mechanisms that transfer water through either the sale or lease of water rights have been used to reallocate water among users and, on occasion, to restore and protect instream flows. Based on data from both the *Water Strategist* and *Water Intelligence* between 1987 and 2008, there were just over 400 sales and leases of water rights in the western states (figure 6.6).[6] The vast majority of transactions to enhance environmental flows were sales or leases of agricultural water rights.

Many groups are involved in purchasing water for instream flows, including the federal government, states, and private organizations (table 6.1). In the Pacific Northwest, the Bureau of Reclamation accounted for just over 80 percent of all expenditures on water sales and leases and 90 percent of the total quantity of water acquired between 1990 and 1997 (Landry and Peck 1998). The bureau is actively purchasing water for instream flows in Idaho, California, and Washington.

In the Pacific Northwest, the Columbia Basin Water Transactions Program has brokered over 200 water transactions (A. Purkey, director of the Columbia Basin Water Transactions Program, pers. comm., October 23, 2008). Whereas the majority of these are short-term leases of water rights, close to 60 have been permanent purchases or long-term leases. According to the director, the Columbia Basin Water Transactions Program's success has been largely due to funding from the Bonneville Power Administration, required for mitigation of the federal hydropower project's impact to endangered fish species protected by the ESA, and to working within an adjudicated basin where water rights have been clearly delineated.

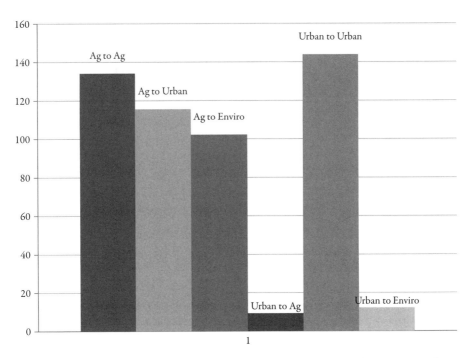

FIGURE 6.6. Water transfers by source and destination within the 12 western states between 1987 and 2008
Source: Based on the Water Transfers Database maintained by the Bren School at the University of California, Santa Barbara (2011).

Market-based mechanisms have been used to protect instream flows in several other states as well. In Montana, a state-run water leasing program forged an unlikely partnership between environmental and agricultural interests as farmers throughout the region received more than $10 million for 490,000 acre-feet of agricultural water that was then allocated to instream flows (Landry and Peck 1998). In Washington, the state Department of Ecology launched a water acquisition program in collaboration with the Washington Water Trust, which increased instream flows in 16 watersheds with vulnerable salmon and trout populations. Between 2000 and 2003, the program completed 80 temporary or permanent direct transfers, representing 9,304 acre-feet of water per year at a cost of about $2 million. In California, Trout Unlimited recently launched the California Water Initiative, which includes a private water acquisition program and American Rivers is developing the Sierra Water Trust.

Market-based mechanisms offer some advantages over regulatory solutions. For example, they usually rely on existing institutions and legal mechanisms, and they can circumvent contentious struggles over water allocation because they are voluntary. However, they also have some significant limitations. In a perfect market, demand and supply determine price, and resources are efficiently allocated to their highest value use. Unfortunately, water markets are imperfect, transaction costs can be high, prices rarely reflect noneconomic values such as ecosystem services and cultural, historical, or aesthetic value, and water is not easily transferred from one physical location to another (Brewer et al. 2007; Howitt and Hanak 2005; Dellapenna 2000). In addition, market-based mechanisms are limited in their ability to restore key aspects of a natural flow regime, such as providing particular magnitude flows at particular times, because they are often working within existing water-rights systems, which permit diversions for extended time periods, such as over an entire water year or growing season.

TABLE 6.1.

Market-Based Instream Flow Protection by Federal, State, and Private Interests in the Pacific Northwest between 1990 and 1997

	Federal	State	Private
Lease expenditures	$26,745,410	$3,684,619	$96,482
Purchase expenditures	$5,038,975	$702,200	$61,700
Total expenditures	*$31,784,385*	*$4,386,819*	*$158,182*
Lease quantity (AF)	1,563,088	111,672	22,083
Purchase quantity (AF)	57,396	10,000	507
Donation quantity (AF)	0	18,000	13,756
Total quantity	*1,620,484*	*140,049*	*36,347*

Note: AF = acre-foot.

Source: Water Strategist and Water Intelligence (1987–2008)

In coming years, market-based mechanisms will continue to be used in a limited fashion, particularly in adjudicated basins and small streams with only a few diverters where water rights are fairly clear and uses can be easily monitored. But a significant expansion of market-based mechanisms will require more information about ecosystems water needs (discussed previously), improved monitoring and enforcement of instream rights, and federal guidance on standard practices for defining and applying market tools.

TECHNOLOGY AND MANAGEMENT IMPROVEMENTS

Changing dam operations

Dams have a number of adverse impacts on aquatic ecosystems including altering flow regimes, modifying sediment availability and distribution, changing water temperature, and impeding fish passage. The federal government owns and operates nearly 2,000 dams. Many have a set of operating rules for how much water gets released and when. An option for providing reliable instream flows for ecosystems is designing and implementing new operations and management criteria for federal dams.[7]

General principles for operating federal facilities are found in umbrella statutes and in authorizing legislation for specific projects, such as the Reclamation Act of 1902 and the Water Resources Development Acts that are passed every two years or so. Project purposes often include flood control, irrigation, municipal and industrial water supply, navigation, and hydropower, but rarely do they include fish and wildlife. Congress, typically, has not assigned priorities among these uses, leaving it to the operating agencies to determine the precise balance of uses (Gillilan and Brown 1997). Policy changes that direct these agencies to give greater priority to environmental flows could prove effective at helping restore aquatic ecosystems.

In 2002, the Army Corps of Engineers and The Nature Conservancy entered into a partnership, known as the Sustainable Rivers Project, to examine ways to manage the Army Corps dams to reduce their environmental impacts while maintaining social benefits (TNC 2008). These projects involve multiple agencies and stakeholders in an adaptive management planning process for defining environmental flows and dam operations. Projects have been initiated on 11 rivers (TNC 2008),[8] following a pilot project on the Green River (see box 6.2: Dam reoperation efforts).

In the coming years, more and more federal dam relicensing efforts offer the opportunity to redress past ecosystem damages and improve future river health, but such efforts will have to be carefully planned and implemented. Hydropower operators worry about loss of revenue or power generation and their concerns need to be addressed. In some cases, it is difficult to release adequate water from dams to mimic natural hydrologic variability, particularly if it may cause flooding in developed areas. In addition, the majority of dams built in the United States were authorized for multiple purposes; thus, without changes to these individual authorizations, dam reoperation may be confined to small changes in the timing and magnitude of releases in order to continue to provide the multiple, stated project benefits.

New legislation should require that environmental flow requirements be given equal consideration with other project purposes, similar to the 1986 amendments to the Federal Power Act that gave habitat conservation goals "equal consideration" with power and development interests. In addition, federal agencies should institute a program of periodic review of dam operations to make recommendations to Congress about changing authorized purposes where appropriate and necessary. Richter and Thomas (2007) have developed an assessment framework to evaluate the benefits that might be restored through dam reoperation. This assessment begins by characterizing the dam's effects on the river flow regime and formulating hypotheses about the ecological and social benefits that might be restored by releasing water from the dam in a manner that more closely resembles natural flow patterns.

BOX 6.2.

DAM REOPERATION EFFORTS

On the Green River, The Nature Conservancy and the Army Corps of Engineers used computer models to create a management plan for the Green River Dam in Kentucky that more closely mimicked natural flow patterns (TNC nd). The project has shown some positive preliminary effects on ecosystems. After a three-year period of managing the dams to better mimic natural flow regimes, some plant and animal species, including endangered species of mussel, showed signs of recovery (Turner and Byron 2006). Similarly, on the Bill Williams River in Arizona, local governments, state agencies, the Bureau of Land Management, USGS, and the US Fish and Wildlife Service worked together with TNC and the Army Corps to define ecosystem flows, and they have begun experimental flood releases to test the river ecosystem's response to floods of various magnitudes, duration, and timing (A. Hautzinger, US Fish and Wildlife Service, pers. comm. October 27, 2008). Revegetation of the floodplain by cottonwood was achieved in 2005 after releases of water from the Alamo Dam were made later than normal in order to spread cottonwood seeds (Hautzinger, pers. comm. October 27, 2008). These examples demonstrate positive impacts even where only a few components of the natural flow regime can be restored.

In many cases, dam reoperation was initiated too recently to show conclusive results as to its effectiveness in restoring aquatic ecosystems, but preliminary analyses show positive impacts on some species and indicators of ecosystem health. The Tennessee Valley Authority, for example, initiated a Reservoir Releases Improvement Program in 1991. The Tennessee Valley Authority operates a system of 49 dams and reservoirs on the Tennessee River and its tributaries, which have traditionally caused low flows and low dissolved oxygen levels below the dams. Both structural and management changes have resulted in increased dissolved oxygen, higher minimum streamflows, and increased macroinvertebrate family richness (number of families), whereas the percentage of macroinvertebrates tolerant of poor water quality decreased. These results all indicate improved ecological integrity (Bednarek and Hart 2005).

Removing unsafe dams

In a surprising about-face, a nation that has been focused for decades on building dams has now begun dismantling them. According to the National Inventory of Dams, more than half of the nation's dams are now at or beyond their expected lifetimes (figure 6.7) and will need to be reinforced or removed in the coming years (Aspen Institute 2002). Due to growing pressure from conservation groups, fishermen, tribes, and state and federal agencies, more dams are now being considered for removal than are being built. In the United States, more than 600 dams have been removed to date (American Rivers 2011b).

Dam removal may improve the health of aquatic ecosystems by restoring natural flows to a river, removing barriers to fish movement, reestablishing healthy river habitats for fish and wildlife, exposing submerged river rapids and riverside lands, and improving water quality. Dam removal may also provide social benefits by eliminating safety hazards, providing river recreation opportunities such as fishing and boating, revitalizing community riverfronts, or providing mitigation for the continued operation or building of other dams. Furthermore, dam removal may provide economic benefits by avoiding costs associated with dam safety improvements and environmental impact mitigation and by generating revenue associated with the social benefits of a restored river (Aspen Institute 2002).

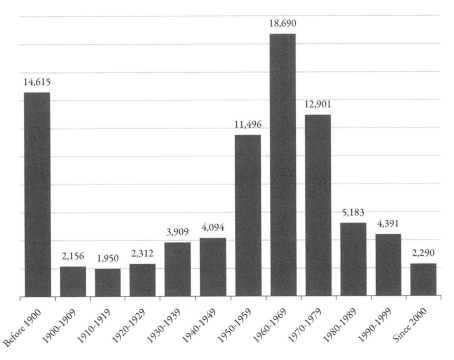

FIGURE 6.7. Dams by completion date
Source: USACE (2011).

One example of this trend is the Elwha River in Washington state (figure 6.8). The Lower Elwha Klallam Tribe, which has lived along the Elwha River for almost three millennia, has consistently objected to the damming of the river by the Elwha and Glines Canyon dams. In 2000, the federal government purchased both dams from Fort James Corporation for $29.5 million and began to consider their removal (American Rivers 2011a). The groundbreaking Elwha Report, submitted by the secretary of the Interior, determined that removing the dams was feasible and necessary to fully restore the fisheries and ecosystem. Removing both dams would open over 70 miles of pristine salmon habitat. The Park Service has since developed the Elwha River Restoration project, which aims to restore natural flows critical to many aquatic species. For instance, anadromous fish such as salmon historically migrated along the Elwha in response to flows of particular magnitudes at particular times.

The project will also remove physical barriers to fish migration, allowing endangered salmon species to once again reach upstream habitat and spawning grounds. A restored, free-flowing river could produce approximately 390,000 salmon and steelhead in about 30 years, compared with less than 50,000 fish if the dams were simply retrofit with upstream and downstream fish passage facilities. In addition, the November 1996 Final Environmental Impact Study found that dam removal would produce significant economic benefits, estimated at $164 million over the 100 years, through increased recreation,

FIGURE 6.8. The Elwha Dam in Washington, removal is scheduled to begin in 2011
Source: Photo courtesy of USGS.

tourism, and sport fishing, and not including additional, albeit hard-to-quantify, benefits from a wide range of cultural, spiritual, recreational, and quality-of-life values. Recently, the project received federal stimulus funding and the demolition of both dams is scheduled to begin in 2011.

In the coming years, improvements will be necessary in the federal approach to managing and evaluating dams, with a focus on more effective consideration of the dam removal option. Until dam removal is considered on an equal basis with other river restoration options, and until dam removal tools are explicitly considered in all federal dam projects, this tool will be underused and underappreciated.

Conclusions

Although there has been significant progress in terms of improving water quality in the United States since the beginning of the 20th century, the health of aquatic ecosystems has continued to decline. The federal CWA's mandate and other official federal objectives include restoring and maintaining the chemical, physical, and biological integrity of the nation's waters; however, there has been a lack of federal leadership in protecting freshwater ecosystems. National assessments of aquatic ecosystems indicate that nearly half of the nation's total stream length is in poor condition. Though there are numerous factors leading to the decline of freshwater ecosystems, alterations of the flow regimes of rivers, withdrawals of water, and degradation of water quality are all key threats. There is a growing consensus within the scientific community that in order to preserve and restore freshwater ecosystems and the essential goods and services that they provide, we need to mimic components of natural flow variability, protect water quality, and restore other components of aquatic ecosystem function (Richter et al. 1996; Poff et al. 1997; Lytle and Poff 2004; Arthington et al. 2006).

This chapter argues that in order to meet 21st-century water challenges, there is a clear role for the federal government to play in guiding and facilitating states' efforts to balance human and ecosystem water needs. Congress already has substantial authority to act to protect the integrity of the nation's waters, but they have so far failed to act effectively to protect our nation's beleaguered aquatic ecosystems. The potential policy solutions provided herein offer a variety of approaches, from collecting better data, to changing legislation or enforcing existing legislation, to using market-based mechanisms, to improving technology and management. These approaches can be applied without compromising state sovereignty over water allocation. The current condition of the water resources in the United States demonstrates the urgent need for federal leadership to improve water management. The most promising opportunities for federal intervention to improve and protect the nation's waters include investing in the collection of basic hydrologic data, bringing environmental flows under existing regulatory frameworks (e.g., the CWA), assisting states in determining and enforcing environmental flows, designating additional wild and scenic rivers, co-ordinating interstate compacts to better manage shared waters, seizing new economic opportunities to permit markets and prices to help reallocate water among users, and, finally, removing unsafe infrastructure and reoperating federal infrastructure to protect aquatic ecosystems.

References

Adler, J. H. 2002. "Fables of the Cuyahoga: Reconstructing a History of Environmental Protection." *Fordham Environmental Law Journal* 14: 89–146.

Adler, R. W. 2003. "The Two Lost Books in the Water Quality Trilogy: The Elusive Objectives of Physical and Biological Integrity." *Environmental Law* 33 (1):29–77.

American Rivers. 2011a. "Elwha River Restoration." American Rivers. http://www.americanrivers.org/our-work/restoring-rivers/dams/projects/elwha-river-tbackground.html.

American Rivers. 2011b. "2011 Dam Removal Resource Guide." American Rivers. http://www.americanrivers.org/our-work/restoring-rivers/dams/projects/2011-dam-removal-resource-guide.html.

Andreen, W. L., and S. C. Jones. 2008. *The Clean Water Act: A Blueprint for Reform*. Washington, DC: Center for Progressive Reform.

Arthington, A. H., S. E. Bunn, N. L. Poff, and R. J. Naiman. 2006. "The Challenge of Providing Environmental Flow Rules to Sustain River Ecosystems." *Ecological Applications* 16: 1311–1318.

Aspen Institute. 2002. *Dam Removal: A New Option for a New Century*. Washington, DC: Aspen Institute. http://www.aspeninstitute.org/policy-work/energy-environment/our-policy-work/dialogue-dams-rivers.

Bednarek, A. T., and D. D. Hart. 2005. "Modifying Dam Operations to Restore Rivers: Ecological Responses to Tennessee River Dam Mitigation." *Ecological Applications* 15 (3): 997–1008.

Bren School, University of California, Santa Barbara. 2011. "California Water Transfer Records." Excel database, available online. http://www.bren.ucsb.edu/news/water_transfers.htm.

Brewer, J., R. Glennon, A. Ker, and G. D. Libecap. 2007. "Water Markets in the West: Prices, Trading, and Contractual Forms." Arizona Legal Studies Discussion Paper No. 07-07, University of Arizona, Tuscon. http://ssrn.com/abstract=964819.

Brooks, D. B., O. M. Brandes, and S. Gurman. 2009. *Making the Most of the Water We Have: The Soft Path Approach to Water Management*. London: Earthscan.

"A California Fish Kill Causes Pollution Worry." 1968. *New York Times*, July 2, 15.

Costanza, R. et al. 1997. "The Value of the World's Ecosystem Services and Natural Capital." *Nature* 387: 253–260.

Dellapenna, J. W. 2000. "The Importance of Getting Names Right: The Myth of Markets for Water." *William and Mary Environmental Law and Policy Review* 25 (2): 317–377.

Evans, J. W., and R. H. England. 1995. *A Recommended Method to Protect Instream Flows in Georgia*. Social Circle, GA: Georgia Department of Natural Resources, Wildlife Resources Division. http://www.georgiawildlife.org/node/722.

Gillilan, D. M., and T. C. Brown. 1997. *Instream Flow Protection: Seeking a Balance in Western Water Use*. Covelo, CA: Island Press.

Graves, A. 1963. "Mystery Fishkill Clogs Bay Waters." *The Washington Post, Times Herald*. August 18, E1.

Howitt, R., and E. Hanak. 2005. "Incremental Water Market Development: The California Water Sector 1985–2004." *Canadian Water Resources Journal* 30 (1): 73–82.

"Huge Fish Kill Blamed on Chemical Dumping." 1970. *Los Angeles Times*, November 11, A2A.

Jelks, H. L., S. J. Walsh, N. M. Burkhead, S. Contreras-Balderas, E. Díaz-Pardo, D. A. Hendrickson, J. Lyons, et al. 2008. "Conservation Status of Imperiled North American Freshwater and Diadromous Fishes." *Fisheries* 33 (8): 372–406.

Karr, J. R. 1991. "Biological Integrity: A Long-Neglected Aspect of Water Resource Management." *Ecological Applications* 1 (1): 66–84.

Kenny, J. F., N. L. Barber, S. S. Hutson, K. S. Linsey, J. K. Lovelace, and M. A. Maupin. 2009. *Estimated Use of Water in the United States in 2005*. US Geological Survey Circular 1344. Reston, VA: US Geological Survey. http://pubs.usgs.gov/circ/1344/pdf/c1344.pdf.

Landry, C. J., and C. Peck. 1998. "Western States Are Creating Water Markets without Compromising the Prior Appropriation Doctrine." *Montana Farmer-Stockman*, December. http://www.waterexchange.com/UserFiles/File/WesternstatesarecreatingwatermarketsbyLandry1998.pdf.

Leavitt, C. 2007. *Troubled Waters: An Analysis of 2005 Clean Water Act Compliance*. Washington, DC: US PIRG Education Fund, 10.

Lytle, D. A., and N. L. Poff. 2004. "Adaptation to Natural Flow Regimes." *Trends in Ecology and Evolution* 19 (2): 94–100.

Mathews, R. 2006. "Instream Flow Protection and Restoration: Setting a New Compass Point." *Environmental Law* 36 (4): 1311–1329

Maunder, D., and B. Hindley. 2005. "Establishing Environmental Flow Requirements: Synthesis Report." Conservation Ontario. http://conservation-ontario.on.ca/projects/flow.html.

McGrath, A. 2009. "Beyond Banning Dams: Benefits of Wild and Scenic River Designation for Northwest and National River Systems." American Rivers. http://www.americanrivers.org/assets/pdfs/dam-removal-docs/beyond-banning-dams.pdf.

National Research Council. 2001. *Assessing the TMDL Approach to Water Quality Management*. Washington, DC: National Academies Press.

Natural Resources Defense Council, et al. v. Kempthorne, Findings of Fact and Conclusions of Law Re Interim Remedies Re: Delta Smelt ESA Remand and Reconsultation, United States District Court, Eastern District of California, 1:05-cv-1207 OWW GSA, 2007.

Neuman, J., A. Squier, and G.l Achterman. 2006. "Sometimes a Great Notion: Oregon's Instream Flow Experiments." *Environmental Law* 36: 1125–1156.

Oregon Water Resources Department (OWRD). 2009. "Instream Accomplishments." Fact sheet. Oregon Water Resources Department, Salem. http://www1.wrd.state.or.us/pdfs/2009_Instream_Accomplishments.pdf.

Pilz, R. D. 2006. "At the Confluence: Oregon's Instream Water Rights Law in Theory and Practice." *Environmental Law* 36 (4): 1383–1420.

Poff, N. L., J. D. Allan, M. B. Bain, J. R. Karr, K. L. Prestegaard, B. D. Richter, R. E. Sparks, and J. C. Stromberg. 1997. "The Natural Flow Regime: A Paradigm for River Conservation and Restoration." *BioScience* 47 (11): 769–784.

Poff, N. L., J. D. Olden, D. M. Merritt, and D. M. Pepin. 2007. "Homogenization of Regional River Dynamics by Dams and Global Biodiversity Implications." *Proceedings of the National Academy of Sciences USA* 104(14): 5732–5737.

Postel, S., and B. Richter. 2003. *Rivers for Life: Managing Water for People and Nature*. Covelo, CA: Island Press.

Ricciardi, A., and J. B. Rasmussen. 1999. "Extinction Rates of North American Freshwater Fauna." *Conservation Biology* 13 (5): 1220–1222.

Richter, B. D., and G. A. Thomas. 2007. "Restoring Environmental Flows by Modifying Dam Operations." *Ecology and Society* 12 (1): 12. http://www.ecologyandsociety.org/vol12/iss1/art12/.

Richter, B. D., J. V. Baumgartner, J. Powell, and D. P. Braun. 1996. "A Method for Assessing Hydrologic Alteration within Ecosystems." *Conservation Biology* 10 (4): 1163–1174.

The Nature Conservancy (TNC). 2008. "Sustainable Rivers Project." The Nature Conservancy. http://www.nature.org/ourinitiatives/habitats/riverslakes/sustainable-rivers-project.xml.

———. nd. "Green River: Southeastern United States." The Nature Conservancy. http://www.nature.org/ourinitiatives/regions/northamerica/unitedstates/kentucky/placesweprotect/green-river.xml.

Turner, W. M., and W. J. Byron. 2006. "Green River Lake: Pilot Project for Sustainable Rivers." In *Operating Reservoirs in Changing Conditions—Proceedings of the Operations Management 2006 Conference*. Edited by D. Zimbelman and W. C. Loehlein, 129–138. Sacramento, CA: American Society of Civil Engineers.

US Army Corps of Engineers (USACE). 2011. "National Inventory of Dams." CorpsMap. http://geo.usace.army.mil/pgis/f?p=397:5:3729961107976069:NO.

US Bureau of Reclamation (USBR). 2005. *10 Years of Progress: Central Valley Project Improvement Act*. Title 34, P.L. 102-575. Sacramento, CA: US Department of the Interior, Bureau of Reclamation, US Fish and Wildlife Service. http://www.usbr.gov/mp/cvpia/docs_reports/docs/cvpia_10yr_progress_final_summ_rpt.pdf.

US Environmental Protection Agency (EPA). 2006. *Wadeable Streams Assessment: A Collaborative Survey of the Nation's Streams*. EPA 841-B-06-002. Washington, DC: EPA Office of Research and Development, Office of Water.www.epa.gov/owow/streamsurvey.

US Geological Survey (USGS). 2009. "Number of USGS Streamgages through Time." USGS. http://water.usgs.gov/nsip/history1.html.

———. 2010. "USGS National Streamflow Information Program: Number of USGS Streamgages through Time." USGS. http://water.usgs.gov/nsip/history1.html.

———. 2011. "National Streamflow Information Program." USGS. http://water.usgs.gov/nsip.

Zellmer, S. 2006. "Instream Flow Legislation." Faculty Publications from the Water Center, University of Nebraska, Lincoln. http://digitalcommons.unl.edu/cgi/viewcontent.cgi?article=1004&context=watercenterpubs.

Zuerlein, G. 2007. "Remember Our Rivers! An Overview of Instream Flows in Nebraska." *Prairie Fire: The Progressive Voice of the Great Plains*, August. http://www.prairiefirenewspaper.com/2007/08/remember-our-rivers.

7

MUNICIPAL WATER USE

Heather Cooley

Introduction

The United States has a remarkably sophisticated and well-developed municipal water system that provides high-quality, reliable water supply and wastewater services to the vast majority of Americans. It was not always this way. In the mid-1800s, most big American cities lacked any kind of comprehensive water delivery infrastructure and struggled to provide safe water to the public. As urban centers were growing rapidly and the Industrial Revolution was gathering speed, thousands of people still died each year from water-related diseases such as cholera and typhoid, largely because of the contamination of drinking water and wide exposure to contaminated wastewater. In 1832, cholera reached New York from Europe and killed over 3,500 people in a city with a population of only 250,000—with today's population, that would be equivalent to more than 100,000. In the 1840s, the disease surged back and forth across Asia, killing tens of thousands at a time, and ships once again carried the disease across the Atlantic to the New World, through the ports of New York and New Orleans. Thousands more died in New York and New Orleans and cholera traveled up the Mississippi River Valley spreading by boat to villages and towns. Ten thousand people died in St. Louis and Chicago, and the disease moved out along the Oregon Trail to the west, where it merged with more cholera brought down by fur traders from Russia through Alaska. President James Polk is reported to have contracted cholera while in New Orleans in 1849, and he died of the disease just a few months after leaving office (Rosenberg 1987; Gleick 2010).

At that time, leading doctors and scientists could not agree on how people were getting ill or the best ways of preventing transmission of most diseases. The sciences of bacteriology, epidemiology, and immunology were rudimentary, and we did not know whether cholera was transmitted through the air as a contagious mist, or miasma, or, as we now know, through contaminated water. By the end of the 19th century, however, science and medicine learned more about the sources and prevention of water-related diseases, and a revolution in thinking about water swept through the rapidly industrializing world, leading to sewage systems, innovative water treatment, new piping and distribution investments, and efforts to clean up and protect drinking water sources.

By the turn of the 20th century, typhoid, cholera, and water-related diarrheal diseases still caused 200 out of every 100,000 deaths, but things were beginning to change. New technology for water filtration and purification was being developed, and new institutional approaches were being tried. After extensive efforts by private investors and companies to develop municipal water systems largely failed, public agencies stepped in and built comprehensive water-treatment and distribution systems, with funding from low-cost, tax-free municipal bonds. In late September 1908, Jersey City, New Jersey, became the first major US city to chlorinate its drinking water in an effort to reduce typhoid and cholera rates. The health benefits were immediate and other cities rapidly followed suit. By 1920, most US cities were filtering and chlorinating municipal supplies. Demographers David Cutler and Grant Miller argue that these innovations in the provision of clean drinking water led to the most rapid improvements in the nation's health ever achieved. They estimate that half of the entire decline in urban death rates and three-quarters of the drop in infant mortality from 1900 to 1940 resulted from improved water quality. Perhaps even more important, the dramatic drop in illness almost certainly contributed to the increase in labor productivity, industrial output, and school attendance that occurred at the beginning of the 20th century and helped the United States become the dominant industrial power of the time (Cutler and Miller 2005). By the middle of the century, water-related diseases had dropped by over 95 percent and have continued to decline (figure 7.1).

Today, US municipalities have some of the safest and most reliable water resource systems in the world, providing low-cost water and sanitation services to the vast majority of the nation's population. But even though traditional water-related diseases have largely disappeared, there are still some important, serious, and growing challenges facing the nation's towns and cities. Pipes laid down a century ago are deteriorating. Infrastructure spending is failing to keep up with need. New contaminants pose health and safety concerns and undermine public trust in the safety of the nation's tap water. And a combination of urban and rural development, climate changes, and old-style institutions undermine our sense of water security.

This chapter reviews some of these challenges. Historical approaches to solving such problems typically relied on building massive, centralized infrastructure. However, experience has shown that these solutions also entailed significant and often unexpected social

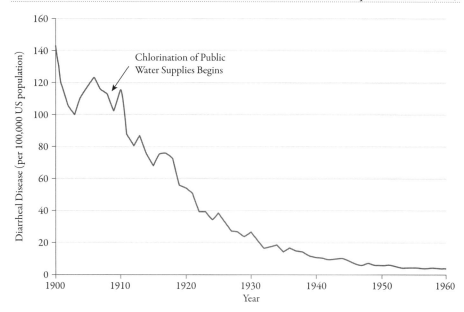

FIGURE 7.1. US deaths from diarrheal disease, 1900–1960
Sources: Vital Statistics of the United States (1945, 1963).

and environmental costs; thus this chapter explores alternative approaches for addressing these concerns, including *soft path* tools and policies that may be especially valuable for moving to a more sustainable water system. The chapter concludes with a series of recommendations on strategies the federal government can take to facilitate these changes.

Municipal Water Use

Municipal water use refers to water withdrawn to meet the needs of people in cities, towns, and small communities. This includes water used in homes for both indoor and outdoor purposes, including cleaning, bathing, cooking, and maintaining gardens and landscapes, as well as commercial and industrial water used to produce the goods and services society desires. Municipal water use also includes water used by institutions, such as schools, municipalities, prisons, and government agencies, as well as water losses due to system leakage, theft, hydrant flushing, and unmetered connections. Such losses are typically about 10 to 15 percent of total withdrawals, although losses can exceed 25 percent of total water use in older systems. Municipal water use in the United States totals about 80 billion gallons each day, or around 20 percent of overall national water use (Kenny et al. 2009) (figure 7.2). This estimate includes self-supplied water for residential and industrial purposes (see box 7.1 for additional discussion on self-supplied water use).

During much of the 20th century, municipal water use increased as the population grew (figure 7.3). This trend, however, suddenly reversed in 1975, when total water use began to level off and then decline, even as the US population and economy continued to grow (Kenny et al. 2009). Although municipal water use has increased slightly from 1980 levels, current (2005) use is still effectively no higher than it was in 1975, despite a nearly 40 percent increase in population. As a result, per capita municipal demand has declined markedly, from 360 gallons per capita [person] per day (gpcd) in 1975 to 262 gpcd in 2005 (figure 7.4). In fact, per capita municipal demand has fallen to levels not seen since the middle of the 20th century.

Reductions in per capita water demand were driven by two major factors. First, the economy shifted from one dominated by water-intensive manufacturing to a less

BOX 7.1
SELF-SUPPLIED WATER SYSTEMS

Nearly 43 million people nationwide, or roughly 15 percent of the population, supply their own water for household uses (Kenny et al. 2009). Total self-supplied water withdrawals for domestic use were about 3.8 billion gallons per day n 2005. Nearly 98 percent of these withdrawals were from groundwater (Kenny et al. 2009). With most private wells or springs, water quality tends to be a larger concern than water availability (although declining water levels in some regions threaten water supplies for rural users). The quality of water from private wells is largely unregulated, placing the burden of maintaining well systems and monitoring water quality with the homeowner. The Safe Drinking Water Act does not apply to systems serving fewer than 25 individuals, and whereas some states and municipalities require testing for domestic wells, a 2009 USGS report finds that "the limited number of contaminants assessed, the small numbers of wells tested, and the infrequent and voluntary nature of the testing do not provide domestic well users with the same level of protection afforded to users of public water systems"(DeSimone 2009, 10).

Recent evidence suggests that this system of regulation is inadequate. A recent USGS analysis of nearly 1,400 wells across the United States found that 23 percent of domestic wells contained one or more contaminants at a concentration exceeding a human health benchmark (DeSimone 2009). Nitrate levels exceeded the Safe Drinking Water Act standard in 5 percent of the sampled wells nationwide and in nearly 10 percent of wells in the Basin and Range Aquifers and California's Central Valley. Microbial contamination was detected in up to one-third of the wells sampled. Organic compounds from anthropogenic sources were detected in about 60 percent of the sampled wells, although concentrations of these compounds exceeded human health benchmarks in less than 1 percent of the sampled wells (DeSimone 2009). For more information and recommendations to address this concern, see chapter 5: Water Quality.

Note: This USGS analysis was conducted on domestic wells. It does not account for indoor plumbing or treatment systems. Treatment can reduce potential health risks although older plumbing systems may increase potential risk.

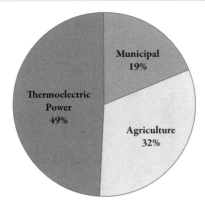

FIGURE 7.2. Water withdrawals by sector in 2005

Note: Municipal water use includes self-supplied water for residential and industrial purposes.
Source: Based on data from Kenny et al. (2009).

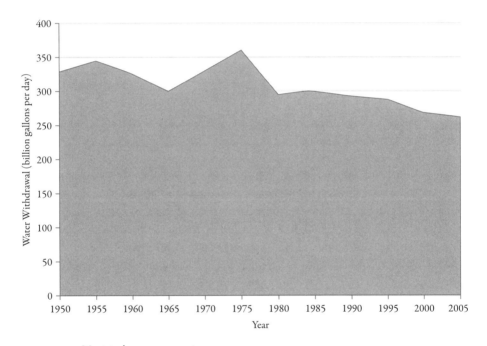

FIGURE 7.3. Municipal water use over time, 1950–2005

Note: We estimate municipal water use by subtracting withdrawals for agriculture and energy production from total water withdrawals. The municipal water use estimate then includes self-supplied water for residential and industrial purposes.
Source: Based on data from Kenny et al. (2009).

water-intensive service-oriented economy. Second, numerous federal policies and actions have facilitated water-efficiency improvements. For example, the Clean Water Act, which was passed in 1973, established water-quality standards for water discharged into the environment that then played a role in encouraging dischargers to adopt more water-efficient technologies to reduce wastewater volumes and costs (see chapter 5:

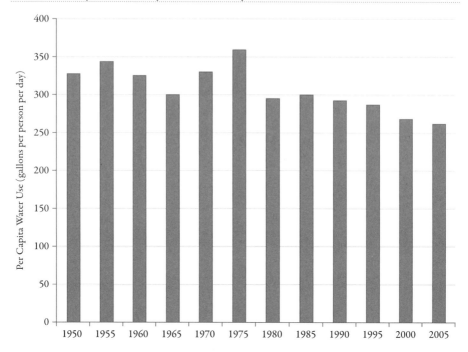

FIGURE 7.4. Municipal per capita water use over time, 1950–2005

Note: We estimate municipal water use by subtracting withdrawals for agriculture and energy production from total water withdrawals. The municipal water use estimate also includes self-supplied water for residential and industrial purposes. *Source:* Kenny et al. (2009).

Water Quality). The National Energy Policy Act of 1992 established efficiency standards for all toilets, urinals, kitchen and lavatory faucets, and showerheads manufactured after January 1, 1994 (table 7.1). Subsequent legislation established additional standards for products not included in the original act, including clothes washers, dishwashers, and a number of commercial products. More recently, the Environmental Protection Agency (EPA) developed the WaterSense program, a voluntary labeling program modeled after the Energy Star program to help customers identify and purchase efficient appliances. Products bearing the WaterSense label use less water than required under the national plumbing standards. Reductions in national per capita water use would likely have been even greater, but this same period saw a rapid shift in population to hotter, drier climates where water use, particularly outdoor water use, is higher.

Pressures and Challenges

Between 2006 and 2009, the southeastern United States—long considered a relatively water-rich region—was gripped by an exceptional drought. By fall of 2007, the metropolitan area around Altanta, Georgia, with a population of more than 4.4 million, was within 90 days of running out of water. In November 2007, Georgia Governor Sonny

TABLE 7.1.

Efficiency Standards Established by Federal Legislation

Fixture/Appliance	Federal Standard (current and future)	Law	Effective Date
Toilet	1.6 gpf	EPAct 1992	January 1, 1994
Showerhead	2.5 gpm at 80 psi	EPAct 1992	January 1, 1994
Faucet	≤2.2 gpm at 60 psi	EPAct 1992	January 1, 1994
Clothes washer	≥MEF 1.26 ft³/kWh/ cycle, WF ≤ 9.5 gal/ cycle/ft³		January 1, 2011
Dishwasher (regular size)	≤355 kWh/yr and ≤6.5 gallons/cycle	Energy Independence and Security Act of 2007	January 1, 2010
Dishwasher (compact)	≤260 kWh/year, ≤4.5 gallons/cycle	Energy Independence and Security Act of 2007	January 1, 2010
Commercial toilet	1.6 gpf	EPAct 1992	January 1, 1994
Urinal	1.0 gpf	EPAct 1992	January 1, 1994
Commercial faucet	2.2 gpm at 60 psi	EPAct 1992	January 1, 1994
Commercial faucet (public lavatory)	0.5 gpm at 60 psi	American Society of Mechanical Engineers standard	2005
Commercial pre-rinse spray valves	1.6 gpm	EPAct 2005	January 1, 2006
Commercial ice makers	sliding scale, based on ice harvest rate	EPAct 2005	January 1, 2010
Commercial clothes washers	≥MEF 1.26 ft³/kWh/ cycle, WF ≤ 9.5 gal/ cycle/ft³	EPAct 2005	January 1, 2007

Note: EPAct = Energy Policy Act; gpf = gallons per flush; gpm = gallons per minute; kWh = kilowatt hour; MEF = modified energy factor; psi = pounds per square inch; WF = water factor.

Perdue staged a prayer vigil on the steps of the State Capitol to ask for God's help to alleviate the drought. Despite these calls, drought conditions persisted for another year before a wet spring in 2009 brought relief.

This was not the first drought that has affected the Southeast and it certainly will not be the last. But why would a comparatively water-rich region with abundant precipitation be so vulnerable to drought? Some parts of Georgia receive up to 50 inches of rain each year in comparison with less than 20 inches in much of the American West. What would happen if drought had persisted another year? Or longer? Has Atlanta implemented policies to support sustainable water management and to reduce vulnerabilities to water scarcity? Or will water managers and decision makers write off these experiences as a fluke? Water managers across the United States, like those in Atlanta, face mounting pressures as a result of rapid population growth and shifting population centers, continued underinvestment in water and wastewater systems, and climate change. In the following sections, we describe each of these challenges in greater detail.

Population Growth

As the Atlanta case highlights, concerns about water scarcity are growing across the United States, even in areas that are not traditionally associated with water-supply constraints. In 2003, the Government Accountability Office surveyed water managers from 47 of the 50 United States (Michigan, New Mexico, and California, all of which are in regions with looming water scarcity problems, did not participate). Of the 47 managers that responded, 36 anticipated that their state would undergo a substantial degree of water shortage before 2013 under normal, non-drought conditions. Forty-six of the 47 state water managers predicted their states would have water shortages if drought conditions occur (GAO 2003).

In many parts of the United States, water scarcity concerns are largely driven by rapid population growth. As shown in figure 7.5, much of this growth is occurring throughout the western and southern United States, where water is already scarce and largely over-allocated. In Nevada, for example, the population is projected to increase by over 114 percent between 2000 and 2030 (US Census Bureau 2005). In comparison, population growth rates in regions with greater water availability, such as the northeastern United States, are far lower.

Overall, the Census Bureau estimates that the US population will grow to 364 million by 2030. Assuming that future municipalities use water at the same rate as today (262 gpcd), municipal water demand would increase by 17 billion gallons per day over 2005 levels, or 1.3 times the average daily flow of the Colorado River. Given the current water stresses already experienced around the nation, meeting this new demand for water—driven solely by population expansion and continued economic growth—with existing water resources will be extraordinarily difficult, expensive, and potentially environmentally damaging.

Our nation's water and wastewater infrastructure consists of thousands of reservoirs and treatment plants and millions of miles of pipes that deliver clean water to homes and businesses and remove wastewater. This infrastructure has provided enormous social, economic, and environmental benefits. As discussed, adequate water and wastewater treatment played the leading role in the decline of waterborne diseases in the United

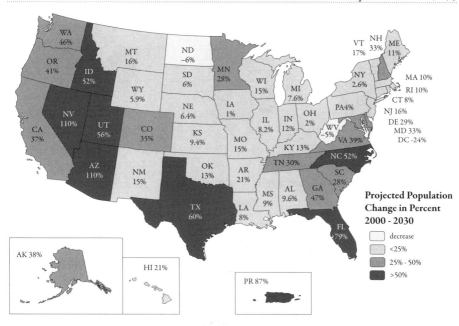

FIGURE 7.5.   Project population change from 2000 to 2030
Source: Based on US Census (2005). Map by Matthew Heberger.

States. Wastewater treatment protects ecosystems from pollution and contamination. Because water is a central element in most economic activities, from the production of steel to microchips, a clean, reliable water supply has fostered continued economic development.

Yet, there is mounting evidence that the nation's water and wastewater infrastructure is deteriorating. Another challenge is new efforts to reduce *combined sewer outfalls* that can overflow when stormwater overwhelms the capacity of municipal wastewater treatment systems, leading to backups and spills of untreated sewage into waterways. According to EPA estimates (cited in CBO 2002), combined sewer outfalls spill an estimated 1.2 trillion gallons of storm- and wastewater into the environment each year, posing a human health and environmental risk. Other evidence of deterioration in current systems includes a high level of leaks and "unaccounted for" water loss. As mentioned earlier, in some regions, urban and rural drinking water systems "lose 20 percent or more of the water they produce through leaks in their pipe networks" (CBO 2002). Newer and better maintained systems can reduce unaccounted-for losses to well under 10 percent. By 2020, the EPA projects that an overwhelming 45 percent of the nation's pipelines will be of poor quality or worse (EPA 2002a) (figure 7.6).

The deteriorating condition of the nation's water and wastewater infrastructure suggests that current funding levels for both repair and upgrading are inadequate. Several governmental agencies and private consortiums have analyzed the size of the water investment shortfall, including the EPA (EPA 2002a), the Congressional Budget Office

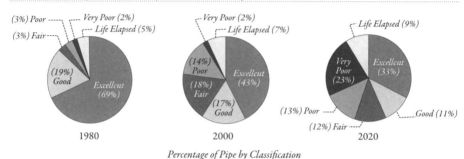

FIGURE 7.6. Likely condition of water pipes in 1980, 2000, and 2020
Source: EPA (2002a).

(CBO 2002), and the Water Infrastructure Network (WIN 2000). A 2002 assessment by the EPA, which is among the most frequently cited, identified major capital and operation and maintenance investment gaps for public water systems. They found that maintaining current spending levels would result in an estimated 20-year capital investment gap of $102 billion for drinking water systems and $122 billion for wastewater systems (EPA 2002a).[1] The operation and maintenance gap was even larger, totaling $161 billion for drinking water systems and $148 billion for wastewater systems (figure 7.7).

Water and wastewater systems represent one of the major components of national infrastructure, and as such, receive a large amount of the nation's infrastructure funding and investment. A common misconception, however, is that these costs are paid for with taxes. In fact, the vast majority of funds for water and wastewater systems come from the utility fees users pay to receive water services. Between 1991 and 2000, investment in water and wastewater systems totaled $670 billion.[2] Local governments and municipalities provided about 90 percent of the funds spent on water and sewer infrastructure development, rehabilitation, and operations nationwide (figure 7.8). States collectively contributed about $25 billion (in 2000$), or about 4 percent of the water and wastewater system investments. In comparison, the federal government allocated $44 billion (in 2000$), 6 percent of the total investment in these systems, mostly for capital improvements, as operations and maintenance costs are not eligible for federal funding. Federal funds were primarily provided through four agencies: the EPA; the Department of Agriculture; Department of Homeland Security; Housing and Urban Development; and the Department of Commerce (GAO 2001). The State Revolving Funds (SRFs), in particular, constitute the majority of federal investments in water and wastewater systems (see box 7.2).

Federal investment in SRFs has declined since the 1990s. In 2007, the federal government provided under $1 billion for Clean Water SRFs, down from over $3 billion in 1991 (in 2007$) (Food and Water Watch 2007). Federal funding for Drinking Water SRFs are about $800 million annually, down from a high of $1.2 billion in 1998 (Palaniappan et al. 2007). Despite the drop in federal investment, however, the total funds available to

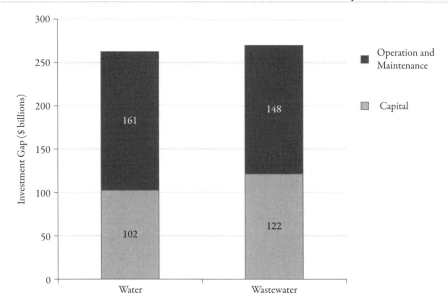

FIGURE 7.7. EPA estimate of the capital and operation and maintenance investment gaps for the water and wastewater sectors, 2000–2019

Note: All estimates shown in 2001$.

Source: Based on data from EPA (2002a).

states has steadily increased due to the revolving loan nature of the program, which has proven to be a very successful financial instrument. Nevertheless, current funding levels are inadequate to meet current needs.

In 2009, the federal government gave a major boost to SRFs—the American Recovery and Reinvestment Act provided $2 billion and $4 billion for local water and wastewater infrastructure improvements, respectively. One-fifth of the American Recovery and Reinvestment Act SRF funds are required to be used for "green" infrastructure or water or energy efficiency projects, thus expanding the traditional definition of water infrastructure. This one-time boost will certainly assist utilities in making much-needed improvements and help provide a short-term boost to local economies but will not address the long-term needs.

Climate Change

Even with a well-designed and maintained municipal water system, new challenges are arising that were unanticipated by the original designers and engineers. One of these challenges is a rapidly changing climate. Rising greenhouse gas concentrations from human activities are causing large-scale changes to the Earth's climate (see chapter 10: Water and Climate). Because the water cycle and the climate cycle are inextricably linked, these changes will have major implications for our nation's water resources, including both natural hydrology and the infrastructure we have built to manage the water cycle.

BOX 7.2
STATE REVOLVING FUNDS

State Revolving Funds (SRFs) are among the most important sources of state and federal funding for water and wastewater infrastructure. The Drinking Water and Clean Water State Revolving Funds were established by the Safe Drinking Water and Clean Water Acts, respectively. SRFs are designed to provide funds for infrastructure projects that help meet the standards set in these acts. These funds are capitalized through EPA grants and 20-percent matching contributions from the states. SRFs use the federal capital (and matching contributions) to provide low-interest loans for various water infrastructure projects. The interest rates for SRF loans are typically less than half of those offered in commercial markets, ultimately providing a cost savings to the utility. For example, the average interest rate for the Clean Water SRF loans is 2.2 percent, compared to a market rate of 4.6 percent, thereby reducing the community's cost for the project by 20 percent (EPA 2010).

The returns on loans are then used to fund additional water infrastructure projects. Over the past two decades, the Clean Water SRF has financed $2.31 in infrastructure projects for every $1 invested by the federal government, providing a remarkable return on federal investment. The EPA has projected that over a 20-year time horizon, the initial federal investment into the Clean Water SRF can result in the construction of up to three to four times as many projects compared to programs that use a one-time federal grant, depending on the allocation of resources to the program (EPA 2008).

When states do not have enough capital to match federal SRF grants, they often "leverage" their funds by borrowing money from private market through the bond market (Food and Water Watch 2007). Though SRFs are one of the primary avenues for the funding of new water infrastructure projects, many communities have been reluctant to use these funds due to the requirements attached, such as meeting state wage rates in accordance with the Davis-Bacon Act (Engle 2009).

Note: The Davis-Bacon Act of 1931 requires that all entities receiving federal funds for construction projects provide workers with prevailing local wages and benefits.

The movement of water is the primary process by which heat is redistributed around the planet. As temperatures rise, the movement of water will accelerate through increases in both evaporation and precipitation. In short, climate change will intensify the water cycle. As shown in figure 7.9, current climate models suggest that wet areas will become wetter and dry areas will become drier across the United States, and though many uncertainties remain, the scientific confidence in these results have been growing as models improve and as physical evidence from the real world accumulates.

Climate change impacts on water resources are already evident across the United States (table 7.2). For example, annual precipitation over the past century has increased for most of the United States but declined in the Central Rockies and southwestern

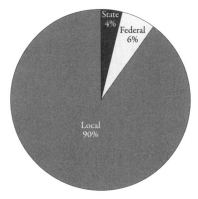

FIGURE 7.8. Local, state, and federal investment in water and wastewater infrastructure, 1991–2000
Source: State and federal estimates are from GAO (2001) and local estimates are from US Conference of Mayors (2007).

United States. As a result, runoff and streamflow have increased for most of the eastern United States but declined for the Columbia and Colorado River basins. Snowpack has begun to diminish in mountains as temperatures rise. The climate has also become more variable. The number of heavy precipitation events has increased, whereas the frequency and intensity of droughts have also increased, particularly in the western United States.

Climate models find that the impacts and economic consequences of climate change will accelerate, particularly if efforts to reduce greenhouse gas emissions continue to be delayed. Climate change will exacerbate challenges already facing the water sector, from aging infrastructure to population and economic growth, especially given that much of the projected population growth is in areas that are projected to become drier. The Intergovernmental Panel on Climate Change concludes that "climate change will constrain North America's already over-allocated water resources, thereby increasing competition among agricultural, municipal, industrial, and ecological uses" (Bates et al. 2008). Although there is growing awareness of these challenges among municipal water managers, and calls from professional water societies to integrate climate risks into long-term water plans, little actual progress has been made in reducing municipal vulnerabilities to these risks.

Moving Toward 21st-Century Solutions

The traditional approach to meeting our water needs has been to focus on supply-side options, including massive, centralized, capital-intensive infrastructure such as large dams and reservoirs, water and wastewater treatment plants, and extensive pipelines and aqueducts. This approach has brought many benefits, permitting the nation to feed an ever-growing global population, reducing the incidence of water-related diseases, mitigating the threat of both floods and droughts, and supporting continued economic growth.

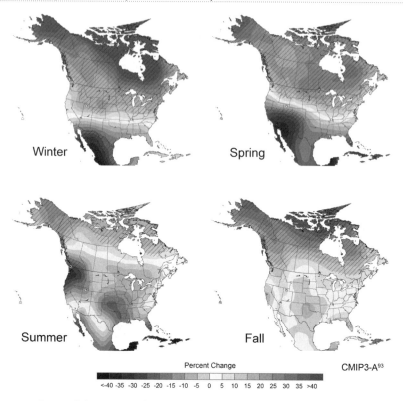

FIGURE 7.9. Projected change in North American precipitation by 2080–2099

Note: The maps show projected future changes in precipitation relative to the recent past as simulated by 15 climate models. The simulations are for late this century under a higher emissions scenario.

Source: Karl et al. (2009).

But it has also come at great social, economic, and environmental costs, many of which were either ignored, undervalued, or unknown at the time. For example, many dams, including Kenzua Dam in Pennsylvania, Shasta Dam in California, the Tennessee Valley Authority dams in the Southeast, and American Falls Dam in Idaho, flooded communities and forced residents to relocate. Nearly 40 percent of North American freshwater and diadromous fish species are imperiled because of physical modifications to rivers and lakes (Jelks et al. 2008). Furthermore, dams have already been constructed on the most appropriate sites; the remaining sites provide fewer benefits at higher and higher costs.

As a result of these constraints, water managers are beginning to look seriously at new ways to enhance water supplies and are rethinking approaches to managing demand to ensure that sufficient water resources are available to meet anticipated needs. The soft path for water, described in the introduction, has emerged as a promising alternative. The term *soft path* was originally coined by Amory Lovins of the Rocky Mountain Institute to describe an alternative path for energy development that emphasized energy efficiency and promoted smaller, decentralized energy systems fueled by renewable sources. The soft path for water, as described by Gleick (2002, 2003), is based on integrating several

TABLE 7.2.

Observed Changes in Water Resources during the Past Century across North America

Observed water resource change	Region affected
Annual precipitation	Most of North America
Annual precipitation	Central Rockies, southwestern United States, Canadian prairies, eastern Arctic
Frequency of heavy precipitation events	Most of United States
Periods of drought	Western United States, southern Canada
Proportion of precipitation falling as snow	Western Canada and prairies, US West
Duration and extent of snow cover	Most of North America
Glacial extent	US western mountains, Alaska, and Canada
Ice cover	Great Lakes, Gulf of St. Lawrence
Mountain snow water equivalent	Western North America
Runoff and streamflow	Colorado and Columbia River basins
Streamflow	Most of the eastern United States
1–4 week earlier peak streamflow due to earlier warming-driven snowmelt	US West and New England regions, Canada
Widespread thawing of permafrost	Most of northern Canada and Alaska
Water temperature of lakes (0.1–1.5°C)	Most of North America
Salinization of coastal surface waters	Florida, Louisiana

Source: Bates et al. (2008).

key principles, including improving the overall productivity of water use rather than seeking endless sources of new supply, matching water quality to the users' needs, meeting basic human and ecosystem water needs as a top priority, and integrating decision making across sectors, for example, water demand, flood management, and land-use planning, to promote projects or facilities that produce multiple services. Furthermore, the soft path seeks meaningful local and community engagement. In the following, we expand on some of the ways that the soft path for water can be applied to municipal water systems and describe appropriate roles for the federal government to help facilitate this transition.

Improve the Productivity of Water Use through Water Conservation and Efficiency Improvements

Despite gains through conservation efforts over the past 25 years, current municipal water use remains wasteful. Inefficient fixtures and appliances are still commonplace, particularly in homes built prior to 1994,[3] and in a range of commercial, institutional, and industrial settings. Even in a dry and populous state like California, where many water agencies have taken the concerns about water supply constraints seriously, far more can be done. A 2003 analysis by the Pacific Institute found that existing, cost-effective technologies and policies can reduce California's urban water demand by more than 30 percent (Gleick et al. 2003).[4] These findings were supported by subsequent studies in other regions. For example, a Seattle study found that installing new, water-efficient fixtures and appliances reduced single-family indoor use by nearly 40 percent. Homeowners rated the performance, maintenance, and appearance of the efficient appliances higher than the older appliances (Mayer, DeOreo, and Lewis 2000). Similarly, a 1997 study by the American Water Works Association found that water conservation and efficiency could reduce indoor water use from 65 gpcd to 45 gpcd for single-family homes, a savings of over 30 percent (AWWA 1997), yet many studies since then show that indoor water use rates remain far above the levels considered achievable. Experience from Australia, for example, which recently suffered 10 consecutive years of severe drought conditions, shows that it is possible to change how people think about and manage their water resources. In Southeast Queensland, Australia, a series of programs targeting residences and businesses resulted in major improvements in their water-use efficiency. In 2009, after drought restrictions were finally relaxed, total urban demand had dropped to only 67 gpcd, and residential demand, including both indoor and outdoor uses, was a low 43 gpcd (Queensland Water Commission 2010).

Australia's success allows for a comparison of what is possible using today's technologies and practices. Future technological improvements and behavioral changes could lower demand even further. Newer, more efficient appliances and management practices continue to be introduced to the market. New, front-loading clothes washers, for example, use as little as 15 gallons per load, compared to more than 40 gallons per load for older top-loading washers. Dual-flush toilets, which are common in Australia and parts of Europe, use 1.6 gallons per flush (gpf) for solid waste but less than a gallon for liquid waste. Installing these devices would reduce per capita demand even further, and California, Texas, and Georgia have recently passed new standards requiring new toilets use no more than 1.28 gpf. Some municipalities are exploring innovative programs to reduce outdoor landscape water use such as paying customers to replace lawns with more water-thrifty plants.

In addition to saving water, water conservation and efficiency provide a number of other cobenefits, including significant energy savings (see chapter 9: Water and Energy). Water is heavy. It also has a high heat capacity—meaning it requires a lot of energy to raise its temperature. As a result, capturing, treating, transporting, and using water requires a tremendous amount of energy. This is particularly true in areas where water supplies and population centers are separated by hundreds of miles or groundwater levels are low. Preliminary studies suggest that it may be cheaper to save energy through water conservation programs than through traditional energy efficiency programs (CEC 2005). This finding is of tremendous importance, particularly as the nation seeks to reduce its greenhouse gas emissions.

Matching the Quality of Supply with the Quality of Demand

Most municipal water systems are designed with a once-through, single-pipe distribution system that provides high-quality potable supply for all uses. The soft path approach raises the possibility of developing water systems that supply water of various qualities, with higher quality water reserved for those uses that require higher quality. For example, storm runoff, rainwater, graywater, and reclaimed wastewater are well-suited for land-scape irrigation, commercial and industrial purposes, toilets, and other nonpotable uses. A growing number of communities across the United States are already beginning to move in this direction. A 2004 report from the EPA estimated that more than 1.7 billion gallons of wastewater are reused each day, and the volume of water reused is growing at 15 percent annually (EPA 2004), with Florida, California, Texas, and Arizona having made the biggest commitment to recycled water.

Today, this number is undoubtedly much higher. A 2010 survey found that in Florida alone, about 659 million gallons of water are reused beneficially each day, up from 584 million gallons per day in 2002 (Florida Department of Environmental Protection 2011). Although seemingly small compared to the total water use across the United States, national and even statewide estimates may hide the importance of recycled water for some communities. For example, the Irvine Ranch Water District in southern California meets nearly 20 percent of its total demand with recycled water (IRWD 2005); whereas in southwest Florida, nearly half of all wastewater is recycled (SWFWMD nd). Significant opportunities exist to expand recycling and reuse throughout the United States, effectively lessening the need to identify and develop new water supplies.

Even though recycled water may be cost-effective in the long-term, constructing a second water distribution system to supply nonpotable water can be expensive. Pumping costs can also be high, as many wastewater treatment plants are located at the lowest point of the utility's service area to take advantage of gravity to deliver wastewater to the treatment plant. There are a variety of ways to reduce these costs. Building smaller, distributed wastewater treatment plants, for example, could reduce pipe length and pumping costs. Installing a second distribution system during initial site development can also help reduce costs. For example, a new residential community in Ventura County, California, was designed with a second water distribution system and now uses recycled water for all of its landscaping needs at an estimated cost of $610 per million gallons (Richards 2006), far below the cost of new surface storage. Indirect potable reuse, whereby recycled water is treated to potable standards and then used to recharge groundwater or surface reservoirs, also tends to be less expensive, although public perception and local or state regulatory requirements may limit application of this option in some areas.[5] Experience shows that involving the public early in the development of the project can help mitigate public perception concerns.

On-site reuse, where a waste stream is treated and reused on site, can also reduce costs. This practice is already fairly common for industrial uses, although more can be done. In addition, households can install small recycling systems that capture water from clothes washers, showers, and faucets, also referred to as graywater, for use on outdoor landscapes or for flushing toilets. States and municipalities have taken a variety of approaches for regulating the use of graywater. Some have adopted strict permitting requirements that greatly increase the cost of installing these systems. Arizona, by contrast, has among the least restrictive requirements: small systems that produce less than 400 gallons per day do not require a permit as long as they meet 13 best management practices, including minimizing surface water accumulation and preventing water from leaving the homeowner's property. Systems producing more than 400 gallons per day, however, must obtain a permit and be approved by a state agency.

Promoting Decentralized Systems

Municipal water systems traditionally consist of massive, centralized systems. The belief was that bigger is better and allows for economies of scale. Smaller, decentralized systems, however, can provide a number of important benefits. The degree of decentralization can vary, ranging from an individual home or business to satellite systems that serve larger numbers of homes and businesses. As mentioned previously, recycled water could be delivered to nearby homes and businesses using smaller satellite systems that rely on the force of gravity, thereby reducing the infrastructure and pumping costs to deliver the water. Whereas managing a larger number of small sites can be challenging, it allows for a number of advantages. First, infrastructure can be added incrementally, reducing the up-front costs and allowing for changes in response to changing conditions. In addition, decentralized systems are less vulnerable to attacks or other catastrophes. Decentralization should be included as a viable alternative when evaluating water and wastewater infrastructure projects.

Integrating Decision Making to Produce Multiple Benefits and Services

Many chapters have detailed the lack of coordination among water management entities at the federal level. Even at the local level, however, water management activities—water, wastewater, and flood management—lack coordination. Water agencies, private water companies, or local governments supply drinking water. Other agencies, companies, or departments supply wastewater treatment services. Yet a third group is charged with flood and storm runoff management. Some utilities provide both water and wastewater services, and others may include all three branches of the water sector. Even when all branches are housed within the same organization, departments may operate in silos, often failing to effectively communicate and coordinate their efforts.

Integration, however, can foster innovative solutions. For example, conventional stormwater management consists of a curb-and-gutter storm drainage system, whereby stormwater is disposed of as quickly as possible. For communities with combined sewer systems, this approach produces tremendous spikes in the volume of water that must be conveyed to and treated at the local water treatment facility during storm events. Treatment of these high flows increases operation and maintenance costs and when these systems are overwhelmed, they often back up, discharging untreated sewage into the environment, as discussed previously. In addition, this approach increases capital costs because these systems are sized to meet peak flows.

Low-impact development is an alternative approach that uses vegetation and permeable surfaces to allow stormwater to infiltrate the ground. According to an EPA analysis, low-impact development is typically less costly than conventional stormwater management techniques, with capital savings of 15 to 80 percent (EPA 2007). In addition, it provides a number of other benefits. It reduces wastewater operation and maintenance costs, minimizes the impacts of urban runoff on local streams and the marine environment, reduces local flooding, recharges local groundwater supplies, and improves water supply reliability and flexibility. Integrated decision making can lead to projects or facilities that provide multiple services and benefits, promoting economic efficiency and public confidence, and improving environmental outcomes.

Integration, however, must extend beyond water management entities. Many of the challenges facing municipal water systems, including population growth and climate change, are outside the direct control of entities responsible for water management. Development decisions, for example, are often made by city or local land-use planning entities. Yet, the responsibility to provide water and wastewater service and flood protection falls on the water sector. Similarly, federal government and state agencies are setting energy policies with little consideration of the implications on water. Cross-sector integration is needed and is one of our overarching recommendations.

Some states and local agencies have developed innovative ways to promote cross-sector integration. Assured supply laws are one such example. Assured supply laws consist of state, county, and municipal measures that require developers to show proof that there is an adequate water supply available to support the proposed development before they are allowed to build. A recent survey found that nearly two-thirds of western states have some form of assured supply law in place (Hanak and Browne 2006). Eastern states are increasingly establishing some form of assured supply laws, although many areas lack any such way to integrate land use and water management. Cross-sector integration must become the rule rather than the exception.

Potential Policy Solutions

Even though much of water management typically occurs at the local or regional level, the federal government plays an important role in setting consistent national standards and regulations, providing funding for issues of national interest, and helping to ensure that municipalities are able to meet future challenges. As mentioned previously, federal regulations have been critical, both directly and indirectly, in encouraging water conservation and efficiency. In the following, we describe specific ways that the federal government can more effectively promote sustainable municipal water use by emphasizing soft-path management strategies.

Expand Data Collection and Monitoring Activities

Measurement and monitoring of our nation's water resource is critical for management of this precious resource. The US Geological Survey (USGS) is responsible for collecting, analyzing, and distributing data on water availability and use. These data include streamflow information from 7,000 national stream gauges, 600 groundwater monitoring wells, and state data on water use to create national water-use estimates. For years, data collection efforts have been severely underfunded. The number of active stations has been declining as USGS has been forced to pull streamflow gauges due to lack of funds (see chapter 6: Protecting Freshwater Ecosystems). Even less information is available on other water resource components, especially groundwater. Additionally, national water-use data are only collected every five years and are not provided in a timely manner due to limited staffing and budgetary constraints. The 2005 data, for example, was not released until late October 2009.

The failure to accurately monitor and measure our nation's water resources contributes directly to the failure to manage it sustainably. In turn, this affects planning, policy making, and ultimately the nation's economic and environmental health. The federal government must ensure that the USGS has sufficient resources to collect and maintain long-term data on key characteristics of water resources, including streamflow, groundwater levels, water quality, and water use. The passage of the Secure Water Act in 2009 is an important step forward in terms of data collection through the requirement for a National Water Census and increased funding for the USGS stream gauge network. Full appropriations should be made to fund these critical programs.

Promote Water Recycling

The federal government has supported water recycling by funding research and development projects and through direct financing for specific projects. As shown in table 7.3, eight federal agencies, ranging from the Bureau of Reclamation to the Bureau of Indian Affairs, provide grants and loans for municipal recycled water projects through 17 different programs. The primary funders are the EPA and the Bureau of Reclamation. These programs typically provide funding for treatment, storage, and distribution of recycled water, whereas funding needed to connect customers to the recycled water system is generally limited and only available at the local level. In addition, most federal

TABLE 7.3.

Federal Programs That Support Municipal Water Recycling Projects

Funding agency	Program
Army Corps of Engineers	Water Resources Development Act, Section 219—"Environmental Infrastructure"
Bureau of Reclamation	Title XVI—Reclamation Wastewater and Groundwater Study and Facilities Act
Department of Agriculture—Rural Development/Natural Resources Conservation Service	Waste and Wastewater Disposal Loans and Grants Program
Department of Commerce, Economic Development Administration	Investments for Public Works and Economic Development Facilities
Department of Health and Human Services Indian Health Service	Indian Health Service Sanitation Facilities Construction Program
Department of the Interior Bureau of Indian Affairs	Bureau of Indian Affairs Facilities Operations and Maintenance
Environmental Protection Agency	Clean Water State Revolving Fund
	Drinking Water State Revolving Fund
	National Estuary Program
	Nonpoint Source Implementation Grants
	Pollution Prevention Grant Program
Department of Housing and Urban Development	Community Development Block Grants Program
	Rural Housing and Economic Development
	Super Notice of Funding Availability—Grant Brownfields Economic Development Initiative

Note: All of these programs can be used for municipal supply, although municipal supply may not be the program's primary target recipient for funding.
Source: Adapted from USBR (2004).

funding occurs through line item appropriations on federal bills. This approach does not ensure that the best projects are constructed; rather politics becomes a determining factor. Federal agencies should be given a budget and the authority to choose what projects are funded based on the project's merits and local needs. In addition, a central database should be developed so that project proponents are able to easily identify which funding programs are most appropriate.

Update National Efficiency Standards

Beginning in the late 1980s and early 1990s, numerous states and municipalities across the country began establishing efficiency standards for certain plumbing fixtures. In an effort to reduce the potential confusion caused by multiple, inconsistent state standards, the Energy Policy Act of 1992 established a single consistent set of national efficiency standards for toilets, urinals, kitchen and lavatory faucets, and showerheads manufactured after January 1, 1994. Although these standards have been effective, they are increasingly outdated as water-efficiency technology has improved. Since the act was adopted, new and more efficient versions of water-using appliances have been developed. Some states are trying to update and expand these standards to reflect these advances. In 2004, for example, the California Energy Commission established a new water conservation standard for residential clothes washers. A federal clothes washer energy standard existed, but it did not include a maximum water flow standard. Under federal law, states can only adopt standards that exceed national appliance efficiency standards in extreme energy emergencies. California applied for a waiver from the Department of Energy but this waiver was denied. California, and now Texas and Georgia, recently made a more successful bid requiring that all toilets and urinals sold in these states use 1.28 gpf and 0.5 gpf or less, respectively.

In order to ensure that new homes and businesses are as efficient as possible, national efficiency standards for appliances and fixtures must be updated to reflect new, more efficient technologies and expanded to include all water-using appliances. Additionally, the federal government should go beyond these standards for all federally managed buildings by requiring these building be equipped with appliances and fixtures that meet Water-Sense specifications.

Develop Sustainable Financing Mechanisms for Water and Wastewater Infrastructure

While the soft path emphasizes some of the nonstructural elements of water management, it also recognizes the importance of maintaining our nation's existing water infrastructure. There are numerous opinions and perspectives on solving the infrastructure challenges. Local groups, including water and wastewater service providers, often call for additional federal investment. For example, the Water Infrastructure Network, a coalition of local officials, water and wastewater service providers, engineers, and environmentalists, recommends "increasing the federal role where needs are great, public health or the environment is at risk, or local resources are inadequate" (WIN 2001, 1). The federal government, including the Congressional Budget Office, however, argues that while substantial federal investment is necessary in some cases, it can also have unintended consequences. They note that "federal subsidies . . . run the risk of undermining the incentives that managers and consumers have to make cost-effective decisions, thereby retarding beneficial changes in the water industry and raising total costs to the nation as a whole" (CBO 2002, ix). Indeed, among the most striking findings of an EPA assessment of the investment gap is that the gap shrinks from $533 billion to $76 billion by increasing local spending by just 3 percent over the inflation rate per year (figure 7.10) (EPA 2002a).

Rather than simply expanding federal investment, we recommend a more comprehensive approach. First, the federal government should continue to encourage local investment through the SRFs and other funding programs. By raising polluter fees, the federal government may even be able to expand federal investment in water and wastewater systems. But whereas modest expansions in federal funding may be warranted, local funding should still be the primary mechanism for funding water and wastewater infrastructure. And given the infrastructure gap, local funding must be expanded.

The federal government can play an important role in promoting sustainable local financing mechanisms. The federal government should develop a standardized method for marginal cost pricing that seeks to include social and environmental costs and then use financial incentives to encourage adoption of these methods. Specifically, the federal government could add stipulations to SRF and other federals funds that require marginal cost-pricing policies. Such stipulations should also require metering and conservation-oriented pricing structures for all customers.

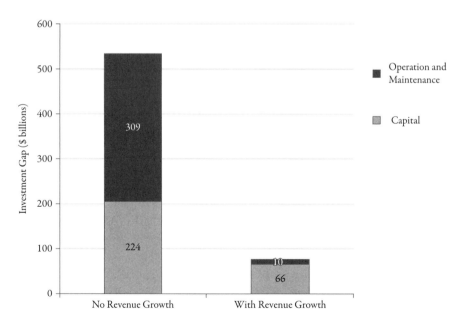

FIGURE 7.10. EPA estimate of the total investment gap for the water and wastewater sectors with and without revenue growth, 2000–2019

Note: All estimates shown in 2001$.
Source: Based on data from EPA (2002a).

Ensure Affordability for Those Unable to Afford Water Services

Affordability is already a major concern for some communities and individuals and emphasizing local financing could exacerbate these concerns. In many communities across the United States, water rates are rising faster than incomes as stricter environmental, health, and safety regulations; replacement of aging infrastructure; and the steady pressure of inflation drive up utility costs (see chapter 3: Water and Environmental Justice). Water affordability concerns are more common in smaller water systems where the general costs of maintenance and infrastructure are spread across fewer customers. Even in large urban systems, however, low-income residents, seniors, and people with disabilities may be unable to afford increases in water bills because of unemployment, underemployment, illnesses, and disability. A 2002 EPA report notes that "it is not unusual for the mean household income affordability indicator to be well under the 2 percent threshold for a system as a whole, but for lower income residents, the financial impact of the rates may range from 4–8 percent of mean household income" (EPA 2002b, 2). Failure to pay bills can have devastating consequences, including the loss of one's home or business and even one's children. In Detroit, for example, water service was shut off to more than 45,000 residents who were unable to afford rising costs (see box 7.3 on the Fight for Affordable Water in Detroit).

In order to ensure that all people have access to water to meet their basic needs at an affordable price, the federal government should take a variety of actions. First, it should establish a Low Income Home Water Assistance Program, similar to what is already in place for energy services. The federal government should also require water suppliers to establish a lifeline rate for low-income water users and make it illegal for a utility company, private or public, to disconnect all water services if a user is unable to afford the bill. Finally, the federal government should target federal investment, including the SRFs, to small, rural, low-income, or other disadvantaged communities.

Target Federal Investment toward "Green" Infrastructure

Federal investment in water and wastewater systems has traditionally funded massive, centralized infrastructure. Greater effort is needed to expand the types of projects funded by the federal government to include small, decentralized systems; water conservation and efficiency improvements; and other forms of green infrastructure. Such techniques, including low-impact development, can produce multiple benefits at lower cost, thereby capturing economies of scope. The federal government can incentivize these approaches through added stipulations on SRFs. The federal government has recently demonstrated interest in such an emphasis with the green reserves for energy and water efficiency measures in the 2009 American Recovery and Reinvestment Act. This set-aside should be made permanent and expanded.

BOX 7.3

THE FIGHT FOR AFFORDABLE WATER IN DETROIT

By Amy Vanderwarker

"Water is a human right" and "Without water I will die" read signs that Detroit residents waved before City Hall in a protest to let their city commissioners know that more than 45,000 Detroiters have been left without water. In the fall of 2000, Michigan Welfare Rights Organization, a union for public recipient workers and low-income workers in the state, began getting telephone calls from residents saying that they could not afford their water bills. "At first we got a couple a week, then we noticed we were getting ten a week; we got more and more, until we were receiving more than ten calls a day," recalls Maureen Taylor, chairperson of the organization. In a city of 837,700 residents, rising water rates have left 5 percent of the population disconnected from this basic need, with hundreds of dollars in unpaid bills and fear of losing their homes, businesses, and families.

In Detroit, water bills have been growing for a number of reasons, including a dwindling city tax base, rising energy costs, ongoing costs of replacing century-old infrastructure, and rigorous regulatory requirements. In response, the Detroit Sewer and Water Department, which provides water to four million people in the city of Detroit and surrounding communities, has been increasing its rates annually. As a result, many low-income or fixed-income residents are paying up to 10 percent of their income on water. Maureen Taylor describes the struggles many Detroiters face: "If you don't pay your water bills, they cut off your water and don't give you an opportunity to appeal. Then they transfer the bills above $100 to property tax rolls for collection. If you can't pay, your house can be foreclosed. . . . People lose their homes, business, and can even lose their children" (M. Taylor, pers. comm. 2005). Child welfare agencies consider lack of water a form of neglect and can take children away from their parents whose water is shut off (National Consumer Law Center et al. 2006).

The community, under the leadership of the Michigan Welfare Rights Organization, put together a Water Affordability Plan. The plan was approved by the City Council in 2004 but has never been fully implemented. In 2006, the city announced the Detroit Residential Water Assistance Program Plan, one element of the Water Affordability Plan, but many essential elements were not included. In particular, funding for the program was cut in half; the administration of the program was passed on to other city departments; and, whereas the original plan served 40,000 people, the adopted plan served only 16,000 (M. Taylor, pers. comm. 2005). Detroit Sewer and Water Department had originally proposed $5 million in funding for the program in fiscal years 2007–2008. Only half of that, or $2.5 million, was actually approved. In 2010, Detroit Sewer and Water Department provided no funds for the program, although customer donations were accepted (Monroe 2010). The fight for affordable water for low-income, elderly, and disabled residents in Detroit continues.

Conclusions

The United States has a remarkably sophisticated and well-developed municipal water system that provides high-quality, reliable, water supply and wastewater services to nearly all people. But these systems are showing evidence of wear. Water managers across the nation face mounting pressures as a result of rapid population growth and shifting population centers, continued underinvestment in water and wastewater systems, and climate change.

In the 20th century, we focused on supply-side options, including massive, centralized, capital-intensive infrastructure such as large dams and reservoirs, water and wastewater treatment plants, and extensive pipelines and aqueducts. Today, we have already built on all the best dam sites and the remaining sites are even more expensive and provide fewer benefits. Freshwater and diadromous fish are severely imperiled. And, in many cases, our existing water resources are already overallocated. The nation needs a 21st-century approach to water management. The soft path for water has emerged as a promising alternative.

Even though much of water management typically occurs at the local or regional level, there is a clear role for the federal government to play in guiding and facilitating efforts to sustainably manage our nation's water resources. Updating national water-efficiency standards, for example, can further promote demand-side management approaches. Shifting federal investment toward green infrastructure can further incentivize alternative water management approaches. Finally, expanding data collection and monitoring efforts can promote long-term sustainable water management.

References

American Water Works Association (AWWA) WaterWiser. 1997. "Household End Uses of Water Without and With Conservation." Residential Water Use Summary—Typical Single Family Home. Denver, Colorado.

Bates, B. C., Z. W. Kundzewicz, S. Wu, and J. P. Palutikof. 2008. *Climate Change and Water*. IPCC Technical Paper VI of the Intergovernmental Panel on Climate Change, IPCC Secretariat. Geneva: Intergovernmental Panel on Climate Change, IPCC Secretariat.

California Energy Commission (CEC). 2005. *2005 Integrated Energy Policy Report*. CEC-100-2005-007-CMF. Sacramento: California Energy Commission. http://www.energy.ca.gov/2005publications/CEC-100-2005-007/CEC-100-2005-007-CMF.PDF.

Centers for Disease Control and Prevention. 1945. Vital Statistics of the United States: *Mortality. Federal Security Agency, US Public Health Service, Part 1*. Washington, DC: US Government Printing Office.

———. 1963. Vital Statistics of the United States: *Mortality. US Dept. of Health, Education, and Welfare*. Washington, DC: US Government Printing Office.

Congressional Budget Office (CBO). 2002. *Future Investment in Drinking Water and Wastewater Infrastructure*. Washington, DC: Congressional Budget Office. t http://www.cbo.gov/ftpdocs/39xx/doc3983/11-18-WaterSystems.pdf.

Cooley, H., J. Christian-Smith, and P. H. Gleick. 2009. *Sustaining California Agriculture in an Uncertain Future*. Oakland: Pacific Institute.

Cutler, D., and G. Miller. 2005. "The Role of Public Health Improvements in Health Advances: The Twentieth-Century United States." *Demography* 42 (1): 1–22.

DeSimone, L. A. 2009. *Quality of Water from Domestic Wells in Principal Aquifers of the United States, 1991–2004*. US Geological Survey Scientific Investigations Report 2008–5227. Reston, VA: US Geological Survey. http://pubs.usgs.gov/sir/2008/5227.

Engle, D. 2009. "It's Raining Money: Recovery-Act Funding Rules May Signal a Longer-Range Policy to Underwrite Water Efficiency." *Water Efficiency*. September/October 2009. http://www.waterefficiency.net/WE/Articles/7908.aspx.

Florida Department of Environmental Protection. 2011. *2010 Reuse Inventory Report. Water Reuse Program*. Tallahassee: Florida Department of Environmental Protection. http://www.dep.state.fl.us/water/reuse/inventory.htm.

Food and Water Watch. 2007. *Clear Water: Why American Needs a Clean Water Trust Fund*. Washington, DC: Food and Water Watch.

Gleick, P. H. 2002. "Soft Water Paths." *Nature* 418: 373.

———.2003. "Global Freshwater Resources: Soft-Path Solutions for the 21st Century." *Science* 302: 1524–1528.

———.2010. *Bottled and Sold: The Story Behind Our Obsession with Bottled Water*. Washington, DC: Island Press.

Gleick, P. H., D. Haasz, C. Henges-Jeck, V. Srinivasan, G. Wolff, K. K. Cushing, and A. Mann. 2003. *Waste Not, Want Not: The Potential for Urban Water Conservation in California*. Oakland: Pacific Institute.

Hanak, E., and M. Browne. 2006. "Linking Housing Growth to Water Supply: New Planning Frontiers in the American West." *Journal of the American Planning Association* 72 (2): 154–166.

Irvine Ranch Water District (IRWD). 2005. *2005 Urban Water Management Plan*. Irvine, CA: Irvine Ranch Water District.

Jelks, H. L., S. J. Walsh, N. M. Burkhead, S. Contrera-Balderas, E. Diaz-Pardo, D. A. Hendrickson, J. Lyons, et al. 2008. "Conservation Status of Imperiled North American Freshwater and Diadromous Fishes." *Fisheries* 33 (8): 372–407.

Karl, T. R., J. M. Melillo, and T. C. Peterson, eds. 2009. *Global Climate Change Impacts in the United States*. New York: Cambridge University Press.

Kenny, J. F., N. L. Barber, S. S. Hutson, K. S. Linsey, J. K. Lovelace, and M. A. Maupin. 2009. *Estimated Use of Water in the United States in 2005*. US Geological Survey Circular 1344. Reston, VA: US Geological Survey.

Mayer, P. W., W. B. DeOreo, and D. M. Lewis. 2000. *Seattle Home Water Conservation Study: The Impacts of High Efficiency Plumbing Fixture Retrofits in Single-Family Homes*. Boulder: Aquacraft, Inc. Water Engineering and Management.

Monroe, L. E. 2010. Memorandum: Detroit Residential Water Assistance Program (DRWAP) to Detroit City Council. November 18, 2010.

National Consumer Law Center, Consumer Federation of America, US PIRG and Consumers Union. 2006. Consumer Groups Comments to EPA's Proposed Revisions to the Existing National-Level Affordability Methodology for Small Drinking Water Systems Variances, Docket ID No. OW-2005-0005.

Palaniappan, M., H. Cooley, P. H. Gleick, and G. Wolff. 2007. "Water Infrastructure and Water-Related Services: Trends and Challenges Affecting Future Development." In *Organisation for Economic Co-operation and Development, Infrastructure to 2010*, Vol. 2: *Mapping Policy for*

Electricity, Water, and Transport. Edited by OECD, 269–340. Paris: Organisation for Economic Co-operation and Development.

Queensland Water Commission. 2010. *The 2009 Water Report.* http://www.qwc.qld.gov.au/about/annualreports.html.

Richards, S. 2006. "Community To Use Reclaimed Water." *Ventura County-Star*, August 15.

Rosenberg, Charles E. 1987. *The Cholera Years: The United States in 1832, 1849, and 1866.* Chicago: University of Chicago Press.

Southwest Florida Water Management District. nd. "Reclaimed Water Use in the District for 2007." Southwest Florida Water Management District. Accessed September 14, 2010. http://www.swfwmd.state.fl.us/conservation/reclaimed/.

United States Bureau of Reclamation (USBR). 2004. Financial Support Opportunities Technical Memorandum. *Southern California Water Recycling Projects Initiative.* Final Draft. Washington, DC: United States Bureau of Reclamation.

US Census Bureau. 2005. *Interim State Population Projections 2000–2030 based on Census 2000.* Washington, DC: US Census Bureau, Population Division.

US Conference of Mayors. 2007. *Who Pays for the Water Pipes, Pumps, and Treatment Works?— Local Government Expenditures on Sewer and Water—1991 to 2005.* Washington, DC: US Conference of Mayors. http://www.usmayors.org/urbanwater/07expenditures.pdf.

US Environmental Protection Agency (EPA). 2002a. *The Clean Water and Drinking Water Infrastructure Gap Analysis.* EPA-816-R-02-020. Washington, DC: US Environmental Protection Agency, Office of Water.

———. 2002b. "Rate Options to Address Affordability Concerns for Consideration by District of Columbia Water and Sewer Authority." White paper prepared by the U.S. Environmental Protection Agency, Region III. Philadelphia.

———.2004. *Guidelines for Water Reuse.* EPA 625-R-04-108. Washington, DC: US Environmental Protection Agency.

———. 2007. *Reducing Stormwater Costs through Low Impact Development (LID) Strategies and Practices.* EPA 841-F-07-006. Washington, DC: US Environmental Protection Agency.

———. 2008. *2007 Annual Report: Clean Water State Revolving Fund Programs.* EPA-832-R-08-001. Washington, DC: US Environmental Protection Agency, Office of Water.

———. 2010. "Clean Water State Revolving Fund." US Environmental Protection Agency, Office of Water. http://www.epa.gov/owm/cwfinance/cwsrf/index.htm. Washington, DC.

US Government Accountability Office (GAO). 2001. *Water Infrastructure: Information on Federal and State Financial Assistance.* GAO-02-134. Washington, DC: US Government Accountability Office. http://www.gao.gov/new.items/d02134.pdf.

———. 2003. *Freshwater Supply: States' View of How Federal Agencies Could Help Them Meet the Challenges of Expected Shortages.* GAO-03-514. Washington, DC: US Government Accountability Office. http://www.gao.gov/new.items/d03514.pdf.

Water Infrastructure Network (WIN). 2000. *Clean & Safe Water for the 21st Century: A Renewed National Commitment to Water and Wastewater Infrastructure.* Washington, DC: Water Infrastructure Network. http://www.win-water.org/reports/winreport2000.pdf.

———. 2001. *Water Infrastructure Now: Recommendations for Clean and Safe Water in the 21st Century.* Washington, DC: Water Infrastructure Network. http://win-water.org/reports/winow.pdf.

WATER AND AGRICULTURE

Juliet Christian-Smith

Introduction

Wallace Stegner's classic treatise *Beyond the 100th Meridian* outlines the struggle of John Wesley Powell, the pioneering American explorer, to educate the nation about the scientific and political implications of the distinction between the wetter eastern states and the drier western states. Hydrologically speaking, the United States is at least two countries, split down the middle along the 100th meridian from North Dakota to Texas. The 100th meridian is a critical dividing line—east of the line states receive an average of 20 inches of rain or more per year, while to the west of the line, states receive an average of 20 inches of rain or less, sometimes much less, per year. As a result, the challenge of economic development of the American West revolved in many ways around the challenges of finding and mobilizing water resources, especially for irrigated agriculture. Irrigation in the 31 eastern states is almost entirely a supplement to natural rainfall. In the West, most crop production would not be possible without large-scale artificial irrigation. The federal government, through federal laws such as the Reclamation Act and other policy initiatives, has been central to efforts to expand irrigated acreage and encourage the settlement of the western United States.

When the first national assessments of irrigation were released from the Census of Agriculture in 1890, there were an estimated 3.7 million acres of irrigated land nationwide. Irrigated land acreage has increased steadily since then (see figure 8.1), with a brief dip through the 1920s to 1930s associated with the Great Depression. Between 1939 and 1949, total irrigated acreage rose by 43 percent, the largest increase ever reported in the

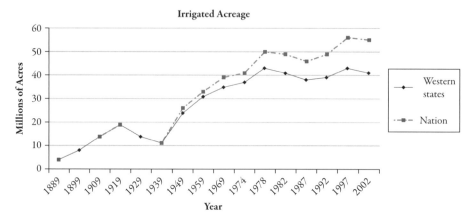

FIGURE 8.1. Irrigated acreage in the 17 western states and total irrigated acreage nationwide, 1889–2007
Source: Based on data from the USDA Census of Agriculture (2007a) and Farm and Ranch Irrigation Surveys (1998, 2003, 2008a).

United States (USDA 1950), largely due to federal and state support for major irrigation and water storage and delivery systems. Texas, for instance, tripled its irrigated acreage from 0.9 to 3.1 million acres, due to groundwater exploitation in the high plains area (associated with tapping the Ogallala aquifer, discussed in chapter 2: Legal and Institutional Framework of Water Management). During the same period, California increased its irrigated acreage from 4.3 to 6.4 million acres, largely due to expansion of irrigation in the state's Central Valley associated with the construction of the Central Valley Project, a massive water infrastructure project funded by US taxpayers through the federal Bureau of Reclamation.

Today, the United States produces a diverse array of agricultural commodities that have varying levels of water demand and irrigation requirements. Figure 8.2 shows the proportion of irrigated acreage in the nation, by different crop types (USDA 2007b). In 2007, 40 million acres were in field crops, accounting for almost 60 percent of irrigated acreage. Pasture accounted for 31 percent of irrigated acreage, while vegetables, orchards, and berries together accounted for 10 percent. Field crops and pasture are often more water-intensive than vegetables, orchards, and berries, requiring up to five times as much water per acre to cultivate, but they remain key staples for livestock feed, basic food needs, exports, and other segments of the nation's food and fiber industries.

Agriculture is the primary user of groundwater and surface water in the United States, accounting for 80 percent of the nation's total water consumption and over 90 percent of water use in many western states (USDA 2004). By the year 2050, the human population is expected to increase by 25 percent in the United States and by as much as 50 percent worldwide, which will drive up the demand for water to meet food, fiber, and fuel needs. Already, the United States is reaching the limit of many of its freshwater

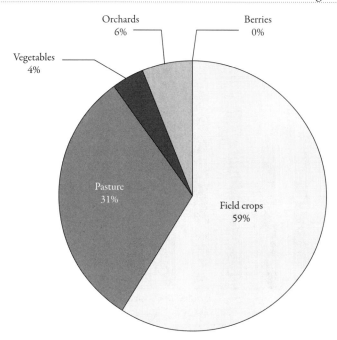

FIGURE 8.2. Proportion of irrigated acreage in different crop types, 2007
Source: Based on data from the USDA (2007b).
Federal Role in Agricultural Water Supply

supplies. Groundwater levels are falling rapidly in many areas, and many river systems are overallocated (Palaniappan and Gleick 2009). Climate change threatens to exacerbate these challenges through warmer temperatures, decreased snowpack, shifting precipitation patterns, increased evapotranspiration (ET), and more frequent and severe floods and droughts.

This chapter discusses historic and current trends in agricultural water use and presents national data in order to understand large-scale, long-term agricultural water supply and quality trends. It then turns to three key 21st-century water challenges: growing competition over freshwater supplies, increased scrutiny of agricultural runoff or nonpoint-source pollution, and climate change. The chapter concludes with a series of recommendations to ensure the continued viability of the agricultural sector in the United States through partnerships and policies promoting agricultural management practices that sustain and protect water resources.

Agricultural Water Use Trends

In 2005, the USGS estimated that agricultural water withdrawals in the United States were around 144 million acre-feet per year or 128 billion gallons per day—almost three times the amount of water withdrawn for public water supplies nationwide. (See

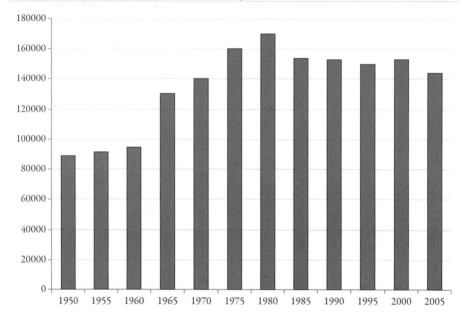

FIGURE 8.3.   Total water withdrawals for irrigation nationwide in thousands of acre-feet, 1950–2005
Source: Based on data from the USGS Estimated Use of Water (1951, 1957, 1961, 1968, 1972, 1977, 1983, 1988, 1993, 1998, 2004, 2009).

box 8.1 for discussion of water use terminology.) Most of the water is applied by an irrigation system to sustain plant growth when natural rainfall alone is inadequate to meet crop water needs. Irrigation can also be useful for frost protection, application of chemicals, field preparation, crop cooling, dust suppression, and leaching salts from the root zone.

Between 1950 and 1980, irrigation demands grew from 90 to 170 million acre-feet, then dropped slightly over the following decades. They have now stabilized around 145 million acre-feet per year (see figure 8.3). This leveling off of demand is the result of several factors, including a slowdown in the expansion of irrigated acreage, changes in the makeup of crops grown, advances in irrigation efficiency, and higher energy costs to transport and supply water.

Surface water from rivers, lakes, and streams has historically been the primary source for irrigation, although data show an increasing reliance on groundwater since 1950 (USGS 2009). In 1950, more than three-quarters of all irrigation withdrawals came from surface water. Between 1950 and 2000, the total volume of groundwater withdrawals for irrigation grew threefold. By 2005, surface-water withdrawals composed just over half of the total withdrawals (58 percent), the remainder being supplied by groundwater wells.

BOX 8.1.
A NOTE ON WATER TERMINOLOGY

A variety of terms are used to describe agricultural water use, including water withdrawal, applied water, and consumptive use.

- Water *use* and *withdrawals* are often used synonymously to refer to water taken from a source and used for agricultural purposes, but it is important to distinguish among *withdrawals, consumptive use*, and *nonconsumptive use. Withdrawals* include groundwater and surface water taken from local sources or water transported via large infrastructure projects. Prior to delivery to a farm, water withdrawn from a source is subject to conveyance losses, in other words, seepage or evaporation from reservoirs and canals.
- *Consumptive use* refers to water that is unavailable for reuse in the basin from which it was extracted, such as through soil evaporation, plant transpiration, incorporation into plant biomass, seepage to a saline sink, or by contamination.
- *Nonconsumptive use* refers to water that is available for reuse within the basin from which it was extracted, typically through return flows.
- *Applied water* is the quantity of water delivered to the farm, that is, water withdrawals minus conveyance losses.

The Federal Role in Agricultural Water Supply and Use

The federal government has long played a central role in agricultural policy and specifically in water policies to promote and support national agricultural production. Although agriculture is quintessentially local—tied to the land and the particularities of its soils, microclimates, pests, and productivity—the federal government has been involved in everything from the construction of reservoirs and irrigation works to providing financial incentives and subsidies for particular crops to helping farmers implement soil conservation practices. Over the 20th century, federal water-resource development programs related to agriculture have had three primary objectives: to supply irrigation water, to protect agricultural land from floods, and to drain wetlands for agricultural use. Diverse federal agencies have had responsibility for administering these programs, including the Department of Interior's Bureau of Reclamation, the Army Corps of Engineers, and the Department of Agriculture. Together, these three agencies have contributed significantly to the expansion of irrigated agriculture in the United States (National Water Commission 1973). In addition, the US Geological Survey plays a central role through the collection and dissemination of data related to water use and quality with the help of the Department of Agriculture.

One of the most transformative pieces of legislation affecting irrigation water development and use in the United States was the passage of the Reclamation Act of 1902. The Reclamation Act set aside public funds to be used for "the construction and maintenance of irrigation works for the storage, diversion, and development of waters for the reclamation of arid and semiarid lands . . ." (The National Irrigation Act of 1902, 32 Stat., 388, §1). Projects included dams, canals, aqueducts, hydroelectric generators, and pumping stations, especially in the western United States. The act also created the US Reclamation Service, later renamed the Bureau of Reclamation, to administer these funds. In so doing, one of the most powerful water supply and management institutions in the nation was established.

Some of the earliest projects in the 20th century ran into problems: Substantial areas of the West include lands unsuitable for irrigation. Repayment of funds was often difficult for irrigators with high costs for land preparation or construction. Waterlogging of poorly drained soils required expensive drainage works. And the science of irrigating arid lands was young and incomplete (Reisner 1986). It was not until 1928, when Congress authorized the Boulder Canyon Project (Hoover Dam) that large appropriations began to flow from Congress, initiating the heyday of western irrigation activities.

Major construction of centralized water storage began in earnest during the Great Depression and lasted through the middle decades of the century (figure 8.4). During the Depression, the Bureau of Reclamation constructed several of the world's largest water infrastructure projects, including the Hoover Dam (1931), the Grand Coulee Dam (1933), and the California Central Valley Project (1935). These projects not only provided millions of acre-feet of irrigation water to arid western lands, but they also served as economic stimuli, generating employment, energy, and investment opportunities—all key aspects of the New Deal and embedded in efforts to restart the American economy.

These projects, financed by the sale of federal lands, were to be repaid by the users *without* interest, establishing a direct subsidy to agricultural water users in the West. These subsidies were justified by the acreage limitations within the act that were meant to target these incentives at small, family farms. However, these limitations were quickly circumvented by large landowners and corporations.

By the end of the century, however, new perspectives on land use and the natural environment began to challenge large-scale western reclamation projects. The environmental movement generated opposition to new water development projects as scientific understanding of the adverse environmental and ecological consequences of existing projects improved. Resistance to large-scale federal dam building also grew for financial reasons. "By the time [Jimmy] Carter became President, the cumulative federal debt was approaching a trillion dollars and inflation had already visited the double digits, but the federal water bureaucracies were still going through $5 billion every year. One of the first things he was going to chop out of the budget was dams" (Reisner 1986,

307–308). President Ronald Reagan continued efforts to reduce federal funding for pork-barrel water projects, and in 1986, Congress passed the Water Resources Development Act, which deauthorized 290 water development projects and, effectively, brought an end to large-scale reclamation works.

Today, the Bureau of Reclamation continues to operate about 180 major reclamation projects in the 17 western states. It remains the largest wholesaler of water in the nation, bringing water to more than 31 million people and one out of every five western farmers. Bureau of Reclamation water irrigates approximately 10 million acres of farmland, which produce 60 percent of the nation's vegetables and 25 percent of its fruits and nuts (USBR 2011). But the focus of its efforts is changing. The Bureau of Reclamation is restructuring its identity, operational approaches, and expertise to focus on more sustainable management of existing water systems, rather than building new ones. The bureau is also struggling to deal with the adverse impacts of its operations on federally threatened and/or endangered species.

In addition, the federal government plays a major role in providing subsidies to agriculture. Agricultural subsidies were first initiated back in the 1920s in response to a severe drop in global and domestic commodity prices after World War I. Today, they are found in various pieces of legislation, especially the US Farm Bill. For example, between 1995 and 2009, the Farm Bill allocated $247 trillion, or on average $20 billion annually to agricultural subsidy programs including direct payments for particular crops (annually accounting for the largest portion of the payments), crop insurance, conservation programs, and disaster programs (figure 8.4). Taxpayer funding for the crop insurance program, in particular, has significantly increased recently (Shields 2010).

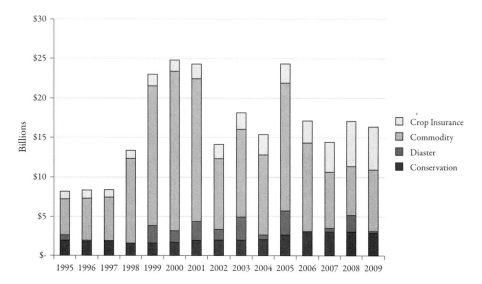

FIGURE 8.4. USDA subsidies to the United States, 1995–2009 (2010$)
Source: Based on data from the EWG (2011).

The 2007 Census of Agriculture reports that 38 percent of farms receive some form of federal subsidy, on average totaling around $10,000 per farm. However, certain crops receive the majority of payments. For instance, over three-quarters of corn, sorghum, soy, and wheat farms receive government payments (USDA 2007a). In addition, large farms receive much more in payments than do small farms. According to the Government Accounting Office (2001), over 80 percent of farm payments are made to large- and medium-sized farms, whereas small farms receive less than 20 percent of the payments. Thus, agricultural subsidies continue to be a major budget item and primarily benefit large-scale production of crops that tend to be low-value and water-intensive.

Twenty-First–Century Challenges

Agriculture will always be a major component of US water use. Farmers have long shown themselves to be flexible, dynamic, and innovative in response to water constraints, technological changes, and market forces. In the 21st century, the challenge will be to envision and develop an agricultural sector that continues to support rural livelihoods and environments, yet is able to respond to growing competition for water, unresolved challenges around water quality, and the rapidly growing threat from climatic change.

Greater Competition

Growing human populations, increased commercial and industrial water demands, new water requirements from the energy sector, and other factors all ensure that there will be greater competition between water users over the nation's finite water supply. In addition, there is a growing understanding of the need to ensure that human water use does not lead to massive and irreversible ecological harm (see chapter 6: Protecting Freshwater Ecosystems). This has led to increasing scrutiny of agricultural and municipal water systems and growing restrictions on the amount of water that can be taken out of many river systems, especially in the western United States where irrigated agriculture dominates water uses.

This problem, however, is not limited to the West. Even in the more humid eastern and southeastern portions of the country, new constraints on agriculture water uses are appearing, as urban populations grow and ecosystems' needs become more apparent. For instance, for more than a decade, Georgia, Alabama, and Florida have been engaged in legal battles over allocations and appropriate uses of the waters of the Apalachicola-Chattahoochee-Flint River Basin, which spans the three states. Due to drought and growing human water demands for urban and agricultural purposes, river flows have decreased drastically, leading to declining populations of Gulf sturgeon, purple bank climber, fat threeridge, and chipola slabshell, which are all now listed as threatened species. Efforts to develop more sustainable energy sources can also compete with the production of food and fiber, with significant impacts on water resources. Biofuels and natural gas have emerged as particularly water-intensive alternatives to traditional energy sources and may begin to affect water supplies in the Midwest, where the majority of corn is grown (see chapter 9: Water and Energy).

Agriculture and Water Quality

Agriculture is the single leading cause of water pollution in the United States today (EPA 2002). The 2000 National Water Quality Inventory conducted by the Environmental Protection Agency (EPA) identified agriculture as a source of pollution for 48 percent of impaired stream and river miles, and for 41 percent of impaired lake waters (EPA 2002). While the Clean Water Act (CWA) successfully reduced point-source pollution, such as industrial discharges, it has not been as successful in reducing nonpoint-source pollutants, such as agricultural runoff (see chapter 5: Water Quality for a more comprehensive discussion of nonpoint-source pollution). The CWA generally exempts many agriculture practices from permitting requirements, as agricultural by-products such as nutrients, salts, and other chemicals are not considered point-source pollutants (National Research Council 2008). As a consequence, the CWA leaves regulation of nonpoint-source pollution to individual states, resulting in varied responses (Ribaudo and Johansson 2006; National Research Council 2008).

In the 1990s, the EPA required states to list waters that were not meeting CWA standards and identify the amount by which point- and nonpoint-sources of pollution must be reduced in order for the water body to meet its stated water-quality standards, known as *total maximum daily loads*. However, these programs still lack enforceable requirements for nonpoint-source pollution (Andreen and Jones 2008; Adler 2011). In coming years, new national efforts will have to be launched to improve our understanding of the links between agricultural practices and national water quality and to improve efforts to address the worst nonpoint sources of contamination.

Climate Changes and US Agriculture

On top of these existing challenges to water availability and quality, a major new threat to agriculture has emerged: global climate change. International, national, and regional studies all indicate that unavoidable climate changes will be particularly important to the agricultural and water sectors, which are vulnerable to expected changes in temperatures, precipitation patterns, the length of growing seasons, the frequency of extreme events, and the distribution of crop pests and diseases (Karl, Melillo, and Peterson 2009; Smith et al. 2007). These impacts will intensify in the future. In the following, we discuss some of the key ways that climate changes will affect the agricultural sector (figure 8.5).

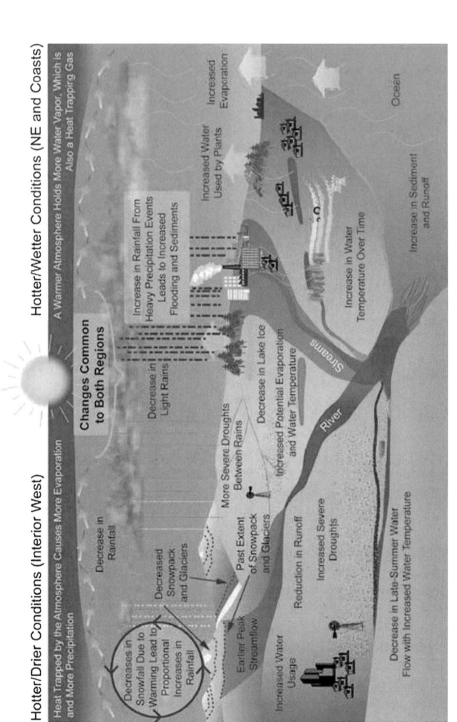

FIGURE 8.5. Graphical representation of the ways climate change will affect freshwater resources

Source: Karl, Melillo, and Peterson (2009).

Increased Agricultural Water Demand and Altered Water Availability

Agricultural water demands are highly sensitive to climatic conditions. Warmer temperatures increase plant transpiration rates, thereby increasing crop water requirements. Higher atmospheric carbon dioxide concentrations in some circumstances can reduce water requirements; in other circumstances, water requirements will grow. More studies can improve our understanding of the complex relationships among temperatures, carbon dioxide concentrations, and soil and crop type.

Just as climate changes will affect water demands, they will alter water availability and the hydrologic cycle. Precipitation patterns are already changing, with different patterns of extreme events. For many parts of the United States, wet areas are expected to become wetter and dry areas drier. In areas that are currently dominated by rain-fed agriculture, the increased uncertainty of precipitation may lead farmers to shift to greater supplemental irrigation, which may increase tensions over scarce surface and groundwater resources. Changes in the timing of flow in many snowmelt dominated rivers are also expected as snowfall and snowmelt patterns shift with warming temperatures. The western United States is especially vulnerable to changes in the timing and quantity of water supplies. With warmer temperatures, more precipitation will fall as rain, which will increase winter flows and reduce the total snowpack. In California, for example, scientists forecast that the total snowpack may decline by as much as 73 to 90 percent by the end of this century (Hayhoe et al. 2004). Because the winter snowpack acts as a natural reservoir that releases water throughout the summer, a reduced snowpack will reduce summer streamflows. Thus, surface water supplies will be increasingly out of phase with agricultural water demand.

Increased Floods and Droughts

Research also suggests that changes in extreme weather events, such as floods and droughts, will have a large effect on crop production. According to Reddy et al. (1999, 852), "unexpected late spring and early frosts and periodic episodes of heat and drought stress are predicted to occur more frequently in the changed weather environment, and these could exacerbate climate change effects on many aspects of crop growth and development, reducing crop yield and affecting quality."

Droughts and floods already have serious implications for agriculture. The Federal Emergency Management Agency estimates that the average cost of drought in the United States is $6 to $8 billion annually. Much of this cost is due to crop loss and other direct and indirect losses. Drought conditions are often favorable for many insects, including grasshoppers and locusts, and drought-stricken crops are also more susceptible to infestations and disease. Wind erosion associated with excessively dry soils can permanently destroy productive agricultural land, such as the long-term impacts of the Dust Bowl. In severe cases, agricultural losses, combined with a lack of food reserves or limited access to aid, could increase the price of food and contribute to a growing risk of food shortages and famine.

Floods can both harm and benefit agricultural production. Floodwaters deposit nutrient-rich sediment on the floodplains, thereby helping to fertilize and enrich soils. But these benefits are offset by the vulnerability of agricultural production to destructive floods that alternately destroy farms and crops. Floods may also cause significant damage to water conveyance and storage infrastructure, further affecting the availability and reliability of water resources.

Developing a 21st-Century Agricultural Water Policy

These new challenges raise questions about how the nation can best maintain a strong agricultural sector that can continue to supply adequate food, fiber, and now fuel for the country and the world. The future of agriculture in the United States depends on addressing both persistent and new water resources management problems in innovative ways. Many of these challenges can be addressed through smart actions at local and state levels, but there are important actions that the federal government must also consider. Specific policies are discussed in the following section with recommendations for federal agencies and actions.

PROVIDE INFORMATION TO ADAPT TO CLIMATE CHANGE

Agriculture is especially vulnerable to climate changes because of its dependence and sensitivity to weather, temperature, rainfall, snowmelt, and other climate-dependent factors. Significant investments are needed in research, technical assistance, and financial incentives to assist farmers and the agricultural sector more broadly in adapting to climate change. In addition, climate change projections must be incorporated into current land- and water-use planning efforts, with an emphasis on both climate change mitigation and adaptation in the agricultural sector.

To keep agriculture viable in the coming decades, greenhouse gas emissions must be reduced *(mitigation)* and unavoidable climate change impacts must be assessed and integrated into planning *(adaptation)*. There are several ways that agriculture can become more resilient. Water-efficiency measures can reduce the dependence of irrigated agriculture on scarce water resources and have been shown to increase crop yields and quality in many crop types. Overall, sustainable agricultural practices offer some of the best opportunities for the sector to become more resilient by reducing or even eliminating the use of synthetic fertilizers (often petroleum-based) and pesticides and by improving soil health and productivity with manure, compost, cover crops, and conservation tillage methods. This not only reduces the carbon costs of growing food, but also benefits water quality by reducing contaminant loads to waterways.

The federal government has a key responsibility to encourage and expand climate change adaptation efforts in the agricultural sector. Specifically, the Department of Agriculture should make climate change mitigation and adaptation a national priority and the Bureau of Reclamation and Army Corps of Engineers, which operate many of the nation's reservoirs and water infrastructure, should reevaluate their operation of these systems and develop new operational rules in light of climate change. Farm Bill conservation programs should be strengthened by enforcing current law that requires agricultural producers who receive federal funds to implement basic soil conservation practices (first introduced in the 1985 Farm Bill) and by expanding eligibility for organic producers.

Farmers and local communities will ultimately be responsible for dealing with climate challenges and for implementing adaptation strategies. But there is much that federal agencies can do to both reduce these challenges and enhance the ability of farmers to adapt. It is critical to communicate information on the nature of climate risks, climate change adaptation options, and technical assistance to agricultural communities. Even though impact studies have been conducted at universities and research centers across the country, in most cases, this information has not been adequately conveyed to farmers. There is a significant gap between top-down analysis and bottom-up implementation. Additional outreach is needed to convey the climate data and information that is available to farmers so that they can begin developing adaptation strategies.

Outreach efforts could be accomplished through existing institutions. In particular, cooperative extension services and the Natural Resource Conservation Service have long-standing relationships with farmers and agricultural organizations throughout the nation. Because cooperative extension agents and the Natural Resource Conservation Service have already established these important relationships, these organizations would serve as ideal conduits for outreach efforts. To encourage these efforts, the Department of Agriculture, in association with the Natural Resource Conservation Service, should develop trainings and provide guidance to extension agents about climate change impacts and adaptation strategies for the agricultural sector.

ENCOURAGE MORE EFFICIENT AGRICULTURAL WATER USE THROUGH IMPROVED IRRIGATION TECHNOLOGIES AND MANAGEMENT

Whereas the agricultural sector has made significant strides in terms of its water-use efficiency, there remains enormous untapped potential. Much of the irrigated acreage in the United States still uses flood irrigation (40 percent, according to the 2008 Farm and Ranch Irrigation Survey [USDA 2008a]) and the majority of farmers are not implementing scientific irrigation scheduling or other advanced water management techniques (less than 30 percent of farmers reported using a soil or plant moisture-sensing device or information about crop water requirements to determine when to irrigate, according to the 2008 Farm and Ranch Irrigation Survey).

By improving agricultural water-use efficiency, farmers can reduce their vulnerability to water-supply constraints. In addition, adopting many of these practices, including drip irrigation and improved irrigation scheduling, can increase crop productivity through better yields and higher quality crops. Agricultural water-use efficiency improvements are part of a soft path approach, which seeks to maximize water productivity in all sectors (Gleick 2009).

Irrigation Technologies

There have been some important shifts in irrigation trends over the last two decades, moving away from flood irrigation. In 1998, flood irrigation was the most common irrigation method but by 2008, the use of gravity flow systems on irrigated acreage had dropped to only 40 percent of irrigated acreage nationwide, while the use of sprinkler systems increased to 56 percent of irrigated acreage (figure 8.6). Drip and microirrigation systems also increased slightly between 1998 and 2008 from 4 to 7 percent of irrigated acreage. Herein, we discuss each of these irrigation methods in turn and then compare their average efficiencies.

Flood irrigation is the oldest form of irrigation—it is simply the application of water by gravity flow to the surface of the field. Either the entire field is flooded (by uncontrolled flood or basin irrigation) or the water is fed into small channels *(furrows)* or strips of land *(borders)* (figure 8.7a). It is most often used on field crops, such as rice and alfalfa. Flooding often requires the least infrastructure and labor and, therefore, is the least

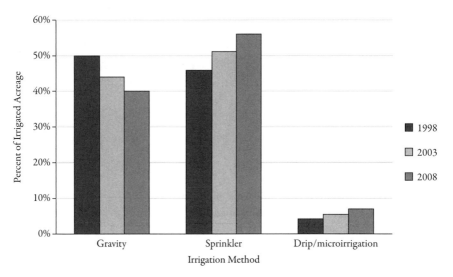

FIGURE 8.6. The fraction of land irrigated with gravity, sprinkler, and drip or microirrigation systems in the United States

Source: Based on data from the USDA Census of Agriculture (2007a) and Farm and Ranch Irrigation Surveys (1998, 2003, 2008a).

expensive; however, it can be challenging where there is sloping terrain or on crops that do not tolerate ponding or that develop moisture-related diseases.

Sprinkler irrigation was introduced in the 1930s. With a sprinkler irrigation system, water is delivered to the field through a pressurized pipe system and is distributed by rotating sprinkler heads or spray nozzles or a single gun-type sprinkler. The sprinklers can be either permanently mounted *(solid set)* or mounted on a moving platform that is connected to a water source *(traveling)*. Low-energy precision application sprinklers are an adaptation of center pivot systems that use drop tubes that extend down from the pipeline (figure 8.7b). Low-energy precision application systems can conserve both water and energy by applying the water at a low pressure close to the ground, which reduces water loss from evaporation and wind, increases application uniformity, and decreases energy requirements. Many row crops and orchard crops are currently irrigated with sprinklers.

Drip irrigation refers to the slow application of low-pressure water from plastic tubing placed near the plant's root zone. Drip systems commonly consist of buried PVC pipe mains and submains attached to surface polyethylene lateral lines (figure 8.8). A less expensive, but also less durable, option is drip tape. Water is applied through drip emitters placed above or below ground, referred to as *surface* and *subsurface drip*, respectively. Microirrigation systems are similar to drip systems with the exception that water is applied at a higher rate (5 to 50 gallons per hour) by a small plastic sprinkler head (Evans et al. 1998).

Despite the success with precision irrigation systems on a wide variety of crops, there are barriers to transitioning to new irrigation technologies. Chief among these barriers is cost, as sprinkler and drip systems often cost over $1,000 per acre to install, and there can also be additional maintenance costs associated with keeping the systems running. In addition, sprinkler and drip systems can impede farm equipment in fields that are cropped multiple times a year. Furthermore, irrigators are limited by their water supply. In most cases, agricultural water suppliers do not provide pressurized water, which is necessary for precision irrigation technologies; therefore, individual irrigators have to buy pumps to pressurize their water. In addition, some agricultural water suppliers are on rotational delivery systems, where each irrigator must take a large amount of water once every few weeks. These delivery systems are designed for flood irrigation.

Nonetheless, flood irrigation is the least efficient because of the larger volumes of unproductive evaporative losses that occur, water application to nontargeted surface areas, and the propensity for deep percolation, which all mean that much of the water that is consumed does not contribute to crop growth. With proper management and design, drip and microirrigation are typically more efficient at maximizing crop-yield-per-unit water use. The *potential irrigation efficiencies* (defined here as the volume of irrigation water beneficially used by the plant divided by the volume of irrigation water applied minus change in storage of irrigation water) for flood irrigation systems range from 60 to 85 percent, whereas for sprinklers, the potential irrigation efficiencies range from 70 to 90

FIGURE 8.7. Border flood irrigation (a) and low-energy precision application sprinkler head (b)
Source: USDA Natural Resources Conservation Service Photo Library.

FIGURE 8.8. Drip irrigation on vines
Source: USDA Natural Resources Conservation Service Photo Library.

percent. Potential irrigation efficiencies for drip and microirrigation systems are even higher, ranging from 88 to 90 percent (table 8.1).

Irrigation Management

Irrigation technologies, however, are only methods to distribute water, not measures of efficiency. A recent University of California Cooperative Extension study, for example, showed that vineyards using drip irrigation systems varied widely in the amount of water applied per acre (from 0.2 to 1.3 acre-feet), suggesting that management practices are an important determinant of applied water (Lewis et al. 2008). A key management practice in terms of water-use efficiency is appropriate irrigation scheduling.

Crop water requirements vary throughout the crop life cycle and depend on weather and soil conditions. Irrigation scheduling provides a means to evaluate and apply an amount of water sufficient to meet crop requirements at the right time. Even though proper scheduling can either increase or decrease water use depending on current practices, it will likely increase yield and/or quality, resulting in an improvement in water-use efficiency because more crops or more revenue can be produced per unit of water (Ortega-Farias et al. 2004; Dokter 1996; Buchleiter, Heermann, and Wenstrom 1996; Rijks and Gbeckor-Kove 1990).[1] Despite the promise of technology-based irrigation scheduling, the vast majority of farmers still primarily rely on visual inspection or personal

TABLE 8.1.

Irrigation Systems and Associated Efficiencies

Type of irrigation system	Efficiency (%)
Flood	
Basin	85
Border	77.5
Furrow	67.5
Wild flooding	60
Gravity	75
Average	73
Sprinkler	
Hand move or portable	70
Center pivot and linear move	82.5
Solid set or permanent	75
Side roll sprinkler	70
Low-energy precision application	90
Average	78
Drip/microirrigation	
Surface drip	87.5
Buried drip	90
Subirrigation	90
Microsprinkler	87.5
Average	89

Note: Efficiency is defined here as the volume of irrigation water beneficially used (equal to ET) divided by the volume of irrigation water applied minus change in storage of irrigation water.

Source: Salas et al. (2006).

experience to determine when to irrigate (USDA 2008a). Soil or plant moisture sensors, computer models, daily evapo-transpiration reports, and scheduling services, which have long been proven effective, are still fairly uncommon, suggesting there is significant room for improving farmer access to these resources. This conclusion is supported by the experience of individual growers who are increasingly linking their irrigation methods and schedules to real-time information on soil moisture and measured water needs.

The traditional irrigation strategy is to supply irrigated areas with sufficient water so that crops transpire at their maximum potential. In other words, water is provided to meet full crop water requirements throughout the season. However, water scarcity and interest in maximizing crop quality have catalyzed a number of innovative approaches to

TABLE 8.2.

Benefits Associated with Regulated Deficit Irrigation for Different Crop Types

Crop type	Quality benefit associated with RDI
Tomatoes	Increase solids
Almonds	Reduce hull splitting
Stone fruits (peaches, plums, apricots, etc.)	Increases shelf life
Pistachios	Increase shell split
Grapes	Improved quality

Source: Chris Higgins, pers. comm. (January 2009).

irrigation management that have been shown to reduce crop water use, including deficit irrigation, tail water recovery, and soil-management practices that increase soil moisture retention (Polaris Institute 2008).

Thus, another promising irrigation management technique is *deficit irrigation.* Deficit irrigation, defined as the application of water below full crop ET requirements, can be an effective tool to reduce applied water and increase revenue (Chaves et al. 2007; Fereres and Soriano 2007). A growing body of international work shows that consumptive water use can be reduced in orchards and vineyards without negative impacts on production. In fact, in some cases, it may improve crop quality. A recent Food and Agriculture Organization report presents a number of deficit irrigation studies focused on various crops in semiarid climates around the world, concluding that substantial water savings can be achieved with little impact on crop yield and quality (Goodwin and Boland 2002). Burt, Howes, and Wilson (2003), however, argue that significant crop stress over multiple years can have a negative impact on yield. These negative impacts may be mitigated, however, by precise management.

Whereas deficit irrigation is uncontrolled, and often unintentional, *regulated deficit irrigation* (RDI) is an irrigation management practice implemented during stress-tolerant growth stages in order to minimize negative impacts on yield (Goldhamer 2007). Because response to water stress can vary considerably by crop, a clear understanding of crop behavior and ecological conditions is required to maintain yields. In pistachios, for example, RDI is imposed during the shell-hardening phase, which is particularly stress-tolerant (and therefore appropriate for reduced irrigation), whereas the bloom and nut-filling stages are not. Additionally, studies indicate that RDI may improve crop quality, particularly for wine grapes (Girona et al. 2006). A summary of benefits associated with RDI is provided in table 8.2.

Water savings associated with RDI depend on many factors, including the crop type and the sensitivity of growth stages to stress, climatic demand, stored available water at bud break, spring-summer rains, and the particular irrigation method.[2] Cooperative extension specialists have hosted a variety of workshops throughout the nation to discuss how to best apply RDI to different crops using local climate data and field-specific information. Thus far, RDI has been more successful with tree crops and vines than with field crops for two reasons (Fereres and Soriano 2007): (1) crop quality, rather than total yield, is an important determinant of economic returns for these crops, and (2) the yield-determining processes in many trees and vines are not as sensitive to water stress during particular growth stages as many field crops.

Soil Moisture Management

In addition to implementing new irrigation technologies and irrigation management practices, a growing number of farms are using mulch, cover crops, conservation tillage, and other soil management techniques to build and conserve soil moisture. These techniques are part of a more holistic approach to farming, often associated with the sustainable agriculture movement and organic agriculture. In traditional agricultural production, soil is tilled between each planting. Conventional tillage involves heavy equipment that removes all of the vegetation from the field and digs furrows in the soil for the next crop seed. In so doing, conventional tillage disrupts the soil biology, leads to soil compaction and impermeability, exposes moist soil strata to evaporation, releases sequestered carbon, and often contributes fine sediments to nearby water courses.

Conservation tillage systems disturb the soil as little as possible; leaving a protective cover of vegetation or mulch on the soil surface. During the growing season, this suppresses weeds, retains soil moisture, and reduces erosion (Baldwin 2009). For example, in a long-term tillage study conducted by the University of Kentucky, researchers observed higher soil moisture under no-till corn production as compared with that under conventional tillage throughout the growing season (Blevins et al. 1971; Blevins and Frye 1993). In addition, significantly less evaporation occurred under no-till early in the growing season, leading the researchers to conclude that conservation of soil water may carry the no-till crop through short drought periods without severe water stress or additional irrigation. Finally, saturated hydraulic conductivity measurements suggest better water movement in no-tillage compared with conventional tillage.

The increased soil permeability and water-holding capacity associated with conservation tillage underscores the importance of conservation tillage practices to increase soil moisture and, therefore, decrease irrigation demand. Conservation tillage is growing in the United States. From 1990 to 2000, the number of US cropland acres planted without tillage more than tripled to 51 million acres. In the Southeast, farmers during the 2000 to 2001 cropping year used no-till systems in planting 39 percent of corn, 20 percent of cotton, and 58 percent of soybeans grown in the region (Baldwin 2009).

PROMOTE CLIMATE-RESILIENT WATER MANAGEMENT OPTIONS

Climate change is already affecting the timing and reliability of our water supplies and historical trends are no longer adequate to understand future water availability (Karl, Melillo, and Peterson 2009). In some seasons and years, we may need more water, in others, less. It is clear that demand will be more variable as extreme weather events become more common. Therefore, it is prudent to develop more climate-resilient water management strategies, which can adapt to changing conditions.

For example, an estimated 38 percent of irrigated agriculture relies on groundwater (Siebert et al. 2010), and this is likely to increase during droughts, when surface water supplies are scarce. Throughout much of the United States, groundwater basins have been mismanaged and are already overdrafted. Whereas overdraft certainly creates challenges, it may also provide an opportunity. In particular, we may be able to store excess surface flows in groundwater aquifers through recharge during wet years for use during dry years.

Better *conjunctive management* of surface water and groundwater supplies can improve supply reliability and flexibility, particularly in the face of more frequent floods and drought, reduce land subsidence, and minimize the impacts of excess runoff on local steams and the marine environment. The federal government should require all states to design and implement comprehensive groundwater monitoring and management programs as part of climate change planning and adaptation efforts.

REALIGN FINANCIAL INCENTIVES IN THE FEDERAL FARM BILL

The wise use of limited natural resources is beneficial in the long run for society, the environment, and the nation's economy. We have inherited an agricultural system based on outdated imperatives to settle the western United States, provide price supports to buoy struggling small farmers, and to provide inexpensive domestic food and fiber. Today, the migration of the population westward is leading to unsustainable population growth in this region relative to water supplies. Farming has become more consolidated and vertically integrated with fewer, larger farms producing products for an international market, which is subject to global market forces. It is critical that we reexamine the incentive structures that were developed in the past in light of these changed circumstances and update structures to reflect new priorities and realities. Incentives that may need to be revisited include those for crop price supports, as well as energy and water subsidies.

For instance, many conservation practices require substantial initial investment (even though a return on investment may be realized over time). Thus, additional financial mechanisms are needed to support water conservation and efficiency improvements. Specifically, the federal government should realign funding in the Farm Bill to make greater and more targeted investments in programs that conserve water resources and protect water quality, for example, by reforming and expanding the Agricultural Water Enhancement Program and by setting up a revolving loan program to provide initial capital to farmers to upgrade irrigation technology and management practices. Instead of requiring new funding for these programs, the federal government could reduce commodity support payments for low-value, water-intensive crops in order to support more sustainable agricultural practices.

In addition, there is a great need for technical assistance and financial assistance programs to accelerate the development and deployment of efficient irrigation technologies and management practices. Technical assistance is necessary to help farmers determine which measures will work best for their particular context and to implement and maintain those measures. There are few public resources to aid the agricultural sector; therefore, many farmers rely on advice from fertilizer and pesticide sales officers and technology manufacturers. To capture untapped potential for water savings through improved management practice, it will be necessary to expand water-efficiency information and evaluation programs through the Natural Resources Conservation Service, Cooperative Extension offices, and local Resource Conservation districts.

AVOID INAPPROPRIATE SUBSIDIES FOR NEW WATER SUPPLIES

Price signals have been shown to provide important incentives for the wise use of resources. In the future, we should avoid inappropriate subsidies for new water-supply options. We should ensure that agricultural water rates better reflect the true cost of water infrastructure and service (with interest) and the effects on water resources and ecosystems. Finally, we must provide support and enforcement for efforts at federal and state scales to require water-rate structures that encourage efficient use of water.

Conclusions

During the 20th century, the federal government played an active role in encouraging the expansion of irrigated agriculture, particularly in the western United States. Between 1930 and 1960, Congress authorized hundreds of water infrastructure projects, in many cases built and operated by the federal government. These projects were critical for the expansion of agricultural production and the settlement of the West, but they also had negative environmental and social impacts, such as creating barriers to fish passage, dislocating people, and providing highly subsidized water, often resulting in inequitable and inefficient water uses. The 20th century also saw the creation of the first federal Farm Bill, originally intended to help small farmers who had seen tremendous losses in the Great Depression. Today, many of these subsidies still exist, although they tend to go to large farms that are not necessarily in financial distress, costing taxpayers around $20 billion annually (in inflation-adjusted 2010$).

At the beginning of the 21st century, agriculture is confronted with several critical challenges, including increased competition over water resources, growing water quality problems, and global climate change. The time is ripe to consider a more comprehensive approach to addressing these persistent and new challenges. A 21st-century agricultural water policy should provide critical information to the agricultural community on climate change impacts and adaptation options, as the agricultural sector is among the most vulnerable to climate change impacts. In addition, a 21st-century agricultural water policy should encourage more efficient water use through improved irrigation technologies and management practices, and climate-resilient water management options such as better conjunctive management of surface water and groundwater resources. Finally, the future requires more integration of historically distinct policy issues, for example, the impact of energy policies on agriculture, and revision of outdated policies, such as agricultural subsidies that can contribute to inefficient water use.

References

Adler, R. 2011. "Rethinking Water Law in a Changing Climate." In *Global Warming: A Reader*. Edited by W. H. Rodgers, pages. Durham, NC: Carolina Academic Press.

Andreen, W. L., and S. C. Jones. 2008. *The Clean Water Act: A Blueprint for Reform*. Washington, DC: Center for Progressive Reform. http://www.progressivereform.org/articles/CW_Blueprint_802.pdf.

Baldwin, K. R. 2009. *Conservation Tillage on Organic Farms*. Center for Environmental Farming Systems. Raleigh, NC: North Carolina State University. http://www.cefs.ncsu.edu/publications/bulletins.html

Blevins, R. L., D. Cook, R. E. Phillips, and S. H. Phillips. 1971. "Influence of No-Tillage on Soil Moisture." *Agronomy Journal* 63: 593–596.

Blevins, R. L., and W. W. Frye. 1993. "Conservation Tillage: An Ecological Approach to Soil Management." *Advances in Agronomy* 51: 33–78.

Buchleiter, G. W., D. F. Heermann, and R. J. Wenstrom. 1996. "Economic Analysis of On-Farm Irrigation Scheduling." In *Evapotranspiration and Irrigation Scheduling: Proceedings of the International Conference*. Edited by C. R. Camp, E. J. Sadler, and R. E. Yoder, 986–991. San Antonio, TX: American Society of Agricultural Engineers.

Burt, C., D. Howes, and G. Wilson. 2003. *California Agricultural Water Electrical Energy Requirements: Final Report*. Prepared for the California Energy Commission by the Irrigation Technology Research Center. ITRC Report R 03-006. San Luis Obispo: California Polytechnic State University.

Chaves, M. M., T. P. Santos, C. R. Souza, M. F. Ortuno, M. L. Rodrigues, C. M. Lopes, J. P. Maroco, and J. S. Pereira. 2007. "Deficit Irrigation in Grapevine Improves Water-Use Efficiency while Controlling Vigour and Production Quality." *Annals of Applied Biology* 150: 237–252.

Dokter, D. T. 1996. "AgriMet—The Pacific Northwest Cooperative Agricultural Weather Station Network." In *Evapotranspiration and Irrigation Scheduling: Proceedings of the International Conference*. Edited by C. R. Camp, E. J. Sadler, and R. E. Yoder, 986–991. San Antonio, TX: American Society of Agricultural Engineers.

Environmental Working Group (EWG). 2011. Farm Subsidies Database. http://farm.ewg.org/.

Evans, R. O., K. A. Harrison, J. E. Hook, C. V. Privette, W. I. Segars, W. B. Smith, D. L. Thomas, and A. W. Tyson. 1998. *Irrigation Conservation Practices Appropriate for the Southeastern United States*. Project Report 32. Atlanta: Georgia Department of Natural Resources Environmental Protection Division and Georgia Geological Survey.

Fereres, E., and M. A. Soriano. 2007. "Deficit Irrigation for Reducing Agricultural Water Use." *Journal of Experimental Botany* 58 (2): 147–159.

Girona, J., M. Mata, J. del Campo, A. Arbonés, E. Bartra, and J. Marsal. 2006. "The Use of Midday Leaf Water Potential for Scheduling Deficit Irrigation in Vineyards." *Irrigation Science* 24: 115–127.

Gleick, P. H. 2009. "Water Soft Path Thinking in the United States." In *Making the Most of the Water We Have: A Soft Path Approach to Water Management*. Edited by D. Brooks, O. M. Brandes, and S. Gurman, 49–60. London: Earthscan.

Goldhamer, D. A. 2007. "Regulated Deficit Irrigation in Trees and Vines." In *Agricultural Water Management: Proceedings of a Workshop in Tunisia*. Edited by L. Holliday, 70–80. Washington, DC: The National Academies Press.

Goodwin, I., and A. M. Boland. 2002. *Scheduling Deficit Irrigation of Fruit Trees for Optimizing Water Use Efficiency in Deficit Irrigation Practices*. FAO Technical Papers, Water Reports 22. Rome: Food and Agriculture Organization. www.fao.org/docrep.

Hayhoe, K., D. Cayan, C. B. Field, P. C. Frumhoff, E. P. Maurer, N. L. Miller, S. C. Moser, et al. 2004. "Emissions Pathways, Climate Change, and Impacts on California." *Proceedings of the National Academy of Sciences USA* 101 (34): 12422–12427.

Karl, T. J., J. M. Melillo, and T. C. Peterson, eds. 2009. *Global Climate Change Impacts in the United States*. New York: Cambridge University Press.

Lewis, D. J., G. McGourty, J. Harper, R. Elkins, J. Christian-Smith, J. Nosera, P. Papper, R. Sanford, L. Schwankl, and T. Prichard. 2008. *Meeting Irrigated Agriculture Water Needs in the Mendocino County Portion of the Russian River*. Davis: University of California Cooperative Extension Mendocino County, University of California Davis, Department of Land Air and Water Resources, and University of California Kearny Agricultural Center.

National Research Council. 2008. *Mississippi River Water Quality and the Clean Water Act: Progress, Challenges, and Opportunities*. Washington, DC: National Academies Press.

National Water Commission (NWC). 1973. *Water Policies for the Future. Final Report to the President and to the Congress of the United States*. Washington, DC: US Government Printing Office.

Ortega-Farías, S., C. Acevedo, A. Acevedo, and B. Leyton. 2004. *Talca Irrigation Management System (TIMAS) for Grapevine. Research and Extension Center for Irrigation and Agroclimatology (CITRA)*. Casilla, Chile: Universidad de Talca.

Palaniappan, M., and P. H. Gleick. 2009. "Peak Water." In *The World's Water 2008–2009, The Biennial Report on Freshwater Resources*. Edited by P. H. Gleick, 1–16. Covelo, CA: Island Press.

Polaris Institute. 2008. *Water Stewardship: Ensuring a Secure Future for California Agriculture*. Sebastopol, CA: California Agricultural Water Stewardship Initiative. http://www.agwaterstewards.org.

Reddy, K. R., G. H. Davidonis, A. S. Johnson, and B. T. Vinyard. 1999. "Temperature Regime and Carbon Dioxide Enrichment Alter Cotton Boll Development and Fiber Properties." *Agronomic Journal* 91: 851–858.

Reisner, M. 1986. *Cadillac Desert: The American West and Its Disappearing Water*. New York: Viking.

Ribaudo, M., and R. Johansson. 2006. "Water Quality: Impacts of Agriculture." In *Agricultural Resources and Environmental Indicators*. Edited by K. Wiebe and N. Gollehon, 33–241. Washington, DC: USDA Economic Research Service. http://www.ers.usda.gov/publications/arei/eib16/eib16_2-2.pdf.

Rijks, D., and N. Gbeckor-Kove. 1990. "Agrometeorological Information for Effective Irrigation Scheduling." *Acta Horticulturae (ISHS)* 278: 833–840.

Salas, W., P. Green, S. Frolking, C. Li, and S. Boles. 2006. *Estimating Irrigation Water Use for California Agriculture: 1950s to Present.* CEC-500-2006-057. Sacramento: California Energy Commission, PIER Energy-Related Environmental Research.

Shields, D. A. 2010. *Federal Crop Insurance: Background and Issues.* R40532. Washington DC: Congressional Research Service.

Siebert, S., J. Burke, J. M. Faures, K. Frenken, J. Hoogeveen, P. Doll, and F. T. Portmann. 2010. "Groundwater use for irrigation – a global inventory." *Hydrology and Earth System Sciences*, 14, 1863–1880.

Smith, P., D. Martino, Z. Cai, D. Gwary, H. Janzen, P. Kumar, B. McCarl, et al. 2007. "Agriculture." In *Climate Change 2007: Mitigation. Contribution of Working Group III to the Fourth Assessment Report of the Intergovernmental Panel on Climate Change.* Edited by B. Metz, O. R. Davidson, P. R. Bosch, R. Dave, and L. A. Meyer, 497–540. Cambridge: Cambridge University Press.

US Bureau of Reclamation (USBR). 2011. About Us. US Bureau of Reclamation. http://www.usbr.gov/main/about/.

US Department of Agriculture (USDA). 1950. *Special Reports, Irrigation 1950: A Graphic Summary.* Washington, DC: US Department of Agriculture. http://www.agcensus.usda.gov/Publications/Historical_Publications/1950/vol5%20Irrigation%201950/41667071v5p7_TOC.pdf.

———. 1998. *Farm and Ranch Irrigation Survey.* Washington, DC: US Department of Agriculture. http://www.agcensus.usda.gov/.

———. 2003. *Farm and Ranch Irrigation Survey.* Washington, DC: US Department of Agriculture. http://www.agcensus.usda.gov/.

———. 2004. *Irrigation and Water Use.* Washington, DC: Economic Research Service. http://www.ers.usda.gov/briefing/wateruse/.

———. 2007a. *2007 Census of Agriculture.* Washington, DC: US Department of Agriculture. http://www.agcensus.usda.gov/Publications/2007/Online_Highlights/Custom_Summaries/Data_Comparison_Major_Crops.pdf.

———. 2007b. *Value Added to the U.S. Economy by the Agricultural Sector via the Production of Goods and Services, 2000–2006.* Washington, DC: Economic Research Service. http://www.ers.usda.gov/Data/FarmIncome/FinfidmuXls.htm.

———. 2008. *Farm and Ranch Irrigation Survey.* Washington, DC: US Department of Agriculture. http://www.agcensus.usda.gov/.

———. 2008. *Western Irrigated Agriculture.* Washington, DC: Economic Research Service. http://www.ers.usda.gov/Data/WesternIrrigation/.

US Environmental Protection Agency (EPA). 2002. "Rivers and Streams," and "Lakes, Reservoirs, and Ponds." In *National Water Quality Inventory: Report 2000*, chaps. 2 and 3. Washington, DC: US Environmental Protection Agency. http://www.epa.gov/305b/2000report.

US Geological Survey (USGS). 1951. *Estimated Use of Water in the United States, 1950.* Circular 115. Reston, VA: US Geological Survey.

———. 1957. *Estimated Use of Water in the United States, 1955.* Circular 398. Reston, VA: US Geological Survey.

———. 1961. *Estimated Use of Water in the United States, 1960.* Circular 456. Reston, VA: US Geological Survey.

———. 1968. *Estimated Use of Water in the United States, 1965.* Circular 556. Reston, VA: US Geological Survey.

————. 1972. *Estimated Use of Water in the United States, 1970.* Circular 676. Reston, VA: US Geological Survey.

————. 1977. *Estimated Use of Water in the United States, 1975.* Circular 765. Reston, VA: US Geological Survey.

————. 1983. *Estimated Use of Water in the United States, 1980.* Circular 1001. Reston, VA: US Geological Survey.

————. 1988. *Estimated Use of Water in the United States, 1985.* Circular 1004. Reston, VA: US Geological Survey.

————. 1993. *Estimated Use of Water in the United States, 1990.* Circular 1081. Reston, VA: US Geological Survey.

————. 1998. *Estimated Use of Water in the United States, 1995.* Circular 1200. Reston, VA: US Geological Survey.

————. 2004. *Estimated Use of Water in the United States, 2000.* Circular 1268. Reston, VA: US Geological Survey.

————. 2009. *Estimated Use of Water in the United States, 2005.* Circular 1344. Reston, VA: US Geological Survey.

US Government Accountability Office (GAO). (2001). Farm Programs: Information on Recipients of Federal Payments. GAO-01–606. Retrieved on February 4, 2011 from http://www.gao.gov/new.items/d01606.pdf.

WATER AND ENERGY

Heather Cooley and Juliet Christian-Smith

Introduction

Water and energy are intricately connected: We use water to produce energy and energy to produce water. Throughout the 20th century, however, these connections were largely ignored. Water and energy managers were separated by well-defined silos and rarely communicated with one another. Water systems were designed and constructed with the assumption that energy would be cheap and abundant. Likewise, energy systems were developed with the assumption that water would be cheap and abundant. And although some have long argued that we would reach peak energy and, more recently, peak water (Gleick and Palaniappan 2010), assumptions about abundance were the status quo.

The era of abundance is coming to an end and is being replaced by the era of limits. Throughout the United States, conflicts between energy production and water availability are on the rise. Some water managers actively seek ways to optimize the efficiency of their water systems in response to rising energy costs and concerns about greenhouse gas emissions. Likewise, there is growing concern that water availability and quality affects the nation's energy security. In January 2008, there was concern that a drought could force a shutdown of nuclear plants across the Southeast United States if water dropped below the level of the intake pipes or if it was too warm to use for cooling. Even though rolling blackouts did not occur, energy prices were expected to spike (Weiss 2008). In September 2010, water levels in Lake Mead dropped to 1,084 feet, prompting the Bureau of Reclamation to reduce Hoover Dam's energy generation by one-third. As water levels continue to drop and the threat of climate change looms on the horizon, dam operators are concerned that more regular or even permanent reductions in the electricity generating capacity will destabilize energy markets in the Southwestern United States (Walton 2008).

Even while we are confronting these limits, however, our policies and management decisions still reflect a 20th-century approach. Water and energy policies are rarely integrated and are based on the assumption that the other resource will remain cheap and plentiful. For example, the federal government, through mandates and subsidies for corn production, has massively increased the production of ethanol, with little concern for the water supply and quality implications of this policy (Energy Policy Act of 2005). Similarly, efforts to reduce greenhouse gas emissions from coal through carbon capture and storage or through expansion of natural gas production using hydraulic fracturing are being pursued with little knowledge of or regard for the water implications of these practices. Likewise, a growing number of water utilities are pursuing seawater desalination or other alternative approaches to water supply. Although there have been significant efficiency improvements in seawater desalination, it remains more energy-intensive than most other water supply-and-demand management options (Wolff, Cohen, and Nelson 2004).

This chapter explores the connections between water and energy and highlights where tensions or conflicts are occurring or are expected in the coming years. We argue that developing rational 21st-century water and energy policies requires policy makers to integrate these connections into their decisions and develop strategies to help mitigate their negative impacts.

Water for Energy

The energy sector has a major impact on the availability and quality of the nation's water resources (table 9.1). Water is used to extract and produce energy; process and refine fuels; construct, operate, and maintain energy-generation facilities; cool power plants; generate hydroelectricity; and dispose of wastes. Some of this water is consumed during operation or contaminated until it is unfit for further use; often much of it is returned to a watershed for use by other sectors of society.

Energy use also affects water quality and ultimately human and environment health. Too often, however, these impacts are ignored. The discharge of waste heat from cooling systems raises the temperature of rivers and lakes, which affects aquatic ecosystems. Wastewaters from mining operations, hydraulic fracturing, boilers, and cooling systems may be contaminated with heavy metals, radioactive materials, acids, organic materials, suspended solids, or other chemicals (EPA 2011; Urbina 2011). Nuclear fuel production plants, uranium mill tailings ponds, and under unusual circumstances, nuclear power plants, have caused radioactive contamination of groundwater and surface water supplies.

TABLE 9.1.

Connections between the Energy Sector and Water Quantity and Quality

Energy element	Connection to water quantity	Connection to water quality
Energy extraction and production		
Oil and gas exploration	Water required for drilling, well completion, and hydraulic fracturing	Impact on shallow or deep groundwater quality
Oil and gas production	Water required for enhanced oil recovery. Large volume of produced, impaired water can be generated during production.	Produced water and spills can contaminate surface and groundwater with diverse pollutants.
Coal and uranium mining	Mining operations can generate large quantities of water.	Tailings and drainage can contaminate surface water and groundwater and destroy watersheds.
Biofuels and ethanol	Water is used for growing biomass.	Pesticides and fertilizers can contaminate surface water and groundwater.
Refining and processing		
Traditional oil and gas refining	Water used during oil and gas refinery operations.	Refinery operations can contaminate water.
Biofuels and ethanol	Water used for refining into fuels.	Refinery wastewater produced.
Synfuels and hydrogen	Water used for synthesis or steam reforming.	Wastewater produced.
Energy transportation and storage		
Energy pipelines	Water needed for hydrostatic testing.	Wastewater produced.
Coal slurry pipelines	Water needed for slurry transport; water not returned.	Slurry water is often highly contaminated.
Barge transport of energy	River flows and stages impact fuel delivery.	Spills or accidents can affect water quality.
Oil and gas storage caverns	Slurry mining of caverns requires large quantities of water	Slurry disposal affects water quality and ecology. Contaminants can leak, polluting surface water and groundwater.

(*continued*)

TABLE 9.1. (*continued*)

Energy element	Connection to water quantity	Connection to water quality
Electric power generation		
Thermoelectric (fossil, biomass, nuclear)	Surface water and groundwater are used for cooling and scrubbing.	Thermal and air emissions alter quality of surface waters and aquatic ecosystems
Hydroelectric	Reservoirs lose water to evaporation.	Dams and reservoir operations alter water temperatures, quality, flow timing, and aquatic ecosystems.
Solar thermal	Surface water and groundwater used for cooling.	Cooling systems can affect surface water and aquatic ecosystems.
Solar photovoltaics and wind	None during operation; minimal water use for panel and blade washing	

Source: Modified from DOE (2006).

Several new trends suggest that the energy sector's impact on water resources may intensify in coming years. In particular, the shift from imported to domestic fuels, especially biofuels and natural gas, is greatly increasing water requirements and creating new water-quality concerns. Efforts to extract energy from marginal sources, such as natural gas from tight sands and shale or oil and liquid fuels from coal and oil shale, require large amounts of water compared to more conventional sources and also raise serious water-quality concerns. In the following section, we provide additional detail on the impacts of the electricity and transportation sectors on water resources.

Water Requirements for Electricity Production

Total water use for electricity production in the United States is substantial. In 2005, thermoelectric power plants withdrew around 200 billion gallons of water each day, which represent nearly half of saline and freshwater withdrawals in the United States (Kenny et al. 2009). This water is primarily used for cooling purposes, although some amount is makeup water that replenishes boiler water lost through evaporation (see box 9.1 for the important distinction between water withdrawal and consumption). About 70 percent of the total amount of water withdrawn by thermoelectric power plants, or 143 billion gallons per day, is freshwater and the remaining 30 percent is saline (Kenny et al. 2009). The use of saline water is largely confined to coastal regions, as nearly all of this water was withdrawn from the ocean (only Hawaii uses saline groundwater to cool power plants). Additional water is required to extract the energy used to generate electricity, although this has not been well quantified.

BOX 9.1
WATER WITHDRAWAL VERSUS CONSUMPTION

There is an important distinction between water withdrawals and consumption. Water taken from the environment is referred to as a *water withdrawal*. For the energy sector, much of this water is returned to the environment, albeit at a higher temperature and of lower quality, and is available for reuse in the same basin. Some water, however, is *lost* through evaporation. Water that is not available for reuse in the same water basin is referred to as *water consumption*. Based on data from 1995, the US Geological Survey estimates that only 2 percent of total water withdrawals for thermoelectric generation were consumed.

It is commonly believed that consumption is a more important indicator than water withdrawal because much of the water withdrawn is returned to the environment and potentially is available for reuse. But under some conditions, water withdrawals are a more important indicator of water use. During a drought or in water-constrained regions, for example, there simply may not be enough water available to sustain the operation of the facility. In addition, surface water temperatures tend to increase as water levels in a stream or river decline, in which case, the water withdrawn is too warm to effectively cool the plant. During a devastating heat wave in 2003, for example, energy utilities in France were forced to scale back or shut down operations at nuclear power plants because water levels were too low in some areas and water temperatures too high for effective cooling in others. At the same time, electricity demand for refrigerators and air conditioners was high. France is particularly dependent on nuclear power, and limits on electricity production may have played a role in the 14,000 deaths that occurred in France during the extreme heat (UNEP 2004). Therefore, it is important we consider here both water withdrawals and consumption associated with electricity generation.

The US Geological Survey estimates that an average of 23 gallons of water, both fresh and saline, were withdrawn for every kilowatt hour generated in 2005 (Kenny et al. 2009). Water requirements, however, vary substantially among fuels and cooling technologies. Thermoelectric power plants using once-through cooling systems produced half of the total power generated by these systems but accounted for 92 percent of total water withdrawals (see box 9.2 for a description of cooling technologies). Thermoelectric power plants that recirculate their cooling water produced about half of the power generated by thermoelectric power plants in the United States but accounted for only 8 percent of total water withdrawn by thermoelectric power plants. Increasingly, new power plants and even some older power plants are installing less water-intensive cooling technologies, such as recirculating or dry cooling systems, suggesting that the volume of water withdrawn to produce each kilowatt hour will decline in the future, although water consumption may increase.

Trends in Water Requirements for Thermoelectric Power Plants

Water withdrawals for thermoelectric generation have declined from their peak in 1980 but have been steadily increasing since 1995 (figure 9.1). There is growing concern that water availability threatens energy security. Beginning in 2004, and in almost every year since, the National Energy Technology Laboratory has conducted an assessment of future water requirements for thermoelectric power generation. These studies are based on future energy scenarios produced by the Energy Information Administration (EIA) and include assumptions about cooling technologies and the use of carbon capture and storage. In the most recent National Energy Technology Laboratory assessment (2010), national freshwater withdrawals are projected to decline in 2035 by 2 percent to 23 percent from their 2010 levels, depending on assumptions about cooling technologies and water sources. During this same period, however, freshwater consumption is projected to increase by 14 percent to 27 percent from their 2010 levels.

These national estimates, however, hide important regional variation. Although water withdrawals are projected to decline nationwide, they are projected to increase in the western United States. All regions are projected to experience an increase in water consumption, with the greatest increases in the Florida and New York regions.

The National Energy Technology Laboratory assessments of the water requirements for future thermoelectric power generation, however, do not account for the potential

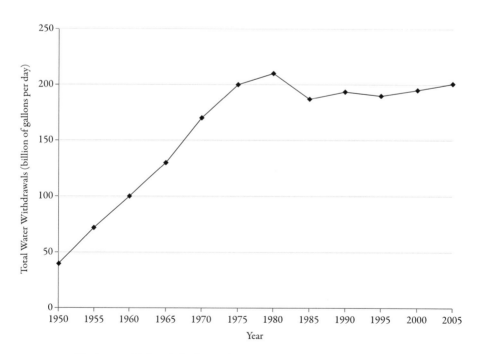

FIGURE 9.1. Total water withdrawals for thermoelectric power generation
Source: Based on data from Kenny et al. (2009).

impacts of energy extraction on water resources. The most recent estimates by EIA, released in December 2010, project that electricity generation under a reference case scenario will increase by 1,160 billion kWh. Coal and natural gas would supply about 40 percent and 30 percent, respectively, of the new electricity generation (figure 9.2). Extracting the coal and natural gas needed to generate this electricity, however, will use and pollute a substantially larger amount of water.

The increase in natural gas production is expected to be largely supplied by unconventional sources, including a fourfold increase in domestic shale gas production (DOE 2010). Although extracting natural gas from unconventional sources is more complex and costly than conventional natural gas recovery, technological improvements have made extraction from unconventional sources more economically viable in recent years. In particular, the combination of horizontal drilling and hydraulic fracturing has greatly increased the productivity of natural gas wells, although, as noted in the following, these technologies have also adversely affected water resources.

Hydraulic fracturing (hydrofracking or fracking) refers to the process by which water, sand, and chemicals, are injected into oil and natural gas wells under high pressure to create cracks and fissures to improve the production of these wells. Hydraulic fracturing was first developed in the early 20th century but was not commercially applied until the late 1940s. It is increasingly applied to natural gas extraction from unconventional sources,

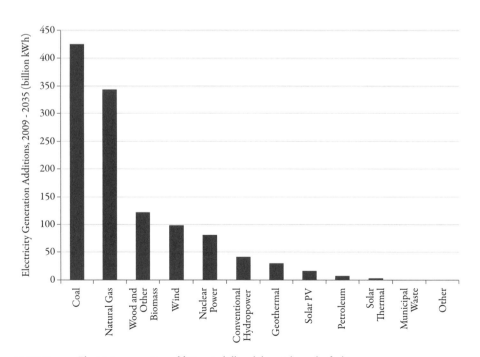

FIGURE 9.2. Electricity generation additions in billion kilowatt hours by fuel type, 2009–2035
Source: DOE (2010) (AEO 2011 reference case).

including coal beds, shales, and tight sands, due to growing interest in developing less-carbon-intensive energy sources and technological improvements.

Hydraulic fracturing requires large volumes of water that may be withdrawn from nearby surface water or groundwater aquifers or purchased from a municipal water system. In most cases, water is transported to the site by tanker trucks or less commonly via a network of pipes and aqueducts (EPA 2011). Once at the well site, the water is mixed with chemicals and a propping agent, such as sand, and injected into a well. After completion of the fracturing process, the well pressure is released and the fracturing fluid, along with some groundwater, flows back to the surface. Some unknown volume of fracturing fluid, along with its chemical additives, remains underground. The flowback and produced water, which can be substantially saltier than seawater, are typically disposed of by underground injection or, less commonly, by evaporation in on-site ponds (EPA 2011). Increasingly, the flowback is being treated on-site and reused for agricultural purposes or additional fracturing (EPA 2011). In rare cases, flowback and produced water are treated at a municipal wastewater treatment plant (GWPC and ALL Consulting 2009), although these systems are not typically designed to deal with this type of wastewater.

Hydraulic fracturing has generated a tremendous amount of controversy in recent years due, in large part, to concerns about its impacts on water resources. Hydraulic fracturing is water-intensive, with water requirements ranging from 50,000 to 350,000 gallons per well for coalbed methane and 2 to 4 million gallons per well for shale gas (EPA 2011). Even though this may be a small fraction of the annual water use in a given basin, this water is typically withdrawn over a short period of time and in one location, potentially conflicting with other uses within the basin. Furthermore, withdrawals of large volumes of water can adversely affect groundwater quality through a variety of means, such as mobilizing naturally occurring substances, promoting bacterial growth, causing land subsidence, and mobilizing lower quality water from surrounding areas. Similarly, withdrawals from surface water can affect the hydrology and hydrodynamics of the source water (EPA 2011).

In addition to impacts associated with water withdrawals, hydraulic fracturing presents a number of water-quality concerns. Chemicals used in the fracturing process, many of which are not known due to proprietary concerns, and methane may contaminate groundwater aquifers (Osborn et al. 2011). This is especially problematic when fracking coalbed methane reservoirs, which may be within or in close proximity to underground drinking water sources (EPA 2011). Additionally, poorly constructed or maintained wells may serve as conduits for the contamination of drinking water reservoirs. Disposal of the recovered fracturing fluid, and even the unknown amount of fluid that is not recovered, could also contaminate groundwater and surface water bodies. The *New York Times* recently released several internal governmental documents that reveal that wastewater from some hydraulic fracturing contains radioactivity at levels higher than previously known, and far higher than can be handled at wastewater treatment plants (Urbina 2011). Additionally, water that is delivered by tanker trucks increases wear on local roads, which not only boosts road maintenance costs but also potentially pollutes nearby water bodies.

Oversight of hydraulic fracturing for oil and gas mining operations is typically done by state oil and gas agencies or state natural resource agencies. Activities on federal land, by contrast, are managed by the Bureau of Land Management and the US Forest Service (GWPC and ALL Consulting 2009). Federal oversight of hydraulic fracturing is largely done by the Environmental Protection Agency through various environmental statutes, although in most cases, states implement these statutes with federal oversight (EPA 2011). Recent exemptions in these regulations, however, have drawn intense criticism from community and environmental groups. In particular, the Energy Policy Act of 2005 exempted hydraulic fracturing from regulation under the Safe Drinking Water Act. Indeed, federal regulators do not know the types or amounts of chemicals used in hydraulic fracturing, although some states are beginning to require facility operators to disclose this information.

In response to growing concerns about hydraulic fracturing and its rapid expansion, the Environmental Protection Agency (EPA) recently launched an investigation of the impacts of hydraulic fracturing on the environment and human health. Given the rapid expansion of the industry, however, more wells will be drilled and fractured before this investigation is complete. In the interim, some states, including New York, have passed laws temporarily suspending hydraulic fracturing "to afford the state and its residents the opportunity to continue the review and analysis of the effects of hydraulic fracturing on water and air quality, environmental safety and public health." In October 2010, Pennsylvania Governor Edward G. Rendell signed an executive order banning further natural gas development on state forest lands.

Transportation Fuels

Efforts to develop more sustainable transportation fuels can have significant impacts on water resources. Biofuels, in particular, have emerged as an alternative to traditional, fossil-fuel energy sources. Biofuels refer to a wide range of solid, liquid, and gaseous fuels derived from plant or animal biomass. First-generation biofuels are primarily based on the conversion of sugar, starch, vegetable oil, and fat—substances that are suitable for human consumption—to a liquid fuel. Advanced biofuels, however, may use feed stocks such as waste biomass, cellulose, and algae.

Ethanol is the primary biofuel produced in the Unites States, and its production has increased dramatically over the past decade, from 1.6 billion gallons in 2000 to 13.2 billion gallons in 2010 (Renewable Fuels Association 2011). Currently, about 98 percent of ethanol produced in the United States is derived from corn (GAO 2009a). The expansion of biofuels is expected to continue over the next decade, driven in part by the Energy Independence and Security Act of 2007. This act mandates that biofuel production increase to 36 billion gallons by 2022, including 21 billion gallons of "advanced biofuels." Although cellulosic ethanol is supposed to account for 45 percent of national production, the EPA recently acknowledged that cellulosic ethanol is not scaling up as quickly as hoped. They recently lowered the interim 2010 cellulosic ethanol requirement from 100 million gallons to only 6.5 million gallons, although it is unclear how this will affect the 2022 target. The rapid expansion of biofuel production has raised a number of concerns about the long-term consequences. These concerns range from the potential impacts on water resources, food production and prices, agricultural diversity, and net greenhouse gas emissions.

The water intensity of biofuel production varies widely according to a variety of factors, including crop type, local climate, and irrigation management practices (table 9.2).

TABLE 9.2.

Water Intensity of Different Transportation Fuels for Light Duty Vehicles

Transportation fuel	Water withdrawal (gallon/mile)	Water consumption (gallon/mile)
Petroleum		
Gasoline	0.63	0.07–0.14
Diesel	0.46	0.05–0.10
Oil shale	0.71–0.86	0.15–0.37
Tar sands	0.76–0.95	0.20–0.46
Electricity		
US grid	7.8	0.24
Wind and solar power	~0	~0
Hydrogen fuel cell		
Electrolysis via US grid	13	0.42
Electrolysis via wind and solar	~0	~0
Natural gas	0.07	0.03
Ethanol		
Irrigated corn grain	6.9–110	1.3–62
Nonirrigated corn grain	0.33–0.56	0.15–0.35
Irrigated "cellulosic" corn stover	5.6–63	2.7–46
Nonirrigated "cellulosic" corn stover	0.41	0.24–0.25
Biodiesel		
Irrigated soybean	1.1–26	0.6–24
Nonirrigated soybean	0.03–0.12	0.01–0.02

Note: Light duty vehicles include cars, four-wheel trucks, and sports utility vehicles.
Source: King and Webber (2008) and King, Holman, and Webber (2008).

Water withdrawals associated with irrigated ethanol production range from 7 to 110 gallons of water per mile traveled for corn grain and 6 to 63 gallons per mile for cellulosic corn stover (King and Webber 2008; King, Homan, and Webber 2008). Water consumption rates are also high. Irrigated ethanol is substantially more water-intensive than traditional transportation fuels. Water withdrawals for nonirrigated biofuels and cellulosic ethanol sources are far lower and even smaller than for traditional fossil fuel–based transportation fuels, although these sources represent only a small proportion of the current fuel mix. To exacerbate these concerns, many existing and planned ethanol production facilities are in areas with limited water supplies (figure 9.3), including the Ogallala Aquifer where pumping extracts water faster than it can be recharged (Guru and Horne 2000).

Interest in biofuels and the resulting higher prices for corn, and possibly soybeans, may make it profitable to grow crops on land previously considered unprofitable. It may also lead to crop shifting on land now used to grow food crops. Growing biofuel crops on previously uncultivated land can increase total water withdrawals and reduce groundwater recharge rates and on-site rainwater retention (in the case of deforestation, particularly). In addition to direct land use changes, biofuel production can lead to indirect changes such as off-site land conversion if increased corn production displaces vegetable or grain

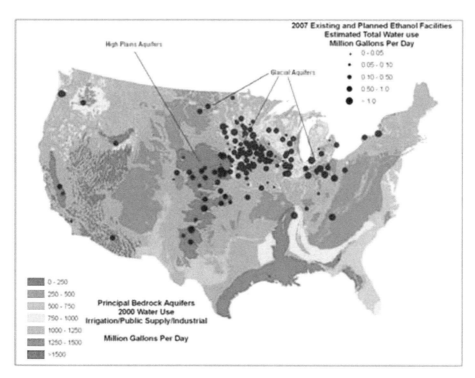

FIGURE 9.3. Existing and planned ethanol production facilities and their estimated total water use per day in comparison to pumping of local bedrock aquifers
Source: National Research Council (2008).

production, and those crops are then grown elsewhere by converting former forested areas or grasslands to agricultural land. Studies typically do not attempt to account for the effect of indirect land-use change even though it is widely recognized that it could be the most significant factor in terms of determining the life cycle implications of biofuels (GAO 2009a).

Crop shifting can also affect the timing and volume of water withdrawals. Whereas corn and soybeans have among the highest water demands of row crops, the net effect of crop shifting will depend on what crops are grown and which are replaced. Currently, corn acreage is growing and replacing other field crops at the national level (figure 9.4). Depending on the crop replaced, biofuel production may lead to a slight decline in water consumption, although regional impacts may be significantly different. If, however, farmers replace dryland farming or native vegetation with irrigated biofuel production, we would expect an increase in water consumption, placing a further stress on water resources in some regions.

In addition to impacts on water supply, increased biofuel production is likely to have consequences for water quality. Corn production, in particular, requires relatively high applications of fertilizers, herbicides, and pesticides. Some of these chemicals make their way to local surface and groundwater sources. The highest instream concentrations of nitrates (associated with fertilizers) and atrazine (a component of some herbicides) occur in the region known as the US "corn belt," which is already the major source of nitrogen loading to the Mississippi River and associated with the Gulf Coast Dead Zone

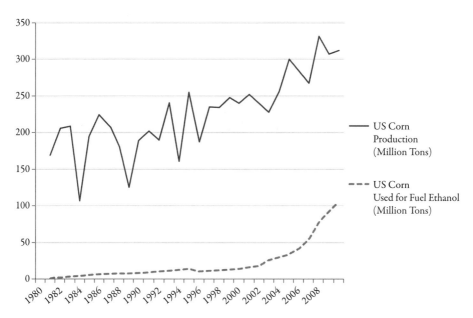

FIGURE 9.4.   US corn production and corn used for fuel ethanol in millions of tons, 1980–2009

Source: Compiled by Earth Policy Institute (2011) with corn used for fuel ethanol from Department of Agriculture Feed Grains Database, www.ers.usda.gov/Data/FeedGrains; and U.S. corn production from USDA, Production, Supply and Distribution, www.fas.usda.gov/psdonline.

(National Research Council 2008). Prior analyses suggest that increases in nutrient loading due to the expansion of ethanol will be in the range of 10 to 37 percent, increasing energy requirements for water treatment (Donner and Kucharik 2008; Simpson et al. 2008; Han, Allan, and Scavia 2009). In addition, increased sediment runoff is a major concern, as increased harvesting and tilling the soil contributes fine sediments to local stream networks. The conversion of more land to biofuel production due to incentives and requirements contained in the Energy Independence and Security Act may further exacerbate these existing problems and, ironically, increase domestic energy consumption (Twomey, Stillwell, and Webber 2010).

Energy for Water

Water provision and use requires energy in all phases, from extraction to treatment to distribution to use, and finally to the treatment of wastewater (figure 9.5). First, water is taken from a source and delivered to a community. In some cases, the force of gravity is sufficient; but in most, water must be pumped from groundwater wells or over long distances and steep terrain. Water must then be treated to drinking water standards through a variety of processes that require energy, including filtration, sedimentation, and disinfection. Treated water is then delivered to the tap, either by gravity or additional pumping. Even more energy is used in our homes, businesses, and institutions to heat, cool, purify, and pump water. Water that is used indoors must then be returned, in some cases pumped, to a wastewater treatment facility where it undergoes further processing that requires energy. Treated wastewater is then either returned to the environment by gravity or pumping or undergoes additional processing and is reused.

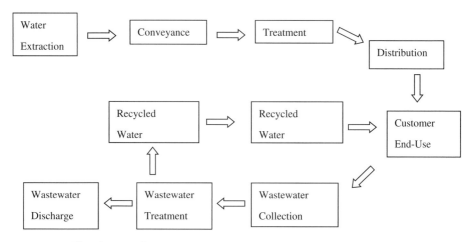

FIGURE 9.5. Flow diagram of energy inputs to water systems
Source: This schematic and method is based on Wilkinson (2000) with refinements by California Energy Commission staff and others.

The water sector is a major user of energy, although the overall energy requirements of the water and wastewater sector remain largely unknown. Among the earliest and most commonly cited report is an Electric Power Research Institute–funded study that estimates that capturing and treating surface water requires an average of around 1,400 kWh per million gallons, whereas groundwater requires 1,800 kWh per million gallons (Burton 1996). That study reported that energy requirements for wastewater treatment vary depending on the type of treatment employed, ranging from under 1,000 kWh per million gallons for basic treatment to more than 1,900 kWh per million gallons for advanced treatment.

More recent assessments, however, suggest that the energy intensity of the water and wastewater sector is even more highly varied and that the average may be much higher. Based on a review of different data sets, including a database maintained by the American Water Works Association, a study from the National Association of Clean Water Agencies, and data from studies in Wisconsin and Iowa, a recent American Water Works Association Research Foundation (2007) analysis estimates that the energy intensity of water systems ranges from 300 kWh to 3,800 kWh per million gallons, whereas the energy intensity of wastewater systems ranges from 800 kWh to more than 3,500 kWh per million gallons. More and better analysis is needed at the state and utility scale to capture this variability and develop a more accurate assessment of the sector's energy use.

An analysis of total energy use by the water sector by the Electric Power Research Institute estimates that public water and wastewater systems use about 52 billion kWh annually and that private water and wastewater systems consume an additional 72 billion kWh annually (EPRI 2002). In total, these systems account for about 3 to 4 percent of the nation's electricity use. Although often cited, these estimates underestimate water-related energy use both because the technology assumptions are too conservative, as noted previously, but more importantly because they exclude end-use energy, such as energy used in homes, businesses, and institutions to pump, heat, and treat water. A 2005 study by the California Energy Commission, which included end-use energy, found that an estimated 19 percent of the state's electricity use, 32 percent of its nonpower-plant natural gas consumption, and 88 million gallons of diesel consumption are water-related. Customer end-use energy represented more than 80 percent of electricity use and 99 percent of natural gas consumption (CEC 2005). Excluding end-use energy consumption in national estimates, therefore, may underestimate the total energy intensity of water by a factor of 4 and suggests that water managers and decision makers could be missing important opportunities to reduce water-related energy use and associated greenhouse gas emissions.

Future Trends

Many factors will influence the energy intensity of the water sector in the near future. Water scarcity has been an ongoing concern in much of the southwestern United States, but even regions not traditionally associated with drought are facing water-supply constraints and pushing water agencies toward new, often more energy-intensive options. In Georgia, for example, 60 percent of the counties were in severe drought conditions in July 2008 (Stooksbury 2008). Continued population growth and climate change will make meeting water demands increasingly difficult over the coming years (see chapter 10: Water and Climate). Between 2000 and 2030, the US population is projected to increase by 30 percent, with much of this growth concentrated in water-scarce regions in the Southwest and Florida.[1] Climate change will further exacerbate these problems, ultimately affecting the supply of, and demand for, water resources.

In order to meet future needs, water suppliers are considering a range of supply-and-demand management options, from traditional surface water and groundwater sources to alternatives such as recycled water, water conservation and efficiency, rainwater harvesting, stormwater capture, brackish and impaired groundwater desalination, and seawater desalination. The traditional approach to solving these challenges has been to import water over longer distances, access water from greater depth, or develop more marginal supplies that require extensive treatment. In Tampa Bay, Florida, for example, water managers recently completed a 15 million gallon per day desalination facility. And in California, 19 seawater desalination plants have been proposed along the coast over the past 10 years. Shifting toward these more energy-intensive supplies will have major energy implications for the water sector.

Similarly, stricter water-quality regulations and emerging contaminants are forcing agencies to adopt more energy-intensive treatment options such as ultraviolet radiation, ozonation, and reverse osmosis. The differences between energy use by traditional and new treatment techniques can be significant. For example, ozone disinfection uses approximately 400 kWh per million gallons, nearly 40 times more than chlorination, the more traditional disinfection method (PG&E 2006).

Potential Policy Solutions

Whereas the energy-water connection presents new national challenges, it also provides opportunities. There are many options for reducing the water intensity of energy systems and the energy intensity of water systems. Additionally, water- and energy-efficiency improvements have the potential to reduce pressures on both resources, creating win-win solutions. In the following, we describe ways that the federal policies can better address water and energy challenges.

Improve Data, Information, and Education on Energy-Water Connections

Water and energy analysts are often frustrated by the lack of available data on the energy needs of water and wastewater systems and the water use and consumption of energy systems. In a 2009 report, the Government Accountability Office outlines some of the major shortcomings of federal data collection efforts on water availability and use as they relate to planning and siting energy facilities (2009b). The US Geological Survey, for example, collects data on water withdrawals by power plants but not water consumption. Streamflow gauges, which provide information on water availability, are disappearing (see chapter 6: Protecting Freshwater Ecosystems). The EIA does not collect data on the use of advanced cooling technologies. No agency collects data on the use of alternative water sources, such as recycled water, for power production. Many of these shortcomings are a result of budget cuts.

Congress has initiated a number of efforts to improve the quality of water and energy data. In 2009, Congress passed the Omnibus Public Land Management Act, which contained the Secure Water Act that, among other things, authorized additional funding to the Department of Interior to report water data, including thermoelectric withdrawals, to Congress. Congress is also considering passage of the Energy and Water Research Integration Act, which would establish an Energy-Water Architecture Council "to promote and enable improved energy and water resource data collection, reporting, and technological innovation" (8). Although this bill passed the House in December 2009, it has not yet been voted on by the Senate. Prompt action is needed to ensure that the important provisions of this bill become law.

Within these efforts, however, less emphasis has been placed on assessing current and future energy requirements for water and wastewater systems. This could be achieved by expanding existing data collection efforts. In particular, the EIA administers the Manufacturing Energy Consumption Survey every four years, collecting energy consumption data by energy source, industry, and census region. This survey could be expanded to include the energy requirements of water and wastewater systems, which would allow for a more robust national estimate of the energy requirements of these systems, an evaluation of any regional differences among these systems, and long-term trends.

Additional data and information are also needed on the impacts of energy production on water quality. Energy production threatens water quality in communities across the United States. In Kentucky, a coal sludge impoundment collapsed and released an estimated 250 million gallons of coal sludge into surrounding waterways, disrupting local water supplies for days and devastating aquatic life along more than 100 miles of streambeds and associated floodplains (EPA 2001). Wastewater from hydraulic fracturing is delivered to public treatment plants that are not designed to remove some drilling waste contaminants, such as radioactive material; the radioactive-tainted wastewater is then discharged into rivers that provide drinking water to downstream communities (Urbina 2011). A *New York Times* analysis of Environmental Protection Agency data finds that power plants are the nation's biggest producer of toxic waste and with efforts to reduce air pollution, many of these pollutants end up in our waterways (Duhigg 2009). Despite the range of impacts that energy production poses to our nation's water quality, few data are available. The EPA should develop and maintain a database that catalogs reported water-quality impacts of energy production, from energy extraction to generation. Additionally, energy companies should have to report all complaints of their operations harming drinking water supplies. Finally, the chemicals and impacts of hydraulic fracturing and other energy-production processes should be monitored and regulated under applicable federal statutes, requiring immediate elimination of special exemptions such as those found in the Energy Policy Act of 2005.

Expand Research and Development on Energy-Water Links

The federal government can play a key role in supporting research and development projects designed to reduce the tension between water and energy management. Key areas for research and development include technologies and management practices to promote the use of alternative water sources, including produced water, brackish groundwater, and municipal wastewater; application of dry- and hybrid-cooling technologies for power plants; technologies and management practices to promote advanced biofuels; improvements in power plant thermal efficiency; the application of decentralized water systems as a means of improving both water and energy efficiency; and the identification of ways by which healthy ecosystems can reduce treatment requirements.

INCENTIVIZE WATER SYSTEM ENERGY EFFICIENCY UPGRADES

Water managers can reduce the energy and greenhouse gas intensity of water systems through a variety of means, including optimizing the efficiency of the existing system by replacing older pumps with newer, more efficient models. Renewable energy generation, especially through biogas recovery at wastewater treatment plants, can also play an important role. A recent EPA report found that 550 wastewater treatment plants across the United States are equipped with anaerobic digesters and are of sufficient size to make cogeneration technically and economically feasible. Less than 20 percent of these facilities, however, use the biogas produced, and most of these only use biogas to generate heat for the digester. Improving operations at existing cogeneration plants and installing new systems in the remaining 80 percent of wastewater treatment plants with anaerobic digesters could produce an additional 340 MW of electricity and reduce carbon dioxide emissions by 2.3 million metric tons per year (EPA 2007).

Even though energy-efficiency improvements can be cost-effective, the needed upfront investment may act as a barrier to implementation. Federal funding can help water and wastewater agencies overcome these barriers. Federal funding for audits, energy-efficiency improvements, and renewable energy systems, including wind power, solar, and cogeneration, is available through a variety of programs, including State Revolving Funds, Rural Energy for America Grants, the Rural Assistance Center, and the Department of Energy's Industrial Technologies Program. Recent federal legislation, such as the Energy Policy Act of 2005, the 2008 Farm Bill, and the

American Recovery and Reinvestment Act of 2009, has sought to expand the number and types of programs available to promote energy efficiency and reductions in greenhouse gas emissions. Most programs are available for a wide range of sectors; only the State Revolving Funds are explicitly dedicated to water and wastewater systems. More targeted funding and outreach are needed to promote efficiency improvement and biogas recovery to reduce the energy intensity of water and wastewater systems and their associated greenhouse gas emissions.

ELIMINATE FUNDING FOR FIRST-GENERATION BIOFUELS

In some cases, more sustainable water and energy integration could be achieved by suspending or redirecting existing financial incentives. In 2005, federal policy on transportation fuels shifted dramatically to provide incentives for greater production of biofuels. The details of the Renewable Fuels Standard policy were crafted to support corn-based ethanol production, moving toward greater production of "advanced" biofuels over time. More recently, however, the government scaled back the production requirements for advanced biofuels, effectively increasing the requirements for the more water-intensive biofuels. Collectively, these policies have profound water implications.

Allowing subsidies for corn-based ethanol to expire would save an estimated $6 billion annually, improve world food supplies, and decrease the implicit irrigation subsidy, according to a bipartisan group of senators (Feinstein et al. 2011). Instead, the federal priority should focus on expanding: (1) nonirrigated advanced biofuels, (2) renewable energy sources, and (3) electric and hydrogen fuel cell vehicle manufacturing and sales. Advanced biofuels use waste products that would otherwise contribute to potent greenhouse gases if left in fields or landfills. Certain renewable energy sources can reduce the water and carbon intensity of the US electrical grid and, in so doing, reduce the water intensity of electrical vehicles and hydrogen fuel cell vehicles.

PROVIDE INCENTIVES FOR SWITCHING TO ALTERNATIVE WATER SOURCES

Alternative water sources can reduce or eliminate freshwater requirements for electricity generation. For example, recycled municipal wastewater is a reliable water source that is available in relative abundance across the United States, suggesting that its use could be dramatically expanded and could contribute to reducing pressure on freshwater systems. In 2007, however, only 57 power plants, most of which were located in California, Florida, and Texas, were using treated municipal wastewater (ANL 2007). Other alternative water sources include produced water from oil and gas wells, mine pool water, and industrial process water.

PROVIDE INCENTIVES FOR ACCELERATING WATER AND ENERGY-EFFICIENCY
IMPROVEMENTS

Saving water saves energy, which in turn saves even more water. Conservation and efficiency can help meet the needs of a growing population, reduce or eliminate the need to develop capital-intensive infrastructure, and provide environmental benefits. Additionally, conservation and efficiency promote both water and energy security by reducing vulnerability to limits on the availability of water and/or energy. All federal funding available for energy-efficiency upgrades should also be available to water conservation and efficiency measures. Research suggests that water-efficiency improvements may be a particularly cost-effective way to reduce energy use and cut greenhouse gas emissions. A 2005 report by the California Energy Commission found that it is cheaper to save energy through water-efficiency improvements than through traditional energy-efficiency measures (CEC 2005). A number of federal incentive programs are available for energy efficiency. The scope of these programs should be expanded to include water-efficiency measures.

ESTABLISH WATER-COOLING TECHNOLOGY REQUIREMENTS

Prior to 1970, most thermoelectric plants were built with once-through cooling systems, which have a low capital cost and high energy efficiency. These systems, however, are highly water-intensive and have been shown to have significant negative environmental impacts. New requirements set by the EPA under Section 316(b) of the Clean Water Act have made permitting requirements for these cooling systems more stringent. Additionally, in regions with limited water resources, plant operators have, out of necessity, moved away from water-intensive cooling technologies. The federal government should continue to tighten water-cooling technology requirements through the federal permitting processes.

UPDATE NATIONAL EFFICIENCY STANDARDS

The federal government has a long history of establishing water and energy efficiency standards for appliances and fixtures. Standards were successfully passed in 1987, 1992, 2005, and 2007 (Neubauer et al. 2009), including the Energy Policy Act of 1992, which established national efficiency standards for toilets, urinals, kitchen and lavatory faucets, and showerheads manufactured after January 1, 1994. Technologies are evolving rapidly, however, and there have been significant lags in federal efforts to update these standards. In order to ensure that new homes and businesses are as efficient as possible, national efficiency standards must be updated to reflect new, more efficient technologies and expanded to include all water- and energy-using devices.

Building efficiency standards are particularly effective for new developments or remodels. Yet, a large number of homes in the United States were constructed before efficiency standards were established and are still equipped with old appliances and fixtures that waste both water and energy. New efficiency standards could be applied to the existing housing stock by requiring water and energy retrofits upon resale as a condition of Federal Housing Administration loans. Additionally, the federal government should update the standards for all federally managed buildings by requiring them to be equipped with appliances and fixtures that meet WaterSense and Energy Star specifications.

ESTABLISH A FEDERAL RENEWABLE PORTFOLIO STANDARD

Shifting from conventional fossil fuels to less water-intensive renewable energy sources would reduce the water-intensity of the nation's electricity sector. This, in turn, would help reduce pressure on the nation's limited water resources and reduce the electricity sector's vulnerability to water-supply constraints. A few states have adopted renewable portfolio standards as a means of transitioning away from fossil-based electricity sources but a federal renewable portfolio standard may be more effective. These standards should prioritize development of less-water-intensive renewable energy sources, such as solar photovoltaics and wind power.

Technology and Management Improvements

SUPPORT BETTER INTEGRATION OF WATER AND ENERGY MANAGEMENT

Many chapters of this book have detailed the lack of coordination within the water management sector as well as among other sectors, including energy, land-use planning, and agriculture. Indeed, some of the unintended consequences of our biofuel policies on water resources are a direct result of a lack of communication and coordination among water and energy planning efforts and decision-making processes. There may be situations where water and energy policies conflict with one another, and trade-offs may be required. However, these trade-offs must be fully understood and mitigated, where possible.

Decision-support tools provide a means to promote integration among water and energy sectors. The EPA and Department of Energy, through the Energy Star program, have developed tools and resources for water and wastewater facility managers to track energy use, costs, and associated greenhouse gas emissions. These tools also allow utilities to compare their facility performance with other facilities. Likewise, scientists at Sandia National Laboratory are working with a variety of stakeholders, including the Western Governors' Association and the Western Electricity Coordinating Council, to develop a water-energy decision-support system that will help energy managers take water availability into account when planning future energy infrastructure. The federal government should expand outreach of its existing decision-support tools by coordinating with water,

BOX 9.2
WATER REQUIREMENTS OF DIFFERENT THERMOELECTRIC POWER PLANT
COOLING TECHNOLOGIES

A variety of cooling technologies are in use in thermoelectric power plants, including once-through, recirculating, and dry-cooling systems. Water withdrawal and consumption vary among each of these cooling technologies. In once-through cooling systems, large volumes of water are withdrawn from a river, lake, aquifer, or the ocean, circulated through heat exchangers once, and then discharged into a nearby water body. With recirculating systems, water is withdrawn from a water body, circulated through heat exchangers, cooled use a cooling tower or pond, and then reused. Recirculating systems withdraw less water than once-through cooling systems do, although much of the water withdrawn is lost through evaporation (EPRI 2002). A small but growing number of power plants rely on air rather than water to cool the steam produced during electricity generation, referred to as *dry cooling*. Plants using dry cooling, however, withdraw and consume a small amount of water for maintaining and cleaning the boiler, including replacing boiler water lost through evaporation. Dry-cooling systems, however, are more expensive to build and operate and reduce the energy efficiency of the power plant.

wastewater, and energy industry groups. Additionally, federal agencies and national labs should convene diverse stakeholder groups to identify what additional decision-support tools are needed.

References

American Water Works Association Research Foundation. 2007. *Energy Index Development for Benchmarking Water and Wastewater Utilities*. Denver: American Water Works Association Research Foundation.

Argonne National Laboratory (ANL). 2007. *Use of Reclaimed Wastewater for Power Plant Cooling*. Argonne, IL: Argonne National Laboratory.

Burton, F. L. 1996. *Water and Wastewater Industries: Characteristics and Energy Management Opportunities*. Report CR-106941. Los Altos, CA: Electric Power Research Institute Report.

California Energy Commission. 2005. *2005 Integrated Energy Policy Report*. CEC-100-2005-007-CMF. Sacramento: California Energy Commission. http://www.energy.ca.gov/2005publications/CEC-100-2005-007/CEC-100-2005-007-CMF.PDF.

Donner, S. D., and C. J. Kucharik. 2008. "Corn-Based Ethanol Production Compromises Goal of Reducing Nitrogen Export by the Mississippi River." *Proceedings of the National Academies of Science* 105: 4513–4518.

Duhigg, C. 2009. "Cleansing the Air at the Expense of Waterways." *New York Times*, October 12.

Earth Policy Institute. "US Corn Production and Corn Used for Fuel Ethanol in Millions of Tons, 1980–2009." Electronic database. www.earth-policy.org/datacenter/xls/book_pb4_ch2_6.xls.

Electric Power Research Institute (EPRI). 2002. *Water & Sustainability. Volume 3: U.S. Water Consumption for Power Production—The Next Half Century*. Palo Alto, CA: Electric Power Research Institute.

Feinstein, D., J. Thune, and A. Klobuchar. July 7, 2011. Letter to the Honorable Harry Reid and Mitch McConnell. http://www.feinstein.senate.gov/public/index.cfm/2011/7/feinstein-statement-on-ethanol-agreement

Gleick, P. H., and M. Palaniappan. 2010. "Conceptual and Practical Limits to Freshwater Withdrawal and Use." *Proceedings of the National Academy of Sciences* 107 (25): 11155–11162.

Ground Water Protection Council (GWPC) and ALL Consulting. 2009. *Modern Shale Gas Development in the United States: A Primer*. Prepared for the US Department of Energy and the National Energy Technology Laboratory. Washington, DC: US Department of Energy.

Guru, M. V., and J. E. Horne. 2000. *The Ogallala Aquifer*. Poteau, OK: Kerr Center for Sustainable Agriculture, Inc.

Han, H., J. D. Allan, and D. Scavia. 2009. "Influence of Climate and Human Activities on the Relationship between Watershed Nitrogen Input and River Export." *Environmental Science and Technology* 43: 1916–1922.

Kenny, J. F., N. L. Barber, S. S. Hutson, K. S. Linsey, J. K. Lovelace, and M. A. Maupi. 2009. *Estimated Use of Water in the United States in 2005*. U.S. Geological Survey Circular 1344. Reston, VA: US Geological Survey.

King, C. W., A. S. Holman, and M. E. Webber. 2008. "Thirst for Energy." *Nature Geoscience* 1: 283–286.

King, C. W., and M. E. Webber. 2008. "Water Intensity of Transportation." *Environmental Science and Technology* 42 (2): 7866–7872.

National Energy Technology Laboratory. 2009. *Use of Non-Traditional Water for Power Plant Applications: An Overview of DOE/NETL R&D Efforts*. Pittsburgh: National Energy Technology Laboratory.

———. 2010. *Estimating Freshwater Needs to Meet Future Thermoelectric Generation Requirements: 2010 Update*. Pittsburgh: National Energy Technology Laboratory.

National Research Council. 2008. *Water Implications of Biofuels Production in the United States*. Washington, DC: National Academies Press.

Neubauer, M., A. Delaski, M. Dimascio, and S. Nadel. 2009. *Ka-BOOM! The Power of Appliance Standards: Opportunities for New Federal Appliance and Equipment Standards*. Research Report A091. Washington, DC: American Council for an Energy-Efficient Economy.

Osborn, S. G., A. Vengosh, N. R. Warner, and R. B. Jackson. 2011. "Methane Contamination of Drinking Water Accompanying Gas-well Drilling and Hydraulic Fracturing," *Proceedings of the National Academy of Sciences* 108 (20): 8172–8176.

Pacific Gas and Electric Company (PG&E). 2006. *Municipal Water Treatment Plant Energy Baseline Study*. Prepared by SBW Consulting, Inc. San Francisco: Pacific Gas and Electric Company.

Renewable Fuels Association. 2011. "2010 Annual Ethanol Production = 13.23 Billion Gallons." Renewable Fuels Association. http://www.ethanolrfa.org/news/entry/2010-annual-ethanol-production-13.23-billion-gallons/.

Simpson, T. W., A. N. Sharpley, R. W. Howarth, H. W. Paerl, and K. R. Mankin. 2008. "The New Gold Rush: Fueling Ethanol Production while Protecting Water Quality." *Journal of Environmental Quality* 37: 318–324.

Stooksbury, D. E. 2008. "Drought Conditions Intensify across Georgia." *Georgia FACES*, July 24.

Twomey, K. M., A. S. Stillwell, and M. E. Webber. 2010. "The Unintended Energy Impacts of Increased Nitrate Contamination from Biofuels Production." *Journal of Environmental Monitoring* 12: 218–224.

United Nations Environment Programme (UNEP). 2004. "Impacts of Summer 2003 Heat Wave in Europe." *Environment Alert Newsletter* 2: 4 pp.

US Department of Energy (DOE). 2006. *Energy Demands on Water Resources. Report to Congress on the Interdependency of Energy and Water*. Washington, DC: United States Department of Energy. http://www.sandia.gov/energy-water/congress_report.htm.

———. 2010. *Annual Energy Outlook 2010*. DOE/EIA-0383(2010). Washington, DC: US Energy Information Administration.

US Environmental Protection Agency (EPA). 2001. *Martin County Coal Corporation, Inez, Kentucky Task Force Report*. Washington, DC: US Environmental Protection Agency. http://www.epa.gov/region4/waste/martincs.pdf.

———. 2007. *Opportunities for and Benefits of Combined Heat and Power at Wastewater Treatment Facilities: Market Analysis and Lessons from the Field*. Washington, DC: US Environmental Protection Agency. http://www.epa.gov/chp/documents/wwtf_opportunities.pdf.

———. 2011. *Draft Plan to Study the Potential Impacts of Hydraulic Fracturing on Drinking Water Resources. Office of Research and Development*. Washington, DC: US Environmental Protection Agency.

US Government Accountability Office (GAO). 2009a. *Biofuels: Potential Effects and Challenges of Required Increases in Production and Use. Report to Congressional Requesters*. GAO-09-446. Washington, DC: US Government Accountability Office. http://www.gao.gov/new.items/d09446.pdf.

———. 2009b. *Energy-Water Nexus: Federal Water Use Data Would Increase Understanding of Trends in Power Plant Water Use*. Report to the Chairman, Committee on Science and Technology, House of Representatives. GAO-10-23. Washington, DC: US Government Accountability Office. http://www.gao.gov/new.items/d1023.pdf.

Urbina, I. 2011. "Regulation Lax as Gas Wells' Tainted Water Hits Rivers." *New York Times*, February 26.

Walton, B. 2008. "Low Water May Halt Hover Dam's Power." Circle of Blue. http://www.circleofblue.org/waternews/2010/world/low-water-may-still-hoover-dam%E2%80%99s-power/.

Weiss, M. 2008. "Drought Could Force Nuke-Plant Shutdowns." WRAL. http://www.wral.com/news/state/story/2343605/.

Wilkinson, R. 2000. *Methodology for Analysis of the Energy Intensity of California's Water Systems, and an Assessment of Multiple Potential Benefits Through Integrated Water Energy Efficiency Measures*. Ernest Orlando Lawrence Berkeley Laboratory, California Institute for Energy Efficiency, Agreement No. 4910110. Santa Barbara: Ernest Orlando Lawrence Berkeley Laboratory, California Institute for Energy Efficiency. http://sustainca.org/sites/default/files/WPuUSA-CA-LBNL.pdf.

Wolff, G., R. Cohen, and B. Nelson. 2004. *Energy Down the Drain*. New York and Oakland: Natural Resources Defense Council and Pacific Institute.

WATER AND CLIMATE

Heather Cooley

Introduction

In addition to a wide range of old, unresolved water challenges facing the nation and federal water policy makers, several new threats are emerging, especially the growing consequences for water resources and developed water systems from a rapidly changing climate. Rising greenhouse gas concentrations from human activities are causing large-scale changes to the Earth's climate. Because of a time lag between greenhouse gas emissions and climate impacts, we know that these changes will continue even if we stop emitting greenhouse gases today. Given our economic dependence on fossil fuels and the difficult political issues associated with emissions-reduction strategies, it now appears inevitable that significant climatic changes will continue to intensify over the next several decades.

Because the water cycle and the climate cycle are inextricably linked, these changes will have major implications for our nation's water resources. The movement of water is the primary process by which energy is redistributed around the planet. As temperatures rise, the flows of water in the hydrologic cycle will accelerate. In short, climate change will intensify the water cycle, altering water availability, timing, quality, and demand. Indeed, all of the major international and national assessments of climate changes have concluded that freshwater systems are among the most vulnerable sectors of society (Compagnucci et al. 2001; SEG 2007; Kundzewicz et al. 2007; Bates et al. 2008). An Intergovernmental Panel on Climate Change (IPCC) technical report on freshwater resources released in 2008 concludes with a very high confidence that "climate change will constrain North America's already overallocated water resources, thereby increasing competition among agricultural, municipal, industrial, and ecological uses" (Bates et al. 2008, 102).

Early research on climate change and water was largely centered on identifying the impacts of rising atmospheric greenhouse gas concentrations. These impacts informed discussions about greenhouse gas mitigation strategies. Given that some degree of climate change is unavoidable (and mitigation activities have been largely unsuccessful thus far), the discussion about climate change has shifted to include adaptation—actions or policies that reduce vulnerability or increase resilience to climate change impacts. As noted by Frederick and Gleick (1999, 33), "the socioeconomic impacts of floods, droughts, and climate and non-climate factors affecting the supply and demand for water will depend in large part on how society adapts." If evaluated holistically, adaptation can not only serve to minimize our vulnerability to climate change impacts, it can also reduce our vulnerability to other water challenges and promote sustainable development.

This chapter examines the projected impacts of climate change on water resources. It discusses various adaptation practices, as well as the process of evaluating and implementing those practices. The chapter concludes with a discussion of the federal government's role in promoting adaptation to climate change.

Climate Change and US Freshwater Resources

Changing climate conditions will affect the supply of and demand for water resources. Indeed, all of the IPCC and other synthesis reports on climate vulnerability conclude that freshwater systems are especially vulnerable (Compagnucci et al. 2001; SEG 2007; Kundzewicz et al. 2007; Bates et al. 2008). Yet climate change is but one of many stressors on our water management systems. Population growth, land-use change, and pollution may have an equally or even larger impact on our water resources in the coming years. These risks must be understood relative to one another and in synergy with one another. Here, we describe current understanding of the projected impacts of climate change on the freshwater resources of the United States.

Surface Water

Climate change will alter the volume of surface water runoff, although specific regional projections vary widely from model to model. In general, it is expected that wet areas will become wetter and dry areas will become drier. For example, an assessment of model outputs from general circulation models by Milly, Dunne, and Vecchia (2005) suggests greater runoff in the eastern United States, little-to-no change in the Missouri and Mississippi basins, and reduced runoff in the western United States. Results from separate regional studies of the eastern and southwestern United States are generally consistent with the overall conclusions of this assessment (Hayhoe et al. 2007; Rosenzweig et al. 2007; Seager et al. 2007; Cayan et al. 2010; Seager and Vecchi 2010). Additional regional assessments are needed in Alaska, Hawaii, the central United States, and the southern United States to better evaluate potential climate impacts. Even with better regional assessments, however, some degree of uncertainty will remain, highlighting the need for water resource managers to pursue flexible strategies and processes that perform well under uncertain conditions.

Not everything is equally uncertain. Models are in general agreement that increasing temperatures will affect the timing of runoff, particularly in snow-dominated basins, which are found throughout the western United States. In snow-dominated basins, hydrologic studies have long agreed that warming will lead to a shift from rain to snow, faster melting of snowpack, earlier peak streamflows, greater winter flows, and lower summer flows. These effects are more pronounced in basins at or near the current snowline. For example, scientists forecast that as much as 70 percent of California's snowpack will be lost due to warming by the end of this century (Hayhoe et al. 2004). In rain-dominated basins, however, such as those found throughout much of the eastern United States, studies suggest that changes in precipitation will have a greater effect on flows than warming temperatures.

Groundwater

The potential impacts of climate change on groundwater are less understood than are the impacts on surface water. Several different kinds of impacts are likely. Climate change will affect groundwater recharge rates, but these effects are site-specific. In some areas, recharge rates will increase, whereas in other areas, they will decline. Higher evaporation rates will likely lead to salinization of groundwater, and sea-level rise will likely increase saltwater intrusion into coastal aquifers. Additionally, demand for groundwater may increase as a means of offsetting reduced surface water flows in some regions (Kundzewicz et al. 2007).

The 2008 Climate Change Science Program report notes that no analyses have yet evaluated impacts on groundwater using results from the 2007 IPCC assessment, although previous studies have been conducted on a limited number of groundwater basins in the continental United States. Results from these studies are mixed. For example, higher precipitation rates can increase recharge, whereas elevated evapotranspiration can reduce recharge. The Climate Change Science Program report concludes that "the interaction of groundwater recharge with climate is an area that requires future research" (Lettenmaier et al. 2008, 145). A lack of data on groundwater use and recharge, however, constrains our understanding of this system and thus limits our ability to examine and adapt to these climate impacts.

Floods and Droughts

Climate models suggest that warmer temperatures will lead to greater climate variability and an increase in the risk of extreme hydrologic events such as floods and droughts. The frequency and intensity of droughts are expected to increase in some regions (Gutowski et al. 2008). Most regions are expected to see an increase in the intensity of precipitation events, thereby increasing the risk of floods (Gutowski et al. 2008). Where warmer temperatures will cause more precipitation to fall as rain rather than snow, there is an increasing likelihood of winter floods. To make matters worse, the higher temperatures mean that what does fall as snow will melt faster and earlier, increasing the risk of summer drought and extreme winter flows. Midcontinental regions are also expected to be drier during the summer as rising temperatures increase evapotranspiration rates, thereby increasing the risk of drought or supply constraints.

Water Quality

The connections between climate change and water quality are less understood than are the impacts on water quantity, although the literature on these connections is growing. Climate change is expected to increase water temperatures in lakes, reservoirs, and rivers, leading to more algal blooms and lower dissolved oxygen concentrations. As temperatures rise and oxygen levels decline, the habitat available may decline for some cold water species but expand for some warm water species (Lettenmaier et al. 2008). More intense precipitation events could increase erosion rates and wash more pollutants and toxins into waterways, thereby threatening the health of freshwater species and humans (Lettenmaier et al. 2008), increasing water treatment costs, and raising water rates (GAO 2007). Reductions in summer flows may further exacerbate water-quality concerns. And in coastal systems, rising sea levels could push salt water further into rivers, deltas, and coastal aquifers, threatening the quality and health of these systems.

Water Demand

The effects of climate change on water demand are far less studied than are the impacts on hydrology. Indeed, the Climate Change Science Program report fails to mention impacts on water demand. Overall, however, demands for water in some sectors are sensitive to climate, particularly agriculture and urban landscapes, and are likely to increase. Plants typically require more water as temperatures rise, although higher atmospheric carbon dioxide concentrations can reduce water requirements under some conditions. Because agriculture accounts for about 60 percent of water use in the United States (Kenny et al. 2009),[1] demand changes in this sector may have broad implications.

In some urban areas, lawns and other outdoor uses are major consumers of water, accounting for up to 70 percent of total residential water use in some hot, dry areas, and these demands would increase under hotter temperatures. Warmer temperatures will also increase the amount of water needed for cooling systems. More research is needed on these kinds of climate-sensitive demands, on a regional basis.

Vulnerability to Climate Change Impacts

The ultimate vulnerability of US water resources and systems to climate change will vary across regions, sectors, and socioeconomic groups (Olmos 2001). According to the IPCC, "vulnerability to climate change is the degree to which these systems are susceptible to, and unable to cope with, adverse impacts" (Schneider et al. 2007, 781). For example, the lack of access to a vehicle or other means of transportation was an unexpected factor in the overall human impacts of a natural disaster such as Hurricane Katrina. New thinking about climate risks and these "intervening conditions" not tied to a specific hazard could facilitate disaster preparedness, response, and recovery. Figure 10.1, from Heberger et al. (2009), provides a conceptual framework of the connections between demographics and

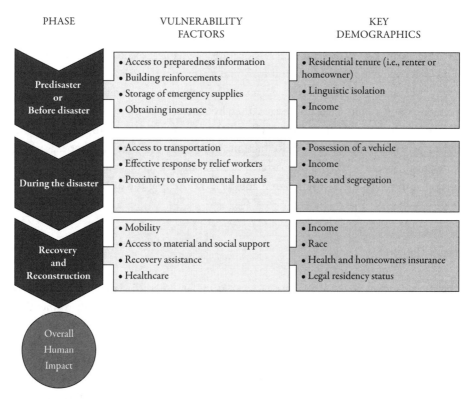

PHASE	VULNERABILITY FACTORS	KEY DEMOGRAPHICS
Predisaster or Before disaster	• Access to preparedness information • Building reinforcements • Storage of emergency supplies • Obtaining insurance	• Residential tenure (i.e., renter or homeowner) • Linguistic isolation • Income
During the disaster	• Access to transportation • Effective response by relief workers • Proximity to environmental hazards	• Possession of a vehicle • Income • Race and segregation
Recovery and Reconstruction	• Mobility • Access to material and social support • Recovery assistance • Healthcare	• Income • Race • Health and homeowners insurance • Legal residency status

Overall Human Impact

FIGURE 10.1. Relationship between demographics and vulnerabilities
Source: Heberger et al. (2009).

BOX 10.1.

CLIMATE JUSTICE AND FRESHWATER FOR ALASKA NATIVES BY PETER SCHULTE

Alaska has already experienced climate change impacts earlier and more drastically than much of the world. Since 1906, the global average temperature has increased by 1.3 °F (IPCC 2007). In comparison, Alaska's mean annual temperature increased by 3.1 °F since 1949. Furthermore, mean winter temperatures increased even more—by 6 °F statewide and over 8 °F in some regions during this same period (Alaska Climate Research Center 2009). Thus, in Alaska, the rate of climate change is much greater than in much of the rest of the world, just as climate models have long forecasted.

Alaska Natives are especially vulnerable to climate change impacts. Fishing is a major source of employment and sustenance, and salmon, in particular, are an important part of native livelihoods and culture. Salmon, however, are a cold-water species. Warmer temperatures increase disease susceptibility and physiological stress, provide a thermal barrier to migration, and favor warm-water species that compete with salmon (Mantua, Tohver, and Hamlet 2009). Thus, climate change impacts on fish populations in Alaska will likely be particularly damaging, both economically and culturally, for Alaska Natives.

Flooding and erosion also pose a major risk for Alaska Native villages. A 2003 GAO report found that 86 percent of Alaska's 200 Native villages are already affected by flooding and erosion. The GAO concluded, "While many of the problems are long-standing, various studies indicate that coastal villages are becoming more susceptible to flooding and erosion caused in part by rising temperatures" (2003, "What GAO Found"). In Kivalina, for example, a barrier of shore ice has protected the village from sea storms and heavy waves during the fall and winter for more than 150 years. The disappearance of the shore ice is now forcing the residents of Kivalina to relocate. Since 2003, federal, state, and village officials have identified 31 villages that, like Kivalina, face imminent threats (GAO 2009). Many of these villages have decided to relocate or are considering it. Unfortunately, federal programs are limited or unavailable for many Alaska Native villages (GAO 2009).

specific vulnerability factors during various phases of a disaster. For example, access to a vehicle can help transport those living within areas at risk to safety, but a vehicle and all of the associated payments is a luxury for many who are struggling to make ends meet. Similarly, flood insurance can allow a homeowner to make repairs after extreme hydrologic events and ensure speedy recovery, yet, many low-income families are unable to afford additional monthly payments needed to purchase insurance. In addition, communities dependent on natural resources for sustenance, including many Native Alaskan communities, are also highly vulnerable to climate change (see box 10.1 for a discussion of the impacts of climate change on Alaskan Native communities).

Climate Change Adaptation

Some degree of climate change is now unavoidable and all regions and sectors are vulnerable to climate change impacts to varying degrees. Thus, adaptation must be a central element of climate change policy. The IPCC (2007) defines adaptation as "initiatives and measures to reduce the vulnerability of natural and human systems against actual and expected climate change effects" (76). There is a wide variety of adaptation options for the various water management activities (table 10.1), ranging from building or expanding reservoir capacity to improving water-use efficiency. These adaptation activities can take many forms; for example, they can be—proactive or reactive, structural or nonstructural, supply-side or demand-side, and more. A recent IPCC report notes that "traditions and institutions in North America have encouraged a decentralised response framework where adaptation tends to be reactive, unevenly distributed, and focused on coping with rather than preventing problems" (Bates et al. 2008, 104). Thus, developing a proactive adaptation strategy will very likely require the United States to chart a new course.[2]

Rigid, expensive, and irreversible actions can increase vulnerability to climate change and ultimately the long-term costs (see following section). Given the uncertainty associated with climate change, planners should support those policies that provide social, economic, and environmental benefits, regardless of climate change impacts—referred to as "no regret" policies. An analysis of impacts and adaptation for the water sector in Canada, for example, identifies several *no-regret* adaptation options, including greater emphasis on water conservation, improved weather-monitoring efforts, and better planning and preparedness for floods and droughts (Lemmen and Warren 2004). While the available no-regret options may not be sufficient to address the full range of climate change impacts, these options should be given priority.

Climate Change Mitigation

While we must begin planning to adapt to those climate impacts that are unavoidable, we must also work to try to avoid severe climate impacts to which we cannot adapt. The good news is that the strong connections between water and energy offer some unique opportunities to both reduce greenhouse gas emissions and to use water more sustainably.

As noted in chapter 7, water is heavy and it has a high heat capacity. Increasing its temperature requires a large amount of energy input. Likewise, and due to these two factors, a significant amount of energy is required to capture, treat, and transport water for use (see chapter 9: Water and Energy for additional discussion of this topic). In the western part of the country, where water supplies and municipalities are often separated by hundreds of miles of land and thousands of feet in elevation, this is a particularly problematic issue. In California, for example, an estimated 19 percent of electricity use, 32 percent of all natural gas consumption, and 88 million gallons of diesel fuel consumption

TABLE 10.1.

Examples of Supply-Side and Demand-Side Adaptation Options for Various Water Management Activities

Water management activity	Supply-side measure	Demand-side measure
Municipal water supply	Increase reservoir capacity	Employ incentives to reduce water use (e.g., through pricing or rebates)
	Extract more water from rivers or groundwater	Enact legally enforceable water use standards (e.g., for appliances)
	Alter system operating rules	Increase use of graywater
	Interbasin water transfer	Reduce leakage
	Capture more rain water (e.g., through low-impact development)	Increase use of recycled water
	Desalination	Develop non-water-based sanitation systems
	Improved seasonal forecasting	
Irrigation	Increase irrigation source capacity line canals	Increase irrigation-use efficiency
		Increase use of drought-tolerant plants
		Alter cropping patterns
Industrial and power station cooling	Increase source capacity	Increase water-use efficiency and water recycling
	Use low-grade water	
Hydropower generation	Increase reservoir capacity	Increase efficiency of turbines; encourage energy efficiency
Navigation	Build weirs and locks	Alter ship size and frequency
Pollution control	Enhance treatment works	Reduce volume of effluents to treat (e.g., by charging for discharges)
		Manage catchment to reduce polluting runoff
Flood management	Increase flood protection (levees, reservoirs)	Improve flood warning and dissemination of information
	Use catchment source control to reduce peak discharges	Curb floodplain development

Source: Adapted and modified from Compagnucci et al. (2001) and Kundzewicz et al. (2007).

Note: To pay an estimated $400 million in relocation costs, the residents of Kivalina have filed suit against 5 oil companies, 14 electric utilities, and a coal company, whom they believe are responsible for their relocation as a result of their greenhouse gas emissions.

each year are water-related.[3] Even though California's water supplies may be more energy-intensive than the national average due to the particularly long distances and elevation changes that the water is subject to, about 83 percent of California's water-related energy use is due to customer end-use, for example, the energy required to pressurize and/or heat water prior to use. Because end-use energy requirements are similar across the United States, water-related energy use is likely high in all regions.

Water-related energy use may increase in the future. Water agencies throughout the county are facing stricter water-quality regulations, forcing some to adopt more energy-intensive water and wastewater treatment technologies. For example, ozone disinfection requires approximately 400 kWh per million gallons, nearly 40 times more than chlorination, the more traditional disinfection method (SBW Consulting 2006). Additionally, some agencies are pursuing energy-intensive water supplies, such as seawater desalination, to meet rising water demands related to population and economic growth and to provide an increasing fraction of water supply less vulnerable to climatic variability. A seawater desalination plant that can process 15 million gallons per day is now operational in Tampa Bay, Florida. In California, more than two dozen plants have been proposed over the past decade. And in some regions, declining groundwater levels are forcing water agencies and farmers to pump water from greater depths at a growing energy cost.

Although the connection between water and energy presents challenges, it also provides opportunities. Water and wastewater agencies throughout the United States are, or will, be subject to greenhouse gas emissions reductions. Because of the energy intensity of water management, saving water saves energy. Recent analysis suggests that energy can be saved through water conservation at lower cost than through traditional energy efficiency measures (CEC 2005). As discussed previously, water conservation and efficiency is also a no-regrets climate change adaptation strategy, thereby providing a win-win situation. Likewise, recycled water is both a mitigation and no-regrets adaptation option because it is less energy-intensive and less vulnerable to climate conditions.

Potential Policy Solutions

A wide range of institutions are responsible for water management activities and will be required to alter their activities in response to climate change. These institutions include both public and private entities that operate at the local, state, and federal level. Local agencies and governments, for example, provide water and wastewater services to urban and agricultural customers, oversee flood management activities, store and deliver irrigation water, and approve land-use activities. Private companies operate water and hydropower systems. Local, state, and federal agencies operate water systems for water supply, flood management, and recreational purposes. All of these institutions will need to adapt to climate change.

Water managers and farmers across the United States already implement a variety of technologies and practices to adapt to current climate- and weather-related risks. For example, water managers implement water-conservation and -efficiency measures to reduce demand, thereby reducing vulnerability to water supply constraints. Farmers shift the timing and types of crops grown according to seasonal weather forecasts. Though it is important to build on these traditional risk mitigation measures, we cannot assume that existing approaches are sufficient to adapt to future climate conditions. Action is needed now. As noted by Robert Repetto, "saying that the U.S. *can* adapt does not imply that it *will* adapt, at least not in the efficient and timely way needed if major damages are to be avoided" (2008, 2). The United States must become a global leader in smart preparation and adaptation to climate change. After years of inaction, the federal government is slowly moving in this direction. In the following section, we provide recommendations on how to expand and accelerate these efforts.

COLLECT BASIC HYDROLOGICAL DATA

The lack of long-term data sets hampers our ability to understand climate change impacts on water resources and develop appropriate adaptation strategies. As noted by Lettenmaier et al. (2008), "observations are critical to understanding the nature of past hydrologic changes and for interpreting the projections of potential effects on future changes" (146). With few exceptions, however, data on water resources are inadequate. Long-term scientific observations are needed to understand Earth's system processes and develop and test models. A recent Government Accountability Office analysis found that federal resource managers lacked adequate data and information "to plan for and manage the effects of climate change on the federal resources they manage" (GAO 2007, "What GAO Found").

Measurement and monitoring of our nation's water resource is critical for management of this precious resource. The US Geological Survey (USGS) is responsible for collecting, analyzing, and distributing data on water availability and use. These data include streamflow information from 7,000 national stream gauges, 600 groundwater monitoring wells, and state data on water use to create national water-use estimates. Data collection activities, however, have been severely underfunded. Streamflow gauges designed to monitor response to long-term climate variability and change are underfunded and have declined by 25 percent since the late 1960s (figure 10.2). Even less information is available on other water resource components, especially groundwater and water use. National water-use data are only collected every five years and are not provided in a timely manner due to limited staffing and budgetary constraints. The 2005 data, for example, was not released until late October 2009.

In order to understand the potential impacts of climate change and plan adaptation efforts, the federal government must ensure that the USGS has sufficient resources to collect and maintain long-term data on key characteristics of water resources, including

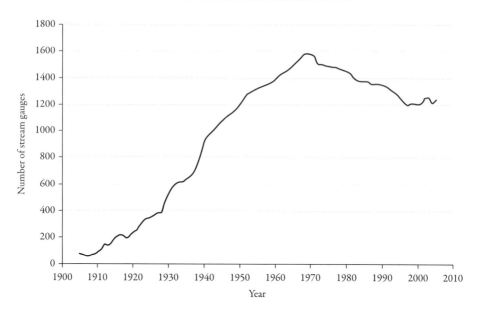

FIGURE 10.2. Number of active stream gauge stations with adequate data for assessing climate variability
Note: HCDN = Hydro-Climatic Data Network.
Source: Based on data from Lettenmaier et al. (2008).

streamflow, groundwater levels, water quality, and water use. The Secure Water Act in 2009 calls for a National Water Census and increased funding for the USGS stream gauge network, which is an important step forward. Full appropriations, however, have not been provided. Congress must ensure that the National Water Census and the monitoring networks receive full funding.

SUPPORT CLIMATE DATA AND INFORMATION NEEDS

Relevant climate data, information, products, and services are not widely available or easily accessible. This may be changing. The Consolidated Appropriations Act of 2010 directed the National Academy of Public Administration to explore options for a National Oceanic and Atmospheric Administration (NOAA) climate service. In February 2010, NOAA and the Department of Commerce announced their intent to establish the National Climate Service, which would be designed to provide climate data, products, and services to fisheries managers, farmers, state governments, water managers, and other users. A more detailed report outlining the vision, mission, and strategic plan for the National Climate Service was released in September 2010 (NOAA 2010). In February 2011, President Obama released a budget request that would fund the National Climate Service. Congress should ensure that this request is approved so that federal agencies, including NOAA, Environmental Protection Agency (EPA), Army Corps of Engineers, National Resources Conservation Service, and USGS, can expand and coordinate the range of climate services available.

CONDUCT VULNERABILITY ASSESSMENTS

Although climate change is a global problem, its impacts are local. Accordingly, detailed assessments of climate change risks require thorough analysis at local and regional scales. Whereas climate change impact studies have been done in some areas, such as California and Washington, good assessments are lacking in others. Additional analysis is needed at the regional level to better understand climate change impacts. Without significant investment to generate the information needed to understand projected impacts, climate change will remain a vague and unwieldy threat. The federal government must take an active role in coordinating and cataloguing impact and vulnerability assessments to ensure that all regions are given adequate attention. Additionally, the federal government must work directly with local water managers to ensure that the information generated by these assessments is disseminated widely.

DEVELOP ANALYTICAL AND DECISION-SUPPORT TOOLS

Analytical and decision-support tools are needed to help communities and governments make informed decisions. In Secretarial Order 3289, released in February 2010, Interior Secretary Ken Salazar committed to using scientific tools to understand and adapt to the impacts of climate change on resources that the Department of the Interior manages. This order established regional Climate Science Centers to synthesize and integrate climate change impacts data and develop tools for managing the department's land, water, fish and wildlife, and cultural heritage resources. Information from the Climate Science Centers is then delivered to Landscape Conservation Cooperatives, who will work with partners to develop resource management goals, monitor progress toward achieving those goals, and identify adaptive management strategies. The Landscape Conservation Cooperatives will work across landscapes to connect science with conservation planning and design. The EPA is also developing a series of tools targeting water managers to help them prepare for the impacts of climate change. The BASINS Climate Assessment Tool, for example, allows for a watershed-based assessment of the potential implications of climate variability and change on water and watershed systems. The EPA is also developing the Water Utility Climate Change Awareness and Risk Assessment Tool, which will assist utilities in evaluating climate change impacts, threats, and adaptation options for their individual system.

The Department of the Interior, EPA, and other federal agencies must continue to develop these tools as a means of improving our understanding of climate change impacts and adaptation strategies. These tools should be developed in collaboration with stakeholders to better understand their planning needs. As these tools are developed, federal agencies must ensure that they are used effectively through workshops and other outreach strategies.

Support Additional Research and Development Efforts

In addition to long-term climate modeling, agencies such as NOAA and the National Weather Service routinely prepare weather forecasts at multiple time scales, from daily to multiseasonal outlooks. These forecasts provide valuable information that water managers use to operate their water systems. Short- and intermediate-term weather forecasts also provide important information to farmers, allowing them to alter their planting regimes and implement other management practices in response to changing weather conditions. The predictive abilities of these forecasts have improved over time, providing farmers and water managers with reliable information over longer periods, for example, from 3- to 5-day forecasts to 8- to 14-day forecasts. Improved forecasting would provide farmers and water managers with better information to make more informed decisions. Funding for research programs to support this research, however, is declining. Congress should restore and expand this funding to support improved weather forecasting.

Expand Outreach Efforts

Information on climate risks and adaptation strategies must be effectively communicated to local stakeholders. Local communities will ultimately be responsible for identifying vulnerabilities and implementing adaptation strategies. Even though impact studies have been conducted at universities and research centers across the country, in most cases, this information has not been adequately conveyed to local stakeholders. Thus, there is a significant gap between top-down analysis and bottom-up implementation. Additional outreach is needed to convey what information is available to inform local and regional decision-making processes.

Outreach efforts would be best accomplished by building on existing institutions. For example, both Land Grant and Sea Grant programs have long-standing relationships with local stakeholders throughout the nation and would serve as ideal conduits for outreach efforts. In coastal areas of the United States, many Sea Grant programs are beginning to develop projects and initiatives to bridge the gap between climate change research and local stakeholders (for a description of some of these initiatives, see NOAA [2009]). Fewer efforts, however, have been initiated by Land Grant programs, although significant opportunity exists here, as well. NOAA and the Department of Agriculture, which oversee the Sea Grant and Land Grant programs, respectively, should develop trainings and provide guidance to local agents about climate change impacts and adaptation strategies with a focus on freshwater resources. The EPA, through its state and regional partners, can also play a role by conveying information to local and regional stakeholders through its regional offices.

New outreach efforts may also be required. In the mid-1990s, NOAA established the Regional Integrated Sciences and Assessments (RISA) Program, which are university-based efforts that support research and product development and provide outreach to a broad community of potential users. There are 10 RISAs in existence across the United States. RISAs, however, have not been established in the midwestern or in much of the northeastern United States. Efforts are needed in these regions. Additionally, the effectiveness of all RISAs should be assessed periodically and adjusted as necessary.

ENSURE CLIMATE CHANGE IS INTEGRATED INTO THE DESIGN, CONSTRUCTION, AND OPERATION OF WATER SYSTEMS

Water managers and policy makers must consider climate change as a factor in all decisions about water investments and the operation of existing facilities and systems. Existing state, federal, and local water systems should be tested under a range of potential future climate conditions to see how they respond and the extent to which they are vulnerable to expected changes. Water managers must then reevaluate engineering designs, reservoir operating rules, contingency plans, and water-allocation policies.

The federal government can facilitate the integration of climate change in water systems in a number of ways. The Bureau of Reclamation and Army Corps of Engineers, which operate many of the nation's reservoirs and water-related infrastructure, should reevaluate their operation of these systems and develop new operational rules in light of climate change. Based on these experiences, the federal government should then provide guidance and oversight to local and state agencies so that they can conduct similar assessments. Additionally, the Federal Emergency Management Agency (FEMA), which evaluates flood risk and develops flood risk maps, should alter their policies and methodologies to ensure that climate change is adequately integrated into their activities.

All new water infrastructure, including levees, reservoirs, and wastewater treatment facilities, must be designed and built incorporating projected climate change impacts over the expected life of the project. The federal government should issue an executive order directing all agencies to integrate projected climate change impacts into long-term planning and all new water-related investments. If an executive order is unsuccessful, follow-up legislation may be required. The federal government can further encourage this by requiring all new and existing projects receiving federal money to integrate projected climate change impacts into facility design and operation.

Ensure the Agricultural Community is Prepared for Climate Change

The nation's agricultural sector is particularly vulnerable to climate change because it is directly tied to land and water resources. Even modest changes in temperature and precipitation patterns, the length of growing seasons, or the frequency of extreme events will have large consequences for many farmers. Farmers already implement a variety of technologies and practices to adapt to current climate- and weather-related risks, such as installing irrigation systems in response to periodic droughts. These response measures are a starting point for developing comprehensive adaptation strategies, but more can, and should, be done. In particular, the Department of Agriculture must actively engage with the agricultural community to develop information, tools, and financing mechanisms to promote climate change education and adaptation.

Improve Disaster Preparedness, Response, and Recovery

Even with the best planning efforts, disasters are inevitable. Given this inevitability, agencies responsible for disaster preparedness, response, and recovery must adequately integrate climate change into their planning efforts. This must occur at the local, regional, state, and national level. FEMA, under the Department of Homeland Security, is responsible for emergency management at the federal level. FEMA must begin planning for the inevitable increase in the frequency of floods, droughts, fire, and other hazards. This planning must begin with a detailed evaluation of how climate change will affect all of FEMA's policies and activities, including floodplain mapping and management, insurance programs, and disaster recovery. Rebuilding efforts should seek to improve climate resilience rather than assume that past climatic conditions will be repeated. Additionally, FEMA should also seek ways to improve preparedness, response, and recovery among states, local, and regional partners.

Support Integration across Water Management Entities

Water management is often spread among multiple agencies that operate with little communication or coordination. Climate change adaptation efforts, however, may provide opportunities for integrating water management entities and developing win-win solutions. For example, climate change is projected to increase the frequency of both floods and droughts in many regions. Alternative stormwater management techniques, including low-impact development, may allow us to capture stormwater and use it to recharge local groundwater aquifers, thereby reducing flood risk and vulnerability to drought. The EPA has supported integrated water management at the watershed scale for decades and has developed guidelines for developing watershed plans. To further encourage integration, the federal government should develop new or prioritize existing funding mechanisms, for example, the State Revolving Fund, for planning and implementation of projects developed through an integrated planning process. These planning analyses and efforts must include the range of potential climate change impacts and be based on meaningful engagement with local stakeholders, especially vulnerable communities. As these planning efforts become more common, they should be required for all projects receiving federal support.

Provide Funding for Climate Change Adaptation

There is tremendous variability in the range of climate change impacts, available adaptation strategies, and sociopolitical context in which decisions are made. As a result, effective climate change adaptation strategies and planning efforts implemented in Salt Lake City, Utah, will be different than those implemented in Miami, Florida. Our understanding of climate change adaptation, however, is limited. As a result, the federal government should support pilot programs in communities across the United States to identify adaptation strategies and develop adaptation plans. As our understanding grows, the federal government should then promote information sharing among communities and establish a clearinghouse that describes the range of potential approaches available and the conditions under which they would be most appropriate.

For many communities, a key issue for adaptation planning will be funding. Adapting to climate change may require significant modifications in existing infrastructure and construction of new infrastructure. The federal government should establish an Adaptation Fund to assist local communities in financing climate change adaptation projects. Financing of the Adaptation Fund could come from a variety of sources, including revenue generated through a cap-and-trade system or a fee on greenhouse gas–producing activities. The Adaptation Fund should, in no way, discourage local or state funding. Rather, it should seek to leverage these existing mechanisms. Additionally, it should prioritize no-regret adaptation strategies and those projects identified through an integrated planning process and include requirements for meaningful community participation and engagement. Finally, set-asides should be included for low-income and disadvantaged communities.

Conclusions

Water resources are especially vulnerable to climate change. Rising temperatures will accelerate the flows of water in the hydrologic cycle, altering water availability, timing, quality, and demand. Even though water managers already practice a variety of measures to reduce the risks of climate variability, we cannot assume that existing approaches are sufficient to adapt to future climate conditions. Action is needed now to improve our understanding of water-related risks from climate change and to explore and implement strategies to reduce these risks.

This chapter argues that in order to meet 21st-century water challenges, there is a clear role for the federal government to play in guiding and facilitating state and local efforts to respond to climate change. In many cases, the federal role is centered on collecting data, providing information, and developing decision-support tools. However, the federal government, through the Bureau of Reclamation and the Army Corps of Engineers, also operate many of the nation's reservoirs, irrigation systems, and other water-related infrastructure. These agencies must evaluate their operation of these systems and develop new operational rules in light of climate change. Based on the experiences gained, the federal government must also support state and regional entities in taking similar actions at local levels.

References

Alaska Climate Research Center. 2009. "Temperature Change in Alaska." Alaska Climate Research Center. http://climate.gi.alaska.edu/ClimTrends/Change/TempChange.html.

Bates, B. C., Z. W. Kundzewicz, S. Wu, and J. P. Palutikof, eds. 2008. *Climate Change and Water*. IPCC Technical Paper VI of the Intergovernmental Panel on Climate Change. Geneva: Intergovernmental Panel on Climate Change, IPCC Secretariat.

California Energy Commission (CEC). 2005. *2005 Integrated Energy Policy Report*. CEC-100-2005-007-CMF. Sacramento: California Energy Commission. http://www.energy.ca.gov/2005publications/CEC-100-2005-007/CEC-100-2005-007-CMF.PDF.

Cayan, D. R., T. Das, D. W. Pierce, T. P. Barnett, M. Tyree, and A. Gershunov. 2010. "Future Dryness in the Southwest US and the Hydrology of the Early 21st Century Drought." *Proceedings of the National Academy of Sciences USA* 107 (50): 21271–21276.

Climate Change Science Program (CCSP). 2008. *Weather and Climate Extremes in a Changing Climate. Regions of Focus: North America, Hawaii, Caribbean, and U.S. Pacific Islands. A Report by the U.S. Climate Change Science Program and the Subcommittee on Global Change Research.* Edited by T. R. Karl, G. A. Meehl, C. D. Miller, S. J. Hassol, A. M. Waple, and W. L. Murray. Washington, DC: Department of Commerce, NOAA's National Climatic Data Center.

Compagnucci, R., L. da Cunha, K. Hanaki, C. Howe, G. Mailu, I. Shiklomanov, E. Stakhiv, and P. Doll. 2001. *Hydrology and Water Resources. Climate Change 2001: Impacts, Adaptation and Vulnerability*. Contribution of Contribution of Working Group II to the Third Assessment Report of the Intergovernmental Panel on Climate Change. Geneva: Intergovernmental Panel on Climate Change.

Frederick, K. D., and P. H. Gleick. 1999. *Water and Global Climate Change: Potential Impacts on U.S. Water Resources*. Arlington, VA: Pew Center on Global Climate Change.

Gutowski, W. J., G. C. Hegerl, G. J. Holland, T. R. Knutson, L. O. Mearns, R. J. Stouffer, P. J. Webster, M. F. Wehner, and F. W. Zwiers. 2008. "Causes of Observed Changes in Extremes and Projections of Future Changes in Weather and Climate Extremes in a Changing Climate." In *Regions of Focus: North America, Hawaii, Caribbean, and U.S. Pacific Islands*. Edited by T. R. Karl, G. A. Meehl, C. D. Miller, S. J. Hassol, A. M. Waple, and W. L. Murray, 81–116. Washington, DC: US Climate Change Science Program and the Subcommittee on Global Change Research.

Hayhoe, K., D. Cayan, C. B. Field, P. C. Frumhoff, E. P. Maurer, N. L. Miller, S. C. Moser, et al. 2004. "Emissions Pathways, Climate Change, and Impacts on California." *Proceedings of the National Academy of Sciences USA* 101 (34): 12422–12427.

Hayhoe, K., C. Wake, T. G. Huntington, L. Luo, M. D. Schwartz, J. Sheffield, E. F. Wood, et al. 2007. "Past and Future Changes in Climate and Hydrological Indicators in the U.S. Northeast." *Climate Dynamics* 28 (4): 381–407. doi:1007/s00382-006-0187-8.

Heberger, M., H. Cooley, P. Herrera, P. H. Gleick, and E. Moore. 2009. *The Impacts of Sea-Level Rise On the California Coast*. Oakland: Pacific Institute.

Intergovernmental Panel on Climate Change (IPCC). 2007. *Climate Change 2007: Synthesis Report, Summary for Policymakers. Fourth Assessment Report of the Intergovernmental Panel on Climate Change*. Cambridge: Cambridge University Press.

Kenny, J. F., N. L. Barber, S. S. Hutson, K. S. Linsey, J. K. Lovelace, and M. A. Maupin. 2009. *Estimated Use of Water in the United States in 2005*. USGS Circular 1344. Washington, DC: US Geological Survey.

Kundzewicz, Z. W., L. J. Mata, N. W. Arnell, P. Döll, P. Kabat, B. Jiménez, K. A. Miller, T. Oki, Z. Sen, and I. A. Shiklomanov. 2007. "Freshwater Resources and Their Management. Climate Change 2007: Impacts, Adaptation and Vulnerability." In *Contribution of Working Group II to the Fourth Assessment Report of the Intergovernmental Panel on Climate Change*. Edited by M. L. Parry, O. F. Canziani, J. P. Palutikof, P. J. van der Linden, and C. E. Hanson, 173–210. Cambridge: Cambridge University Press.

Lemmen, D. S., and F. J. Warren, eds. 2004. *Climate Change Impacts and Adaptation: A Canadian Perspective*. Ottawa, Ontario: Natural Resources Canada. http://adaptation.nrcan.gc.ca/perspective/pdf/report_e.pdf.

Lettenmaier, D., D. Major, L. Poff, and S. Running. 2008. "Water Resources." In *The Effects of Climate Change on Agriculture, Land Resources, Water Resources, and Biodiversity*. Washington, DC: US Climate Change Science Program and the Subcommittee on Global Change Research.

Mantua, N., I. Tohver, and A. Hamlet. 2009. "Impacts of Climate Change on Key Aspects of Freshwater Salmon Habitat in Washington State." In *The Washington Climate Change Impacts Assessment: Evaluating Washington's Future in a Changing Climate*. Edited by Climate Impacts Group, chap. 6. Seattle: Climate Impacts Group, University of Washington.

Milly, P. C. D., K. A. Dunne, and A. V. Vecchia. 2005. "Global Pattern Trends in Streamflow and Water Availability in a Changing Climate." *Nature* 438: 347–350.

National Oceanic and Atmospheric Administration (NOAA). 2009. *Sea Grant: Helping Communities Adapt to Climate Change*. Washington, DC: National Oceanic and Atmospheric Administration. http://www.masgc.org/pdf/workshops/slr/climate.pdf.

———. 2010. *A Climate Service in NOAA: Draft Vision and Strategic Framework*. Washington, DC: National Oceanic and Atmospheric Administration. http://www.noaa.gov/climateresources/resources/NCS_Vision_and_Strategic_Framework_Draft.pdf.

Olmos, S. 2001. *Vulnerability and Adaptation to Climate Change: Concepts, Issues, Assessment Methods*. Winnipeg, Canada: Climate Change Knowledge Network. http://www.cckn.net/pdf/va_foundation_final.pdf.

Repetto, R. 2008. *The Climate Crisis and the Adaptation Myth*. Working Paper 13. New Haven, CT: Yale School of Forestry and Environmental Studies.

Rosenzweig, C., D. C. Major, K. Demong, C. Stanton, R. Horton, and M. Stults. 2007. "Managing Climate Change Risks in New York City's Water System: Assessment and Adaptation Planning." *Mitigation and Adaptation Strategies for Global Change* 12 (8): 1391–1409. doi: 10.1007/s11027-006-9070-5.

SBW Consulting, Inc. 2006. *Municipal Water Treatment Plant Energy Baseline Study*. San Francisco: Pacific Gas and Electric Company.

Schneider, S. H., S. Semenov, A. Patwardhan, I. Burton, C. H. D. Magadza, M. Oppenheimer, A. B. Pittock, et al. 2007. "Assessing Key Vulnerabilities and the Risk from Climate Change." In *Climate Change 2007: Impacts, Adaptation and Vulnerability. Contribution of Working Group II to the Fourth Assessment Report of the Intergovernmental Panel on Climate Change.* Edited by M. L. Parry, O. F. Canziani, J. P. Palutikof, P. J. van der Linden, and C. E. Hanson, 779–810. Cambridge: Cambridge University Press.

Scientific Expert Group on Climate Change (SEG). 2007. *Confronting Climate Change: Avoiding the Unmanageable and Managing the Unavoidable.* Edited by R. M. Bierbaum, J. P. Holdren, M. C. MacCracken, R. H. Moss, and P. H. Raven. Report prepared for the United Nations Commission on Sustainable Development. Research Triangle Park, NC, and Washington, DC: Sigma Xi and the United Nations Foundation.

Seager, R., M. Ting, I. Held, Y. Kushnir, J. Lu, G. Vecchi, H. Huang, et al. 2007. "Model Projections of an Imminent Transition to a More Arid Climate in the Southwestern North America." *Science* 316 (5828): 1181–1184.

Seager, R., and G. A. Vecchi. 2010. "Greenhouse Warming and the 21st Century Hydroclimate of Southwestern North America." *Proceedings of the National Academy of Sciences USA* 107 (50): 21277–21282.

US Government Accountability Office (GAO). 2003. *Alaska Native Villages: Villages Affected by Flooding and Erosion Have Difficulty Qualifying for Federal Assistance.* GAO-04-895. Washington, DC: US Government Accountability Office.

———. 2007. *Climate Change: Agencies Should Develop Guidance for Addressing the Effects on Federal Land and Water Resources.* GAO-07-863. Washington, DC: US Government Accountability Office.

———. 2009. *Alaska Native Villages: Limited Progress Has Been Made on Relocating Villages Threatened by Flooding and Erosion.* GAO-09-551. Washington, DC: US Government Accountability Office.

11

UNITED STATES INTERNATIONAL WATER POLICY

Peter H. Gleick

Introduction

A comprehensive national water policy must take into account the international aspects of freshwater, from agreements with neighboring countries on how to manage and share transboundary water resources to the role of international development assistance in helping address water challenges for humanitarian, economic, or political purposes. An international water policy must also include and tackle issues of water poverty and inequity in an integrated way. None of the comprehensive national water "assessments" prepared in the 20th century systematically addressed these international aspects of water (see, for example, WRPC 1950, NWC 1973), and although this chapter is limited in scope, it presents a set of major links, key issues, and initial recommendations for how the United States might better integrate national and international water-policy objectives.

The United States has fewer international neighbors sharing watersheds than many other countries do, and it has made considerable effort to develop formal treaties and agreements covering many of these water resources and transboundary watershed management. Nevertheless, these efforts and policies could be more effective and comprehensive. Moreover, many of the issues tackled in 20th-century agreements will have to be modified in light of improved information about water availability and use, the growing risks of climate changes, and new international principles for how to effectively manage shared water.

National foreign policy priorities are also constantly changing, as are the tools for identifying and addressing those priorities. In the field of water, improved understanding of the links among water, poverty, development, and conflict has led international security scholars and economic development experts to explore new approaches to overseas development funding and new pressure to shift financial resources and attention to water (and related resource) problems as a growing part of US foreign policy. On World Water Day in March 2010, Secretary of State Hillary Clinton said:

> In the United States, water represents one of the great diplomatic and development opportunities of our time. It's not every day you find an issue where effective diplomacy and development will allow you to save millions of lives, feed the hungry, empower women, advance our national security interests, protect the environment, and demonstrate to billions of people that the United States cares, cares about you and your welfare. Water is that issue. . . . Water challenges are most obvious in developing nations, but they affect every country on earth. And they transcend political boundaries. As water becomes increasingly scarce, it may become a potential catalyst for conflict among—and within—countries (Department of State 2010b).

Water and US National Security Interests

Just as states have fought over oil and other resources, so too water plays a role in national security concerns and in international politics and conflicts (Gleick 1993). Political borders and boundaries rarely coincide with the geophysical borders of watersheds, ensuring that politics inevitably intrudes on water policy. Indeed, approximately half of the land area of the planet is in an "international river basin"—shared by two or more nations (Wolf 2007), and even though the United States has few international neighbors, it shares major water resources with both Canada and Mexico. There is an extensive literature on the connections between internationally shared water resources and political tensions, conflicts, and disputes and the Pacific Institute maintains an online database of water conflicts.[1] Interstate conflicts over water are a function of many things, including religious tensions and animosities, economic disputes, conflicting visions of development, ideology, and more. Water and water infrastructure have been the roots and instruments of war. Access to shared water has been manipulated for political and military reasons. Water-supply systems have been targeted during conflicts. Inequities in access to water have been the source of increasing regional and international frictions and tensions. And there is growing concern about the possibility of terrorist acts against water targets (Gleick 2000, 2006). Such conflicts can occur at local, subnational, and international levels. These are all issues of concerns to national governments, including diplomatic and military agencies.

Water disputes are generally resolved diplomatically, and shared water resources can be an effective source of cooperation and negotiation. Serious challenges remain, however, in improving the ability of current international law and multilateral frameworks to reduce disputes over water. The classic tools for managing shared international river basins are formally negotiated international treaties or related agreements. Hundreds of such treaties are in effect around the world (see the valuable International Freshwater Treaties Database maintained by Oregon State University [OSU 2010]), and the evidence suggests that these are often highly effective at reducing the risks of conflicts over water quality and quantity disputes (Wolf 2007). Nevertheless, new tensions and new forms of water disputes continue to materialize, adding to the urgency of developing effective tools for reducing water and security conflicts.

US Transboundary Water Resources

Many countries are completely, or largely, made up of international river basins. Approximately 15 nations, including Austria, Botswana, Nepal, Paraguay, and Armenia have 100 percent of their land area in international river basins, making water and land management issues of intense international interest. The United States, unlike many other smaller countries especially in Africa, Europe, and Asia, has relatively few water resources that are shared with other nations. But over 60 percent of the nation's land area is in an international river basin or watershed, and these resources are of growing economic and political importance. The vast majority of US international watersheds are almost entirely in the United States, including the Mississippi, Columbia, Rio Grande, and Colorado River basins (shared with either Canada or Mexico), and some of the larger basins lie in relatively water-abundant regions. Several other large river basins are shared between Canada and the state of Alaska, where water demands and competition are very low, but some major basins are in areas of growing water scarcity. Table 11.1 lists the major shared international rivers in North America. All together, 18 major river systems are shared by the United States and its neighbors.

Several of the major shared water systems in North America are covered under formally negotiated international treaties and agreements, reducing the risks of political conflict over water between the United States and its neighbors. There are two important examples of functioning transboundary agreements that have helped the United States manage transboundary water resources with its neighbors: the 1944 agreements with Mexico over the Colorado and Rio Grande River basins, and the several agreements with Canada over joint management of the Great Lakes. Each is described briefly herein.

The United States and Mexico share more than a border; they share several major river basins, including the Colorado and Rio Grande rivers. In 1944, the two countries signed a treaty to define water allocations, set a framework for managing these allocations, and address shortages (typically defined as droughts) and water-quality concerns (US Government 1946; Mumme 2003). The treaty also established a joint institution where disputes and management issues could be negotiated and addressed—the International Boundary and Water Commission (IBWC).

TABLE 11.1.

North American International Rivers

Alesek	Chilkat
Colorado	Columbia
Firth	Fraser
Mississippi	Nelson-Saskatchewan
Rio Grande	St. Croix
St. John	St. Lawrence
Stikine	Taku
Tijuana	Whiting
Yaqui	Yukon

Source: Wolf et al. (1999).

The IBWC is divided into two sections: one for the United States and one for Mexico. Each section consists of one engineer commissioner who acts as the primary representative of each country, two principal engineers, a legal advisor, and a secretary appointed by their respective governments. Each government funds its own section and joint expenses are divided evenly between the two sides (Jones 1999). The 1944 Water Treaty authorized the IBWC to manage the following activities (Marin 2003):

1. Demarcation of the land boundary of the watersheds.
2. Preservation of the Rio Grande and Colorado River as the international boundary.
3. Protection of lands along the rivers from floods by levee and floodway projects.
4. Distribution between the two countries of the waters of the Rio Grande and the Colorado River.
5. Regulation and conservation of the waters of the Rio Grande for their use by the two countries by joint construction, operation, and maintenance of international storage dams, reservoirs, and hydroelectric generating plant.
6. Delivery of Colorado River waters allocated to Mexico.
7. Solution of border sanitation and other border water-quality problems.

The treaty also determines the division of the shared portions of the Rio Grande between the two nations and the allocations of water from the Colorado and Rio Grande owed to each country. Among other provisions, it requires that the United States delivers an average of 1,500,000 acre-feet of Colorado River water to Mexico each year, and Mexico must allot 1,750,000 acre-feet of water from the Rio Grande every five years (an average of 350,000 acre-feet per year) to the United States (University of Texas 2003).

The IBWC has proven effective at addressing technical water issues at the border and at maintaining a functional relationship between the two nations. Mumme (2003) argues that the IBWC is among the best examples of shared management of natural resources across international borders. Despite its success, however, new challenges are complicating joint river basin management. These challenges include rapid industrialization and urbanization, growing demand for water, worsening water-quality problems, ecosystem management, and climate change (Jones 1999). The population of the border region has increased by 400 percent since 1945, and there are now major concerns about both nations' abilities to meet promised water allocations to all parties. Some tensions have also arisen due to Mexico's inability to meet their water allocations to the United States from the Rio Grande in many years, and over the quality of water delivered to Mexico on the Colorado River (University of Texas 2003).

IBWC has also long been criticized for its failure to aggressively address problems before they become critical, having few specific provisions for ensuring compliance of its own stipulations, a lack of environment sensitivity, and a lack of transparency with state and local governments and nongovernmental organizations (Ingram and White 1993). Part of the difficulty is that the IBWC was designed largely to address political concerns rather than today's major environmental and social problems, and new efforts or approaches may become necessary to address them in the coming years. Reviewing these challenges and needs is a key role for the federal government.

SHARED US AND CANADA WATER RESOURCES

The United States and Canada share many watersheds along their extensive border, but only a few are of major economic and political importance, in particular, the Great Lakes system. The Great Lakes are the largest surface freshwater system on Earth, containing nearly 85 percent of the fresh water in North America, and about 21 percent of the world's total freshwater supply (EPA 2006). The population of the basin includes about 10 percent of the US population (around 30 million people) and over 30 percent of the Canadian population. Seven percent of American farm production and 25 percent of Canadian farm production comes from this region (EPA 2006). The Great Lakes–St. Lawrence River Basin Water Resources Compact, commonly known as the Great Lake Compact (and not to be confused with the Great Lakes Basin Compact of 1968), is a regional binding agreement between the states and provinces of the Great Lakes Basin regarding the sustainable use and management of the region's freshwater resources. It provides a forum and process to help states and provinces collaborate on the sustainable management of their shared water resources. The compact covers eight states (Illinois, Indiana, Michigan, Minnesota, New York, Ohio, Pennsylvania, and Wisconsin) and two Canadian provinces (Ontario and Quebec) and coordinates the joint management of the water of the entire Great Lakes–St. Lawrence River Basin, defined as the Great Lakes, the St. Lawrence River, all interconnections between them, and all bodies of water that

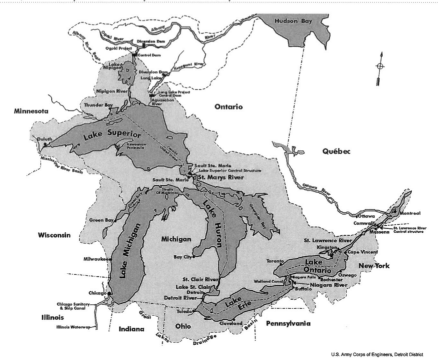

FIGURE 11.1. The Great Lakes Basin
Source: U.S. Army Corps of Engineers, Detroit District

feed into the lakes, as well as the groundwater within this area (see figure 11.1) (Council of Great Lakes Governors 2005).

Integrated water management of the Great Lakes Basin began with the Boundary Waters Treaty of 1909, which established the International Joint Commission to solve disputes between the United States and Canada over use of the Great Lakes water resources (Squillace 2007). The Great Lakes Commission, created by the original Great Lakes Basin Compact of 1968, collects data, conducts related research, publishes reports, and makes recommendations on technology and policy for the Great Lakes Basin. The recent push to collaboratively manage the Great Lakes water resources with a focus on sustainability began in 1985 with the establishment of the Great Lakes Charter—a voluntary (nonbinding) agreement and set of guiding principles outlining what was considered "good practice" at the time for watershed management (Council of Great Lakes Governors 2005).

As we have seen along the US-Mexico border, new challenges are emerging that the existing US-Canadian agreements fail to address. For example, in 1998, the Nova Group from Ontario was issued an initial permit to export to Asia 600 million liters of water a year from Lake Superior, raising questions about bulk water export authority and rights and public/private control. The permit was later revoked due to concern from the International Joint Commission, Canadian public concern, and international legal questions.

In 2001, the Great Lakes governors and premiers of Ontario and Quebec signed "Annex 1" to the original 1985 Great Lakes Charter, which agreed to establish a binding agreement for management of basin waters (Council of Great Lakes Governors 2005). In late 2005, the governors and premiers of the Great Lakes states and provinces followed up on this annex by signing the Great Lake–St. Lawrence River Basin Sustainable Water Resources Agreement. During 2007 and 2008, each of the eight Great Lakes state legislatures ratified the compact. Legislative approval was completed by the US Senate on August 1, 2008, and by the US House of Representatives on September 23, 2008. In October 2008, President George W. Bush signed the joint resolution of Congress granting consent to the compact. The 2005 agreement calls on the parties to (Council of Great Lakes Governors 2005):

- Remove causes of present and future controversies
- Provide for cooperative planning and action by the member states with respect to such water resources
- Facilitate consistent approaches to water management across the Basin while retaining State management authority over water management decisions within the Basin
- Facilitate the exchange of data, strengthen the scientific information on which decisions are made, and engage in consultation on the potential effects of proposed withdrawals and losses on the water resources of the basin.
- Prevent significant adverse impacts of withdrawals and losses on the basin's ecosystems and watersheds
- Promote interstate and state-provincial comity
- Promote an adaptive management approach to the conservation and management of basin water resources.

Unlike the original Great Lakes Basin Compact of 1968, which was largely consultative in nature, this new compact is legally binding. Among the new issues addressed in the compact are a ban of bulk diversions outside the basin and a regulatory standard prohibiting individual withdrawals of more than 100,000 gallons per day, including groundwater. The main governing body of the compact is the Great Lakes–St. Lawrence River Basin Water Resources Council, which consists of the 10 governors and premiers of the member states. Each member of the council has one vote and decisions are decided by simple majority. The council may create advisory committees and hire staff to ensure the efficient implementation of the compact provisions.

The compact has been widely supported and lauded for its approach to the sustainable and collaborative management of shared water resources. In particular, it is among the first legally binding agreements to comprehensively manage an entire water system across both state and national boundaries. One criticism of the compact is that it promotes a movement toward total public ownership of water, including groundwater supplies that have traditionally been considered a right associated with land ownership. Others note that the compact does not initiate public ownership of all waters because groundwater is not owned by land owners in the first place (Kroll 2008). These kinds of public-private disputes are common to transboundary water debates and must be resolved in each case.

Other US Transboundary Water Concerns

Despite the relative success of the Colorado River/Rio Grande River basins and Great Lakes efforts at cooperative transboundary water cooperation, water is playing an increasing role in US international politics, in part because the State Department and other relevant agencies have not developed adequate political or diplomatic tools for consistently and systematically addressing these risks. For example, there are ongoing arguments over energy and water developments along the Flathead River, which flows from British Columbia into Montana; unresolved questions about the management of water releases and quality in the Devils Lake watershed between North Dakota and Manitoba; and disputes about water management, quality, and control along the Rio Grande River. New energy projects, including coal and coalbed methane, tar sands, and hydraulic fracturing of shale formations all have the potential to both reduce and contaminate water flows on shared rivers (see chapter 9: Water and Energy). There are also concerns associated with neighboring national parks in both Canada and the United States and endangered species of fish in shared river basins. Among the unresolved questions are legal obligations of upstream and downstream parties, whose environmental assessment and management laws should apply, and a wide set of jurisdictional issues (Ingelson, Mitchell, and Assie 2010).

In order to reduce these problems, the federal government, under the auspices of the Department of State, should designate competent federal water agencies or authorities to implement cooperative management policies (for both surface and groundwater) for waters shared by the United States and neighboring nations and not currently covered by treaty or agreement. These agencies must ensure coordination and cooperation among all stakeholders and bodies concerned with water management and facilitate the development of water management plans or explicit treaty agreements.

Water, Economic Development, and US Foreign Policy

Water also plays a role in US foreign policy far beyond our immediate borders in both diplomatic arenas and in the form, direction, and nature of foreign assistance. United States international aid and development assistance have always been part of national foreign policy objectives. Rarely, however, have those objectives included systematic efforts to address basic human needs for water, including water management, water and poverty, or other important related issues. Perhaps the greatest failure of international economic development efforts of the 20th century was the failure to meet basic human needs for water for the entire population of the planet. Poverty takes many forms, and one of the most harmful to human and environmental health is the lack of access to safe drinking water and adequate sanitation. Billions still lack these fundamental services. The best estimate of the World Health Organization in 2010 was that more than 880 million people lacked reliable access to safe drinking water and over 2.6 billion still lacked access to sanitation (WHO 2010). In the past few years, this problem has become one of the most important international political problems associated with water.

What should be the role of the United States in addressing these basic needs? In the past few decades, new debates have sprung up over the connections between water and foreign affairs as our understanding of the links between water, poverty, economic development, and national interests has improved (Gleick 2005). An increasing number of nations, international water conferences, and aid organizations have announced efforts to improve global access to these fundamental water services. In September 2000, the United Nations General Assembly adopted the Millennium Development Goals in broad efforts to reduce poverty, including a goal for water. In August 2002, at the second Earth Summit in Johannesburg, the international community added a new goal for sanitation. The objectives are to halve the proportion of people without sustainable access to safe drinking water and basic sanitation.

The legal and ethical implications of a "human right to water" have also been taken up by the United Nations and recently given formal legal standing. Major international conferences focusing on water are growing in scope and influence. And as already noted, nations and regions fight, politically and diplomatically, over shared water resources. As these issues take on new importance, policy makers and the public in the United States are working to better understand and integrate all aspects of water, from the ecological to the political.

Individual nations, including the United States, have launched programs to focus more international aid effort to tackle these objectives. Although no recent US administration has played a particularly active or effective role in this area, the opportunities to do so are large, and the risks of failing to do so are growing. Included among the opportunities are vast improvements in human health, economic gains that can be made by expanding markets for US goods and services, reductions in social and political unrest in unstable regions, and restoration of global goodwill.

Politicians are also taking increasing notice. In November 2004, Senate Majority Leader Bill Frist made a speech on the floor of the US Senate decrying the terrible human and political costs of failing to meet water needs in developing countries and urging greater efforts on the part of nations and nongovernmental organizations:

> unsafe water poses a clear security threat. Water basins do not follow national borders, and conflict over them will escalate as safe water becomes even scarcer. These conflicts may come to threaten our own national security. Modest, pragmatic, clean water projects that yield real measurable benefits will make things better (US Congress 2004, 25301).

US Strategy for International Water Policy: Objectives and Approaches

The US government has laid out several objectives and goals for the nation's international water policy, along with strategies for reaching those objectives. In support of these objectives, various legislative tools have been created to facilitate funding and the operation of federal agencies. Some of these are described herein. According to the State Department (Department of State 2008, 2010a), the primary US objectives for global development on water are to:

- Increase access to, and effective use of, safe drinking water and sanitation to improve human health
- Improve water resources management
- Increase the productivity of water resources

The primary approaches applied by federal agencies for meeting these goals are:

- Capacity building
- Institutional strengthening
- Policy/regulatory reform
- Diplomatic engagement
- Direct investment
- Investment in science and technology
- Working through partnerships

Federal Agencies with a Role in International Water Policy

More than 15 different federal agencies play a role in international water issues or water-related economic development. Of these, three receive direct appropriations related to water in developing countries: US Agency for International Development (USAID), the Millennium Challenge Corporation (MCC), and the Department of Defense. Many of the rest—including the US Geological Survey, Department of Agriculture, Centers for Disease Control, Environmental Protection Agency, US Army Corps of Engineers, National Oceanic and Atmospheric Administration, and the Peace Corps—provide technical support, data collection and analysis, modeling, and on-the-ground programs often in partnership with aid agencies. Some of the agencies are described herein, but for a more comprehensive list of US government agencies involved with international water-related aid and projects, see Center for Strategic and International Studies (2005).

US AGENCY FOR INTERNATIONAL DEVELOPMENT

USAID is an "independent agency that provides economic, development and humanitarian assistance around the world in support of the foreign policy goals of the United States" (USAID 2011). USAID is the lead agency responsible for international development and humanitarian assistance, and even though it is independent, USAID receives foreign policy guidance from the State Department.

USAID was created in 1961 by Congress when it passed the Foreign Assistance Act. The Foreign Assistance Act, with subsequent amendments, is the major legal tool authorizing economic assistance programs abroad, and it provides the policy framework for aid activities. The Foreign Assistance Act reorganized disjointed US foreign assistance programs and explicitly separated military and nonmilitary aid. The act mandated the creation of an agency to administer economic assistance programs, and on November 3, 1961, President John F. Kennedy established the USAID (USAID 2010).

USAID's primary emphasis is long-term economic- and social-development assistance efforts. The agency integrated existing US aid efforts, combining the economic and technical assistance operations of the International Cooperation Agency, the loan activities of the Development Loan Fund, the local currency functions of the Export-Import Bank, and the food activities of the Food for Peace program of the Department of Agriculture.

USAID's work with water began in the 1960s with a focus on irrigation and large hydropower and dam projects. Its emphasis shifted in the 1970s from dam construction to community water and sanitation with some assistance to community organizations. In the 1980s, USAID further extended its activities to work on water pollution and quality and watershed management. In the 1990s, USAID began supporting efforts around coastal zone management and Integrated Water Resources Management. Overall, a geographical priority of the agency has been the Middle East.

MILLENNIUM CHALLENGE CORPORATION

The MCC is a US government corporation established in 2004 to reduce global poverty through the promotion of sustainable economic growth, in part through the extension of water services and sanitation. The MCC provides countries with large grants to programs that reduce poverty through sustainable economic growth as a complement to other US international development programs. The MCC is managed by a chief executive officer, who is part of the nine-member board of directors consisting of the secretary of State, the secretary of the Treasury, the US trade representative, and the USAID administrator along with four private sector representatives. Since its creation, the MCC has approved over $7.4 billion in programs in sectors including agriculture and irrigation, transportation (such as roads, bridges, ports), water supply and sanitation, education, and anticorruption initiatives (MCC 2011).

DEPARTMENT OF STATE

The Department of State serves as the lead agency for US foreign policy and diplomacy, including efforts to reduce risks over water conflicts. It also provides funding for watershed management and water supply and sanitation systems. In recent years, secretaries of state have spoken out on the need for US involvement in alleviating water poverty (see the quote from Secretary of State Clinton in the introduction to this chapter).

DEPARTMENT OF DEFENSE AND THE US INTELLIGENCE COMMUNITY

While the primary role of the Department of Defense is military actions in support of national security, it also plays an important role in disaster relief operations, including short-term rapid response for water provision. Various elements of the US intelligence community—a complex and ever-changing group of agencies and organizations—look at long-term challenges facing the security of the United States, including the risks of climate change, resource depletion, environmental disruptions, and other nontraditional security threats. Among their concerns have been the issue of water resources and the extent to which water shortages, disputes, and inequities might contribute to political instability that leads to a US security threat.

PEACE CORPS

The Peace Corps's water-related activities include hygiene and sanitation education and a wide range of projects to improve water quality and sanitation in over a dozen countries.

US International Funding for Water and Sanitation

The US total average annual overseas development assistance (ODA) commitment for water comes from a variety of agencies and sources and fluctuates very significantly from year to year.[2] US government water- and sanitation-related activities are funded almost entirely through USAID and the MCC. USAID provides funding for water and sanitation activities in three sectors: water, sanitation, and hygiene projects (WASH); water resources management; and water productivity, with minor additional funding through the International Disaster Assistance and Food for Peace programs. MCC water funding is concentrated on basic water and sanitation projects located primarily in Sub-Saharan Africa. MCC also has supported irrigation projects in Armenia and Mali for efforts to rehabilitate infrastructure and improve the effectiveness of irrigation systems, water supply agencies, and user associations.

Figure 11.2 shows that water-related spending between 1990 and 2004 (in 2003 dollars) averaged around $229 million per year (Clermont 2006), before beginning a substantial expansion in the water and sanitation area. For a short period from 1990 to 1993, US ODA on water averaged roughly $400 million annually. Between 1994 and 2003, this figure only went above the $229 million annually on one occasion and was below $150 million for 7 of the 10 years (CSIS 2005). Since 2005, US ODA for water has begun to increase again in part due to congressional legislative efforts (see the following section).

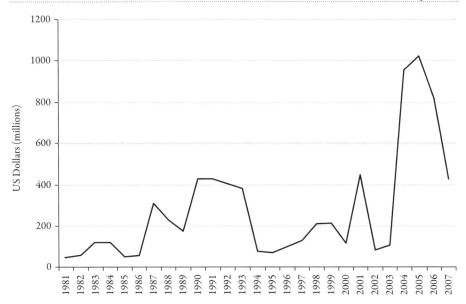

FIGURE 11.2. US Overall ODA on Water Supply and Sanitation, 1967–2007
Sources: Based on data from Clermont (2006) and OECD (2010).

In Fiscal Year (FY) 2009, the United States committed about $774 million worldwide for all water- and sanitation-related activities in developing countries, primarily through two agencies: USAID and the MCC. USAID obligated just under $600 million for water- and sanitation-related activities in more than 60 countries, an increase of over $100 million from 2008 funding. The MCC obligated $121.3 million for all water sector and sanitation-related activities—a major drop from previous years' obligations. USAID obligated $481.8 million and MCC obligated $31.9 million for basic water and sanitation funding, for a combined 2009 total of $513.7 million. In this same year, USAID WASH funding dropped to under $10 million for Sub-Saharan Africa (State Department 2010a).

Between 1990 and 2004, the United States was the world's fourth largest donor for ODA on water, behind Japan ($912 million), the World Bank's International Development Association ($445 million), and Germany ($362 million) (OECD 2010).[3] Over that period, the United States provided 7.3 percent of the world's ODA on water. US ODA on water was heavily concentrated in countries in the Middle East: Egypt, Palestinian administrative areas, Jordan, and Iraq received 88 percent of all US ODA on water. Those same countries received only 11.6 percent of all total international ODA on water with US funds composing 55 percent of their total ODA on water received (Clermont 2006).

USAID FUNDING

USAID categorizes its WASH funding into two broad types of interventions: direct service delivery, such as providing community standpipes for household water and building latrines, and institutional, policy, and behavioral interventions, such as educational program for hygiene and improving utility operations of drinking-water service providers.

USAID's current efforts address a wide range of water resources management activities spread across 4 primary sectors and 12 technical subsectors. These include:

- Water supply, sanitation and wastewater management
  - Drinking water supply
  - Sanitation
  - Wastewater management
  - Pollution and water resources
- Natural Resources Management
  - Watershed management and Integrated Water Resources Management
  - Coastal resources management
  - Freshwater ecosystems management
- Economic development and food security
  - Irrigation
  - Fisheries, mariculture, and aquaculture
  - Hydropower
- Disaster preparedness
  - Monitoring/forecasting
  - Vulnerability assessments

The period of 2003–2009 saw a shift of emphasis within water-related priorities at USAID. In 2003, about 40 percent of USAID's water-related funds were directed toward drinking water supply, sanitation, and hygiene, with the rest focused on water resources management and water productivity. By 2009, over 80 percent of all USAID water-related funds went to water supply, sanitation, and hygiene. This shift of emphasis has come at the cost of a steadily declining percentage of USAID funds being spent on water (excluding supplemental appropriations for the wars in Iraq and Afghanistan and for disaster relief) until the passage of the Paul Simon Water for the Poor Act. The amount of annual obligations from USAID on water dropped from 2004 to 2007, before growing again in recent years (though water obligations at the MCC have dropped substantially in recent years). Whereas both water-resources management and water-productivity activities received between 20 and 30 percent of USAID water-related funding in 2003, by 2009 both these figures had declined to below 10 percent (see table 11.2) (State Department 2008, 2010a). In 2007, most water spending was directed to Africa and Asia and the Near East regions, and most of this spending was for water supply and sanitation projects (see table 11.3 and figure 11.3).

TABLE 11.2.

Estimated USAID Water Obligations FY 2003–2009

	2003	2004	2005	2006	2007	2008	2009
Water supply, sanitation, and hygiene	$159.8	$239.8	$216.9	$265.0	$212.7	$389.9	$481.6
Water resources management	$105.7	$82.5	$60.7	$56.0	$27.4	$58.6	$30.3
Water productivity	$115.6	$68.4	$45.4	$22.5	$17.4	$38.9	$45.3
Disaster risk reduction	$20.6	$10.0	$6.8	$5.8	$5.6	$2.2	$41.3
Total	$401.7	$400.7	$329.8	$349.3	$263.1	$489.6	$598.8

Note: In millions of dollars. Amounts *exclude* supplemental appropriations for Iraq, Afghanistan, and disaster relief.

Source: Department of State (2008, 2010a).

TABLE 11.3.

Estimated USAID Water Obligations in FY 2007, by Region

	Africa	Asia and Near East	Europe and Eurasia	Latin America and the Caribbean	Central Programs	Total	Percent of total
Water supply, sanitation, and hygiene	$103.9	$88.4	$3.7	$10.1	$6.9	$212.7	81
Watershed management	$2.6	$12.5	$2.6	$5.3	$4.4	$27.4	27.4
Water productivity	$2.6	$1.5	$2.7	$8.5	$2.1	$17.4	17.4
Disaster preparedness	$0.2	$0.2	$0.0	$0.0	$5.3	$5.7	5.7
Total	$109.3	$102.6	$9.0	$23.8	$18.7	$263.1	—
Percent of total	42%	39%	3%	9%	7%	—	

Note: In millions of dollars.

Source: Department of State (2008).

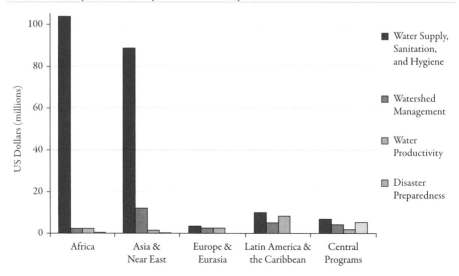

FIGURE 11.3. Estimated USAID Water Obligations in FY 2007, by Region (in Millions of Dollars)
Source: Based on data from the Department of State (2008).

MCC FUNDING

In 2007, MCC provided an additional $655.5 million in commitments and $407.7 in obligations for water-related activities (see table 11.4 and figure 11.4, note that "obligations" may be disbursed over five years) (Department of State 2008). This dropped to $546.9 million of obligations in 2008 and then dropped again, substantially, in 2009, when MCC water obligations totaled only $121 million. Examples of MCC water and sanitation projects in 2007 included a $203 million project in Mozambique on urban and rural water services and a $164 million project in Lesotho to provide water infrastructure for local businesses.

SENATOR PAUL SIMON WATER FOR THE POOR ACT

In the early years of the 21st century, new efforts were made to refocus the priorities of US international aid programs on the issue of water and sanitation in developing countries, as an explicit aspect of national foreign policy. In December 2005, Congress passed, and President George W. Bush signed into law, the Senator Paul Simon Water for the Poor Act of 2005. This act was named in honor of the late Senator Paul Simon—one of the few elected officials with a long-term commitment to national and international water issues. The act requires the secretary of state, in consultation with the USAID and other agencies, to develop and implement a strategy "to provide affordable and equitable access to safe water and sanitation in developing countries." It also sought to increase US assistance for international sanitation and hygiene (WASH) projects and mandate national efforts aimed at reaching the UN Millennium Development Goals.

TABLE 11.4.

MCC FY 2007 Commitments and Obligations for Water-Related Activities

	Drinking water supply, sanitation, and hygiene	Water resources management	Increased productivity	Total
Commitments from MCC	$383.3	$16.7	$255.5	$655.5
Obligations from MCC	$96.9	$6.8	$304.0	$407.7
Obligations from MCC (% of total)	23.8	1.7	74.6	—
Obligations from USAID	$212.7	$27.4	$17.4	$263.1[a]
Obligations from USAID (% of total)	80.8	10.4	6.6	—

Note: In millions of dollars.

[a] Total is more than sum of parts because "Disaster Risk Reduction" is not counted here.

Source: Department of State (2008).

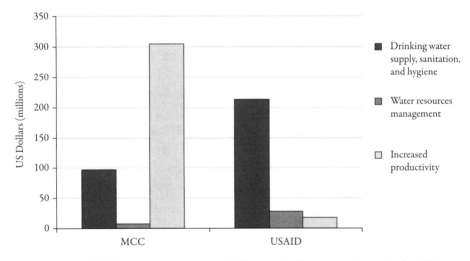

FIGURE 11.4. MCC FY 2007 Commitments and Obligations for Water-Related Activities (in Millions of Dollars)
Source: Based on data from the Department of State (2008).

The Water for the Poor Act establishes water and sanitation as key development priorities but it did not initially appropriate specific funds (Department of State 2008). Funds for the act have been appropriated via annual congressional budgets. The Congressional Appropriations Committee provided $200 million for the program in FY 2006 (the first year with the act in effect). In implementing this appropriation, the State Department used an overly broad definition of *water* and in reality only $70 million of this (35 percent) was new funding made available for water aid specified in the language of the act. Though the act directed that funds be spent on regions with the most need, of this $70 million in FY 2006 only $10 million went to Sub-Saharan Africa (Shandling 2008). In the past few years, overall water and sanitation funding from USAID has grown, as has the total committed to Sub-Saharan Africa, but commitments from MCC, the other major water aid funder, have declined. As a result, there has been no substantial change in US water aid.

More than five years after the passage of the act and with the deadline for the Millennium Development Goals looming, overall progress has been limited by a lack of strategic water planning, inadequate prioritization of WASH in US development policies, inadequate expertise with water within USAID and the State Department, and insufficient financial appropriations (GAO 2010). The act does seem to have led to an increase in international water aid specifically from USAID. USAID obligations of funds for WASH activities increased by approximately 82 percent from $265 million in FY 2006 to $482 million in FY 2009, with the majority of funding supporting WASH activities in three USAID regions—Sub-Saharan Africa, the Middle East and North Africa, and Asia and the Pacific. In FY 2008 and FY 2009, Congress directly linked the annual appropriations directives to the Paul Simon Water for the Poor Act, requiring USAID to obligate at least $300 million for such activities, with the additional requirement that no less than $125 million of the $300 million appropriations directives be obligated in Sub-Saharan Africa. In those years, USAID reported that about $337 million and $495 million, respectively, of their obligations for water and sanitation activities could be attributed to these congressional directives (GAO 2010).

Like most foreign aid programs, distribution of WASH assistance is influenced more by US international geopolitical factors and priorities than by actual levels of need or the potential effectiveness at reaching especially underserved or vulnerable communities (Allen, Folse, and Keene 2010). According to the Government Accountability Office, most of the 31 countries designated as high priority for development assistance by the State Department in 2009 do not have the greatest water and sanitation needs. Table 11.5 shows the 10 largest recipients of USAID water-related obligations for 2007. More recent data for 2009 show that, on average, the USAID obligations have continued to be directed largely to countries in the Middle East, Afghanistan, and Pakistan, where other political priorities dominate, rather than in the countries and regions with the greatest water needs. In 2009, the United States gave, on average, more than 20 times as much WASH funding per capita to the Middle East, Afghanistan, and Pakistan as it did to Sub-Saharan Africa, despite the fact that average needs in Sub-Saharan Africa are more than twice as high (State Department 2010a). In fact, the Government Accountability Office reported that five regions strategically important to the United States—the West Bank and Gaza, Jordan, Pakistan, Sudan, and Afghanistan—received 54 percent of all USAID water funding in 2009 (GAO 2010).

TABLE 11.5.

Ten Largest Recipients of Estimated USAID Obligations in FY 2007 for Water Supply, Sanitation, Hygiene Activities

Country	Water supply and sanitation	IDFA water and sanitation	Total	Percentage of total
Sudan	$7.0	$42.7	$49.7	23.4
Pakistan	$23.0	$0.6	$23.6	11.1
Jordan	$19.0	—	$19.0	8.9
West Bank/Gaza	$11.7	—	$11.7	5.5
Indonesia	$8.8	$0.0	$8.8	4.1
Somalia	$0.6	$8.0	$8.6	4.0
Uganda	$2.5	$5.0	$7.5	3.5
Ethiopia	$3.0	$3.4	$6.4	3.0
Iraq	—	$5.5	$5.5	2.6
Lebanon	$2.8	$1.7	$4.5	2.1
Top 10 total	$78.4	$66.9	$145.3	68.3
All other recipients	$57.1	$10.2	$67.4	31.7
All regions total	$135.5	$77.1	$212.7	—

Note: In millions of dollars. As described in the text, USAID obligations are only part of total US ODA on water. IDFA = International Disaster and Famine Assistance.
Sources: Department of State (2008) and USAID (2007).

Additional US Efforts to Support for International Water Organizations

In addition to providing money for federal agencies focused on international aid, the federal government also provides some funds directly to international organizations for such purposes, including efforts in support of UN agencies. These water-related contributions are modest. In FY 2007, we estimate that water-related contributions to international organizations were only around $11 million (see table 11.6 and figure 11.5). Official government estimates are somewhat higher, but these include contributions to international organizations that do little or nothing on basic water systems or services, such as the International Atomic Energy Agency.

Ideas for a 21st-Century US International Water Policy

The United States could be a powerful, effective, and influential voice for sustainable water management and for the use of the tools of cooperation and conflict resolution in managing water disputes around the world. Applying these tools consistently

TABLE 11.6.

Approximate US Financial Support for Select International Organizations in FY 2007

Organization	US contribution to core budget	Approximate percent of core budget spent on water	US contribution to water-related projects
UN Children's Fund	$125.7	4.7	$5.4
FAO	$91.0	3.0	$2.7
UNESCO	$80.8	1.4	$1.1
WHO	$97.0	0.4	$0.4
World Meteorological Organization	$11.0	4.7	$0.5
UNEP	$5.8	11.4	$0.7
UNDP	$100.0	0.4	$0.4
Total			$11.2

Note: In millions of dollars. FAO = Food and Agriculture Organization; UNDP = United Nations Development Programme; UNEP = United Nations Environment Programme; UNESCO = United Nations Educational, Scientific, and Cultural Organization; WHO = World Health Organization.

Source: Department of State (2008).

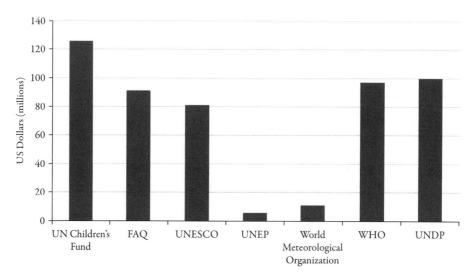

FIGURE 11.5. Estimated US Financial Support for Select International Organizations in FY 2007 (in Millions of Dollars)

Note: FAO = Food and Agriculture Organization; UNDP = United Nations Development Programme; UNEP = United Nations Environment Programme; UNESCO = United Nations Educational, Scientific, and Cultural Organization; WHO = World Health Organization.

Source: Based on data from the Department of State (2008).

would be beneficial to the US economy, human health, and foreign affairs. There are several critical areas where federal involvement and responsibility are key to effective and efficient international water policy.

Negotiate and Support International Water Agreements

Every major watershed in the United States spans two or more states, and many cross our borders with Mexico and Canada. The federal role in negotiating compacts and agreements that address navigation, trade, water allocation, and water quality is enshrined in constitutional principles, but should be reinforced with resources to permit a more active effort to resolve disputes. The recent work of federal agencies in helping alleviate interstate water disputes between the states that share the Colorado River shows the importance of federal involvement in ongoing disputes that states are unable to resolve alone (Adler and Straube 2000). Similarly, expanded federal involvement is needed for resolving disputes with both Canada and Mexico.

Provide Diplomatic Support to Reduce Water Conflicts

As conflicts and tensions over shared freshwater resources continue to grow outside the United States, the need for effective diplomatic interventions also grows. At the moment, no independent organization consistently plays this role, though various international organizations have intervened in specific regions in the past. For example, the dispute between India and Pakistan over the Indus River was resolved by the strong participation of the World Bank in the 1960s. The ongoing Nile River Basin Initiative—an effort to reach an agreement with all 10 Nile Basin countries—has been supported by the African Development Bank, the Canadian International Development Agency, the United Nations Development Programme, and the World Bank.

The United States has also played an important role in diplomatic interventions in water-related disputes, although not in recent years. One example was the role the United States played in the multilateral peace talks in the Middle East in the 1990s, which contributed to the Treaty of Peace signed by Jordan and Israel in 1994 with its special annex on water sharing. US diplomatic initiatives should be further encouraged in this area, especially given our ability to bring scientific, hydrologic, financial, and legal expertise to the table. Overall, however, the Department of State has given inadequate attention to the politics of shared water in the past and should create a permanent water office staffed with a competent water scientist/advisor and career diplomats with experience in international environmental diplomacy.

Expand Efforts to Develop and Implement a Comprehensive WASH Strategy

The State Department is required by congressional legislation to create a comprehensive WASH strategy. Five full years after the congressional deadline, no strategy has been produced. A Framework for Action created in 2009 is a first step but lacks specific and measurable goals, benchmarks, and timetables (Department of State 2009). A strategy should be created immediately that satisfies these mandates and includes clear indicators to measure the effectiveness of US water-related assistance and to identify and obtain the financial and institutional resources needed to implement such a strategy.

The administration must also work with Congress to ensure adequate funding for water-related activities is provided in the foreign assistance budgets in order to avoid having to shift money from other important priorities. The United States could be a leader in efforts to help meet basic human needs for water for all, but current US financial contributions remain small.

BROADEN THE GLOBAL HEALTH INITIATIVE TO INCLUDE WATER

The US Global Health Initiative is a significant and coordinated effort to address a wide range of health threats (Kates et al. 2009), but includes inadequate attention to the effect of contaminated water and inadequate sanitation. Water problems are fundamental underlying causes of disease and death. Between 2 and 5 million people—mostly small children—die every year from preventable water-related diseases. This toll is comparable to that from human immunodeficiency virus/acquired immunodeficiency syndrome (HIV/AIDS) and far easier to reduce with financial and medical resources. Funding for WASH within separate health interventions has not been commensurate with its role in disease and death. Recent international health initiatives in the area of HIV/AIDS and malaria must remain active and aggressive in their efforts to tackle these major diseases, but more attention should be given to an integrated water and health initiative. US financial and organizational investment in these health initiatives is critical with a focus on education on the links between safe water and improved health, funding of hygiene education programs and the construction of community sanitation infrastructure, and medical research on tools for prevention and treatment of a wide range of parasitic, bacterial, and chemically related water illnesses.

INVEST IN NEW, SMART US WATER TECHNOLOGY FOR OVERSEAS MARKETS

Although water problems are the result of complex economic, political, social, cultural, and environmental factors, and must be addressed in these terms, technology also has an important role to play. New small-scale technologies are increasingly needed to help monitor water quality, to deliver water at the community scale, and to treat water to standards appropriate for safe and healthy use. Technological innovation in the United

States can play an important role and can expand jobs here in the United States, as well as exports of US-made equipment and expertise. The United States should increase its support of small business developments of low-cost water quality and supply technologies, as well as public-private partnerships with innovative entrepreneurial nongovernmental organizations.

References

Adler, R. W. and M. Straube. 2000. "Watersheds and the Integration of U.S. Water Law and Policy: Bridging the Great Divides." *William & Mary Environmental Law and Policy Review* 25 (1): 1–67.

Allen, H., M. Folse, and B. Keene. 2010. *U.S. Implementation of the Senator Paul Simon Water for the Poor Act: Small Steps for a Crisis that Calls for Great Strides.* New York: WaterAid America. http://www.wateraidamerica.org/includes/documents/cm_docs/2010/w/water_for_the_poor_act_report_2010.pdf.

Center for Strategic and International Studies (CSIS). 2005. *Addressing Our Global Water Future.* Washington, DC: Center for Strategic and International Studies, Sandia National Laboratory. http://www.csis.org/media/csis/pubs/050928_gwf.pdf.

Clermont, F. 2006. *Overseas Development Assistance for Water, 1990–2004.* Marseille, France: World Water Council. http://www.worldwatercouncil.org/fileadmin/wwc/Library/Publications_and_reports/FullText_Cover_ODA.pdf.

Council of Great Lakes Governors. 2005. "Great Lakes-St. Lawrence Water Resources Basin Compact: Agreement." Council of Great Lakes Governors. http://www.cglg.org/projects/water/docs/12-13-05/Great_Lakes-St_Lawrence_River_Basin_Water_Resources_Compact.pdf.

Gleick, P. H. 1993. "Water and Conflict." *International Security* 18 (1): 79–112.

———. 2000. "How Much Water Is There and Whose Is It?" In *The World's Water 2000–2001: The Biennial Report on Freshwater Resources.* 19–38. Washington, DC: Island Press.

———. 2005. "Freshwater and Foreign Policy: New Challenges." In *Great Decisions.* Edited by Foreign Policy Association, 95–104. New York: Foreign Policy Association.

———. 2006. "Water and Terrorism." *Water Policy* 8: 481–503.

Ingelson, A., L. Mitchell, and S. Assie. 2010. "Coal and Coalbed Methane Development in the Flathead—An International Water Dispute." *Global Business and Development Law Journal* 22: 155.

Ingram, H., and D. R. White. 1993. "International Boundary and Water Commission: An Institutional Mismatch for Resolving Transboundary Water Problems." *Natural Resources Journal* 33: 153–175.

Jones, P. 1999. "The U.S. Mexico Boundary Waters Regime and North American Environmental Agreements: What Lessons for International Water Agreements' Compliance Mechanisms?" *CEMMLP Annual Review 3*, article 7. Dundee: The Centre for Energy, Petroleum and Mineral Law and Policy. University of Dundee, Scotland, United Kingdom. http://www.dundee.ac.uk/cepmlp/car/html/car3_article7.htm.

Kates, J., J. Fischer, and E. Lief. 2009. *The U.S. Government's Global Health Policy Architecture: Structure, Programs and Funding.* Menlo Park: Kaiser Family Foundation. Available at: http://www.kff.org/globalhealth/7881.cfm.

Kroll, J. 2008. "Great Lakes Water Compact Weighs on Region's Future." *The Plain Dealer*, April 6.

Marin, C. 2003. "Bi-National Border Water Supply Issues from the Perspective of the IBWC." *11 United States-Mexico Law Journal* 35: 39.

Millennium Challenge Corporation (MCC). 2011. "About MCC." Millennium Challenge Corporation. http://www.mcc.gov/pages/about.

Mumme, S. P. 2003. "Revising the 1944 Water Treaty: Reflections on the Rio Grande Drought Crises and Other Matters." *Journal of the Southwest* 45 (4): 649–670.

National Water Commission. 1973. *Water Policies for the Future.* Final Report to the President and to the Congress of the United States. Washington, DC: US Government Printing Office.

Oregon State University (OSU). 2010. International Freshwater Treaties Database. http://www.transboundarywaters.orst.edu/database/interfreshtreatdata.html.

Organization for Economic Cooperation and Development (OECD). 2010. OECD StatExtracts, ODA by Sector. http://stats.oecd.org/Index.aspx. (Data available under "Development: Aggregate Aid Statistics: ODA by Sector").

Shandling, K. 2008. "Paul Simon 'Water for the Poor' Act Receives Funding." MaximsNews Network. http://www.maximsnews.com/news20080504waterforpoorfunding10805040801.htm.

Squillace, M. S. 2007. "Rethinking the Great Lakes Compact." *University of Colorado Law School. Michigan State Law Review* 2007. http://papers.ssrn.com/sol3/papers.cfm?abstract_id=960574.

US Agency for International Development (USAID). 2010. "USAID History." USAID. http://www.usaid.gov/about_usaid/usaidhist.html.

———. 2007. "Investments in Drinking Water Supply Projects and Related Water Resources Activities: Report to Congress Fiscal Year 2007." US Agency for International Development, Washington DC. http://www.ehproject.org/PDF/ehkm/usaid-wss_investments2007.pdf

———. 2011. "Frequently Asked Questions." US Agency for International Development. http://www.usaid.gov/faqs.html.

US Congress. 2004. *U.S. Congressional Record,* vol. 150, pt. 19, 25301. Washington, DC: US Government Printing Office.

US Department of State. 2008. *Senator Paul Simon Water for the Poor Act, Report to Congress.* Washington, DC: US Department of State. Bureau of Oceans, Environment, and Science. http://www.state.gov/documents/organization/105643.pdf.

———. 2009. *Addressing Water Challenges in the Developing World: A Framework for Action.* Washington, DC: Bureau of Economic Growth, Agriculture, and Trade, US Agency for International Development, US Department of State.

———. 2010a. *Senator Paul Simon Water for the Poor Act Report to Congress.* Washington DC: US Department of State. http://www.state.gov/documents/organization/146141.pdf.

———. 2010b. "World Water Day Remarks by Secretary Hillary Rodham Clinton." US Department of State. http://www.state.gov/secretary/rm/2010/03/138737.htm.

US Environmental Protection Agency (EPA). 2006. "Great Lakes: Basic Information." US Environmental Protection Agency. http://www.epa.gov/glnpo/basicinfo.html.

US Government. 1946. The Mexican Water Treaty: Treaty Series 994 (59 Stat. 1219): Utilization of waters of the Colorado and Tijuana Rivers and of the Rio Grande. Washington, DC: US Government Printing Office. http://www.usbr.gov/lc/region/pao/pdfiles/mextrety.pdf.

US Government Accountability Office (GAO). 2010. *U.S. Water and Sanitation Aid: Millions of Beneficiaries Reported in Developing Countries, But the Department of State Needs to Strengthen Strategic Approach.* GAO 10–957. Washington DC: US Government Accountability Office. http://www.gao.gov/new.items/d10957.pdf.

University of Texas. 2003. "US-Mexico Water Issues." CE397 Transboundary Water Resources. http://www.caee.utexas.edu/prof/mckinney/research/rio-grande-research.html.

Water Resources Policy Commission (WRPC). 1950. *A Water Policy for the American People: Volume 1: General Report."* The Report of the President's Water Resources Policy Commission. Washington, DC: US Government Printing Office.

Wolf, A. T. 2007. "Shared Waters: Conflict and Cooperation." *Annual Review of Environment and Resources* 32 (3): 1–29.

Wolf, A. T., J. A. Natharius, J. J. Danielson, B. S. Ward. and J. K. Pender. 1999. "International River Basins of the World." *International Journal of Water Resources Development* 15 (4): 387–427.

World Health Organization (WHO). 2010. *WHO/UNICEF Joint Monitoring Report 2010: Progress on Sanitation and Drinking Water*. Geneva: World Health Organization. http://www. who.int/water_sanitation_health/monitoring/fast_facts/en/index.html.

12

CONCLUSIONS AND RECOMMENDATIONS

Summary

The preceding chapters have described the persistent and emerging water challenges that the United States faces and have offered suggestions for overcoming them. We are approaching limits on our renewable water supply and overpumping some groundwater aquifers. Key water laws are out of date and are not effectively or equitably enforced. An increasing number of aquatic ecosystems are in danger of collapse. Many cities, businesses, and farms are not taking advantage of existing, cost-effective water conservation technologies and practices and are confronting water-supply constraints. Much of our infrastructure has not been adequately maintained and will become increasingly strained by climate change and continued population growth. Rising energy demands and shifts toward domestic fuels add additional pressures on the nation's food and water resources. And, as mentioned in the introduction, our current institutions for water management are, in many cases, inadequate, inefficient, and uncoordinated.

These persistent and emerging challenges are being felt worldwide and have served as the basis for many governments to reassess their approach to water management. Beginning with South Africa's water reform efforts in the mid-1990s, many other countries have followed suit in the last decade by passing innovative water laws that share a common commitment to more holistic water management, including Australia, the European Union, and Russia. Although these initiatives have differing cultural dimensions and political imperatives, they share a commitment to many soft path water solutions.

As discussed in the introduction, the soft path defines a new approach to water resources that recognizes that there are limits to our ability to develop new water supplies while continuing to benefit from critical ecological services such as nutrient cycling, flood protection, aquatic habitat, and waste dilution and removal (Gleick 2002). Conventional management approaches in the United States have created a variety of obstacles to the implementation of a soft-path approach, including the disconnection between human systems and ecological systems, ineffective water-pricing structures and markets, and the segregation of agencies and policies into "silos" (Brooks, Brandes, and Gurman 2009). Many of the recommendations that we have provided in the individual chapters are part of a soft-path approach in that they encourage better integration across sectors and scales, equitable access to water, proper application and use of economics, incentives for efficient use, social objectives for water quality and delivery reliability, and public participation in decision making (Wolff and Gleick 2002).

In response to the growing concerns around current and future water quality and supply, the federal government should act now to remove some of the largest obstacles to developing a more comprehensive approach to sustainably manage the nation's precious water resources. Each chapter provides specific recommendations, and here we list 10 overarching conclusions of our national assessment of water policy and management and summarize the key recommendations for improvement.

Conclusions and Recommendations

COMBINE AND COORDINATE FRAGMENTED FEDERAL WATER AGENCIES AND PROGRAMS

Over 30 federal agencies and numerous independent boards and commissions have water-related programs and responsibilities. The complex legal and institutional framework of water management has evolved over two centuries and has never undergone thorough review and integration. The result is an incomplete, and often inefficient, approach to water management at the federal level (Rogers 1993; Leshy 2009; Neuman 2010). Given the persistent and emerging challenges of the 21st century, the time is ripe for a more integrated and comprehensive approach to national water policy. Even though many water issues will remain local, to be resolved by community efforts, the federal government has the responsibility to protect national interests. In particular, federal involvement in water management is needed and appropriate where federal water is provided; states are in legal conflict; national standards for water quality or efficiency are involved; and where unsustainable water uses threaten the nation's economic productivity, environmental integrity, or national security. We recognize that previous national water reviews have also recommended improved integration and management among disparate federal agencies, with limited success. Nevertheless, there are some new opportunities and actions that we think are achievable and that would result in more efficient and effective federal water programs.

DEVELOP A NATIONAL STRATEGY FOR WATER RESOURCES

The Office of Science, Technology, and Policy's Committee on Environment, Natural Resources, and Sustainability should be tasked with developing a national strategy for ensuring the long-term sustainability of our nation's water resources. Although another group could be created to do this, the Office of Science, Technology, and Policy's committee already exists and has been effective in previous efforts. Such a national strategy would define a protocol to assess existing pressures and potential threats to interstate surface and groundwater resources; recommend amendments, new legislation, or improved administrative approaches to reduce pollution and manage interstate watersheds; develop a framework for systematic collection and dissemination of national water data; and serve as a focus for improved communication among federal agencies.

REVIVE RIVER BASIN COMMISSIONS AND REQUIRE RIVER BASIN PLANNING ON RIVERS SHARED BY TWO OR MORE STATES

Increasingly, state and tribal water-resource professionals are turning to watershed management as a means for achieving greater results from their programs. The federal government once had several active river basin commissions, but they were eliminated by President Reagan in 1981 (Executive Order 12319). River basin commissions have proven effective and could again serve a national purpose. River basin commissions were first devised by the Hoover Commission on the Reorganization of the Executive Branch and were consistently supported in bipartisan recommendations of the Cooke Commission, the Presidential Advisory Committee on Water Resources Policy, the National Water Commission, and the Western Water Policy Review Advisory Committee (Neuman 2010).

Given increasing tensions over water and the new challenges identified in this book, we recommend that the US river basin commissions be reinstituted and revitalized as a rational locus for organizing water-management responsibilities and prioritizing key projects and programs to address major threats. These commissions should develop watershed management plans that can serve as a gateway for federal funding. Grants for improved water management that are now dispersed through separate agencies and programs, such as the Farm Service Agency, the Environmental Protection Agency, and State Revolving Funds, among others, could instead be integrated and restricted to priority projects developed through comprehensive river basin management plans.

TASK A NATIONAL WATER COMMISSION OR COUNCIL WITH GUIDING RIVER BASIN PLANS AND REVIEWING WATER-RELATED BUDGETS AND PRIORITIES

Numerous studies, books, and boards have recommended a national water commission or council that reports directly to the president (e.g., NWC 1973; Rogers 1993; Gleick 2009). We support the development of such a commission, which would be composed of diverse, nonfederal experts representing a broad range of disciplines, including leaders of the environmental justice movement. The commission's first task should be to develop guidelines and requirements to ensure that river basin management plans are scientifically rigorous and participatory, identify key threats and stressors to the basin's water resources, and recommend methods for selecting projects to address those threats. The council's responsibilities would also include reviewing all water-related budgets and making recommendations for key priorities. This review would provide a much needed, independent analysis of gaps and overlaps in existing water-related programs.

A national water commission or council would be authorized by Congress; would be composed of nongovernmental water experts from across the many disciplines involved and communities affected, including the sciences, economics, public policy, law, governments, public interest groups, and appropriate private sectors; would have a fixed term and specific mandate; and would serve as a neutral third party. Such a commission should offer both Congress and the Office of Management and Budget advice on improving the efficiency with which federal agencies fund and conduct water research and priorities. Additional efforts of such a commission could include providing guidance on national water science, research, and policy priorities; strategies for increasing protection of aquatic ecosystems; new approaches for financing water infrastructure and improving water-use efficiency and conservation; steps to improve the physical security of the nation's water and reduce risks of international tensions over shared water resources; and strategies for helping prepare the nation's water resources systems for the risks of climate change.

SUPPORT AN IMPROVED UNDERSTANDING OF WATER SUPPLY, USE, AND FLOWS

Measurement and monitoring of our nation's water resources is critical for responsible management. In 1889, the US Geological Survey (USGS) began measuring the flow in the nation's rivers and continues to play a leading role in water data collection and analysis. These data are used to guide many water- and land use planning decisions. For example, hydrologists routinely use federally collected water data to understand rainfall-runoff relationships, return intervals, flood forecasts, and drought risks. For years, these data collection efforts have been severely underfunded. A vast amount of water data are still not collected, and large numbers of existing, long-term stream gauges are being lost. In 2009 alone, nearly 100 long-term gauges were discontinued due to budgetary constraints (USGS 2011), and cuts in satellite observing systems have opened up serious gaps in data availability and advance warning of disasters.

Ensure the USGS has sufficient funding for stream gauges and the Secure Water Act

The failure to accurately monitor and measure our nation's water resources contributes directly to the failure to manage it sustainably. In turn, this affects planning, policy making, and ultimately the nation's economic and environmental health. The federal government must ensure that the USGS has sufficient resources to collect and maintain long-term data on key characteristics of water resources, including streamflow, groundwater levels, water quality, and water use. The passage of the Secure Water Act in 2009 (P.L. 111-11) is an important step forward in terms of data collection through the requirement for a National Water Census and increased funding for the USGS stream gauge network. The act authorized appropriations of $20 million for the national water census effort. This is a key priority not only for improving the nation's data collection but also to provide valuable information to states about water availability and water use. Recent funding constraints, however, will cripple some of these efforts. We recommend full appropriation for the Secure Water Act for its provisions, especially for the National Water Census.

Ensure new monitoring techniques are developed and deployed and existing systems are supported

The Office of Science, Technology, and Policy should develop a protocol for incorporating a new generation of remotely sensed water monitoring techniques into national water data systems. For instance, National Aeronautics and Space Administration's Gravity Recovery and Climate Experiment satellites, which take detailed measurements of the Earth's gravity fields, are valuable for tracking the movement and storage of water around the planet, including poorly understood groundwater systems. In addition, Landsat satellites record thermal infrared radiation that can be used to estimate evapotranspiration, energy balances, and water flows, and polar orbiting satellites provide crucial weather forecasting, emergency warning, military planning, and hydroclimatological data on extreme events such as droughts, floods, hurricanes, tornadoes, and more. Remote sensing can be far less expensive and more comprehensive than land-based networks, yet 2011 cuts in National Oceanic and Atmospheric Administration (NOAA) funding may lead to an 18-month gap in polar satellite observations. We urge greater financial support for National Aeronautics and Space Administration and NOAA programs focused on collecting, storing, analyzing, and disseminating national water, weather, and climate data.

USE INNOVATIVE ECONOMIC STRATEGIES AS A TOOL TO ENCOURAGE SUSTAINABLE WATER PRACTICES

Numerous past assessments of the nation's water resources have urged the adoption of sensible economic strategies at the federal level. In 1973, the National Water Commission recommended discontinuing subsidies for new irrigation projects: "Direct beneficiaries of Federal irrigation developments should pay in full the costs of new projects allocated to irrigation" (148–149). Peter Rogers, who participated in an assessment of the nation's water resources in 1993, concluded: "Charging users what water really costs to produce, manage, treat, deliver, and dispose of after use is so sensible a concept that it hardly merits elaboration. But the fact is that few water delivery systems follow such a policy today" (185). Nearly 20 years later, there has been little progress in appropriate water pricing and markets or applying the user-pays principle, and water continues to be inappropriately subsidized or undervalued in many sectors and regions.

At the same time, the nation's water and wastewater infrastructure is in decline and requires major investment by a combination of users and local, state, and federal sources. Left to the federal government alone, the infrastructure gap would grow by more than $500 billion by 2019 (EPA 2002).[1] However by increasing local spending by just 3 percent over the inflation rate per year, the Environmental Protection Agency (EPA) estimates that the gap would only grow to $76 billion by 2019. Thus, rather than suggesting expanded federal investment, we recommend an approach that requires: increased local cost shares to reduce the amount spent on federal grants, continued federal capitalization of state revolving fund programs, better local cost recovery through appropriate water-pricing policies, and higher user and polluter fees. This strategy would continue to support state revolving loans, but would require more local funding as well. At the same time, we urge the gradual but comprehensive elimination of federal subsidies that promote activities that pollute or waste water.

Increase local cost share for federal grants

The Army Corps of Engineers, Bureau of Reclamation, and Natural Resources Conservation Service typically share costs of water resources development with nonfederal groups. Federal cost-sharing arrangements are inconsistent, and such inconsistencies can induce local groups to select water development options that are not cost effective. In particular, some rules for cost-sharing can encourage local groups to demand projects that, although beneficial for the local community, are not most beneficial for society. In 2010, the Congressional Research Service found that the Army Corps requires only a 35 percent local match for construction of agricultural water storage projects and 25 percent for the construction of some municipal and wastewater infrastructure (Carter and Stern 2011), when other options such as local conservation and efficiency improvements may be much more cost-effective. Local cost shares should be increased; this would encourage local governments to pursue a broader range of cost-effective options.

Continue or expand current levels of funding for State Revolving Funds

Given the high return on investment with state revolving funds, we recommend expanding current levels of funding for these programs. Over the past two decades, the Clean Water State Revolving Fund has financed $2.31 in infrastructure projects for every $1 invested by the federal government, providing a remarkable return on federal investment. The EPA (2008) has projected that over a 20-year time horizon, the initial federal investment into the Clean Water State Revolving Fund can result in the construction of up to three to four times as many projects as programs that utilize a one-time federal grant. The Clean Water State Revolving Fund also requires states to prioritize the most important projects and to have set-asides for green infrastructure and disadvantaged communities. These set-asides should be maintained and increased, respectively.

Use proper water prices to improve cost recovery and build reserves for infrastructure maintenance and improvement

Water pricing is often thought of as a local or state concern. However, the federal government directly provides water to users through the Bureau of Reclamation, Army Corps of Engineers, and Tennessee Valley Authority, among other entities. As the largest wholesaler of water in the West, the federal Bureau of Reclamation plays an important role in setting water rates. The United States should reform pricing policies that promote the inefficient use of water, prevent adequate cost recovery, and limit the ability to create financial reserves to cover future costs.

For instance, the Central Valley Project Improvement Act passed by Congress in 1992 required the Bureau of Reclamation to institute tiered water rates to encourage conservation. This requirement for conservation pricing should be extended to all federal projects and should be designed carefully so that tiered rates actually encompass current levels of water use and provide incentives for improving water-use practices. In addition, new criteria for federal grants and loans should require water suppliers to recover the full cost of service through their water and wastewater pricing policies and provide programs to assist those on low incomes and ensure that they have access to a basic level of service at affordable prices. We also recommend increasing charges for water extraction and fines for pollution and reinvesting these funds in water and wastewater infrastructure.

INTEGRATE THE RISKS OF CLIMATE CHANGE INTO ALL WATER FACILITY PLANNING, DESIGN, AND OPERATION

The growing risks of climate change for water resources and systems must be directly and explicitly integrated into all federal water planning, designs, and system operations. The federal government can play a central role in guiding and facilitating state and local efforts to respond to climate change and prepare federal water facilities for those changes. This role includes collecting data, assessing future risks as part of the legislatively mandated National Climate Assessment program, providing information to the public and water managers, and developing decision-support tools. The federal government also has a role in building and operating water-related infrastructure that is at risk from climate change. As a result, they have a responsibility to identify the most vulnerable national water systems, regions, and communities and to improve disaster response. Unless the risks of climate change are integrated into these responsibilities, federal water projects will be at increasing threat of failure.

Develop better climate information and decision-support tools to assist states

Relevant climate data, information, products, and services are not yet widely available or easily accessible. NOAA launched the NOAA Climate Services Portal in February 2010 to provide climate data, products, and services to fisheries managers, farmers, state governments, water agencies, military planners, and other users. The purpose of the NOAA Climate Services Portal is to bring together climate science data that is now maintained by various NOAA branches and to improve the efficiency of existing programs and services. Similar programs have proven effective and valuable, including the National Weather Service, Marine Fisheries Service, Ocean Service, and Coastal Service. The federal government must provide the necessary funding and support so that federal agencies, including NOAA, EPA, the Army Corps, Natural Resources Conservation Service, and USGS, can expand and coordinate the range of climate services available. Funding for the Climate Services was explicitly targeted for elimination in 2011, and it should be reinstated.

In addition, analytical and decision-support tools are needed to inform decision making. In Secretarial Order 3289, released in February 2010, Interior Secretary Ken Salazar committed to using scientific tools to understand and adapt to the impacts of climate change and created the regional Climate Science Centers to synthesize and integrate climate change impacts data and develop tools for better managing resources. The EPA is also developing a series of tools targeting water managers to help them prepare for the impacts of climate change. The BASINS Climate Assessment Tool, for example, allows for a watershed-based assessment of the potential implications of climate variability and change on water and watershed systems. The EPA is also developing the Water Utility Climate Change Awareness and Risk Assessment Tool, which will assist utilities in evaluating climate change impacts, threats, and adaptation options for their individual system. The Department of the Interior, EPA, and other federal agencies must continue to develop these tools as our understanding of climate change impacts and adaptation strategies improves. As these tools are developed, federal agencies must ensure that they are used effectively through workshops and other outreach strategies.

Ensure climate change is integrated into the design, construction, and operation of water systems

At a minimum, all new water infrastructure, including levees, reservoirs, and wastewater treatment facilities, must be designed and built to incorporate projected climate change impacts over the expected life of the project. The president should issue an executive order directing all federal agencies to integrate projected climate change impacts into long-term planning and all new water-related investments. The administration can further encourage this by requiring all projects receiving federal money to integrate projected impacts into facility design and operation.

Require states to conduct climate and weather vulnerability assessments

The federal government must take an active role in coordinating and cataloging impact and vulnerability assessments to ensure that all regions are given adequate attention. The federal government should require states to develop adaptation planning documents. States should develop and submit these plans every five years to the Interagency Climate Change Adaptation Task Force for review. New financing available for adaptation efforts should be predicated on the approval of plans by the Interagency Climate Change Adaptation Task Force.

Improve disaster preparedness, response, and recovery efforts

Even with the best planning efforts, flooding and drought disasters are inevitable. Given this inevitability, and given that there is growing evidence that climate change will worsen the frequency and intensity of some extreme events (including heat extremes, floods, droughts, and fires), agencies responsible for disaster preparedness, response, and recovery must adequately integrate climate risks into their planning efforts. This must occur at the local, regional, state, and national level. The Federal Emergency Management Agency, which is responsible for emergency management at the federal level, must play a central role in these efforts.

UPDATE CURRENT FEDERAL WATER LAWS AND EXPAND MONITORING AND ENFORCEMENT

Today, many communities and tribes still lack access to safe, affordable water. Violations of our nation's strongest water laws occur too often. Even with weak monitoring, a recent survey of national water quality data found that more than 50 percent of regulated facilities sometimes violated the CWA. Enforcement actions against polluters are infrequent (Duhigg 2009). Similarly, water utilities regularly report violations of the Safe Drinking Water Act (SDWA) and some are beginning to detect new contaminants not covered by law. Clear and immediate action is needed to expand the enforcement and scope of established water law.

Update existing water laws, improve enforcement, and expand their scope

The SDWA is the main federal law protecting drinking water quality; it authorizes the EPA to set standards for drinking water quality and to oversee the states, localities, and water suppliers who implement those standards. Yet, the standards have not kept pace with the emergence of new contaminants in drinking water and have not addressed synergistic impacts. Standards should be updated to apply to emerging contaminants and to address the combined effects of common chemicals. Furthermore, equality of access to safe drinking water should be included in the SDWA's mandate.

The CWA establishes the basic structure for regulating discharges of pollutants into the waters of the United States. The act made it unlawful to discharge any pollutant from a point source into navigable waters without a permit and set a goal of eliminating those discharges altogether. Over three decades later, the act has not reached its goal of zero discharge and has largely failed to reduce nonpoint-source pollution. The federal government should tighten controls on point sources, increase fines for violating National Pollutant Discharge Elimination System permits, rescind or deny renewal of permits of repeat violators, and accelerate efforts to address nonpoint-sources of water contamination. The traditionally broad scope of the CWA could be restored by Congress, bringing water bodies such as ephemeral streams and wetlands with no "nexus" to a navigable water body back under its jurisdiction. The authority and administration of the CWA should also be expanded to adequately regulate groundwater quality.

Finally, federal standards that define the efficiency of water-using appliances are also out of date. Many were put in place by the EPA over two decades ago, but there have since been substantial improvements in technology. Updates and revisions should be considered every five years to ensure that regulations keep pace with available technology.

Give environmental benefits "equal consideration" under the law

Many of the nation's waterworks and regulations were created before we fully understood the extent and value of the ecological services provided by intact river systems. New legislation is needed to ensure that these benefits and the water required to sustain them be given equal consideration with other project purposes. This approach is similar to the 1986 amendments to the Federal Power Act that gave habitat conservation goals "equal consideration" with power and development interests.

DEVELOP FEDERAL POLICIES TO ENCOURAGE DEMAND MANAGEMENT AND ALTERNATIVE APPROACHES TO EXPANDING WATER SUPPLIES

The traditional approach to meeting water needs has been to focus on supply-side options, especially massive, capital-intensive infrastructure such as large dams and reservoirs, centralized water and wastewater treatment plants, and extensive pipelines and aqueducts. This approach has brought many benefits, permitting the nation to produce more food and fiber, reduce the incidence of water-related diseases, mitigate the threat of both floods and droughts, and support continued economic growth. But it has also come at great social, economic, and environmental costs, many of which were either ignored, undervalued, or unknown at the time. For example, many dams, including Kenzua Dam in Pennsylvania, Shasta Dam in California, the Tennessee Valley Authority dams in the Southeast, and American Falls Dam in Idaho, flooded communities and forced residents to relocate. As the country runs out of ideal locations, dams provide fewer benefits at higher economic and environmental costs. Nearly 40 percent of North American freshwater and diadromous fish species are imperiled because of physical modifications to rivers and lakes (Jelks et al. 2008).

In response, water managers are beginning to look seriously at new, nontraditional ways to enhance water supplies and are rethinking approaches to managing demand. Two key principles of the soft path for water, as described by Gleick (2002), are expanding innovative sources of supply such as water recycling, advanced treatment, rainwater harvesting, and conjunctive use, and improving the productivity of water use while matching water quality to the users' needs. Furthermore, the soft path requires meaningful local and community engagement.

Promote new supply approaches

There is a need for expanded and more diverse water supplies without the adverse environmental, social, economic, and political costs of traditional dams, reservoirs, and groundwater extraction. New approaches are being explored throughout the United States and include finding innovative ways to reuse municipal water that is now treated as waste, increasing groundwater storage and conjunctive use, harvesting local rainwater, reusing graywater, and employing appropriate desalination technologies. The federal government should support basic research into these alternatives as prioritized by a national water commission, create and enforce consistent standards for graywater and wastewater reuse, and encourage states to clarify and update health ordinances and laws that inappropriately restrict the use of alternative water sources. In addition, the federal government should continue its support for the Bureau of Reclamation's Title XVI program, with a focus on supporting the public benefits of wastewater reclamation and reuse, and continue to promote "green infrastructure" through State Revolving Funds. As with all federal water projects, we support appropriate local cost-share requirements.

Increase water-use efficiency

There is a need for increased efforts to promote the use of water-efficient technologies and practices through updated federal standards for appliances and fixtures, along with expanded education and technical assistance. As part of its water-efficiency standards, the EPA should pursue residential indoor and outdoor water-use targets (for both single- and multifamily homes), promoting best available technologies or practices, per capita water-use standards adjusted for regional differences, and rate structures that promote both cost-recovery and -efficiency. Such efforts will help municipal water suppliers and water users shift efforts from pure supply-based strategies to broader and more cost-effective efforts to manage both supply and demand. In addition, technical assistance programs to agricultural landowners should be targeted at accelerating the adoption of water conservation and efficiency practices in priority agricultural areas.

Build the capacity of community-based organizations

Community-based organizations play a central role in encouraging and promoting the effective involvement of community residents in water policy and in understanding and resolving community concerns. Federal agencies should support these organizations by increasing resources for community-based organizations and grant programs to technical assistance providers working on critical water issues, such as the EPA's program to support small water systems and the Natural Resources Conservation Service's Watershed Protection and Flood Prevention Program. Federal water projects should also be more responsive to community input and move beyond what has often been perceived to be perfunctory and insincere efforts to solicit and address local concerns.

INTEGRATE US WATER POLICY WITH OTHER FEDERAL RESOURCE POLICIES

Many chapters of this book have detailed the lack of coordination within the water management sector as well as among other sectors, including energy, land-use planning, and agriculture. Indeed, some of the unintended consequences of national policies come from this lack of coordination. For example, US biofuel policies and efforts to rapidly expand natural gas production through hydraulic fracturing are designed to address the very real threats to national security from continued dependence on imported sources of petroleum. Yet these same policies have led to unanticipated adverse impacts on national and international food prices, water use, and water quality (Twomey, Stillwell, and Webber 2010, Osborn et al. 2011). These impacts are a direct result of a lack of communication and coordination among water- and energy-planning efforts and decision-making processes. There may be situations where water and energy (and other) policies conflict with one another, and trade-offs may be required. However, improved coordination at all levels can greatly reduce these conflicts by identifying them early and implementing strategies to mitigate them through cross-sector cooperation and action. Some specific recommendations follow.

Manage water and energy together

Energy and water are closely linked. Although there is an increasing understanding of the water requirements for energy production, major gaps still remain, such as the water risks associated with hydraulic fracturing. Efforts to understand the energy requirements of water systems should be greatly expanded, as should efforts to understand the water implications of energy policies. National energy policy must include a comprehensive analysis of national water quality and quantity risks and strategies that take those risks into account. There have been some modest steps in the right direction recently. Proposed legislation such as the Energy and Water Integration Act would direct the National Academy of Sciences to conduct an in-depth analysis of the impact of energy development and production on the water resources of the United States. In addition, it would require the secretary of the Interior and the administrator of the EPA to identify best available technologies to maximize water and energy efficiency in the production of electricity. The EPA must move more aggressively to protect water quality from energy-related developments under existing authority provided by the CWA and the SDWA and must seek additional authority when necessary.

Similarly, the energy requirements of federal water policies are poorly understood. For instance, new water supplies and treatment technologies, such as desalination, can be energy intensive. Changes in federal water strategies, such as efforts to enhance instream flows or modify license conditions at federal dams have implications for hydroelectricity generation. The secretary of the Interior should work with other federal agencies to evaluate the quantities of energy used in water storage, management, and delivery operations in major federal projects. Legislation that calls for programs to better understand and reduce the overall energy costs of federal water programs is needed, as is national research on how to reduce linked energy and water use in all sectors.

Integrate water and climate change policy

Just as water and energy are linked, so are water and climate change. Two key advantages result from more integrated climate and water policies: New opportunities for reducing greenhouse gas emissions can be developed, and new policies to reduce the vulnerability of US water systems to unavoidable climate impacts can be identified and implemented.

Substantial amounts of energy are used in operating US water systems. As a result, there are large but poorly quantified emissions of greenhouse gases produced from these activities. Though the connection between water and energy presents challenges, it also provides opportunities. Saving water can reduce greenhouse gas emissions. As noted in chapter 9: Water and Energy, new analyses suggest that substantial amounts of energy can be saved through water-efficiency improvements, often at lower costs than through traditional energy-efficiency measures. Water conservation and efficiency is also a no-regret climate change adaptation strategy. Likewise, reuse of recycled water can be both a mitigation and an adaptation option because it can be less energy-intensive and less vulnerable to climate conditions. It is clear that incorporating water into other policy areas provides multiple benefits that would not be captured if dealt with separately.

It seems inevitable that policies will be put in place to reduce greenhouse gas emissions. Such policies are already in place in many other countries and some states are moving forward in this area as well. Because the federal government also operates and maintains diverse water systems, such strategies will be needed at the national level. Water and wastewater agencies throughout the United States are already beginning to assess their contributions to climate change and implement strategies for reducing such contributions as a way to save energy, money, and overall emissions. Federal agencies should do the same.

Conversely, despite efforts to reduce emissions, some significant climate impacts are now unavoidable, including wide-ranging impacts on both water resources and on water infrastructure. Federal policies must quickly be developed to assess the risks of likely climate impacts on water systems, followed by strategies to reduce those risks before they occur. This includes the growing risk of both floods and droughts due to the intensification of the hydrologic cycle, effects of sea-level rise on coastal water systems, changes in streamflow to federal reservoirs, altered hydroelectric generation from changes in rainfall and snowmelt dynamics, and more.

Link water and agricultural policies

Despite the fact that nearly half of the water withdrawn in the United States and nearly 80 percent of the water consumed goes to agriculture, there has been little effort to integrate national water and food policies. At the beginning of the 21st century, US agriculture is confronted with several critical challenges, including increased competition over water resources, urbanization, growing water-quality problems, rapidly changing global market conditions, and climate changes that will change the reliability of water supplies. Subsidies have long played a major role in agricultural policy. Today, the Farm Bill provides substantial subsidies for the production of primarily low-value, water-intensive crops. Other practices that made sense in the 20th century, such as providing low-cost water from irrigation systems built with taxpayer money, are now causing perverse impacts, such as slowing the rate of conversion to high-efficiency irrigation technologies or encouraging unnecessary excess irrigation.

National agricultural policies should consider approaches that strengthen agricultural communities while improving water use. These can include shifting money away from practices that encourage water-intensive crops or inefficient irrigation techniques that exacerbate regional water challenges and toward conservation title programs that provide funding to enhance agricultural productivity while also reducing pressures on water supplies or improving water quality (e.g., the Agricultural Water Enhancement Program). Even though conservation title programs provide multiple benefits, they currently are allocated less than 5 percent of the total Farm Bill budget. We recommend at least doubling this allocation, with a longer range shift toward 20 to 25 percent of the Farm Bill budget in conservation title programs.

APPLY ENVIRONMENTAL JUSTICE PRINCIPLES COMPREHENSIVELY IN FEDERAL WATER POLICIES

Many federal agencies, including the EPA and Department of the Interior, already have the statutory authority to address the concerns raised by environmental justice communities in permitting, project review and construction, and financing activities. Through the work of the National Environmental Justice Advisory Council and other efforts of the Office of Environmental Justice, there are many documents providing guidance on how to achieve this in a variety of agencies. However, renewed effort is needed to fully integrate environmental justice into federal water policy.

Target federal funding toward environmental justice communities

Programs such as the Clean Water State Revolving Fund, the Safe Drinking Water Revolving Fund, and the Department of Agriculture's Rural Loan and Grant program should prioritize funding and expand current programs specifically for low-income communities and communities of color to fund critical water supply, water quality, and wastewater projects.

Ensure water quality laws consider sensitive populations

The EPA should ensure water-quality permits and programs, such as the Underground Injection Control and the Total Maximum Daily Load programs, are based on numeric standards that are protective of the most sensitive populations. In addition, it will be increasingly critical to update standards to address synergistic impacts, which are often prevalent in environmental justice communities. Finally, in order to better understand public health impacts, federal research entities such as the National Institutes of Health should prioritize comprehensive and long-term epidemiological research that explores the health implications of synergistic interactions among common and emerging water contaminants.

Review policies and programs

A national water commission should conduct an environmental justice review of federal water-related funding programs. Entities receiving federal funding should be required to demonstrate collaboration with affected communities and ongoing efforts to address disproportionate impacts in order to continue receiving funding. This would apply to both grant and loan programs such as the Department of Agriculture's Environmental Quality Incentives Program, State Revolving Funds, and the Bureau of Reclamation's water-supply projects.

Support tribal water management institutions and educate Congress about tribal water issues

Tribal water governance does not rely heavily on statutory law, with a few notable exceptions. Rather, water management depends on effective tribal water governance. Effective tribal water governance must include stable institutions and policies, a fair and effective dispute resolution system, separation of politics from business management, a competent bureaucracy, cultural legitimacy, and strategic partnerships. Despite a history of colonization and assimilation, tribes can and are developing, implementing, monitoring, and enforcing their own environmental standards and playing a critical role in the sustainability of these resources for the benefit of Indians and non-Indians alike.

It is important that Congress provide adequate federal funds for tribal water governance, just as it does to states through programs such as the State Revolving Funds. In addition, policy makers and the public generally have little knowledge about contemporary tribal matters or even understand basic differences between tribes and would benefit from education aimed at improving understandings about tribal water issues and governance. A rigorous educational initiative that tackles tribal water matters could provide unforeseen dividends.

Conclusions

In summary, the 21st century brings with it both persistent and new water challenges, including growing human populations and demands for water, unacceptable water quality in many areas, weak or inadequate water data collection and regulation, outdated laws and regulations, and growing threats to the timing and reliability of water supply from climate change. Several countries have reformed their water policies to better address these challenges—it is time the United States did as well. Although the political and cultural contexts of international water reforms have varied, they each reflect a greater focus on soft path water solutions, including new concepts of water supply, expanded efforts at improving water conservation and efficiency, smarter water pricing and economic strategies, and more participatory water management. The United States has not followed suit and continues to rely on a fragmented and outdated approach to water policy based on a patchwork of old laws, competing institutions, and aging infrastructure. New and effective solutions are available and are being explored at local, state, regional, and national levels. That experience should inform efforts to develop a new, integrated federal water policy for the 21st century. In this book, we have laid out a path toward such a policy. Progress will be slow as we learn how best to identify and overcome barriers, but effective and sustainable water management is a necessity. It is urgent that the nation accelerate efforts to improve water management for the sake of future generations.

References

Brooks, D. B., O. M. Brandes, and S. Gurman, eds. 2009. *Making the Most of the Water We Have: The Soft Approach to Water Management.* London: Earthscan Books.

Carter, N. T., and C. V. Stern. 2011. *Army Corps of Engineers Water Resource Projects: Authorization and Appropriations, R41243.* Washington, DC: Congressional Research Service.

Duhigg, C. 2009. "Millions in US Drinking Dirty Water, Records Show." *New York Times,* December 8.

Gleick, P. H. 2002. "Soft Water Paths." *Nature* 418: 373.

———. 2009. "On 21st Century Water Planning: The Need for Integrated National Water Actions." Testimony to the House Committee on Science and Technology. US Congress. Washington, DC, March 4, 2009. http://www.pacinst.org/publications/testimony/gleick_testimony_hr1145.pdf.

Jelks, H. L., S. J. Walsh, N. M. Burkhead, S. Contreras-Balderas, E. Díaz-Pardo, D. A. Hendrickson, and J. Lyons, et al. 2008. "Conservation Status of Imperiled North American Freshwater and Diadromous Fishes." *Fisheries* 33 (8): 372–406.

Leshy, J. 2009. "Notes on a Progressive National Water Policy." *Harvard Law and Policy Review* 3 (1): 133–159.

National Water Commission (NWC). 1973. *Water Policies for the Future. Final Report to the President and to the Congress of the United States.* Washington, DC: US Government Printing Office.

Neuman, J. 2010. "Are We There Yet? Weary Travelers on the Long Road to Water Policy Reform." *Natural Resources Journal* 50: 139–166.

Osborn, S. G., A. Vengosh, N. R. Warner, and R. B. Jackson. 2011. "Methane Contamination of Drinking Water Accompanying Gas-Well Drilling and Hydraulic Fracturing." *Proceedings of the National Academies of Sciences* 108 (20): 8172–8176. http://www.pnas.org/cgi/doi/10.1073/pnas.1100682108.

Rogers, P. 1993. *America's Water: Federal Roles and Responsibilities.* Cambridge, MA: The MIT Press.

Twomey, K. M., A. S. Stillwell, and M. E. Webber. 2010. "The Unintended Energy Impacts of Increased Nitrate Contamination from Biofuels Production." *Journal of Environmental Monitoring* 12: 218–224.

US Environmental Protection Agency (EPA). 2008. *2007 Annual Report: Clean Water State Revolving Fund Programs—Yesterday, Today, and Tomorrow, 20 Years of Progress, EPA-832-R-08-001.* Washington, DC: Office of Water.

———. 2002. *The Clean Water and Drinking Water Infrastructure Gap Analysis, EPA-816-R-02-020.* Washington, DC: Office of Water.

US Geological Survey (USGS). 2011. National Streamflow Information Program. USGS. http://water.usgs.gov/nsip.

Wolff, G., and P. H. Gleick. 2002. "The Soft Path for Water." In *World's Water 2003–2003: The Biennial Report of Freshwater Resources.* Edited by P. Gleick, pages. Covelo, CA: Island Press.

Key Pieces of Federal Legislation

WATER RESOURCE DEVELOPMENT ACTS

The Water Resources Development Acts are a set of omnibus legislation that include Flood Control Acts, Rivers and Harbors Acts, and Water Resources Development Acts. Typically passed biennially, these acts collectively give the US Army Corps of Engineers (USACE) their mandate, and fund and authorize USACE projects. Together, these acts give the USACE jurisdiction over a wide range of water management activities.

Passed in the early 1800s the Rivers and Harbors Acts were the first water-related federal legislation. These acts authorized USACE to survey and improve the navigability of rivers and harbors. Regulatory authority over obstructions to navigation (including physical obstruction by dams, dikes, the dumping of dredged or other materials, or hazards created from dumping contaminants) was given to USACE under section 13 of the Rivers and Harbors Act of 1899 (also known as the Refuse Act). Enforcement of the Refuse Act was strengthened in 1971 when President Nixon issued Executive Order 11574, calling for a permit program under this act to regulate the discharge of refuse, including pollutants, into navigable waters. The statute is still in effect today, but sections 402 and 405 of the Clean Water Act shifted the authority to grant permits that allow discharges into waters to the administrator of the Environmental Protection Agency (EPA) and to states.

Flood control came under the jurisdiction of the USACE in 1917 when the first Flood Control Act was passed. The USACE's authority was expanded again when the Flood Control Act of 1944 set a new precedent for multipurpose dam projects that provided for irrigation, municipal water supply, hydropower, and recreation, in addition to navigation and flood control. By this time, the Bureau of Reclamation was already building dams in the western United States primarily for expanded irrigation. In 1974, Rivers and Harbors Acts and Flood Control Acts began to be combined into Water Resources Development Acts.

In the 1970s, USACE projects came under considerable scrutiny both as "pork-barrel" spending and for their negative environmental impacts. In recent years, USACE inadequacies have been highlighted by events such as a USACE economist revealing that the agency falsified information to justify a billion-dollar lock system project, and the failure of multimillion dollar floodwalls and levees that contributed to the massive and tragic destruction caused by Hurricane Katrina (GAO 2005). The 2005 Water Resources Development Act included reform measures, such as the requirement that proposed projects that are controversial or cost more than $40 million undergo independent review, and improved mitigation requirements (Carter et al. 2007).

THE CLEAN WATER ACT

The Clean Water Act is the main law that regulates and protects the quality of surface water in the United States. Administration of the act is achieved through a partnership between the federal EPA and states or tribes, where states or tribes can be granted "primacy," thereby becoming primarily responsible for daily implementation and enforcement tasks. The chapters on water quality (chapter 5) and freshwater ecosystems (chapter 6) discuss the administration of the act at length, so we focus here on the legislative history and important programs administered under the act.

Originally passed in 1948 as the Federal Water Pollution Control Act, the law was significantly restructured and revised by a 1972 amendment, and after a 1977 amendment, became known as the Clean Water Act. While the 1948 Federal Water Pollution Control Act was the first statement of federal interest in water quality beyond that affecting the navigability of US waters, it was difficult to enforce and largely ineffective. The 1972 amendment drastically changed the structure of the statute. It also set up several ambitious goals including zero-discharge of pollutants by 1985 and an interim "fishable" and "swimmable" goal by mid-1983, although these goals have still not been met.

The act has both regulatory and financial assistance components, and operates under the conception that all discharges into water are illegal unless permitted. The act's two main regulatory components are: permits requiring technology-based standards for point sources of pollution, and ambient water quality standards for each water body. Point sources of pollution are regulated under National Pollutant Discharge Elimination System permits. These permits mandate specific monitoring and reporting requirement for permittees, and set technology-based standards for discharges of pollutants.

The Water Quality Standard program has three main components: designated uses, water quality criteria, and antidegradation. As part of this program, states establish designated uses for water bodies, which must include uses that have existed at any time since 1975. In addition to establishing designated uses, they also determine the water quality criteria, including the chemical, physical, and biological conditions required to maintain and support these uses. For waters that meet Water Quality Standard criteria, antidegradation policies under the Clean Water Act are meant to ensure that water quality is maintained. Waters that do not meet Water Quality Standard criteria are considered to be *impaired*. This special status requires states or tribes to establish total maximum daily loads for each pollutant present in the impaired water body.

Section 404 of the act requires a permit for the placement of dredged or fill materials into US waters, which are granted under the USACE with the guidance of the EPA, National Marine

Fisheries Service, and the Fish and Wildlife Service. This section has had particular importance to wetlands. Section 404 requires a stepwise consideration process for filling wetlands: first, impacts to a wetland should be avoided to the extent practicable; unavoidable impacts should then be minimized to the extent practicable; and finally, for the area that is negatively affected, an equal area of wetlands should be restored or created to result in "zero net loss" of wetlands. A section addressing nonpoint-source pollution (section 319) was added to the act in 1987. Under this section, grants are available to states that create and implement an approved nonpoint-source pollution management program. However, it does not contain any enforceable standards or regulations.

The Clean Water State Revolving Fund was set up in 1987 to fund clean water projects, such as municipal sewer plan upgrades. States are given low- or no-interest federal loans for water quality projects, and states must match funds with $1 of state money for every $5 of federal funds. Nationwide, between several billion dollars are loaned to states annually under the program.

THE SAFE DRINKING WATER ACT

The Safe Drinking Water Act is the primary law regulating the quality of public drinking water in the U.S. Passed in 1974 and amended various times, the Act authorizes and directs the EPA to set standards for drinking water contaminants that pose a public health risk. The Safe Drinking Water Act was passed by Congress after studies of water systems in the United States revealed widespread public health risks and generally inadequate facilities and procedures (Tiemann 2007). Although it originally focused primarily on treatment to provide safe drinking water, the act was expanded to emphasize the role of protection of drinking water sources, funding water system improvements, and public awareness in drinking water safety.

The Safe Drinking Water Act requires that the EPA create health-based concentration limits for contaminants found in drinking water, and that water systems supplying water to the public comply with these limits as well as various monitoring and reporting requirements. The EPA sets limits for contaminants that may have negative public health impacts, are present in public water supplies, and for which the administrator of the EPA determines that regulation would present a "meaningful opportunity" to protect public health; currently, 91 contaminants are regulated under the act.

THE ENDANGERED SPECIES ACT

The Endangered Species Act (ESA) protects species that are endangered or threatened with extinction, and the habitat that is critical to their survival. Although the act was not specifically created to regulate water resources, in practice it often does, as freshwater ecosystems are critical habitats for many threatened and endangered species. Furthermore, as outlined in chapter 6: Protecting Freshwater Ecosystems, the ESA is often considered the strongest environmental law in the United States (Postel and Richter 2003).

The act mandates federal action and encourages states to aid in the recovery of endangered species of plants and animals. Federal agencies are given the authority to determine and list species as threatened or endangered, to acquire land for conservation of listed species (using land and water conservation funds), to establish cooperative agreements with states, and to assess civil and criminal penalties for violating the act. The secretary of the Interior, acting under the auspices of the Fish and Wildlife Service, is responsible for listing species as threatened or endangered, except in the case of species that live at least part of their life in the ocean, for which the secretary of the Interior under the National Marine Fisheries Service, is responsible.

Section 7 of the act requires that federal agencies ensure that their actions will not jeopardize endangered species or modify their critical habitat. When there is uncertainty regarding whether a federal action will result in jeopardy of a species, agencies must seek counsel from the Fish and Wildlife Service or the National Marine Fisheries Service (depending on the species). In addition, the act makes it illegal for anyone to take, possess, sell, or transport endangered species without authorization. *Take* has been defined to mean, "to harass, harm, pursue, hunt, shoot, wound, kill, trap, capture, or collect, or to attempt to engage in any such conduct" (16 U.S.C. § 1532(19)).

Significant changes to the law were made in 1978 amendments. For the first time, a process for obtaining exemptions from the law was set up through the establishment of the cabinet-level Endangered Species Committee. The Endangered Species Committee has the authority to grant exemptions to the ESA on economic grounds. However, this committee is rarely used and has convened on only three occasions.[1] The amendment also required that economic impacts be considered when designating critical habitats and required public notification and hearings prior to the listing of a species.

A 1988 amendment also made significant changes, requiring the secretary of the Interior to monitor all species that were candidates for listing and to develop and implement recovery plans without showing preference for certain taxonomic groups. Public review and biennial reporting to Congress are also required for all recovery plans. In addition to the federal ESA, many states have passed their own endangered species laws. State ESAs vary widely and, in many cases, their effectiveness is limited (Matsumoto et al. 2003).

THE RECLAMATION ACT

One of the most transformative pieces of legislation in terms of shaping water use in the American West was the passage of the Reclamation Act of 1902, which set up a fund to finance irrigation projects in the arid western states.[2] Irrigation projects included dams, canals, hydroelectric generators, and pumping stations. At the time, irrigation was seen as a necessity for settling the West, as private and local irrigation projects had largely failed. The act appropriated money from the sale of public lands to finance the construction of irrigation projects, which was to be later repaid, without interest, by project users or hydropower produced by the project. The Reclamation Service, which later became the Bureau of Reclamation, was established soon after the act was passed to oversee its implementation.

In the beginning, the program faced numerous problems. Projects were constructed in areas not fit for farming. For this and other reasons, users were unable to repay grants over the allotted 10-year repayment period. Subsequently, the repayment period was extended to 20 years by legislation in 1914 and then to 40 years by legislation in 1926 (GAO 1996). In 1928, Congress authorized the bureau to construct the Boulder Canyon Project (Hoover Dam), signaling the beginning of large-scale reclamation projects throughout the West. During the Depression years, the bureau financed the construction of the Grand Coulee Dam (1933), the California Central Valley Project (1935), and the Bonneville Dam (1937), among others. The last major project authorization occurred in the late 1960s as environmental legislation such as the Water Resources Development Acts and the ESA began to require environmental review of irrigation works.

In an effort to provide benefits of the reclamation projects to family farmers and to limit land speculation, project water was to be given to land owners of no more than 160 acres. Additionally, in order to be eligible for project water, the land owner needed to be a resident on the land or in the neighborhood of the land and needed to use at least one-half of the irrigable area of their land for agricultural purposes. However, these requirements were largely ignored, resulting in a lawsuit against the federal government in the 1970s. In response to this, the Reclamation Reform Act of 1982 was passed, increasing the amount of land that farmers could own to 960 acres and requiring that acres in excess of this be charged a higher rate for water (USBR nd). However, a recent study by the Environmental Working Group shows that reclamation projects still disproportionately benefit large land owners (EWG 2004).

FEDERAL POWER ACT

The Federal Power Act, passed in 1920, set up a standard process for licensing private hydroelectric power projects and created the Federal Energy Regulatory Commission, an independent regulatory agency that oversees the natural gas, oil, and electricity markets, regulates the transmission and sale of these energy resources (except for oil), provides licenses for nonfederal hydroelectric dams, and addresses environmental matters arising in any of these areas (16 U.S.C. § 791). The act's authority over water pertains primarily to privately owned dams that occupy federal lands, are located on navigable waters, use surplus water or hydropower from a federal dam, or affect interstate commerce interests. Licenses are limited to 50-year periods, after which the commission can decommission or relicense the project.

Before 1986, dam licenses issued by the Federal Energy Regulatory. Commission primarily considered a river's power generation potential, often without regard for the project's environmental impacts. The 1986 amendments to the Federal Power Act required the commission to give equal consideration to other values such as energy conservation, protection of fish and wildlife, recreational opportunities, and preservation of general environmental quality. Since 1993, more than 400 projects have been relicensed (Hydropower Reform Coalition 2011).

THE NATIONAL ENVIRONMENTAL POLICY ACT

The National Environmental Policy Act requires federal agencies to complete certain environmental review procedures for actions that "significantly affect the quality of the human environment." The act does not include standards or require that federal actions adopt the least environmentally damaging alternative, but simply that potential impacts be considered before major federal actions are taken. Public input is a required part of this review process. As stated in the preamble (42 U.S.C. 4321), the purposes of this act include developing a nation policy that will "encourage productive and enjoyable harmony between man and his environment," promoting efforts to prevent or eliminate environmental damage, and increasing knowledge of ecosystems. National Environmental Policy Act reviews are required for federal agency actions that potentially affect water resources, for example, constructing dams or levees or issuing discharge permits to new water polluters.

An environmental review can take one of three forms depending on the severity of the environmental impact that a federal agency action will have: a categorical exclusion, an environmental assessment, or a full environmental impact statement.

- A *categorical exclusion* is used for actions that have been determined to not have a significant impact on the human environment and, therefore, do not require further analysis. Minor routine agency actions are a typical example of actions falling under this category. Each agency must publish a list of their categorical exclusion activities, and each activity is subject to a public review process. Categorical exclusions cannot be used in the presence of an "extraordinary circumstance," such as instances that involve wetlands or endangered species.
- *Environmental assessments* determine whether an action will have significant environmental impacts. These documents are intended to be relatively brief and to determine whether a more in-depth review is necessary. If an EA determines that an action will result in significant environmental impacts, an Environmental Impact Statement (EIS) must be conducted.
- EISs require a much more thorough and lengthy analysis and often take years to complete. Public input is encouraged during an early scoping process for EISs, and a draft EIS is also required to be made available for public comment. Any public comments must be addressed in the final version of the document.

In practice, an agency rarely goes through this entire process. Typically, mitigation measures are included in an action to reduce the environmental impacts to a point where an EIS is not needed. If an agency determines that this cannot be achieved, it will often forego the environmental assessment and instead prepare only an EIS.

All federal government agencies are responsible for complying with the act. The Council on Environmental Quality is responsible for overseeing implementation. Under the Clean Air Act (section 309), the EPA is required to review and publicly comment on the environmental impacts of major federal actions, including actions that are the subject of EISs. The EPA also carries out the operational duties associated with the administrative aspects of the EIS filing process.

References

Carter, N. T., H. S. Hughes, P. A. Sheikh, and J. A. Zinn. 2007. *CRS Report for Congress: Water Resources Development Act (WRDA): Corps of Engineers Project Authorization Issues.* Washington, DC: Congressional Research Service. http://www.cnie.org/NLE/CRSreports/07Nov/RL33504.pdf.

Environmental Working Group (EWG). 2004. "California Water Subsidies." Environmental Working Group. http://archive.ewg.org/reports/Watersubsidies/execsumm.php.

Hydropower Reform Coalition. 2011. "The Federal Power Act: Hydropower Licensing and Consideration of Environmental Values." Hydropower Reform Coalition. http://www.hydroreform.org/policy/fpa

Matsumoto, S., C. Pike, T. Turner, and R. Wan. 2003. "Citizens' Guide to the Endangered Species Act." San Francisco, CA: *Earthjustice*. http://www.earthjustice.org/library/reports/Citizens_Guide_ESA.pdf.

Postel, S., and B. R. Richter. 2003. *Rivers for Life: Managing Water for People and Nature*. Covelo, CA: Island Press.

Tiemann, M. 2007. *CRS Report for Congress: Safe Drinking Water Act: A Summary of the Act and Its Major Requirements*. Washington, DC: Congressional Research Service. http://assets.opencrs.com/rpts/RL31243_20080521.pdf

US Bureau of Reclamation (USBR). nd. "Reclamation Reform Act of 1982." Reclamation: Managing Water in the West. http://www.usbr.gov/rra/.

US Government Accountability Office (GAO). 1996. *Information on Allocation and Repayment of Costs of Constructing Federal Water Projects*. GAO/RCED-96-109. Washington, DC: US Government Accountability Office. http://www.gao.gov/archive/1996/rc96109.pdf.

———. 2005. *Army Corps of Engineers: History of the Lake Pontchartrain and Vicinity Hurricane Protection Project*. GAO-06-244T. Washington, DC: US Government Accountability Office. http://www.gao.gov/products/GAO-06-244T.

Notes

CHAPTER 1

1. Data table 1 in Gleick (2006) identifies US annual renewable water supply as 3,069 km³/yr.

2. We note that estimates of drought losses are notoriously difficult to calculate and often miss indirect losses.

CHAPTER 2

1. The Bureau of Reclamation is perhaps the only federal agency created specifically for freshwater water-related purposes. A handful of agencies, for example the National Ocean Service, focus exclusively on oceans.

2. Definitions of beneficial use can change over time, illustrated by the increasing inclusion of instream or environmental uses (*State Dept. of Parks v. Idaho Dept. of Water Administration,* 1974).

3. California Water Code §1011(a) and §1011(b) attempt to address this disincentive by allowing appropriators to keep water saved from use of recycled, desalinated, or polluted water or water salvaged by conservation efforts.

4. Reasonable use has been defined by the courts in regard to surface water such that each owner of riparian land is allowed to use water regardless of the effect on natural flow so long as each user does not transgress the equal right of other riparians to the use of that water. In other words, one riparian water user cannot inflict "substantial harm" or "unreasonable injury" on another (Beck and Kelley 2009).

5. Currently, the Arizona Department of Water Resources is preparing the fourth of five management plans for the Active Management Areas.

CHAPTER 3

1. See, for example, Ringquist (2005), Szasz and Meuser (1997).

CHAPTER 4

1. The terms, *American Indian tribes,* or simply, *tribes* are used throughout this chapter because these are commonly used and there is no universally preferred term for the diverse and complex indigenous groups within the United States. Because of space limitations (and the vast differences) the focus here is on federally recognized tribes within the continental United States. I have not addressed equally difficult water issues for tribes that are not federally recognized, Alaska Natives and tribal members, or Native Hawaiians.

2. In order these decisions are: *South Dakota v. Bourland* 508 U.S. 679 1993; *Seminole Tribe v. Florida* 517 U.S. 44 1996; *Idaho v. Couer D'Alene Tribe* 117 S Ct. 2028 1997; and *Arizona v. California* 2000.

3. The discussion about the Wind River reservation is taken from a section in Berry (2006b), which was published in Czech language.

CHAPTER 5

1. States develop priority rankings and create and implement TMDL programs for prioritized waters first.

2. The SDWA defines *public water system* as a facility—both publicly and privately owned—that serves piped water to at least 25 persons or 15 service connections for at least 60 days each year.

3. Reporting and monitoring failures can also result in noncompliance; however, only actual discharge exceedances are included in figures in this section (Leavitt 2007).

4. Other funding sources for small water systems are grants, loans, and loan guarantees through the Department of Agriculture's Rural Utilities Service, grants from the Department of Housing and Urban Development's Community Development Block Grants Program, and loans through the Rural Community Assistance Partnership Revolving Loan Fund.

5. In some cases, the EPA will require a treatment technology be used by water suppliers instead of setting a maximum contaminant level.

CHAPTER 6

1. These conservation categories are defined as follows: *Endangered*—"a taxon that is in imminent danger of extinction throughout all or extirpation from a significant portion of its range." *Threatened*—"a taxon that is in imminent danger of becoming endangered throughout all or a significant portion of its range." *Vulnerable*—"a taxon that is in imminent danger of becoming threatened throughout all or a significant portion of its range" (Jelks et al. 2008).

2. Arizona, California, Colorado, Idaho, Montana, Nevada, North Dakota, Oregon, South Dakota, Utah, Washington, and Wyoming.

3. Reporting and monitoring failures can also result in noncompliance; however, only actual discharge violations are included in this section (Leavitt 2007).

4. The Pittman-Robertson Wildlife Restoration Act (1938) and the Dingell-Johnson Sport Fish Restoration Act (1950) provide federal funding through excise taxes on hunting and fishing

equipment to the states for the management and restoration of wildlife and fish. In 2008, nearly $500 million were available to states through the Fish and Wildlife Service's Division of Federal Aid.

5. In 2008, the Fish and Wildlife Service awarded approximately $66 million to states for protection and restoration of endangered species habitats through the Cooperative Endangered Species Conservation Fund (authorized by Section 6 of the Endangered Species Act).

6. Data compiled by the Bren School at the University of California, Santa Barbara.

7. In addition to impacts on the flow regime of rivers, dams have a number of other adverse impacts on aquatic ecosystems, including altering the sediment regime, changing water temperature, and impeding fish passage.

8. Rivers currently included in the program include the White, Black and Little Red in Arkansas and Missouri, the Bill Williams in Arizona, the Savannah in Georgia and South Carolina, the Green in Kentucky, the Roanoke in North Carolina and Virginia, the Willamette in Oregon, the Big Cypress Bayou in Texas and Louisiana, and the Connecticut River Basin in New England.

CHAPTER 7

1. This need includes cost for projects to expand, replace, or repair existing infrastructure and to construct new infrastructure to provide drinking water to existing customers. It does not include an estimate of the investment needed for new or future customers.

2. State and federal estimates are from GAO (2001) and local estimates are from US Conference of Mayors (2007).

3. National water-efficiency standards for some fixtures were signed into law in 1992; implementation began in 1994.

4. Additional work on California's agricultural sector suggests that efficient technology and management practices can reduce that sector's water use by 4.5 million acre-feet in a wet year to 6.0 million acre-feet in a dry year, or around 17 percent of that sector's current use (Cooley, Christian-Smith, and Gleick 2009). See chapter 8 for additional discussion on the agricultural sector.

5. Indirect potable reuse is practiced in communities across the United States, although it is often not called by this name. Any community whose water intake is downstream of another community's wastewater discharge is practicing unplanned indirect potable reuse.

CHAPTER 8

1. *Water-use efficiency* is defined here in both agronomic terms (as crop yield divided by applied water) and economic terms (revenue divided by applied water).

2. Water savings are described in comparison to a control that received full irrigation to meet ET requirements (estimated by the Penman-Monteith method).

CHAPTER 9

1. Population projections available at http://www.census.gov/population/www/projections/projectionsagesex.html.

CHAPTER 10

1. Excluding water use for thermoelectric generation.

2. Note that federal efforts should complement and be done in coordination with state and local adaptation efforts.

3. To put these numbers in perspective, consider that leaving the hot water running for 5 minutes uses as much energy as operating a 60-W light bulb for 14 hours.

CHAPTER 11

1. See the Pacific Institute's Water Conflict Chronology: http://worldwater.org/chronology.html.

2. ODA is typically define as financial flows to "developing" countries and to multilateral institutions provided by official governmental agencies, with the objective of promoting economic development and human welfare. ODA is concessional in character and conveys a grant element of at least 25 percent. ODA on water refers to a wide range of projects, including: water resources policy and administrative management, water resources protection, water supply and sanitation (large systems), water supply and sanitation (small systems), river development, waste management/disposal, and education and training in water supply and sanitation. As used here, ODA for water does not include money spent on large water infrastructure projects, though the categories used for accounting often overlap.

3. All figures in 2003$.

CHAPTER 12

1. This includes both operation and maintenance and capital costs for both wastewater and water infrastructure.

APPENDIX

1. The Endangered Species Commission, also known as the "God Squad" because it ostensibly has the ability to determine whether a species will become extinct, has been convened three times to examine the cases of the snail darter, whooping crane, and Northern spotted owl.

2. States originally included under the act were Arizona, California, Colorado, Idaho, Kansas, Montana, Nebraska, Nevada, New Mexico, North Dakota, Oklahoma, Oregon, South Dakota, Utah, Washington, and Wyoming. Texas was added after it acquired federal lands in 1906.

About the Authors

JULIET CHRISTIAN-SMITH is a senior research associate with the Pacific Institute's Water Program. Dr. Christian-Smith is a National Academy of Sciences Frontiers of Science Fellow, has been a Community Forestry and Environmental Research Fellow, a Fulbright Fellow, a winner of the National Science Foundation Undergraduate Research Award, and was honored by the Environmental Protection Agency for Outstanding Achievement along with colleagues Peter Gleick and Heather Cooley.

Peter H. Gleick is the recipient of a MacArthur Foundation "Genius" award, member of the US National Academy of Sciences, and widely considered a global expert on freshwater resources. Dr. Gleick is the cofounder and current president of the Pacific Institute in Oakland, California. He is also the author of *Bottled and Sold: The Story Behind Our Obsession with Bottled Water*, author and editor of *The World's Water*, a biennial book on fresh water and the author and editor of *Water in Crisis*.

Heather Cooley is the codirector of the Pacific Institute's Water Program. Ms. Cooley has been a contributor to multiple editions of *The World's Water*, writing chapters on the energy implications of water supply and the impact of climate change on water resources, and *The Water-Energy Nexus in the American West*. She manages several water projects at the institute associated with the science and policy of water efficiency, desalination, climate change, and more.

Lucy Allen is a research associate with the Pacific Institute's Water Program. Her current research interests include water quality and drinking water regulation, and the links between water, energy, and climate change. She graduated with high distinction from

University of California, Berkeley, where she completed an honors research project on soil organic carbon cycling.

Amy Vanderwarker has worked in the environmental justice movement for almost a decade, with experience in both local community-based campaigns and statewide policy initiatives. She worked for four years at the Environmental Justice Coalition for Water, a California-based coalition of community-based organizations, tribes, and nonprofits working to address water issues impacting low-income communities and communities of color, and as a consultant on water justice campaigns and communications. She currently serves as cocoordinator of the California Environmental Justice Alliance, a statewide co-alition of grassroots environmental justice organizations working on air quality, land use, renewable energy and climate change issues.

Kate A. Berry is professor of geography and director of the Core Curriculum at the University of Nevada, Reno. Dr. Berry's work focuses on the analysis of water governance and policy, with an emphasis on research about intergovernmental relations in water con-flicts, participation in water management, and the cultural and political dimensions of water issues. She has worked extensively on indigenous resources issues, including tribal and Native Hawaiian water issues. Dr. Berry is a former president of the Association of Pacific Coast Geographers, has been a Fulbright Fellow, and is currently the chair of the International Advisory Panel for the Dutch Program on Conflict and Cooperation in Natural Resources Management in Developing Countries.

Index

DATE DUE